A FIELD GUIDE TO COMMON

TEXAS INSECTS

GULF PUBLISHING

An imprint of

ROWMAN & LITTLEFIELD PUBLISHERS, INC

Lanham • New York • Oxford

A FIELD GUIDE TO COMMON
TEXAS INSECTS

BASTIAAN M. DREES, Ph.D.
JOHN A. JACKMAN, Ph.D.

GULF PUBLISHING FIELD GUIDE SERIES:

A FIELD GUIDE TO COMMON
TEXAS INSECTS

Published by Gulf Publishing
An Imprint of the Rowman & Littlefield Publishing Group
Lanham, Maryland 20706

Distributed by National Book Network

Library of Congress Cataloging-in-Publication Data

Drees, Bastiaan M. (Bastiaan Meijer)
    Gulf publishing field guide series : a field guide to common Texas insects / Bastiaan M. Drees and John A. Jackman.
        p.   cm.   — (Texas Monthly field guide series)
    "August 1997."
    Includes bibliographical references and index.
    ISBN 0-87719-263-4 (alk. paper)
    1. Insects—Texas—Identification.   I. Jackman, J. A.   II. Title.   III. Title: Common insects of Texas.
    IV. Series.
    QL475.T4D74   1998
    595.7'09764—DC21   97-39473
                                                    CIP

Printed in the United States of America.

Printed on acid-free paper (∞).

CONTENTS

Acknowledgments   ix

Foreword   xi
    by Horace Burke, Ph.D.

Introduction   1
    How to Use This Guide 2. Terminology, Classification,
    and Use of Scientific Names 3

COLLEMBOLA
Springtails   6

THYSANURA
Silverfish, Firebrats, and Bristletails   8

EPHEMEROPTERA
Mayflies   10

ODONATA
Dragonflies and Damselflies   13

PHASMIDA
Walkingsticks   17

ORTHOPTERA
Grasshoppers, Crickets, and Katydids   19

MANTODEA
Praying Mantids   25

BLATTARIA
Cockroaches   27

ISOPTERA
Termites 30

DERMAPTERA
Earwigs 35

PLECOPTERA
Stoneflies 37

PSOCOPTERA
Psocids, Booklice, and Barklice 39

PHTHIRAPTERA
Lice 42

HEMIPTERA
True Bugs 45

HOMOPTERA
Cicadas, Leafhoppers, Planthoppers, Treehoppers,
Psyllids, Whiteflies, Aphids, Mealybugs, and
Scale Insects 63

THYSANOPTERA
Thrips 86

NEUROPTERA
Dobsonflies, Fishflies, Mantidflies, Lacewings,
Antlions 90

COLEOPTERA
Beetles, Lightningbugs, Borers, Weevils 94

MECOPTERA
Scorpionflies 198

SIPHONAPTERA
Fleas 200

DIPTERA
Flies, Gnats, Mosquitoes, and Lovebugs 202

TRICHOPTERA
Caddisflies 224

LEPIDOPTERA
**Butterflies, Moths, Caterpillars, Bagworms,
Webworms, Cutworms, and Leafrollers** 226

HYMENOPTERA
Sawflies, Wasps, Bees, Hornets, and Ants 272

NON-INSECT ARTHROPODS 291

SCORPIONIDA
Scorpions 292

UROPYGI
Vinegaroons 294

ARANEAE
Spiders 295

OPILIONES
Harvestmen 300

ACARI
Ticks, Mites, and Chiggers 301

PSEUDOSCORPIONES
Pseudoscorpions 308

SOLIFUGAE
Windscorpions 309

ISOPODA
Sowbugs and Pillbugs 310

CHILOPODA AND DIPLOPODA
Centipedes and Millipedes 311

Appendix A: Collecting and Preserving Insects 312

Appendix B: Threatened and Endangered Insects
in Texas 317

Appendix C: Threatened and Endangered Arachnids
in Texas 319

Bibliography 321

Index 343

ACKNOWLEDGMENTS

We would like to thank the following individuals for their assistance in reviewing various sections of earlier versions of the manuscript for this book:

Brant A. Baugh
Dr. Horace R. Burke
Dr. Charles L. Cole
Dr. Roger E. Gold
Dr. Harry N. Howell, Jr.
Dr. Clifford E. Hoelscher
Dr. Rodney L. Holloway
Dr. Allen E. Knutson
Dr. Garland McIlveen, Jr.
Dr. Forrest L. Mitchell

Dr. Jimmy K. Olson
Dr. John D. Oswald
Dr. Carl D. Patrick
William O. "Bill" Ree, Jr.
Dr. James A. Reinert
Edward G. Riley
Dr. Marlin E. Rice
Dr. James V. Robinson
Dr. Robert A. "Bob" Wharton
Dr. Mary K. Wicksten

The valued support of Anna Rodriguez, Kathy Hopkins, and other members of our Extension Entomology Project Group is also acknowledged. We are particularly grateful for the help, guidance, and bibliographic contributions provided by Dr. Horace R. Burke; and the review of figures and order characters by Edward G. Riley. Dr. Burke also provided his bibliography of publications documenting Texas' insect fauna which has been incorporated in this book.

Individuals that contributed photographs are credited in the plates, and are also listed below to acknowledge their contributions:

Dr. Charles T. Allen
Dr. Charles L. Barr
Dr. Darrell E. Bay
Dr. Harold W. Browning
Emory P. Boring, III
Dr. Charles L. Cole
Gregory P. Cronholm
James Hamer
Dr. Clifford E. Hoelscher
Dr. Allen E. Knutson
J. Lee
Dr. Roger W. Meola
Dr. Michael E. Merchant
Nick Mirro

Dr. William P. "Pat" Morrison
Dr. Glen R. Needham
Dr. Roy D. Parker
Doug Paxton
R. Randall
William O. "Bill" Ree, Jr.
Dr. Marlin E. Rice
Dr. James V. Robinson
Dr. Alton N. "Stormy" Sparks, Jr.
Dr. Beverly Sparks
Dr. Winfield L. Sterling
Dr. J. W. Stewart
H. A. Turney

We have tried as much as possible to seek approval from, cite, and give credit to the original photographers. However, in some cases photographs from the historic files at the Texas Agricultural Extension Service Entomology Project Group were used when no others were available. We apologize if any photographers were not cited correctly or given proper credit. We also thank Dr. Dick Weber, whose training in close-up photography allowed the authors and our colleagues to take better photographs of insects and their tiny relatives.

Finally, we wish to thank our families, Carol, Carly, and Erin Drees; and Linda, Paul, Kevin, and Ben Jackman, for their patience and support as we spent the many hours away from our family duties to complete the manuscript for this book. Without their understanding, this book certainly would not have been completed.

Bastiaan M. Drees, Ph.D.
John A. Jackman, Ph.D
Texas A&M University
College Station, Texas

FOREWORD

Insects and man in Texas have been acquainted for a long time. From the first human colonization in what is now Texas to the present day, insects have played an important role in the lives of man. Insect-borne diseases such as malaria, yellow fever, and dengue plagued Texans well into the present century, causing untold suffering and loss of life as well as costly social and economic disruptions. The boll weevil, imported fire ant, and other introduced pests of man, crops, and livestock have joined with native species to extract a heavy cost in reduced production, as well as increased monetary and environmental expenses due to pesticide usage. There seems to be no end to the surprises inflicted upon us by these new pests. The diverse environments and favorable climates of Texas seem to invite insect immigrants of the worst sort. Furthermore, once these unwelcomed invaders establish residence they show no willingness to leave. Coping with so many native and immigrant pests tends to strongly color our views about the overall importance of the insect world. Only occasionally do we have time to think of the many "good bugs" that affect our daily lives—those that pollinate crops, prey upon their pestiferous cousins, serve as food for birds, reptiles, mammals, and fishes, and sometimes even dazzle us with their beauty and unusual behavior.

In this day of heightened environmental consciousness there is a general realization of the need to know more about the physical and biological world in which we live and the interrelationships of all of its inhabitants. This quest for a balanced ecological view must consider the conspicuous elements of our flora and fauna as well as the more "lowly" and often unseen creatures that make up the vast majority of species of organisms occurring in Texas. Insects comprise a very large part of the latter category.

Knowing the name of an animal or plant is the key to unlocking the store of accumulated knowledge about its life history, distribution, and relationships to man. The name is absolutely essential to accessing the knowledge of an organism as well as to communicating with others about it. Some groups of animals and the plants of Texas are sufficiently well known so that obtaining their names is a relatively easy process. This may be achieved either through use of the keys and illustrations of a field guide designed for such a purpose or by asking someone who is already able to recognize species of the group in question.

Unfortunately, most insects are not easily identified to species by the general student. The reasons for this are obvious when it is recognized that perhaps 30,000 or more species of insects occur in Texas, several times more than all of the kinds of birds, mammals, reptiles, fishes, and plants of the state combined. Insects are often minute or small in size and lead rather secluded lives which further contributes to the likelihood that most of them will not be much noticed. Even the most dedicated of insect specialists find it difficult, and sometimes impossible, to identify some species they encounter. It is still not uncommon to find species of insects in Texas that are unnamed or, in other words, new to the scientific world. Butterflies are sufficiently well known and have been treated in field guides that make their identification to species relatively easy; however, they are the exception rather than the rule. Other Texas insects are sometimes included in taxonomic monographs and journal articles that in a rather technical way treat a genus or family occurring over a wider geographic area. If one is sufficiently motivated to track down such literature and is willing to learn the terminology and intricacies of descriptions and identification keys, it may be possible to obtain names of some of the more elusive species. But the latter process does not lend itself to easy usage by the general public and, as a consequence, the insect in question often remains identified only as a "bug." Such an imprecise identification is not very satisfying to the inquisitive person who may want a species name to be able to learn more about the creature's life history and behavior or simply to satisfy a curiosity to know what things are.

Many entomologists study diverse aspects of Texas insects today and numerous professionals and amateurs alike collect and survey the insect fauna in the state. There is certainly an ongoing effort to increase our knowledge about these organisms. Thousands of specimens are in private and institutional collections in the state waiting to be incorporated into data bases that will provide up-to-date taxonomic, biological, and distributional information about our fauna. However, there is still a long way to go before a reasonably large percentage of Texas insects are collected, studied, described, and illustrated so that they can be identified by nonspecialists. Even though knowledge of Texas insects in general is woefully incomplete, many species are relatively well known and can be readily identified by the general student if the essential information is available. This information is best presented in the form of illustrated field guides and local manuals that emphasize readily visible recognition characters. Once the goal of identification is achieved, the information can be expanded to provide a broader perspective of the life history and behavior of the insects covered. This is exactly the procedure adopted by the authors of the present guide. They initially made the very difficult decisions about which of the many thousands of species of Texas insects should be included. The selected "common" species, a mixture of both pests and nonpests, were then described, illustrated, and their life histories and habits discussed.

One of the great strengths of this book is the extensive information presented on the biologies of the insects covered; I am not aware of any other field guide on insects that covers this subject so thoroughly. Bart Drees and John Jackman are eminently qualified to undertake the task of accumulating and presenting diverse information about insects to a general audience. They both have worked extensively for many years to inform citizens of Texas about the various aspects of insect biology and control. During the course of this work, they have built a strong base of knowledge on the general occurrences of Texas insects, their relationships to man, and the public's interest in them. The authors are further qualified because of their special involvement in the more technical aspects of systematics (taxonomy), both having contributed to the primary literature on this subject.

There will be moments when the natural curiosities of users of this guide are unfulfilled. They may either want to know more about a particular species covered in the guide or have a question about an insect that is not included in the book. Because it is highly unlikely that there will ever be a single publication that contains recognition characters of all of the Texas insects, it is important to realize that the present work is but a first step in the process of accumulating a reasonably complete base of knowledge on the subject. The numerous references included here will lead the user to other sources of information on Texas insects. This field guide is especially useful for introducing a broader general audience to the great diversity of insects and their truly fascinating behavior. Perhaps it will encourage others with interests in Texas insects to treat their special groups in a similar way to extend the knowledge of the Class Insecta in the state. Many smaller groups of Texas insects lend themselves to coverage in guides and manuals that provide handy sources of essential information about their names and lives. Publications on insects are conspicuous by their absence in the growing body of literature on Texas natural history. This field guide to the common insects of Texas serves notice that there is a vast, and to a great degree unexplored, world of creatures out there that are worthy of attention by any lover of nature. Armed with the information presented here, one has to go no further than their own backyard to begin the wonderful journey of insect study.

Horace R. Burke, Ph.D.
Professor of Entomology
Texas A&M University

About the Authors

Bastiaan "Bart" M. Drees, Ph.D., is a professor and extension entomologist in The Texas A&M University System. Dr. Drees presents educational programs to promote the adoption of integrated pest management (IPM) in urban environments and agricultural production systems. In addition, he conducts applied research and has coordinated extension programs relating to the management of arthropods of commercially-produced ornamental plants, rice, and soybeans. He currently coordinates the Texas Imported Fire Ant Research and Management Project, implementing a six-year, multi-agency, statewide plan.

Dr. Drees' awards include the Texas A&M University College of Agriculture's Vice Chancellor's Award in Excellence (1995); the Texas A&M University System's Distinguished Achievement Award in Extension and the Award for Superior Service (1996); and the Distinguished Achievement Award in Extension from the Entomological Society of America (1997).

John A. Jackman, Ph.D., is a professor and extension entomologist in The Texas A&M University System. He presents educational programs on insects and their management. Dr. Jackman's areas of expertise include biological control of weeds in rangeland and aquatic ecosystems, pest surveys, youth programs for extension entomology including 4-H, and vegetable insect management. He has written dozens of articles for scientific journals and public use on a variety of agricultural and urban pest related topics.

Dr. Jackman has extensive computer background and focuses this on computer applications that support integrated pest management. He has coordinated over 20 custom computer programs to support decision making in agriculture using population simulations, data base management, decision support, expert systems, and geographic information systems. He is currently the webmaster for the departmental web site at: **http://entowww.tamu.edu,** which is the most comprehensive site on entomology in Texas.

INTRODUCTION

There are about 25,000 to 30,000 insect species in Texas, with 6,000 being beetles (Coleoptera) and 5,000 being moths and butterflies (Lepidoptera). Although this book will help you to identify many insects to groups (i.e., class, order, family, genus, species), there are too many species to be able to present them all in this field guide. This text includes only the more "common" insects found in Texas. Many insect species are widespread in occurrence and often become numerous during certain periods of the year. However, their populations often fluctuate from year to year, with only a few years during which an "outbreak" occurs. Other species may be restricted in statewide distribution, but occasionally become locally abundant. Still others are neither numerous or rare, but attract attention because of their unique appearance or habits. The species cited in this book are commonly reported to the Texas Agricultural Extension Service. Sections present biological information on individual species or species groups. References are provided for those interested in pursuing additional information.

We designed this book for people with no formal training in the science of entomology: the study of insects. Insects are the most common form of "animal life" that we encounter on a daily basis, yet many people cannot identify them or determine which ones are harmful or beneficial. Most insects encountered are harmless and a natural part of our environment. The assumption that every insect is a pest that needs to be eliminated can lead to unnecessary and over-use of insecticides. The more one knows about insects, the more we appreciate them.

Insects are the most diverse terrestrial animals on earth. They are found in all terrestrial ecosystems and fresh-water habitats around the world. They fill the roles of predators, herbivores, scavengers, and detritivores (feed on decomposing organic matter) in our ecological communities. In short they are valuable components of our ecosystem. Insects are so diverse that a person may specialize in a single group, making it his or her life time work. To organize and make sense of insects it is necessary to have them grouped into orders, families, genera, and species. This scheme of grouping insects together by similar characteristics allows us to access information about insects once we know a group. This is known as systematics or taxonomy.

We study insects for many reasons. They are important pests of crops and livestock; transmit diseases to man and animals; pollinate our crops; and produce honey, lacquer, and other valuable substances. Insects are used as laboratory animals for many kinds of studies and are useful as indicators of environmental quality. They are beautiful in their own right and marvelous for behavioral studies. Understanding insects is a key to living in harmony with them. Many people are prone to hate insects without good reason. In fact, most insects are beneficial or have no really impact on human lives.

We hope this guide will foster fascination with insects and their relatives. It should be a great help to all interested in learning about the insects around them, and especially those who collect insects. (Appendix A at the end of this guide provides tips for collecting and preserving insects.) Casual amateur insect collecting does not endanger species as does habitat destruction or other factors. Only rare species with very localized distributions can be threatened by over-collection. Preparing insect collections promotes science and education. However, be aware that current laws prohibit collection of insects and other arthropods in state and federal parks without written permission.

How to Use this Guide

This guide has two main parts—photographs of common Texas insects and related arthropods, and descriptions of specific families, genera, and species. When studying insects, try to use all of the information that is available. Often clues about host plants or habitat are as useful for insect identification.

There are four basic ways to identify insects: (1) ask an expert; (2) compare a specimen to authoritatively identified specimens; (3) compare the specimen to the original descriptions, illustrations, or photographs; (4) use identification keys. Entomologists and identified collections are seldom readily available. Original descriptions of insects are often tedious to use and require a good knowledge of insect anatomy, a considerable collection of literature, and experience. Identification keys may demand an understanding of specific characters, which may be hard to see and require that a preserved specimen is at hand.

Short-cut methods like quick recognition characters are provided in the book, at least those pertaining to order. These methods rely on recognition of specific features that define a group but may lead to less definitive identifications than an authority would provide. However, with observation and careful deduction, one can become reasonably confident with quick recognition methods, although identification to a higher level of taxa may be all that is achieved. It is always better to be cautious with the identification than jump to conclusions quickly. Often a family name or a genus name still provides sufficient and useful information.

Identification is just as much a process of elimination as it is one of recognition. Like Sherlock Holmes on a case, eliminate the possibilities and what remains is the likely answer. Insect names are continually changing as scientists learn more about them. You will find that some of the names now used do not agree with those in older books. Similarly some names used here will certainly be outdated in years to come.

While an understanding of insect naming systems (nomenclature) is a challenge and a worthy goal, it should not be an end point. There is still much to be learned about the basic biology of insects and their role in our ecological communities. Careful observation of insects can provide some useful information that can add to our existing knowledge. We have provided some key references at the back of this guide that will facilitate further study of insects.

Terminology, Classification, and Use of Scientific Names

Animals are classified into the animal kingdom. This kingdom is then divided into increasingly smaller groups based on similarities between organisms. The different levels of groups are named by the convention of taxonomists (scientists who study classifications). Using the standard groups in a typical complete classification of species, for example, a honey bee, *Apis mellifera* Linnaeus, would be classified as follows:

KINGDOM: Animal

PHYLUM: Arthropoda

CLASS: Insecta or Hexapoda

ORDER: Hymenoptera

FAMILY: Apidae

GENUS: *Apis*

SPECIES: *mellifera*

AUTHOR'S NAME: Linnaeus

There are often additional groups used that are intermediate to the groups listed. These groups can use a prefix of super- (above) or sub- (below) to indicate the position of the new group in the above list. Thus, superfamily groups fall between order and family, while subfamily groups fall between family and genus. An insect name is complete if the genus, species, and author name(s) are given because of the rules that govern taxonomy. The author is the person who first described the species as new to science—Linnaeus in the case of the honey bee.

No capital letters are used in common names unless they contain a proper noun. Common names are written as two words if the species actually belongs to that classification, e.g., honey bee, or as one word if not within the classification, e.g., sawfly is not in Diptera, the order containing true flies.

Scientific names (genus, species, and subspecies) are italicized or underlined with the genus (first) name capitalized. Then, the names of the species' authors follow. Authors' names are in parentheses if the classification of the species has changed since it was described.

This guide uses approved common, scientific, and authors' names according to the Entomological Society of America (ESA), (Stoetzel 1989). Whenever possible, other common names presented are those used by authors cited, or those names associated with the family or genus. Common names are presented here in bold letters, although not all are approved common names. Scientific names of higher taxa (orders, families) are arranged according to the taxonomic groups in Borror et al. (1989).

Insects belong to a larger group or phylum called Arthropoda, which includes all animals with segmented legs, segmented bodies, and exoskeletons, such as spiders, ticks, mites, centipedes, millipedes, shrimps, lobsters, and many other organisms. Entomology is concerned primarily with the study of organisms belonging to the Class Insecta or Hexapoda, but may include the study of other groups, such as the Class Arachnida (spiders, ticks, mites, scorpions, and relatives). However, some other arthropod classes like Diplopoda (millipedes) and Chilopoda (centipedes) are often considered by entomologists. Even a few non-arthropod groups like snails and slugs (Phylum–Mollusca) are sometimes referred to entomologists.

Class Insecta or Hexapoda—Insect Characteristics

Most adult insects have the following characteristics:

- Three body segments (head, thorax, and abdomen) that are usually distinct during at least part of the life cycle.
- Head commonly has a pair of antennae, usually compound eyes (and simple eyes), and mouthparts.
- Thorax usually has 3 pairs of true legs, which are occasionally highly modified or absent to some degree during all or part of the life cycle.
- Abdomen terminates in reproductive structures and occasionally has other appendages (cerci, prolegs, cornicles, etc.).

Life Cycle: Simple or complete metamorphosis with some intermediate or specialized types.

Insect Orders

The Class Hexapoda is generally studied under a classification system with approximately 30 orders. Many of these are of minor importance and are studied only from the standpoint of scientific interest. Considered here are some of the more important orders you are likely to encounter. Many taxonomists disagree on the number of orders and their names. Thus, this scheme will often vary with different authors.

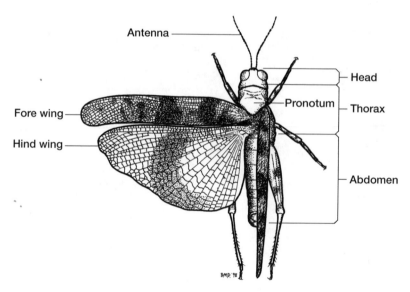

Identifying characteristics of insects

ORDER COLLEMBOLA
Springtails

DESCRIPTION

- Collembola are tiny, wingless insects, which jump by means of a forked tail-like appendage that folds under the body.
- Bodies are elongate or globular, usually white, but some are yellowish brown or gray and covered with scales that may appear metallic in color.
- Mouthparts are formed for chewing.
- Young (nymphs) resemble adults except for size.
- Bodies are microscopic to ¼ of an inch long.

LIFE CYCLE

- Metamorphosis is simple (egg, nymph, adult).

PEST STATUS

- Some species are important pests in greenhouses and mushroom cellars.

HABITAT

- Springtails are common in moist locations, in leaf litter, and under loose bark.
- Springtails are abundant at the soil surface, but are easily overlooked.

1 SPRINGTAILS

Collembola   Many species

Description: Springtails are small, ½₅ to ⅕-inch-long, wingless insects. Color varies, depending on species, and ranging from black to gray to white, yellow, lavender, red, green or gold. Some are patterned or mottled and some are iridescent or metallic due to the scales that cover the body. In addition to antennae and three pairs of true legs, springtails jump with an unusual forked structure (furcula) on the end of their abdomen (fourth abdominal segment). This structure functions like a catapult and is normally underneath the body and held in place with a clasp-like structure (tenaculum). Some springtails can jump 3 to 4 inches.

The **garden springtail**, *Bourletiella hortensis* (Fitch) (Sminthuridae), is a black and yellow species that commonly occurs in large numbers and damages flowers and vegetables. Occasionally, springtails gather in puddles, ponds, and swimming pools, especially the **water springtail,** *Podura aquatica* (Linnaeus) (Poduridae), which is a gray species.

Springtails are occasionally misidentified as fleas because they can occur in the home and jump. However, springtails are round and soft-bodied instead of dark brown and flattened. Springtails have normal hind legs, whereas fleas have hind legs modified for jumping.

Life cycle: There is little difference between immature and adult forms except size.

Pest status: They occur in soil in house plants and around the home where they can be a nuisance when numerous. Occasionally, large numbers of springtails occur in greenhouse crops where they can injure young plants.

Habitat and food source(s): Mouth parts are elongate, concealed within the head. They feed on algae and decomposing vegetable matter, bacteria, and fungi. Springtails prefer dark, damp areas such as leaf mold, damp soil, and rotting logs. Some species injure sprouting seeds, roots and tender shoots.

Literature: Borror et al. 1989; Cole and Hamman 1984.

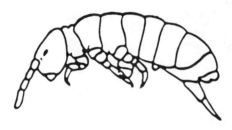

Springtail

ORDER THYSANURA
Silverfish, Firebrats, Bristletails

DESCRIPTION

- Thysanura are wingless insects with flattened elongate bodies.
- Head has long antennae.
- Abdomen usually has three, long, tail-like appendages.
- Young (nymphs) resemble adults except for size.
- Mouthparts are formed for chewing.
- They are up to ¾ of an inch long.

LIFE CYCLE

- Metamorphosis is simple (egg, nymph, adult).

PEST STATUS

- Silverfish can be a nuisance in houses.
- Occasionally they damage bookbindings, curtains, wallpaper, etc.

HABITAT

- They are usually found in moist locations around houses or out-of-doors under stones, bark and boards.
- They run rapidly and hide in cracks and crevices.
- They are secretive and usually are most active at night.

2 SILVERFISH

Thysanura: Lespismatidae

Lespisma saccharina
(Linnaeus)

Description: Silverfish are always wingless and are silvery to brown in color because their bodies are covered with fine scales. They are generally soft bodied. Adults are up to ¾ inch long, flattened from top to bottom, elongated and oval in shape, and have three long tail projections and two long antennae. The **firebrat**, *Thermobia domestica* (Packard), is quite similar in habits but is generally darker in color.

Life cycle: Females lay eggs continuously after reaching the adult stage and may lay over 100 eggs during her life. Eggs are deposited singly or in small groups in cracks and crevices and hatch in about 3 weeks. Silverfish develop from egg to nymph to adult within 4 to 6 weeks and continue to molt throughout their life. Immature stages appear similar to adults except they are about ¹⁄₂₀ inch long when they first hatch and whitish in color, taking on the adults' silver coloring as they grow. They are long-lived, surviving from two to eight years.

Pest status: They are primarily a nuisance inside the home or buildings; can contaminate food, damage paper goods and stain clothing.

Habitat and food source(s): Silverfish are chewing insects and general feeders but prefer carbohydrates and protein, including flour, dried meat, rolled oats, paper and even glue. They can survive long periods, sometimes over a year, without food but are sensitive to moisture and require a high humidity (75 to 90%) to survive. They prefer temperatures of 70–80°F. They are fast running, mostly active at night, and generally prefer lower levels in homes, but may be found in attics.

Literature: Jackman 1981.

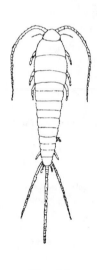

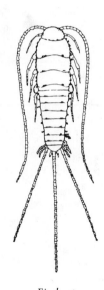

Silverfish   *Firebrat*

ORDER EPHEMEROPTERA
Mayflies

DESCRIPTION

- Ephemeroptera are delicate insects with 2 pairs (less commonly just 1 pair) of triangular-shaped wings with many veins; the front pair is large, and the hind pair is small. Wings are held together and upright over the body when at rest.
- They have long front legs that are often held forward.
- The adults have non-functional mouthparts and do not feed.
- The antennae are very short.
- Abdomen usually has 3 (less commonly only 2) long, tail-like appendages.
- Immature mayflies have elongate bodies with long legs, short antennae and usually 3 tails on the abdomen (some have only 2).
- They have leaflike gills on the sides of the abdomen.
- Adults and immatures can be up to about 1 inch long.

LIFE CYCLE

- Mayflies have simple metamorphosis (egg, nymph, subimago, and adult).
- Adult mayflies mate and lay eggs during their short (1–2 days) adult life.
- Mayflies are the only insect group that molts after the wings are fully developed.
- The first winged stage is called the subimago and this stage typically has cloudy wings.

PEST STATUS

- Adults may emerge in large numbers around water, especially in spring.
- Both the immatures and adults are an important fish food.

HABITAT

- Nymphs are found in aquatic habitats, often found on rocks or other substrates.
- They do not feed during their adult life and are attracted to lights at night.

3, 4 MAYFLIES

Ephemeroptera (several families)   Many species

Description: Subimagoes (pre-adults) and adults (imagoes) have large triangular front wings with many cross veins with the wings held upright and together over the thorax. Subimagoes have the cloudy wings while imagoes have clear wings. Some species may have patterned wings. Hind wings are much smaller than the fore wings and may even be absent in a few (mostly small) species. The thorax and the abdomen of mayflies is bare and often shiny. Legs are of various sizes, with the front legs the longest and held forward when at rest. Body color varies with species, including yellow, green, white, and black. Adults and immatures are quite delicate. Aquatic immature stages are elongate, and flattened or cylindrical. Immature mayflies (nymphs) have long legs and plate-like gills on the sides of the abdomen, they usually have three, long, thin, tail projections (cerci) but a few species only have two. They have short antennae. Their body color may be green or brown but may vary by the food that is eaten. Flattened forms attach themselves to rocks or other substrates in streams. Cylindrical forms are better swimmers.

Our largest species is *Hexagenia limbata* (Serville) (Ephemeridae), which can be nearly an inch long not including the tails. This species is yellow or yellow-green and may be found along the edges of lakes where the nymphs burrow into mud. Some of the most abundant species are in the family Baetidae. Caenidae and Tricorythidae are also common and some of these are barely a quarter of an inch long as adults.

Life cycle: Adult mayflies are very short lived, surviving only one or two nights. During that time the adults mate in swarms in the air. They are also attracted to lights. Eggs are deposited by females while flying low over the water, or by dipping the abdomen on the water surface. Some females even submerge themselves and lay eggs underwater. Afterward, they often die on the water surface. Immatures develop through several stages (instars) by molting during development. The number of molts depends on the species, temperature, and water conditions. Immature stages then swim to the water surface or crawl onto rocks or plants. There, in seconds or minutes they molt into subimagoes with wings and fly quickly from the water to nearby plants where they molt again into adults (imagoes). Mayflies are the only group of insects that molt after they have wings. In all other orders wings are only found on adults, the last stage of development. A typical life cycle will last one year.

Pest status: These common aquatic insects generally go unnoticed, occasionally, large numbers of adults (and subimagoes) emerge during certain times of year in synchrony and are sometimes abundant enough to be a nuisance. Most problem situations occur when they are attached to electric lights at night. Immature mayflies are an important food source for fish. Many lures and artificial flies are patterned after them.

Habitat and food source(s): Immature stages (nymphs) have chewing mouthparts; adult mayflies do not feed and have non-functional mouthparts. Nymphs are aquatic and feed by scavenging small pieces of organic matter such as plant material or algae and debris that accumulates on rocks or other substrates in streams. Most Texas species prefer flowing or highly oxygenated water situations. A few species develop in lakes or ponds and their distribution in water is usually limited by oxygen content of the water.

Literature: McCafferty 1981.

Drees

Mayfly

ORDER ODONATA
Dragonflies and Damselflies

DESCRIPTION

- Dragonfly adults have 2 pairs of large membranous wings that can be clear, colored or marked with patterns, depending on species. The hind pair of wings is slightly larger than the front wings in dragonflies and almost identical in size and shape in damselflies. Dragonflies hold their wings flat (or nearly so) extending them outwards from the body when at rest. Damselflies tend to hold their wings together over the abdomen.
- Adults and nymphs have large well developed compound eyes and short antennae.
- The abdomen of adults is very long and variously colored depending on the species.
- Adult and immature Odonata have chewing mouthparts.
- Damselfly nymphs (immature stages) have elongate tails with 3 flattened extensions. Dragonfly nymphs lack the tail extension and are oval or flattened in shape.
- Nymphs have elongated extensible lower lip (labium) with piercing jaws used to capture prey.
- They are 1 inch to over 3 inches in length. Wingspread can reach about 4 inches.

LIFE CYCLE

- Odonata have simple metamorphosis (egg, nymph, and adult). Immature stages are aquatic and do not resemble the adults.

PEST STATUS

- Nymphs feed on aquatic insects and other organisms (even small fish).
- Adults are also beneficial because they feed on mosquitoes, flies and other small flying insects.

HABITAT

- Nymphs live in flowing or still water.
- Adults are common around ponds, lakes and streams.
- Adult dragonflies and damselflies can hover like a helicopter or fly and dart around rapidly.

5, 6 DRAGONFLIES

Odonata (Suborder Anisoptera)   Many species

Description: Dragonfly adults have two pairs of large membranous wings that can be clear, colored, or marked with black patterns, depending on the species. The hind pair of wings is slightly larger than the front wings. Wings are held flat or nearly so and extend outward from the body when at rest. The abdomen is very long and variously colored depending on the species. Nymphs (6) can be elongate, rounded, or even flattened. They have long legs, are cryptically colored, and have an internal anal pouch for exchanging oxygen.

Our largest dragonflies are in the family Aeschnidae and are high fliers. These species may wander long distances from water. The **common green darner**, *Anax junius* (Drury), is perhaps the most common in this family. **Clubtails** (Gomphidae) are usually a little smaller and typically have an enlarged tip of the tail. **Common Skimmers** (Libellulidae) (5) are the most common and most colorful of the dragonflies. Male and female adults of many of these species are different in appearance (they are dimorphic) and can be separated at a glance. They also change color with age. They are called skimmers because they tend to fly low over water. They often follow the same path and return to a familiar perch. Dragonflies are sometimes called "mosquito hawks" or "snake doctors."

Dragonflies and damselflies can sometimes be confused with antlions and owlflies (Neuroptera). Owlflies have long antennae with clubs on the end. Antlion adults have shorter antennae with clubs at the ends, but these are longer than the hair-like antennae of Odonata.

Life cycle: Adults emerge in the spring, summer or fall. They live for a few weeks to a few months and they fly mostly during the day (diurnal activity). Their mating technique is unusual: Males deposit sperm in a secondary genitalia structure on the second and third abdominal segment by bending the abdomen forward. The male then clasps the female behind the head with claspers on the tip of his abdomen and mating pairs can be seen flying in tandem. The female then loops her abdomen forward and picks up the sperm from the male. Eggs are deposited in emergent plants or floating vegetation or directly into the water. Some dragonflies just drop eggs into the water by dipping their abdomen into the water surface. Nymphs develop in the water and take several months or even years to develop to maturity. They typically develop through 10 to 12 stages (instars), but there may be more or fewer instars, depending on the species and habitat. Once mature, they climb from the water onto plants, rocks, or other structures where they molt into adults. Emerging dragonflies (and other insects that are emerging) are very susceptible to predation or mechanical damage. They must emerge, extend their wings and harden enough to allow them to fly away to safety. Most species have one generation per year. Dragonfly nymphs have rectal gills and expand and contract the rectal wall to move water over the gills. They can move rapidly forward by sudden expulsion of water from the anus which acts like jet propulsion.

Pest status: Dragonflies are beneficial insects. They are predacious on a wide variety of flying insects, and help keep populations of other insects in check.

Habitat and food source(s): Nymphs feed using an extendable lower "lip" (labium) like damselflies. They have teeth on the end of the "lip" that are used to capture and hold prey, which includes other aquatic insects and occasionally small fish. Adult dragonflies can capture prey and feed while flying using their hair-fringed legs as a basket to capture and hold prey. Our species have nymphs that are obligate aquatic insects. They are not strong swimmers and prefer slow moving or still water. They can be found in vegetation and hiding around underwater structures. Some species can be found in flowing streams or rivers. Adults feed on a wide variety of small to medium-sized flying insects such as mosquitoes, midges, other flies, and winged ants.

Literature: Borror et al. 1989; McCafferty 1981.

7,8   DAMSELFLIES

Odonata (Suborder Zygoptera)   Many species

Description: Damselflies have four large membranous wings of nearly equal size, which are held together over their back when they are at rest, except for the Lestidae, which hold them slightly open. Wings are usually clear except for a spot at the end of the wing called a stigma. Some species have black or red coloration in the wings. Damselflies have long thin bodies that are often brightly colored with green, blue, red, yellow, black, or brown. They have oblong heads with bulging eyes and very short antennae. Aquatic immature damselflies (nymphs) (8) have elongate bodies, long legs, and three leaf-like appendages or gills on the tail. These appendages are used for oxygen transport.

There are four families of damselflies (including the Protoneuridae). The largest species in Texas is *Archilestes grandis* (Rambur) in the family Lestidae. **Spreadwing damselflies** in the family Lestidae hold their wings somewhat open when at rest. Calyopterygidae are **blackwinged damselflies,** *Calopteryx,* (some have half black wings) and the **ruby spots,** *Hetaerina,* which has red at the base of the wings. Most of our species are in the family Coenagrionidae, which commonly are found around ponds and streams. They can be found with many body colors but they always have clear wings. The Protoneuridae are small damselflies inhabiting streams in far south Texas.

Life cycle: Adults emerge in the spring, summer or fall. They live for a few weeks to a few months and fly mainly during the daytime (diurnal). Like dragonflies, their mating technique is unusual; see the dragonfly section for a description. Immature damselflies (nymphs) hatch from eggs and live in water. They develop through 10 to 12 immature stages (instars), although there may be more or fewer instars depending on the species and habitat. The last immature stage crawls out of the water onto vegetation before the adult emerges. Most species have one generation per year.

Pest status: Damselflies are beneficial insects; adults catch and eat insects while they fly.

Habitat and food source(s): See dragonflies for the discussion of feeding of the immature stages. Aquatic immature stages are not strong swimmers. They occur on aquatic vegetation and on the bottom of streams and ponds. They feed on aquatic insects and other arthropods that are found in the water. Damselfly adults use their hind legs, which are covered with hairs, to capture prey as they fly. They hold the prey in their legs and devour it by chewing. Adults are commonly found near water.

Literature: Johnson, C. 1972; McCafferty 1981.

Dragonfly

ORDER PHASMIDA
Walkingsticks and Leaf Insects

DESCRIPTION

- They have extremely elongate and stick-like bodies with long legs and long antennae.
- Texas species are wingless as adults.
- Adults and nymphs have chewing mouthparts.
- Immature stages (nymphs) resemble adults but are smaller.
- Females of one species may be over 7 inches long.

LIFE CYCLE

- They have simple metamorphosis (egg, nymph, adult).
- They have one generation per year.

PEST STATUS

- These insects feed on leaves and can occasionally cause defoliation.

HABITAT

- Walkingsticks are slow moving and are generally found on trees or shrubs.

9, 10   WALKINGSTICKS

Phasmida   Several species

Description: Walkingsticks are slow-moving, wingless, and stick-like, with long, slender legs and long thread-like antennae. Their color, form and behavior allow them to hide from predators. They vary in color from green to brown and may grow to be almost 4 inches long e.g., *Anisomorpha buprestoides* (Stoll), although one Texas species, *Megaphasma dentricus* (Stål), grows to almost 7 inches long, the longest insect in the United States!

No other species can be confused with walkingsticks. They do not have front legs modified for capturing prey as do praying mantids and the thread bugs (Hemiptera: Reduviidae).

Life cycle: Black or brown, seed-like eggs, are dropped by females to the litter below host plants in the fall. Nymphs hatch in the spring and develop through several stages (instars) before becoming sexually mature adults. One generation is produced each year.

Pest status: Occasionally, walkingsticks are numerous enough to defoliate some types of shrubs and trees. When disturbed, walkingsticks can emit a foul smelling defensive odor—or in some species a milky, caustic secretion—from glands on the thorax.

Habitat and food source(s): Nymphs and adults have chewing mouthparts and feed on leaves. In the spring, young nymphs feed mainly on understory shrubs. Later instar nymphs and adults feed throughout the crown of host plants. Host plants include apple, basswood, birch, dogwood, hackberry, hickory, locust, oak, pecan and wild cherry. Outbreaks are cyclic.

Literature: Borror et al. 1989; Johnson and Lyons 1988; Swan and Papp 1972.

Walkingstick

ORDER ORTHOPTERA
Grasshoppers, Crickets, and Katydids

DESCRIPTION

- Orthoptera generally have 2 pairs of wings with many veins. Front wings are generally elongate and the hind wings are usually wider and membranous. Wings may be held tent-like over the body or more flattened and overlapping like in crickets. Adults of some Orthoptera, such as cave crickets, never develop wings.
- Antennae may be long and thread-like (crickets and katydids) or shorter (most grasshoppers).
- Hind legs are generally long and modified for jumping.
- Nymphs resemble the adults but lack fully developed wings.
- Adults and nymphs have chewing mouthparts.
- Orthoptera are ¼ to almost 4 inches in length as adults.

LIFE CYCLE

- Metamorphosis is simple (egg, nymph, adult).

PEST STATUS

- Some members of this group are quite destructive to crops (grasshoppers).
- Nearly all Orthoptera in Texas are plant feeders. However, a few are actually predaceous on other insects.

HABITAT

- They may be found in grass, shrubbery, trees or crops.
- Some are attracted to lights as adults.

11   DIFFERENTIAL GRASSHOPPER

Orthoptera: Acrididae   *Melanoplus differentialis*
(Thomas)

Description: Adult differential grasshoppers are brown to olive green and yellow and up to 1¾ inches long. Some individuals are melanistic (black) in all instars. The hind legs (femora) are enlarged for jumping and are marked with chevron-like black markings.

There are several grasshopper species common in Texas, including the **redlegged grasshopper,** *Melanoplus femurrubrum* (DeGeer); the **white-whiskered grasshopper,** *Ageneotettix deorum* (Scudder), the **bigheaded grasshopper,** *Aulocara elliotti* (Thomas). Other grasshoppers that may be recognized are the **high plains grasshopper,** *Dissosteira longipennis* (Thomas); **twostriped grasshopper,** *Melanoplus bivittatus* (Say); **migratory grasshopper,** *Melanoplus sanguinipes* (Fabricius); **eastern lubber grasshop-**

per, *Romalea guttata* (Houttuyn); and **American grasshopper,** *Schistocerca americana* (Drury).

Life cycle: Winter is spent in the egg stage, or during mild winters as an adult. Eggs are deposited in 1-inch-long packet-like masses or pods ½ to 2 inches deep in the soil and sod clumps. Each packet can contain many (over 25) eggs. Eggs are laid in grassy areas of uncultivated land such as roadsides, field margins, and pastures. Tiny grasshopper nymphs hatch from eggs in the spring. Nymphs resemble wingless adults and develop (molt) through 5 or 6 stages (instars) as they grow larger and develop wing pads. Nymphs develop into adults in 40 to 60 days. There is generally one generation per year.

Pest status: This is one of the most common grasshopper species; large numbers can damage a wide variety of plants. Grasshoppers make excellent fishing bait!

Habitat and food source(s): Most grasshoppers are general feeders on the leaves and stems of many types of plants. When numerous, they can damage or destroy many crops including corn, cotton, forage grasses, soybeans, and rice. Large numbers of grasshopper nymphs can develop in tall weedy areas, attracting little attention. However, when they become winged adults, they can fly and disperse greater distances, and suddenly appear to consume a variety of vegetation.

Literature: Helfer 1972; Metcalf et al. 1962.

12   BANDED-WINGED GRASSHOPPER

Orthoptera: Acrididae   *Arphia pseudonietana*
                                              (Thomas)

Description: The adult is 1 to 1¼ inches long, grayish-brown to black and mottled with numerous spots. Hind wings, seen only when they fly, are bright orange-red. A clicking sound is usually made during erratic flight, though not during controlled flight.

Several other species of grasshoppers occur with colorful hind wings. For instance, those of the **pallid-winged grasshopper,** *Trimerotropis pallidipennis* (Burmeister), are pale yellow with a black band beyond the middle. The **Carolina grasshopper,** *Dissosteira carolina* (Linnaeus), has black hind wings with a narrow yellow outer border.

Life cycle: Mated females lay egg pods containing about 20 eggs in soil during the fall. Wingless nymphs hatch in the spring and develop through 5 stages (instars) during the late spring and early summer months. Adults appear in late summer and fall.

Pest status: Often encountered in natural, open, sandy areas and along trails; usually not considered to be a plant pest.

Habitat and food source(s): This species feeds on range grasses, although other plants are also fed upon. They commonly occur in dry sandy or gravely areas with sparse vegetation.

Literature: Capinera and Sechrist 1982.

13   LUBBER GRASSHOPPER

Orthoptera: Acrididae   *Brachystola magna* (Girard)

Description: Adults are large (1½ to 2½ inches long) with short front wings (tegmina), but they are flightless. The body is reddish-brown and marked with greenish-brown although the tegmina are marked with reddish and black spots and each abdominal segment is marked with a row of light dots.

The **rainbow** or **pictured grasshopper (14)**, *Dactylotum* sp. is sometimes confused with the lubber grasshopper.

Life cycle: Eggs are laid in the ground in "pods" of about 20 eggs. Wingless nymphs hatch in late spring or early summer and develop through five stages (instars). Adults occur throughout the summer and fall.

Pest status: Usually not considered to be a serious pest of grasslands.

Habitat and food source(s): The main food plants of this species are forbs (e.g., sunflowers, blanket flower, ragweed, cotton, lettuce, feverfew), although they will also consume live or dead insects. They are usually found in weedy vegetation along roadways, vacant lots, and field margins in areas with rocky or gravely soil.

Literature: Capinera and Sechrist 1982.

15   KATYDIDS AND LONG-HORNED GRASSHOPPERS

Orthoptera: Tettigoniidae   Many species

Description: Tettigoniids are predominantly medium to large (1 to 2½ inches long), winged or short-winged, green to brownish insects with long, hair-like (filamentous) antennae, and hind legs modified for jumping. Wings of adults of some species appear leaf-like, allowing katydids to hide in foliage. Males are capable of generating sound and do so by rubbing their wings together (stridulating). Females hear them with an "ear" (tympanum-covered auditory structure) at the base of the second segment (tibia) of each front leg. Most adult females possess a sword-shaped egg-laying structure (ovipositor).

Some species of "false" katydids of the genera *Microcentrum* and *Scudderia* (Phaneropterinae) **(15)** produce a double row of flattened, grayish-brown, ¼-inch oval, overlapping eggs on twigs in the fall and feed on orange (citrus) leaves during the summer. **Meadow grasshoppers,** *Conocephalus* spp., are numerous in wet grassy meadows and rice fields and feed on pollen. However, they are seldom numerous enough to cause serious plant damage. A few species are predatory on other insects.

Life cycle: Depending on species, females insert oval, flattened eggs into bark of trees, on twigs or along the edges of leaves in the fall. Wingless nymphs hatch in the spring and develop through several stages (instars) as wing pads develop. Adults of most species have fully-developed, functional wings. One generation per year.

Pest status: Most feed on leaves and tissues of various plants; a few are predaceous. If held improperly they can bite. Katydids are named for the sounds resembling, "Katy-she-did" or "Katy did, Katy didn't," produced by males of some species (e.g., the **northern true katydid**, *Pterophylla camellifolia* (Fabricius) (Pseudophylinae). Each species has a unique song.

Habitat and food source(s): Most katydids and long-horned grasshoppers are general plant feeders, consuming foliage, stems, flowers, fruit of trees, weeds and crops.

Literature: Borror et al. 1989; Drees et al. 1995; Helfer 1972; Metcalf et al. 1962; Swan and Papp 1972; Westcott 1973.

16   TREE CRICKETS

Orthoptera: Gryllidae   *Oecanthus* spp.

Description: Adults are winged, but otherwise resemble nymphs. Tree crickets are whitish to light green, slender-bodied with long antennae. The **snowy tree cricket**, *Oecanthus fultoni* Walker, has black spots on the first 2 antennal segments.

Life cycle: In the fall, females lay eggs in shoots of 2-to-4-year-old twigs and stems of trees, shrubs, and vines. Eggs overwinter where laid and hatch in spring. Nymphs develop through 5 stages (instars) before becoming winged adults.

Pest status: More often heard than seen; tree crickets inhabit trees and shrubs but are not usually considered damaging. Egg-laying habits of females in nurseries occasionally damage woody ornamental plants and fruit trees. Treehoppers and cicadas also deposit eggs in twigs and branches, causing some damage when high numbers occur, but usually not sufficient to justify control.

Habitat and food source(s): In late summer, male crickets produce a high-pitched whine or "song." Tree crickets are active at dusk (crepuscular) and at night (nocturnal), inhabiting trees, shrubs, and high weeds, feeding on plant parts, some insects (e.g., aphids, scales) and other materials (e.g., fungi, pollen). Egg-laying activities can affect plant health by injuring growth on twigs and branches or introducing certain plant diseases (e.g., introducing canker-forming fungi); one generation is produced per year.

Literature: Helfer 1972; Johnson and Lyons 1988; Swan and Papp 1972.

17   FIELD CRICKETS

Orthoptera: Gryllidae   *Gryllus* spp.

Description: Field crickets are dark brown to black and ⁹⁄₁₆ to over 1 inch long.

House crickets, *Acheta domesticus* (Linnaeus), are similar to field crickets but are smaller (about ¾ inch long) and yellowish-brown with three dark bands on the head and prothorax. **Cave** and **camel crickets (18)** (Gryllacrididae) are dark brown, wingless, and have long antennae, long well-developed hind legs for jumping. The head is bent down and the back is arched up, giving these insects a humped-back (camel) appearance.

Life cycle: Adult females are recognizable because of the sword-like egg laying structure (ovipositor) in addition to the 2 appendages (cerci) at the end of the abdomen, and their fully developed wings. Females deposit eggs in moist soil or sand. After 15 to 25 days, nymphs hatch from the eggs. They resemble adults except for their smaller size and lack of wings. Nymphs develop to adults in about 12 weeks, depending on temperature. As many as three generations may be produced per year in southern areas. Winter is spent in the egg stage in cold climates and also as nymphs in warmer areas. Crickets can be kept alive for an extended period of time under cool conditions. Adult males chirp to mark territory and attract females.

Pest status: Field crickets feed on plant material, but are less of a plant pest problem than a nuisance when found in large numbers; prefer outdoors, but will be attracted to lights in large numbers and invade homes. Crickets are one of the more effective fish baits.

Habitat and food source(s): Outdoors, high numbers of crickets can damage garden plants. Indoors, crickets can damage natural and synthetic fabrics, furs and carpeting. Chicken laying mash or dry dog food is excellent feed for raising crickets. Crickets spend the day in warm, dark cracks and crevices and emerge at night to feed. Camel crickets live in cool dark and damp habitats like caves, plumbing, under rocks, damp basements and inside privies.

Literature: Davis 1981; Helfer 1972; Leser 1980.

19   SOUTHERN MOLE CRICKET

Orthoptera: Gryllotalpidae   *Scapteriscus borellia*
                                                   Giglio-Tos

Description: Southern mole crickets have front legs that are enlarged, shovel-like and modified for digging. Adults are cylindrical, nearly 1½ inches long and dull brown. The shield-like segment just behind the head (pronotum) is marked with two pairs of pale spots. There are 2 finger-like projections (dactyls) on the terminal segment of the front leg (tibiae) separated by a U-shaped gap, and the hind tibiae is longer than the pronotum. Adults have well-developed wings covering ¾ of the abdomen when held at rest. They fly at night, can run quickly, but are poor jumpers. Nymphs resemble adults but are smaller and do not have fully-developed wings.

The **northern mole cricket,** *Neocurtilla hexadactyla* (Perty), is a native species throughout the eastern part of Texas. It can be identified by 4 dactyls on the digging claw. The **tawny mole cricket,** *Scapteriscus vicinus* Scudder, has only recently been detected in Texas. In contrast to the southern mole cricket, the tawny mole cricket lacks pale spots on the pronotum and the space between the pair of dactyls on the front tibiae is smaller, appearing V-shaped.

Life cycle: Winter is spent as partially-grown nymphs and as adults. In spring and early summer, mating and dispersal flights occur and afterwards females lay eggs in cells dug in the soil. Eggs hatch in about 2 weeks and nymphs develop through 8 stages (instars) during the summer months. One generation is produced per year, although a second generation may occur in southern Texas.

Pest status: This species feeds primarily on other insects and earthworms as nymphs and adults; their prey-searching activities involving digging shallow tunnels in soil, resembling small mole runs, which disrupt root systems of turf grass and crops. The southern mole cricket occurs in the eastern one-third of the state, having spread westward after being accidentally introduced into Galveston and other southeastern locations from South America around 1900. The small mounds and tunnels or ridges of soil are a particular problem on golf course putting greens.

Habitat and food source(s): This insect invades soil in pastures, gardens, field crops, and turfgrass. Infestations are usually very spotty and localized. Mole crickets prefer sandy soil and are often found in golf courses, living in ½-inch-diameter burrows. They are active at night and either tunnel just beneath the surface, up to 20 feet per night when soil is moist in search of insect prey, or come to the surface and run about freely. Tunneling activities can be very disruptive to many plants. They loosen the soil around the root system, causing the roots to dry out. Bermuda grass and bahia grass, particularly in areas with sandy soil, are often more affected than St. Augustine grass. Reduction of plant stand is common.

Literature: Brandenburg and Villani 1995; Brook et al. 1982; Crocker and Beard 1982; Niemczyk 1981; Sailer et al. 1984.

Mole cricket

ORDER MANTODEA

Mantids

DESCRIPTION

- Mantodea are rather large, elongate and slow-moving insects.
- Mantids have the prothorax unusually elongate.
- Their front legs are modified for grasping prey.
- Their wings are held flat over the back and overlap when at rest.
- Adults and nymphs have chewing mouthparts.
- They may be up to 4 inches long.

LIFE CYCLE

- Metamorphosis is simple (egg, nymph, adult).

PEST STATUS

- They feed on a large variety of insects and other arthropods.
- Mantids are well known as valuable predators and are sold as biological control agents.

HABITAT

- Mantids are often found in foliage.
- They usually wait motionless for their prey to venture within striking distance.

20, 21   PRAYING MANTID

Mantodea: Mantidae   *Stagmomantis* and
                                            Tenodera species

Description: Several mantid species occur in Texas. The common name comes from the way nymph and adult mantids hold their front legs, as though in prayer. The front legs are designed for grasping prey. Adults are green to grayish brown, have well developed wings, and may reach 2 to 4 inches in length. Egg masses (**21**) of common Texas species such as the **Carolina mantid**, *Stagmomantis carolina* (Johannson), are somewhat rectangular in shape, usually about 1 inch long, ⅜ inches wide, with rounded sides. Each mass contains dozens of eggs encased in a frothy material produced by the female that hardens and is tan or occasionally white on top with darker sides.

The species most commonly sold by suppliers for biological control, the **Chinese praying mantid**, *Tenodera aridifolia sinensis* Saussure, does not occur naturally in the state. Egg masses of this species are spherical hardened frothy masses glued around twigs.

Life cycle: In the fall, adult female mantids lay eggs on twigs, vines, and other sites such as under eaves of homes. Eggs hatch in the spring. Nymphs develop through several wingless stages (instars) before becoming sexually mature winged adults. Only one generation is produced per year.

Pest status: Mantids are beneficial insect/natural enemy; predaceous on insects.

Habitat and food source(s): Nymphs and adults feed actively on many pest and beneficial insects, including each other! Older mantids can feed on flies, honey bees, crickets, and moths. They are not effective for the control of aphids, mites, or caterpillars. Older mantids are territorial and are only found alone. The lore related to female mantids eating the heads of males in order for them to successfully copulate has more recently been questioned. Apparently, the original research was conducted with starved specimens.

Literature: Helfer 1972; Henn and Weinzeri 1990; Metcalf et al. 1962; Westcott 1973.

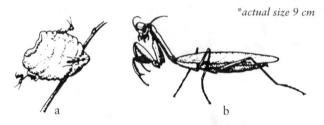

*actual size 9 cm

The Chinese praying mantid, Tenodera aridifolia sinensis: (a) Egg case with newly hatched nymphs. (b) Adult. (From Henn and Weinzeri 1990)

ORDER BLATTARIA
Cockroaches

DESCRIPTION

- They have flattened bodies and their head is mostly concealed from above.
- They have 2 pairs of wings, but in some species the wings are greatly reduced. Wings are held flat over the back. Fore wings are thickened, while hind wings are membranous.
- Immature stages (nymphs) resemble adults but lack fully developed wings.

LIFE CYCLE

- Cockroaches have simple metamorphosis (egg, nymph, adult).
- They deposit their eggs in a capsule called an ootheca.

PEST STATUS

- Cockroaches are somewhat general feeders but have a preference for materials high in fats and starches.
- They have an unpleasant odor and can be very annoying in the home.
- Allergic reactions can occur to cockroach remains and feces.

HABITAT

- Several species invade homes where they can contaminate food.
- They are adapted for running (cursorial) and move rapidly.

22   AMERICAN COCKROACH

Blattaria: Blattidae   *Periplaneta americana*
                                        (Linnaeus)

Description: This is one of the largest common cockroaches in Texas, reaching 1½ to 2 inches. They are reddish-brown and the shield portion behind the head (pronotum) is margined with light brown or yellowish.

The **smokybrown cockroach (23)**, *Periplaneta fuliginosa* (Serville), is similar to the American cockroach in size and color, but differs because the shield behind the head (prothorax) is all brown rather than having light brown margins. This roach frequently enters homes but primarily lives outdoors. Another similarly-sized, black-brown, common indoor species is the **oriental cockroach**, *Blatta orientalis* Linnaeus, but it differs because the wings on adults are rudimentary on the female and only cover 75% of the abdomen of the male. Other cockroach species come in a variety of sizes and shapes. Most are dark brown with or without color patterns on the body. Occasionally, a whitish cockroach is observed and incorrectly thought to be an "albino" form. These are roaches that have just molted and have not yet had time to darken their "new" exoskeleton. There is, however, a pale green cockroach species, the **Cuban cockroach,** *Panchlora nivea* (Linnaeus) (Blaberidae), that is occasionally encountered in the Houston area. Other common outdoor species include the **wood roaches,** *Parcoblatta* spp. (Blatellidae), and the **pale-bordered field cockroach (24),** *Pseudomops septentrionalis* Hebard (Blattellidae).

Life cycle: Female cockroaches glue or drop ¼-inch-long bean-like egg capsules (oothecae) containing about 15 eggs on or around infested areas. Nymphs hatch from the egg case and resemble small grayish-brown adult cockroaches without fully-developed wings. Nymphs molt 10 to 13 times in over a year (470 to 600 days, depending on temperature) before becoming adults.

Pest status: Although not shown to be direct carriers of disease, they can contaminate food and kitchen utensils with excrement and salivary secretions and leave an unpleasant odor.

Habitat and food source(s): Although they occur indoors, this is generally an outdoor species, living in wood piles, decaying trees, palm trees, and in sewer systems. Cockroaches have flattened bodies that allow them to enter homes through cracks around loose-fitting doors and windows, and where electric lines or pipes pass through walls. They are mainly active at night and hide in cracks and crevices during the day, preferring dark moist sites in attics and basements. Cockroaches eat almost anything including meats, grease, starchy foods, sweets, baked goods, leather, wallpaper paste, book bindings and sizing. Adults are capable of gliding flights.

Literature: Ebeling 1978; Hamman and Turney 1983.

25   GERMAN COCKROACH

Blattaria: Blattellidae

Blattella germanica
(Linnaeus)

Description: The adult German cockroach is about ⅝ inch long, overall light brown in color with wings that cover the abdomen. The thoracic shield just behind the head (pronotum) is marked with two prominent black stripes. Immature stages (nymphs) are smaller, wingless and have a pale stripe (on at least the second and third thoracic segments in first stage nymphs) running lengthwise down the middle of the darker brown body.

The **field cockroach,** *Blattella vaga* Hebard, is similar to the German cockroach in appearance, but it occurs primarily outdoors where it feeds on decaying plant materials. Compared to the German cockroach, it is more active during daylight hours and will be found around lights. They also are known to fly when disturbed. The **brownbanded cockroach,** *Supella longipalpa* (Fabricius), is about the same size as the German cockroach, but appears "banded" because the wings are marked with a pale brown band at the base and another about a third of the distance from the base.

Life cycle: Mated females produce an egg capsule attached to the end of the abdomen for up to a month before being dropped a day or so before eggs hatch. Each 5/16-inch-long, brown egg capsule contains 30 to 40 eggs which hatch in 2 to 4 days after being deposited. Nymphs hatching from eggs are less than 1/8 inch long and wingless. They develop through 6 to 7 stages (instars) over 74 to 85 days (varying with temperature) before becoming adults. There may be four generations per year.

Pest status: One of the most common household cockroach pests in the state; their presence in homes is a nuisance and they may spread food contaminants. Some people have allergic reactions to cockroaches or cockroach residues (e.g., feces, body extracts).

Habitat and food source(s): This is mainly an indoor species although they will also migrate outdoors from one structure to another. Occasionally, new infestations begin by bringing in cartons and other materials from infested structures that harbor the roaches or their eggs. Kitchens, bathrooms, and other locations that provide food, moisture, warmth, and shelter are preferred habitats. German cockroaches are mainly active at night, when they search for food and water. During the day, they remain concealed in cracks and crevices unless they are over-crowded, with all developmental stages occurring together. They also can occur in attics, wall voids, crawl spaces, foundation cracks, garbage areas and around the landscape.

Literature: Ebeling1978; Hamman and Owens 1981; Olkowski et al. 1991.

ORDER ISOPTERA
Termites

DESCRIPTION

- Colonies consist of 3 castes: workers, soldiers and swarmers (reproductives).
- Workers and soldiers are soft-bodied, pale-colored, and wingless and never leave the intact colony.
- Swarmers, or the reproductive forms, have dark bodies and 4 long, many-veined wings. The front and hind wings of termites are nearly identical in size and venation.
- Termites also have bead-like antennae and thick "waists" between the thorax and abdomen, which distinguishes them from ants.
- Termites have chewing mouthparts.
- Most termite workers are under ⅜ of an inch long.

LIFE CYCLE

- Termites undergo simple metamorphosis (egg, nymph, and adults).
- Swarmers leave the colonies on sunny days to mate and establish new colonies.

PEST STATUS

- Termites are important because they do millions of dollars in damage to buildings each year. However, in nature they play an important beneficial role because they decompose wood and other cellulose-containing items, thereby helping to recycle these materials in nature.

HABITAT

- Termites feed on dead wood including structural timber.
- Termites eat wood but cannot digest the cellulose without the microorganisms (protozoan) that live in their gut.

26–29   DRYWOOD TERMITE

Isoptera: Kalotermitidae   *Incisitermes* spp.

Description: Drywood termite swarmers are light yellow to black with clear to smoky gray wings, about ⁷⁄₁₆ inch long. Worker termites (nymphs), are up to ⅜ inch long, wingless, white to grayish with white to yellowish-brown heads, and soldiers are similar but with large rectangular darker heads bearing well-developed jaws (mandibles) used to defend the colony.

   Termites, which are occasionally confused with winged ants (Hymenoptera: Formicidae), have body segments that are similar in width,

COMPARE THESE FEATURES

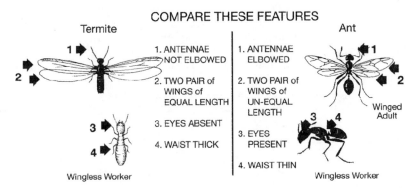

Termite		Ant
1. ANTENNAE NOT ELBOWED	1. ANTENNAE ELBOWED	
2. TWO PAIR of WINGS of EQUAL LENGTH	2. TWO PAIR of WINGS of UN-EQUAL LENGTH	Winged Adult
3. EYES ABSENT	3. EYES PRESENT	
4. WAIST THICK	4. WAIST THIN	

Wingless Worker

Wingless Worker

Termite vs. ant comparison

Drywood termite soldier

Termite fecal pellets

straight (non-elbowed) antennae and, when present, four wings of equal length; ants have narrow waists, elbowed antennae, and when present, fore wings that are longer than hind wings.

The differences between drywood termites (Kalotermitidae) and subterranean termites (Rhinotermitidae) (26) are easiest to see in the venation of the wings of the adult reproductive caste: Wings of drywood termites have three heavy veins along the basal part of the front edge of the fore wing and the crossveins near the wing tip are angled, making trapezoidal cells; subterranean termite wings have just two major veins along the front edge of the fore wing and the cross veins towards the wingtip are perpendicular to these veins, making square and rectangular cells. Soldier and worker castes are more difficult to distinguish, but are generally larger than subterranean termites. However, other characteristics of infested wood can be used for identification.

Life cycle: Winged male and female termites swarm and mate, usually in late summer and early fall. Males and females remain together to start a new colony and mate periodically thereafter to assure continued egg production. Eggs, produced by the mated female reproductive or queen, hatch in about two weeks. Nymphs develop through two stages (instars) and become workers (nymphs). Additional molts produce adults including soldiers; winged forms called alates or primary reproductives; and wingless forms (dealates, secondary reproductives), which are capable of replacing deceased primary reproductives in an existing colony. A colony requires several years to become mature, an event marked by the production of winged reproductives. Mature colonies may contain up to 10,000 individuals.

Pest status: These termits occur in Texas coastal counties, with local infestations in Uvalde and San Antonio and north to Collin County, causing a great deal of concern to homeowners who discover an infestation in their homes. The drywood termites biology differs from the more common subterranean termite because it does not nest in the ground and thus requires a different, more expensive treatment approach.

Habitat and food source(s): Colonies of this social insect occur in sound, dry wood. Swarming occurs at dusk or early evening and the swarmers are attracted to lights. The mated pair starting a colony seeks a crack and crevice in wood, such as the spaces between wood shingles. The queen and male (king) produce and tend the first brood. Afterwards, worker termites care for the queen and male, tend the brood (eggs and immature forms), gather food, build and maintain the colony. Termite workers eat cellulose-containing materials found in plant products, which is digested by one-celled animals (protozoan) living in their digestive system. Workers share food with the other members of the colony. Tunnels or galleries that house the colony are produced by workers in dry, cured wood clean and free of debris. Tunnels can run across the grain of the wood. Those reaching the wood surface end in "kick" holes, where fecal pellets are expelled from the colony and pile up below infested timbers. These pellets are hard, ½s inch long, elongated seed-like particles with six lengthwise ridges between depressed surfaces. Soldier termites defend the colony from intruders.

Literature: Borror et al. 1989; Hamman and Gold 1992.

SUBTERRANEAN TERMITES

Isoptera: Rhinotermitidae   *Reticulitermes* spp.

Description: Subterranean termites, *Reticulitermes* species (Isoptera: Rhinotermitidae), include *R. flavipes* (Kollar) and *R. tibialis* Banks, found throughout Texas, and *R. hageni* Banks and *R. virginicus* Banks, which occur in the eastern part of the state. They are social insects. There are three types (castes) of termite adults in a colony: (1) reproductives, (2) workers, and (3) soldiers. Reproductives can be winged, primary reproductives called alates or swarmers, or wingless, secondary reproductives. Winged reproductives have ¼-to-⅜-inch long pale yellow-brown to black bodies and bear four wings of equal size that may be smoky gray to brown and have few wing veins. Termite workers are white and soft-bodied. Soldiers resemble worker termites, except that they have enlarged brownish heads and strong, well-developed jaws. Soldiers defend the colony from invaders, primarily ants.

Another subterranean species, **Formosan termites,** *Coptotermes formosanus* Shiraki, is found primarily in the greater Houston-Galveston area and Beaumont-Port Arthur. (They can be transported to some major inland areas in landscape timbers.) They are larger than subterranean termites and have a pale yellow body color; the head shape of the soldier caste is more oval; and the wings of reproductives are hairy. Colonies, found in spaces such as wall voids or in hollows dug in wood both in or on the ground, are built of a mixture of chewed wood and soil cemented together, called carton. Reproductives swarm in late afternoon and evening, and are attracted to lights.

Life cycle: Subterranean termites nest in the soil. Winged male and female reproductives swarm from the nest in daylight during the spring, usually after a rain when proper conditions (heat, temperature, and light) occur. Male (king) and female (queen, **28**) termites mate and seek a colony site and stay together because periodic mating is required for continuous egg production. Development from egg to adult takes 2 to 7 weeks. Eggs, produced by the queen develop into wingless nymphs that develop through three stages (instars), requiring 10–14 days, 2–3 weeks, and 3–4 weeks, respectively. At first, only worker termites are produced. Thereafter, there can be three types of nymphs: (1) false workers or pseudergates with no wing pads that molt continuously; (2) nymphs with wing pads that develop into winged male and female reproductives; and (3) soldier nymphs. Reproductive termites can develop from nymphs with wing pads (primary reproductives) as well as from false worker nymphs in the absence of primary reproductives due to the death of the queen or colony fractionation. A termite colony matures (forms reproductives, **29**) in 2 to 4 years and may contain 21,000 to 365,000 termites.

Pest status: Worker termites tunnel into structural timbers and other sources of cellulose on which they feed. Soldier termites can bite.

Habitat and food source(s): Worker termites gather food, maintain the nest, and feed and care for other members of the colony. Paper, cotton, burlap and other plant products as well as the stems of some plants (e.g. okra) serve as food sources. Workers returning to the colony share food with the rest of the colony. Workers feeding above ground construct tunnels or tubes made of soil and wood particles and salivary secretions. These tubes protect the workers and retain moisture in the nest.

Literature: Ebeling 1978; Hamman 1989; Haney 1993; Howell et al. 1987; Pawson 1995.

30   DESERT TERMITES

Isoptera: Termitidae   *Gnathamitermes*
                                                  tubiformans (Buckley)

Description: Surface active worker termites are wingless ⅜-inch-long creamy-white soft-bodied insects with brown heads.

Life cycle: Like other termites, this species is a social insect that lives in colonies deep (up to 4 feet) in the soil and contain thousands of individuals. Their biology is similar to the subterranean termite.

Pest status: Also known as "woodlice," desert termites are common in southern and western Texas and noticeable in rangeland where they construct fragile mud tubes and sheets of mud around the surfaces of herbaceous and woody plants, litter, dung, fence posts, and similar objects. In pastures, their feeding activities can reduce forage for livestock.

Habitat and food source(s): These termites do not tunnel into wood, but rather, remove surface matter from plant matter (cellulose), which they encase. They consume living or dry forage grasses, legumes and other plants, which is digested by symbiotic flagellated protozoans living in the termites' digestive system. In some areas, "carton" tubes can cover about 6% of the soil surface during May through September on shortgrass rangeland in southwest Texas, particularly in overgrazed areas or during dry years. Workers are active on the soil surface at night or during cooler parts of the day. They are active from March through September, particularly after rainy periods.

Literature: Borror et al. 1989; Fuchs et al. 1990.

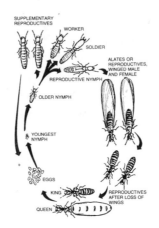

Termite life cycle

ORDER DERMAPTERA
Earwigs

DESCRIPTION

- Dermaptera are medium-sized insects usually with 4 wings. The front pair of wings is short, leathery and meet down the center of the back, which leaves most of the abdomen exposed. The hind wings are folded under these and are membranous.
- A pair of non-poisonous pinchers is found at the end of the abdomen. The pinchers are not segmented but consist of a single piece. The pinchers often are asymmetric, i.e., the right and left sides are shaped differently.
- Immature stages (nymphs) resemble adults but lack fully developed wings.
- Adults and nymphs have chewing mouthparts.
- Most earwigs are about ½–1 inch long as adults.

LIFE CYCLE

- Earwigs undergo simple metamorphosis (egg, nymph, and adults).
- Some earwigs provide some parental care for the young.

PEST STATUS

- They are a nuisance when they enter homes.
- Earwigs in Texas are rarely destructive in greenhouses and field crops.

HABITAT

- Usually earwigs are found out-of-doors hiding in leaf litter, under boards or in cracks during the day. They are active at night when they search for food.
- They release a bad smelling substance when crushed or disturbed.

Earwig

31 EARWIGS

Dermaptera: several families   Several species

Description: Adults and nymphs have characteristic "pinchers" or forceps-like structures on the back end of their brown to black somewhat flattened bodies. Adult males have larger, more curved forceps than do females. They may be up to 1 inch long and have three pairs of well-developed legs. Nymphal stages are wingless, but adult earwigs have hind wings neatly folded underneath short fore wings. About 10 species occur in Texas, but only a few are common. The **ringlegged earwig,** *Euborellia annulipes* (Lucas) (Labiduridae) has yellow legs with dark bands or rings on the segments. Other common species include the **striped earwig,** *Labidura riparia* Pallas; the **linear earwig,** *Doru lineare* (Eschscholtz); and the **brown-winged earwig,** *Vostox brunneipennis* (Serville).

Earwigs are occasionally confused with rove beetles (Coleoptera: Staphylinidae), which are often elongate and have an exposed abdomen and short fore wings (elytra). However, these beetles have no forceps-like structure on the end of the abdomen, but may have short segmented cerci. Many sap beetles (Coleoptera: Nitidultidae) have short front wings as well.

Life cycle: All developmental stages are able to overwinter. Eggs are produced in clusters and hatch in about 2 weeks. Female earwigs stay with the eggs and young nymphs. Nymphs leave the nest in a few days and thereafter develop through five stages (instars) over about 45 to 176 days, depending on temperature. One to two generations are produced annually.

Pest status: Earwigs feed mainly on arthropods and decaying organic matter. They can be a nuisance when they invade homes.

Habitat and food source(s): Earwigs are active at night and seek dark places during the day such as underneath rocks, bark, and plant debris. They also occur indoors, particularly during periods of unfavorable weather conditions. They feed mainly on both dead and living insects, mosses, lichens, algae, and fungi. Indoors, their food consists of sweet, oily, and greasy foods. One earwig, the **European earwig,** *Forficula auricularia* Linnaeus (Forficulidae), feeds at night on leaves of plants. Some species emit a fowl odor when crushed. Earwigs may be found around lights.

Literature: Brook et al. 1982; Jackman 1981.

ORDER PLECOPTERA
Stoneflies

DESCRIPTION

- Adult stoneflies have 2 pairs of wings, which are held together flat over the abdomen when at rest and extend beyond the abdomen. The hind wings are much larger than the front and are folded fan-like under the front wing.
- Stoneflies have long antennae on the head and 2 long appendages (cerci) at the end of the abdomen.
- Adults and nymphs have chewing mouthparts.
- Nymphs are aquatic and have elongate bodies with long legs and long antennae.
- They usually have only 2 "tails" (cerci) on the end of the abdomen.
- The gills on the nymphs are feathery or branched fleshy extensions often under the base of the legs or on the head.
- They are ½ to over 1 inch in length.

LIFE CYCLE

- Stoneflies have simple metamorphosis (egg, nymph, and adults).
- Nymphs develop slowly in water typically taking a year to develop, but adults are short lived.

PEST STATUS

- Stoneflies are scavengers or predators and are generally considered beneficial.
- They are eaten by fish.

HABITAT

- Nymphs occur in fast flowing water that is well oxygenated.

32, 33   STONEFLIES

Plecoptera: several families   Several species

Description: Adults are rather soft-bodied, elongate, and have two pairs of wings that may be highly pigmented and are folded over the back when at rest. The hind wing is quite wide and is folded fan-like over the back. The head bears long slender antennae. The abdomen ends with the two "tails" (cerci). Immature stages (nymphs, **33**) are elongate and flattened or cylindrical. They are ³⁄₁₆ to 1⅜ inches long. The head has widely separated eyes, long slender antennae and chewing mouthparts. Legs are long and end in two claws. They have gills that are finger-like or filamentous and may be branched. Gills are usually found at the base of the legs but may also be found on other parts of the head and thorax. They also have two "tails."

There are only about 20 species of stoneflies known in Texas.

Life cycle: Mating occurs on the ground or on vegetation. Females may carry eggs on their abdomen before laying (ovipositing). Eggs are deposited into the water in many ways: in flight, on the water's edge, or even by crawling below the surface. Nymphs develop in the water over 3 months to one year or more. They usually have 12 to 22 stages (instars). Thereafter, they move to the edge of streams and crawl out on rocks or vegetation and molt into adults. Adults appear in winter or spring, depending on the species.

Pest status: They are uncommon and restricted to aquatic habitats, and are good food for fish.

Habitat and food source(s): Immatures (nymphs) are restricted to fresh water. They are usually associated with well oxygenated streams or sections of lakes with plenty of wave action. They are predatory on a variety of other aquatic insects and invertebrates. However, some are scavengers (detritivores) that contribute to the breakdown of leaf litter and plant material in the stream. Adults can be found along the edges of streams on vegetation or attracted to lights. Adult daily (diurnal) activity patterns vary with species. Adults can be found at lights or on stream side vegetation. They may only be present for a few weeks because some adults are short lived.

Literature: McCafferty 1981.

ORDER PSOCOPTERA
Psocids, Booklice, and Barklice

DESCRIPTION

- Psocoptera are tiny insects that have either 4 wings or none at all. When present, wings are held tent-like over the back of the body.
- They generally have long antennae and soft bodies.
- They have chewing mouthparts.
- Microscopic to ¼ of an inch in size.

LIFE CYCLE

- They undergo simple metamorphosis (egg, nymph, adult).

PEST STATUS

- May be a nuisance when they become locally abundant.
- Some booklice occur indoors and feed on stored grains while others are library pests, which eat glue on old books. Barklice are considered beneficial, even though one species forms webbing on tree trunks and branches.

HABITAT

- Most live out-of-doors and are found resting in soil litter, on and around dead tree branches, or on vegetation, stones, logs and fences.
- Booklice are found in and around old books, papers, stored food, and in damp, dark rooms.

BOOKLICE

Psocoptera: Liposcelidae   *Liposcelis* spp.

Description: Booklice are not true lice. They are small (⅟₁₆ inch long), free-living, pale cream-colored to grayish or brownish, soft-bodied insects resembling tiny termite workers. Booklice species include *Liposcelis corrodens* Heymons and the **cereal psocid**, *L. divinatorius* (Muller).

Another family of psocids, the Trogiidae, also contains species occurring indoors considered to be booklice: The **larger pale trogiid**, *Trogium pulsatorium* (Linnaeus), also known as the "deathwatch" because the female makes a ticking sound by striking her abdomen against surfaces on which she is resting; and *Lepinotus inquilinus* Heyen, which occurs in granaries.

Life cycle: The cereal psocid reproduces asexually (parthenogenetically) and males are not known. Eggs hatch into nymphs that resemble adults although they are smaller. Nymphs develop through 3 stages (instars) into

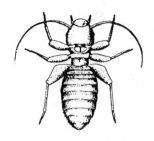

Booklouse

adults over 24 to 110 days, depending on temperature. Up to 8 generations occur per year.

Pest status: Booklice occur indoors where their presence in large numbers can be a nuisance. They do not bite man or animals, but they may contaminate food.

Habitat and food source(s): Booklice prefer warm, dark, and damp indoor habitats, such as on book shelves and in window sills, behind loose wallpaper or in stored dry foods such as flour and cereals. They feed primarily on molds, particularly those growing on the glues and sizing used in book bindings.

Literature: Borror et al. 1989; Ebeling 1978.

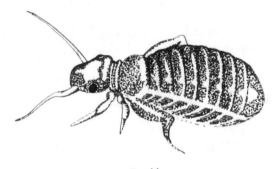

Booklouse

34, 35   BARKLICE

Psocoptera: Archipsocidae   *Archipsocus nomas* Gurney

Description: Barklice are tiny (less then ⅛ inch long) brownish insects. Adults possess 2 pairs of membranous wings, with the fore wing being larger than the hind wing. Wings are held roof-like over the body when at rest. Barklice have long, thin antennae.

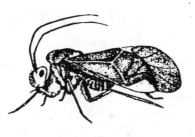

Barklouse

Another common species occurs in Texas: *Cerastipsocus venosus* Burmeister (Psocidae) (35). Members of this species are larger, growing to about ¼ inch long, and adults have shiny black wings. Nymphs appear dark gray and pale banded between abdominal segments. Nymphs are very gregarious, clustering together in a "herd" on the bark.

Life cycle: Eggs of psocids are laid singly or in clusters and are sometimes covered with silk or debris. Nymphs hatching from eggs resemble tiny wingless adults. Most species develop through 6 stages (instars). Barklice are gregarious and live together underneath layers of silken webbing.

Pest status: Barklice are communal web spinners. Layers of silken webbing cause some concern.

Habitat and food source(s): Barklice feed on fungi, algae, dead plant tissues, and other debris. Consequently, they are considered harmless and perhaps beneficial to the trees they infest. Barklice first appear in the spring. However, by late summer, silken webbing can completely wrap a large tree from the base of the trunk to the tips of the branches. Some people consider this webbing to be unsightly. Left undisturbed, these insects apparently eat and remove the silk webbing before populations decline by the end of the year.

Literature: Borror et al. 1989; Little 1963.

ORDER PHTHIRAPTERA

Lice

DESCRIPTION

- Phthiraptera are divided into the chewing lice and sucking lice.
- Chewing lice are wingless parasites that can live on most birds and mammals, although most species are somewhat host specific. They are small, flat, wingless, parasitic insects with mouthparts formed for chewing.
- The **chicken head louse (36)**, *Cuclotogaster heterographus* (Nitzsh) (Philopteridae), is an example of a chewing louse.
- Sucking lice are small, flat, wingless, parasitic insects with mouthparts formed for piercing and sucking.
- The **hog louse**, *Haematopinus suis* (Linnaeus) (Haematopinidae), is an example of a sucking louse.
- Legs and antennae are short and end in claws.
- Immature stages resemble the adults except for size.
- About ⅙ to ³⁄₁₆ of an inch long when mature.

LIFE CYCLE

- Lice undergo simple metamorphosis (egg, nymph, and adults).
- Lice deposit their eggs, called "nits," on the hair or feathers of the host.

PEST STATUS

- Lice are irritating pests that can be carriers of disease.
- Only the sucking lice contain members that attack humans.

HABITAT

- Chewing lice feed upon feathers of birds or on hair and skin of other animals.
- Chewing lice are important pests of domestic fowl and animals.
- Sucking lice feed by sucking blood and are important pests of domestic animals and man.
- Sucking lice are found commonly on domestic animals, but not on birds.

Head Louse and Body Louse

Phthiraptera: Pediculidae

*Pediculus humanus
humanus* Linnaeus and
P. h. capitus De Geer

Description: The **head louse,** *Pediculus humanus capitus* De Geer, and the **body louse,** *Pediculus humanus humanus* Linnaeus, are subspecies that appear similar but infest different parts of the human body. Adult lice are about ¹⁄₁₂ to ¹⁄₈ inch long with six legs that bear claws for grabbing hair. Their abdomens are longer than wide and dirty white to grayish-black in color, depending on the color of the host. Oval shaped eggs, called "nits" (**38**), are glued to the base of hair or fabric fibers and are grayish-white to tan and about ¹⁄₃₂ inch long. After hatching they appear clear. For head lice, nits found on hair more than ¼ inch from the scalp have already hatched or will not hatch, and may be associated with a past infestation. Adult lice are wingless.

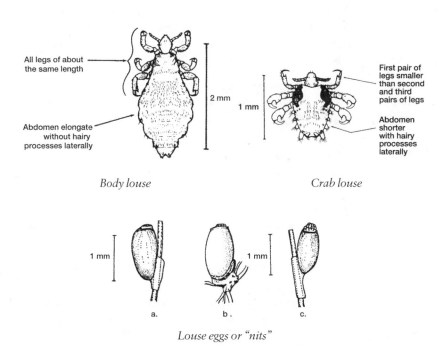

All legs of about
the same length

2 mm

1 mm

First pair of
legs smaller
than second
and third
pairs of legs

Abdomen elongate
without hairy
processes laterally

Abdomen
shorter
with hairy
processes
laterally

Body louse

Crab louse

1 mm

1 mm

a.

b.

c.

Louse eggs or "nits"

The **crab louse**, *Pthirus pubis* Linnaeus (Pthiridae), also occurs on humans, but occurs primarily in the pubic region. The **human louse**, *Pediculus humanus* Linnaeus, is also in this suborder. It is responsible for millions of deaths throughout the centuries because it spreads the organism causing epidemic typhus from one person to another.

Life cycle: Female head lice attach eggs to the hair shafts of the host particularly behind the ears and the nape of the neck, while body lice glue their eggs predominately on clothing fibers. Eggs hatch in 5 to 10 days into nymphs resembling small adults. Nymphs develop through three stages (instars) to adults in 8 to 10 days for head lice and 2 to 2½ weeks for body lice. Adults can live for 3 or more weeks.

Pest status: These lice suck blood, causing skin irritation and itching, and are capable of spreading human disease agents such as those causing typhus and epidemic relapsing fever. They are easily spread, with the head lice often being a problem among school children who are in close daily contact.

Habitat and food source(s): Lice feed every 3 to 6 hours by sucking blood and do not usually survive for more than 48 hours away from the host, although eggs on clothing and other articles can survive off the host longer. Head lice and body lice are parasites only of humans. The head louse is found predominately on the head, while the body louse lives in seams and linings of clothing, blankets and sheets from which they periodically crawl onto the skin to feed. Lice are spread primarily by close personal contact and by sharing personal articles such as brushes, caps, and other headgear, or storing these in shared lockers.

Literature: Hamman and Olson 1985.

ORDER HEMIPTERA
True Bugs

DESCRIPTION

- Hemiptera usually have 4 wings folded flat over the body. The front pair is thickened and leathery at the base with membranous tips or ends. Hind wings, when present, are membranous. There is often a visible triangle at the center of the back that the wing bases do not cover, called the scutellum.
- Mouthparts are formed for piercing and sucking and the "beak" arises from the front part of the head.
- Immature stages (nymphs) resemble adults but lack fully developed wings.
- Most are under ½ of an inch long but some forms, especially aquatic ones, may be over 2 inches in length.

LIFE CYCLE

- Metamorphosis is simple (egg, nymph, adult).

PEST STATUS

- Some true bugs cause considerable plant damage by their feeding; others are beneficial because they prey on other insects.
- Some species can bite humans when mis-handled. A few species feed on the blood of man and other animals.

HABITAT

- They are found in many terrestrial and aquatic habitats, but mostly on plants. Some species occur indoors and are associated with man and animals.

39 GIANT WATER BUGS

Hemiptera: Belastomatidae   *Lethocerus* spp.

Description: Adults can be over 2 inches long, flattened and oval in shape and are basically a green-brown in color. The front wings have a leathery base and the outer areas are more membranous with well defined veins. The abdomen ends in a tube or rod-shaped structure that is used for breathing air while below the surface. The front legs are adapted to capture and hold prey. The second two pairs of legs are used for swimming and have a series of hairs that help in that regard.

Water scorpions (Nepidae) are also large, long-legged aquatic predators. They superficially resemble praying mantids (Mantodea), having more slender, elongated bodies and longer breathing tubes than giant water bugs.

Life cycle: Females may deposit up to 100 eggs or more on the back of the males. Males stroke water over the eggs with their legs and this behavior seems to assist the success of hatching of the offspring. Aquatic immature stages remain in the water often concealed among plants.

Pest status: They can inflict a painful bite if handled improperly.

Habitat and food source(s): Giant water bugs develop in ponds, pools, ditches, and similar habitats with slow-moving water. They are often found among aquatic vegetation. Adults fly well and are attracted to lights, which gives them the common name "electric light bugs."

They capture and hold their prey with their front legs, using their mouthparts to drink body fluids from their prey.

Literature: McCafferty 1981.

40   WATER BOATMEN

Hemiptera: Corixidae   *Corixa* and other genera

Description: Water boatmen are somewhat flattened and elongate in shape. Their hind two pairs of legs are fitted with hairs and the terminal segment, tarsi, of the hind legs are scoop or oar-shaped, which allows them to swim. Adults are from ³⁄₁₆ to ⅜ inch long and are usually dull colored and often mottled.

Water boatmen are the largest group of aquatic true bugs. They are sometimes confused with **backswimmers** (Notonectidae) because they have the same general shape. However, backswimmers swim upside down in the water and the wings are lighter colored than the leg area.

Life cycle: Immatures (nymphs) are similar to the adult and share the habitat.

Pest status: May occasionally be a concern in ponds when numerous; beneficial because they are an important part of the diet of fish.

Habitat and food source(s): Their sucking mouthparts are modified to allow some chewing. Water boatmen often swim in open water. They can be seen in groups or clusters swimming through a pond. They feed on plant material including algae.

Literature: McCafferty 1981.

41, 42   WATER STRIDERS

Hemiptera: Gerridae   *Gerris* and other genera

Description: Water striders are long-legged and slender although some species have more robust bodies. Adults may be winged or wingless. The claws on their "feet" arise before the tip (preapical claws), which allows them to "skate" on the surface film. Part of their hind legs, the femora, are usually very long. Adults are ³⁄₁₆ to ¾ inch long, but the long legs make them appear much larger.

Water treaders (Mesoveliidae) are generally smaller but share similar habitats. **Broad-shouldered water striders** or **riffle bugs** (Veliidae) are similar to water striders but are smaller (less than ¼ inch long), usually wingless, and brown or black in color with silvery markings. They are gregarious, feed on small insects, and occur near or in streams and ponds.

Life cycle: Immatures (nymphs, **47**) and adults share the same habitat.

Pest status: Not a pest, predatory on other insects.

Habitat and food source(s): They sit and skate on the surface of ponds, lakes and slow moving areas of streams. Water striders capture live or dead insects from the water surface. They use the sucking mouthparts to drain body fluids from the insects that they capture.

Literature: McCafferty 1981.

43 AZALEA LACE BUG

Hemiptera: Tingidae   *Stephanitis pyriodes* (Scott)

Description: The adult is about ⅛ inch long, with lacy clear wings marked with brown to black patterns. Nymphs are clear when young, growing darker until they are black, with spines along the edges of their bodies.

Life cycle: Winter is spent in the egg stage. Beginning in February, nymphs hatch from eggs and develop through 5 stages (instars) in about 2 weeks before becoming adults. Adults mate and disperse. Over a period of several weeks, female lace bugs lay smooth, white eggs in the tissue of the underside of leaves, often along a large leaf vein. Nymphs of all stages can occur together because of the extended egg laying period of the female. Two or more generations are produced per year, with periods of high nymphal numbers occurring from March through May and from July through September. Eggs deposited in leaves from September through October hatch the following spring.

Pest status: Nymphs and adults damage leaves on azalea and mountain laurel.

Habitat and food source(s): Evergreen varieties of azalea are preferred, although deciduous varieties and mountain laurel are also host plants. Nymphal and adult stages of the lace bug occur on the underside of leaves. They damage leaves by sucking juices from the undersurface leaves, resulting in yellowish to brownish spotting on the upper surface. Severely injured leaves drop from the plant. Nymphs usually occur in groups and are associated with cast skins from previous stages (instars). Fecal material, appearing as tar-like shiny black specks are apparent on infested leaves.

Literature: Carter et al. 1980.

44 SYCAMORE LACE BUG

Hemiptera: Tingidae   *Corythuca ciliata* (Say)

Description: Adult lace bugs are ⅛ to ¼ inch long and flattened. The wings and flattened areas behind the head are gauze- or lace-like and make these insects appear rectangular and whitish or silvery. Nymphal stages lack fully-developed wings and appear oval, marked with blackened areas and adorned with spines.

There are several other lace bug species in Texas that can become abundant during certain years on particular host plants, such as the **oak lace bug,** *Corythuca arcuata* (Say); **hawthorn lace bug,** *Corythuca cydoniae* (Fitch) (**45**), on hawthorn, quince or pyracantha; **cotton lace bug,** *Corythuca gossypii* (Fabricius); and **lantana lace bug,** *Teleonemia scrupulosa* Stål (**46**), on lantana and Texas sage (ceniza).

Life cycle: Adults become active in the spring when leaves appear on the host plant. Eggs are glued to the underside of leaves among the "hair" (pubescence). Nymphs hatch from eggs in a few days and develop through five stages (instars) before becoming adults. Development from egg to adult occurs in about 30 days depending on temperature and other environmental conditions. Three to five generations can be produced annually. Winter is spent as an adult in crevices of host plant bark.

Pest status: Damage to sycamore leaves is common but rarely affects tree health.

Habitat and food source(s): All life stages occur together on the undersurface of leaves on sycamore, ash, and hickory. The upper surface of infested foliage becomes marked with white to yellowish (chlorotic) and later brown (necrotic) speckles. The undersides of infested leaves become marked with black varnish-like excrement spots and cast skins of previous developmental stages often remain attached to infested leaves.

Literature: Boring 1979; Johnson and Lyon 1988.

47 TARNISHED PLANT BUG

Hemiptera: Miridae   *Lygus lineolaris* Palisot de Beauvois

Description: Adults are oval, flattened insects about ¼ inch long, predominantly coppery-brown with some whitish-yellow markings, particularly near the end of each front wing margin just before wings turn clear and black tinted. Nymphs are similar to adults but lack wings and are greenish and marked with black spots on the thoracic segments.

Another **lygus bug,** *Lygus hesperus* Knight, is a similar species. When nymphs first hatch, they are green with an orange spot in the middle of the abdomen. Adults are marked similar to tarnished plant bug but have a light-colored triangle (scutellum) in the middle of the body between the base of the front wings. This and other species are commonly called "lygus bugs," while members of this family (Miridae) are also called "plant bugs."

Life cycle: Adults overwinter in protected habitats and become active in the spring. Females lay whitish elongated eggs into or on host plants that hatch in about 8 days. Tiny nymphs (½5 inch long) are pale green when they first hatch. They feed and develop through 5 stages (instars) as they grow, change color and develop wing pads before becoming adults. Development from egg to adult takes about 3 to 4 weeks, and 3 to 5 generations can be produced each year.

Pest status: They can damage a wide variety of plants.

Habitat and food source(s): Tarnished plant bugs feed on a wide variety of plants, including alfalfa, beans, beets, cabbage, cauliflower, chard, celery, cotton, cucumbers, pecans, potatoes, salify, turnip, many flowering plants, small fruit and nut trees, grasses and weeds. Plant bugs inject a toxic saliva into the plant during feeding. On fully developed leaves, injury appears as yellowish (chlorotic) spotting, while leaves damaged in the bud stage or during leaf expansion appear distorted. Feeding on cotton squares (buds) or small bolls (fruit) usually causes them to fall off the plant. Damage to buds of developing fruit causes them to become dwarfed and pitted ("cat-facing"). Damage to young peach trees can result in twigs and terminal branches wilting and dying, later causing trees to appear bushy or scrubby.

Literature: Bohmfalk et al. 1982; Metcalf et al. 1962; Slater and Baranowski 1978.

COTTON FLEAHOPPER

Hemiptera: Miridae   *Pseudatomoscelis seriatus*
                                      (Reuter)

Description: Adult cotton fleahoppers are about ⅛ inch long, oval, white to yellowish-green with white spots, and minute black hairs on the fore wings. Immature stages (nymphs) are similar, but lack fully-developed wings. Cotton fleahopper nymphs can be confused with nymphs of other plant bugs.

Life cycle: Eggs are ¹⁄₃₀ inch long and yellow-white, and are inserted under the bark of small stems. This stage survives the winter in wild host plants. During the year, eggs hatch in about 11 days. Nymphs molt five times within a period of about 15 days before becoming adults. Up to 8 generations occur annually.

Pest status: It is both a beneficial insect and a pest, being a predator of eggs and immature stages of insects and a plant-damaging species in cotton fields, where it punctures small cotton squares, causing them to drop from the plants.

Habitat and food source(s): Wild host plants include woolly croton, cutleaf evening primrose, snowy sundrops, woolly tidestromia, beebalm (horsemint), and silverleaf nightshade. One to three generations occur on cotton. Nymphs and adults feed on tender leaf buds of host plants, interfering with normal growth patterns by causing shortened internodes and stimulating the growth of spindly branches or "suckers" from the lower parts of the cotton plant. Feeding on anthers of small cotton squares causes them to turn brown and die, resulting in a "blasted" appearance. Heavy infestations can result in fruit loss on preflowering plants. Fleahoppers also feed on eggs of cotton bollworms and tobacco budworms (Lepidoptera: Noctuidae), each eating about one egg per day.

Literature: Bohmfalk et al. 1982; Slater and Baranowski 1978.

48 GARDEN FLEAHOPPER

Hemiptera: Miridae   *Halticus bractatus* (Say)

Description: Adult garden fleahoppers are tiny (less than ¹⁄₁₆ inch long) and black with long antennae. Males and the long-winged form of the female resemble tiny tarnished plant bugs. Females of the short-winged form are more globular in shape and have beetle-like fore wings with no membranous portions. They generally occur on the underside of leaves and readily jump or hop when disturbed.

This insect superficially resembles flea beetles (Coleoptera: Chrysomelidae) in size and jumping habits, but produces no holes in leaf tissue as do chewing beetles. They may also be confused with some aphids because of their small size. However, aphids do not jump. The **suckfly**, *Cyrtopeltis notata* (Distant) (Miridae), is another small true bug that can similarly damage tomatoes in home gardens and commercial greenhouses. Adults are slender and parallel-sided, ⅛ inch long, green-black bugs with long slender legs (not modified for jumping), and antennae. Nymphs are greenish with red eyes and do not have fully-developed wings. They develop through five molts and feed on the underside of leaves.

Life cycle: Winter is spent in the egg stage (diapausing) in colder regions or as adults in warmer areas. Adults deposit eggs in punctures made by the mouthparts in leaves and stems of host plants. Nymphs hatching from eggs are green and develop through 5 stages (instars) before becoming winged adults in 11 to 41 days depending on temperature. Up to five generations can occur per year.

Pest status: They are common in the garden causing stippling of leaves of a wide variety of plants.

Habitat and food source(s): Nymphs and adults feed on leaves and stems of beans, beets, cabbage, celery, corn, cowpeas, cucumbers, eggplant, lettuce, peas, peppers, potatoes, pumpkins, squash, sweet potatoes, tomatoes, many herbs and other plants including ornamentals such as chrysanthemums. Leaf feeding causes pale (chlorotic) spots that appear as stipples, which detracts from plants grown for use of fresh leaves such as lettuce and herbs. Heavily damaged leaves may die.

Literature: Carter et al. 1982a; Little 1963; Metcalf et al. 1962; Slater and Baranowski 1978.

49   Damsel Bugs

Hemiptera: Nabidae   *Nabis* spp.

Description: Adult damsel bugs are ⅜ to ½ inch long, tan to reddish-brown and slender, with the body tapering toward the head. Nymphal stages are similar but lack fully-developed wings. Legs are relatively long with the front pair enlarged slightly to capture prey. The head bears long four-segmented antennae and a four-segmented beak (rostrum). The beak is held underneath the body when at rest but is capable of being extended to pierce prey.

Life cycle: Adult damsel bugs spend the winter in ground cover and winter crops such as winter grain and alfalfa. Eggs are inserted into plant tissue by females. Nymphs hatching from eggs develop through 5 stages (instars) in about 50 days. They are most abundant from mid-June through mid-August.

Pest status: Species of damsel bugs, including the **pale damsel bug,** *Nabis capsiformis* Germar, are beneficial insects because they feed on a variety of arthropod pests; capable of biting but generally medically harmless.

Habitat and food source(s): Damsel bugs are abundant in gardens, orchards, and field crops such as cotton and soybeans, where they feed on caterpillar eggs, small larvae, aphids, fleahoppers, lygus bugs, leafhoppers, treehoppers, and spider mites. They will also prey on other beneficial insects such as minute pirate bugs and bigeyed bugs. Although they will also feed on some plants, they cause no damage.

Literature: Bohmfalk et al.1982; Irwin and Shepard 1980.

50   Minute Pirate Bug

Hemiptera: Anthocoridae   *Orius tristicolor* (White)

Description: Adults are tiny (⅛ inch) black bugs with white markings at the base of the front wings (hemelytra), resulting in a band-like appearance across the body when wings are at rest. Wingless immature stages (nymphs) are orange. The **insidious flower bug,** *O. insidiosus* (Say), is often the more abundant species in East Texas.

Anthocorids are occasionally mistaken for chinch bugs (Lygaeidae), particularly in the early nymphal stages.

Life cycle: Adults overwinter in protected habitats such as in leaf litter. Female *Orius* spp. insert eggs into plant tissue. Nymphs develop through several stages (instars) before becoming winged adults.

Pest status: Considered beneficial; nymphs and adults prey on small arthropods. They are capable of using their sucking mouthparts to bite man.

Habitat and food source(s): Nymphs and adults prey upon a wide variety of arthropods including aphids, chinch bugs, springtails, plant bugs, thrips, eggs and small larvae of corn earworms, whiteflies, and spider mites. Sucking mouthparts are inserted into prey and body fluids are removed. When corn earworm eggs are plentiful, *Orius* spp. eat about one egg per day. They are important natural enemies of pests of many crops including corn, cotton, sorghum, and soybeans. They may also feed on tender plant parts. Some *Orius* species are sold commercially for augmentive biological control releases.

Literature: Bohmfalk, et. al. 1982; Henn and Weinzeri 1990; Kogan and Herzog 1980; Slater and Baranowski 1978; Swan and Papp 1972.

51, 52   ASSASSIN BUGS

Hemiptera: Reduviidae   *Zelus, Sinea* species, and others

Description: Common species include the **leafhopper assassin bug,** *Zelus renardii* Kolenati, and the **spined assassin bug,** *Sinea diadema* (Fabricius). In both species, the head supports a strong beak. The leafhopper assassin bug is about ½ inch long and red, brown to yellowish-green. The front legs have no spines and are covered with a sticky substance with which they catch their prey. The spined assassin bug is similar in size but is dark brown to dull red-brown, not bicolored. The front legs are slightly swollen and covered with spines. The abdominal margins are expanded and flat with a pale spot on the rear margin of each segment.

Assassin bugs are often mistaken for pests such as the leaffooted bug (Coreidae). Assassin bugs lack the widened portion of the hind legs and are more solitary in habits than plant feeding species.

Life cycle: Assassin bug females periodically deposit masses of brown, cylindrical eggs. Immature nymphs resemble adults but are wingless and develop through five molts (instars) into adults in about two months. Nymphs of the spined assassin bug are distinctly sway-backed.

Pest status: Assassin bugs are beneficial insects/natural enemies; predatory on insect eggs, larvae and adults. They are capable of biting.

Habitat and food source(s): In cotton fields, assassin bugs prey on a wide range of prey including fleahoppers, lygus bugs, aphids, caterpillar eggs and larvae, and boll weevils. They will also eat other predaceous insects such as lady beetles and bigeyed bugs. They occur in gardens on tomatoes, cabbage, and other plants.

Literature: Bohmfalk et al. 1982; Frank and Slosser 1991; Kogan and Herzog 1980; Slater and Baranowski 1978.

BLOODSUCKING CONENOSE AND MASKED HUNTER

Hemiptera: Reduviidae

Triatoma sanguisuga
(LeConte) and *Reduvius*
personatus (Linnaeus)

Description: Adults are ¾ inch long, flattened insects with elongated, cone-shaped heads bearing a pair of five-to-six-segmented, elbowed antennae and prominent "beak" (proboscis). The beak of *Triatoma* is more tapered, slender, and straighter than that of *Reduvius*. Their bodies are dark brown to black, but the abdomen of the bloodsucking conenose is widened, with flattened sides sticking out beyond the margins of the wings and marked with six equally-spaced reddish-orange spots.

The **bloodsucking conenose**, *Triatoma sanguisuga* (LeConte), is also called the "Mexican bed bug." Species of *Triatoma* are also called conenoses or "kissing bugs" because of their habit of biting around the mouth. Bites of kissing bugs are occasionally mis-diagnosed as "spider bites."

Bites of the **masked hunter**, *Reduvius personatus* (Linnaeus), and other predatory assassin bugs can also be painful.

Bed bugs, *Cimex lectularius* Linnaeus (Cimicidae), also feed on human blood, but are not closely related to kissing bugs and are seldom encountered today. These bugs are wingless, grow to be about ¼ inch long and have oval, flattened, brown bodies. They feed on human blood at night and hide during the day in cracks and crevices.

Life cycle: In the Reduviidae, barrel-shaped eggs, some with ornate fringed caps, are deposited singly or in small clusters in areas frequented by females. Tiny wingless nymphal stages hatch in 8 to 30 days, depending on species and temperature. Nymphs develop through five (*Reduvius*) or eight (*Triatoma*) stages (instars) before becoming adults with fully-developed wings. The masked hunter overwinters as a partially-developed nymph. Other species overwinter in the egg or adult stages. Generally, one generation is produced annually, although the bloodsucking conenose requires three years for development.

Pest status: Masked hunters are considered beneficial because they prey on insect pests; this and many reduviid species are medically important because they can "bite" with their sucking mouthparts. The mouthpart system (proboscis) is held bent back under the body when at rest. Piercing stylets are held within a sheath (labium). When feeding, articulation allows the proboscis to be pointed forward. Stylets can be extended beyond the end of the labial sheath into the blood meal host or insect prey.

Triatoma feed only on the blood of vertebrates. In southern Texas and southward, they can transmit the Chagas' disease agent, *Trypanosoma cruzi* Chagas, among small animals, dogs, and man. During blood-feeding, their bites are hardly felt by their hosts. However, bites, usually produced in self-defense, can be quite painful and can cause severe reactions in sensitive people, including burning, itching, swelling, red blotches, welts, rashes, fainting spells, nausea, diarrhea and anaphylactic reactions.

Habitat and food source(s): The masked hunter occurs in and around homes, entering homes to feed on bed bugs, *Triatoma,* and other insects. Adults are often attracted to lights. Nymphal stages "mask" their bodies by picking up debris such as dust and lint on their sticky bodies. The blood-sucking conenose bugs feed on blood of rats and other animals, including humans. They often live in nests of wood rats and other nesting rodents.

Literature: Borror et al. 1989; James and Harwood 1979; Slater and Baranowski 1978; Swan and Papp 1972.

54 WHEEL BUG

Hemiptera: Reduviidae   *Arilus cristatus* (Linnaeus)

Description: Adults are up to 1¼ inch long, dark brown insects with a prominent spiny ridge or "wheel" on the thorax.

Life cycle: Females deposit bottle-shaped eggs in the fall on twigs and other surfaces, and overwinter. Nymphs, with red and black patterns, hatch in the spring. Older nymphs resemble adults but lack fully-developed wings. One generation is produced annually.

Pest status: This large predaceous insect is known for its painful bite.

Habitat and food source(s): Wheel bug nymphs and adults are predaceous on a wide range of insects including honey bees and caterpillars. However, they are rarely numerous, and therefore have minimal impact on prey insect populations in agricultural crops.

Literature: Frank and Slosser 1991; Slater and Baranowski 1978.

55–57 SOUTHERN CHINCH BUG

Hemiptera: Lygaeidae   *Blissus insularis* Barber

Description: Adult chinch bugs are almost ³⁄₁₆ inch long, have black bodies and fully developed wings that appear frosty-white except for distinctive triangular black patch-like markings at the middles of the outer margins. Adults appear as either long-winged or short-winged forms. Newly hatched nymphs appear red-orange with a pale whitish band across their abdomens. As they molt through 5 growth stages (instars), nymphs gradually change color from red to orange to black and develop wing pads.

The **common chinch bug,** *Blissus leucopterus leucopterus* (Say), also occurs in Texas and has a wide range of agricultural crop and wild host plants. Appearance, damage, and life history is very similar to that of the southern chinch bug. **False chinch bugs,** *Nysius raphanus* Howard and *N. ericae* (Schilling) (Lygaeidae), are similar in appearance and habits to chinch bugs, and feed primarily on the seed heads of sorghum and weed seeds. Other common lygaeids are the **large milkweed bug (56),** *Oncopeltus fasciatus* (Dallas), and species in the genus *Lygaeus* (57).

Life cycle: Adult southern chinch bugs overwinter in protected places like weeds and grasses, becoming active in the spring. During mild winters and probably in southern Texas, all developmental stages may survive. Mated females lay eggs singly behind leaf sheaths or in the soil around host plants. Wingless nymphs hatch from eggs in about 2 weeks and develop through 5 stages for about 30 days before becoming adults. The entire life cycle can occur in about 6 weeks or longer, depending on temperature. Two to five or more generations can occur annually.

Pest status: Chinch bugs are capable of damaging plants such as grasses, corn and sorghum.

Habitat and food source(s): St. Augustine grass is the primary host of the southern chinch bug. Other host plants include bermuda grass, bahia grass, centipede grass and zoysia grass. Nymphs and adults use their sucking mouthparts to remove sap from the base (crown) and stolons of plants and inject a toxic substance that prevents the plant from transporting water. In turf grass areas, damage typically appears as yellow or dead drought-stressed or heat-stressed spots in the yard, most commonly in July and August. Infestations are often initially localized because chinch bugs feed in aggregations. Damaged plants occur in spots or patches that enlarge as the population increases and spreads. When infested host plants die, high numbers of chinch bugs migrate by walking to neighboring lawns or turf areas in search of suitable host plants.

Literature: Carter et al. 1982b; Hamman 1979; Olkowski et al. 1991; Randolph and Garner 1961; Reinert et al. 1995.

58, 59   BIGEYED BUGS

Hemiptera: Lygaeidae   *Geocoris* spp.

Description: Several species are found in Texas, with *Geocoris punctipes* (Say), a large gray species, and *G. uliginosus* (Say), a small black species, being common in cotton fields. Species range in size from ⅛ to ¼ inch long and have broad heads with large, curved, backward-projecting eyes. Immature stages (nymphs) resemble adults but do not have fully-developed wings.

Life cycle: Adults overwinter and lay eggs on plants. Nymphs (59) hatching from eggs develop through 5 stages (instars) before becoming winged adults.

Pest status: Predaceous nymphs and adults are beneficial.

Bigeyed bug

Habitat and food source(s): Nymphs and adults are general predators, feeding on small caterpillars and caterpillar eggs, fleahoppers, lygus bugs, mites, thrips, whiteflies. They will also feed on various seeds and suck plant juices but are not considered a threat to plants. They occur in most crops and landscapes.

Literature: Bohmfalk et al. 1982; Kogan and Herzog 1980.

60   LARGUS BUG

Hemiptera: Largidae   *Largus succinctus*
                                       (Linnaeus)

Description: The **largus bug,** *Largus succinctus* (Linnaeus) (Largidae), is about ½ inch long, elongated, oval and flattened, slate blue in color, and has reddish-yellowish markings around margins of the shield behind the head (pronotum) and abdomen. The outer margins of the pronotum are rounded. Immature nymphs are similar in appearance, steel blue, with flattened oval bodies, but lack fully-developed wings. (Also see boxelder bugs.)

Life cycle: Mated females lay eggs on host plants or drop them on the ground near their host plant. Tiny nymphs hatch from eggs and develop through 5 stages (instars) over several weeks before becoming adults.

Pest status: Largus bugs are seed feeders, occasionally a nuisance when in high numbers around the home.

Habitat and food source(s): Although largus bugs are general feeders, they generally cause little damage to plants upon which they feed.

Literature: Borror et al. 1989.

61–64   SQUASH BUG

Hemiptera: Coreidae   *Anasa tristis* (De Geer)

Description: Adults are dark brown, ½ to ⅔ inch long, ¼ inch wide with fully-developed flat wings held over the back of the body. Eggs are shiny brown, oval and usually deposited on their long sides on the underside of leaves in an orderly, tight or loose aggregation forming an angular pattern bordered by larger leaf veins. Developing nymphs (**62**) are wingless and mostly gray with black antennae and legs.

Squash bug

Another coreid common in east Texas gardens and similar to squash bugs is *Phthia picta* (Drury) (**63**). *Hypselonotus* (**64**) is another genus of coreids that is frequently encountered.

Life cycle: During the winter months, adult squash bugs survive in plant debris, under piles of leaf litter, firewood, boards, and other protected sites. They become active in spring after host plants emerge, mate, and lay eggs on the underside of leaves. Nymphs hatch from eggs in about 2 weeks. Upon hatching, they are about ⅛ inch long and green and reddish in color. Initially they aggregate, but as they develop to nearly the size of winged adults through 5 stages (instars), the grayish-white nymphs gradually disperse throughout the plants. Development from egg to adult occurs in 45 to 60 days, and up to 3 generations may occur annually.

Pest status: These insects damage leaves and fruit of squash and related plants, occasionally killing heavily-infested plants or parts of plants.

Habitat and food source(s): Host plants include pumpkin, squash, and other cucurbits. Damaged leaves appear grayish and may wilt and die. Populations increase during the season and large numbers of nymphs may occur on the fruit in the fall. Adults are more solitary and tend to occur around the base of the plant near the ground. When crushed, a disagreeable odor is released by this insect.

Literature: Little 1963; Metcalf et al.1962.

65–68 LEAFFOOTED BUGS

Hemiptera: Coreidae   *Leptoglossus clypealis*
                                     (Heidemann)
                                     L. phyllopus (Linnaeus)
                                     and others

Description: Adults are about ¾ inch in length and are dark brown with a whitish to yellowish stripe across the central part of the back. The hind legs have flattened, leaf-like expansions on the tibia. Nymphal stages look similar to adults except that they do not have fully developed wings.

A leaffooted bug in the genus *Narnia* (**66**) is common on prickly pear cactus. Another species (**67**), *Acanthocephala declivis* (Say), is one of the largest true bugs, being over an inch in length as an adult. Adults are particularly active in the fall. Although some members of this group are predaceous, immature stages can be easily confused with assassin bugs (Reduviidae).

Broad-headed bugs (68) (Alydidae) are similar to Coreidae, but the head is as wide as the widest portion of the thorax. They grow to about ¾ inch long and are yellow to dark brown. Immature stages remarkably resemble ants (Hymenoptera: Formicidae).

Life cycle: Immature stages are gregarious, being found in high numbers on certain fruit where egg masses were laid.

Pest status: Plant feeder; has well developed scent glands and will emit distinctive odor when handled.

Habitat and food source(s): Leaffooted bugs feed on a wide variety of developing fruit, including cotton, peaches and tomatoes, and seeds such as beans, black-eyed peas, and sorghum. They also feed on the stems and tender leaves of plants such as potatoes. Damage produced is similar to that produced by stink bugs.

Literature: Borror et al. 1989; Slater and Baranowski 1978.

69   BOXELDER BUG

Hemiptera: Rhopalidae   *Boisea trivittata* (Say)

Description: Adults are flattened, about ½ inch long and ⅓ inch wide, brownish-gray to black bugs with characteristic red eyes, back and wing markings. The segment behind the head (pronotum) has three red lines running lengthwise. Immatures or nymphs are red and develop black markings and wing pads as they grow.

The **redshouldered bug (69)**, *Jadera haematoloma* (Herrich-Schäffer), is also a pest of shade trees and often enters homes. Another Rhopalid in the genus, *Niesthrea,* occurs on hibiscus.

Life cycle: Overwintered adult females deposit eggs in bark cracks and crevices in the spring at bud break. Nymphs hatch from eggs in about 2 weeks and develop through several stages (instars) during the summer before becoming winged adults. There may be 2 or more generations per year.

Pest status: Feeds on boxelder and several kinds of trees, but are more of a problem when they enter houses in search of overwintering habitats.

Habitat and food source(s): Nymphs and adults suck juices primarily from seeds of boxelder trees, but also suck juices from fruits of other trees, e.g., plum, cherry, apple, peach, grape, chinaberry, western soapberry, ash, and maple. Young fruit may be scarred or dimpled from feeding activities. In the fall, large nymphs and winged adults leave host plants in search of overwintering habitats. They enter homes through cracks and crevices around doors and window frames and around the foundation. They also overwinter in tree holes and in piles of debris around the landscape. In the spring adults reappear and often sun themselves on light colored walls. In homes, the bugs may stain curtains, paper and other objects with fecal material.

Literature: Hamman 1985.

70–72 BURROWER BUG

Hemiptera: Cydnidae   *Pangaeus bilineatus* (Say)

Description: Adults are black, roughly ¼ inch long, and superficially resemble small stink bugs. However, they are more oval and have spines on their leg segments (tibiae). The front wings are clear and membranous (hemelytron) at the tips beyond a black thickened basal part (corium and clavus), and can be seen at the rear end of the body when the wings are held at rest.

Members of the Thyreocoridae (**71**), e.g., *Corimelaena pulicaria* (Germar), are similar to burrowing bugs. However, when at rest, adults lack clear membranous front wing tips because the wings are completely covered by an enlarged shell-like plate (the scutellum, which is normally a small triangular-shaped area between the basal part of the wings just behind the pronotum or shield located just behind the head). Black or with a paler margin along the pronotum and scutellum, they are very beetle-like in appearance because the membranous wings are not easily visible. **Shield bugs (72)** (Scutellaridae) have a similar shell-like plate on the back. They are generally brown to green and often enter homes in the fall.

Life cycle: In Texas, burrower bugs overwinter by burrowing into the soil at a depth of 6 to 8 inches below the surface until the first week of March, at which time they move up to the surface.

Pest status: They can be a pest of crop production; large numbers of adults encountered around lights at night in the fall; found throughout Texas.

Habitat and food source(s): Burrower bugs feed on parts of plants including pepper and spinach seedlings, vegetable crops, cotton and peanuts.

Literature: Borror et al. 1989; Cole 1988; Metcalf et al. 1962; Swan and Papp 1972.

73–78 SOUTHERN GREEN STINK BUG

Hemiptera: Pentatomidae   *Nezara viridula* (Linnaeus)

Description: Adults are about ½ to ¾ inch in length and are solid green. Immature stages vary in color from black for very small nymphs to green for larger nymphs. However, the immature stages have a distinctive pattern of whitish spots on the abdominal segments. Nymphal stages (**74**) are often found together in high numbers because eggs (**75**) are laid in clusters that appear as rows of small barrels on and around suitable food sources.

There are several different species of stink bugs common in Texas, including the **conchuela**, *Chlorochroa ligata* (Say); the **brown stink bug (76)**, *Euschistus servus* (Say); and the **harlequin bug (77)**, *Murgantia histrionica* (Hahn). One group of stink bug species, *Brochymena* (**78**), often called the "rough" or "tree" stink bug, closely resembles the color and texture of tree bark on which they live.

Life cycle: Adults deposit barrel-shaped eggs; immature stages develop through five stages or instars that appear similar to adults except that they do not have fully developed wings. Development from egg to adult requires about 35 days, but varies with temperature. Up to five generations per year may occur with greater numbers appearing in the fall before adults overwinter.

Pest status: Plant feeder; has well developed scent glands and will emit a distinctive disagreeable odor when handled.

Habitat and food source(s): The southern green stink bug feeds on a wide variety of developing fruit, including cotton, peaches, and tomatoes, and seeds such as pecan, sorghum, and soybeans. They also feed on many ornamental and wild plants. In fruit, such as tomatoes, damage is of two types: Young green fruit is damaged, by the bugs' toxic saliva injected into the plant cells, which stop expanding, while the cells around the dead cells continue to expand by increasing their water content. The result is deformed fruit that appears to have dimples. This type of damage has been called "cat facing." The second type of damage occurs when ripened or nearly ripened fruit is attacked. Toxic saliva is injected which merely kills a cluster of cells that later forms an off-color hard mass in the fruit, reducing fruit quality and producing a bad flavor to the fruit. Some plant diseases are spread by stink bug feeding.

Literature: Drake 1920; Slater and Baranowski 1978.

79   RICE STINK BUG

Hemiptera: Pentatomidae   *Oebalus pugnax* (Fabricius)

Description: Adult rice stink bugs are straw-colored, ⅜ to ½ inch long, somewhat elongated and flattened with forward pointing spines on the shield-like segment behind the head (pronotum). Nymphs hatching from eggs are at first bright red with black markings. As they grow, they begin to resemble adults but do not have fully-developed wings or forward-pointing spines; but they have an intricate red and black pattern on the upper surface of their abdomens.

Life cycle: Winter (October through April) is spent in the adult stage near the ground in wild grasses. In April and early May adults become active and mated females lay clusters of 10 to 30 light green barrel-shaped eggs arranged in double rows on leaves and seed heads (panicles) of wild grasses, sorghum, and rice. Nymphs hatch in about five days. They molt 5 times as they grow

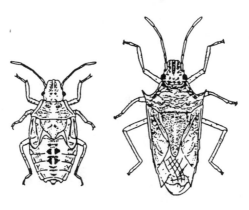

Rice stink bug

over a period of 15 to 28 days before becoming adults. Development from egg to adult occurs in 18 to 50 days, depending on temperature. Up to 5 generations can develop annually, with 2–3 developing on sorghum and rice.

Pest status: Along the Texas coastal counties, rice stink bug nymphs and adults feed on developing sorghum and rice kernels, causing loss of quality (grade) and yield.

Habitat and food source(s): Rice stink bug adults migrate from wild grasses to sorghum and rice when plants begin to develop kernels or develop in and around fields on wild host plants. Nymphal and adult feeding removes contents (endosperm) from developing seeds (milk and soft dough stages) and results in an empty seed coat or shriveled kernels. Yellow to black spots develop at feeding sites on rice kernels injured later (dough stage) and are often associated with plant disease microorganisms. This type of damage is commonly called "pecky rice," and it has been correlated with reduced head yield and increased percent broken kernels in milled rice, a loss in quality or "grade." Wild host plants include barnyard grass and sedge, *Cyperus* sp.

Literature: Drees et al. 1996; Naresh and Smith 1982, 1984; Nilakhe 1976; Peairs and Davidson 1956; Swanson and Newsom 1962.

80, 81   SPINED SOLDIER BUG

Hemiptera: Pentatomidae   *Podisus maculiventris* (Say)

Description: Adults vary in color from yellowish to pale brownish and are covered with small black specks. There is also a short black line on the wing tips that extends beyond the abdomen. A conspicuous spine on the middle of the front leg segment (tibia) may also be noticed. They are about ½ inch long. Eggs are metallic bronze.

This species may be confused with *Euchistus* species, which are common plant-feeding stink bugs. The spined soldier bug has more sharply pointed spines on the edge of the pronotum.

Life cycle: Eggs are laid in small clusters of 20–30 on leaves of plants. Immatures (**81**) may be found clustered around the eggs shortly after they hatch. Young nymphs may feed on plant juices but later stages are predaceous. Each female may lay up to 1,000 eggs. Adults may live for 5 to 8 weeks.

Pest status: This is one of the more prominent predatory stink bugs in North America.

Habitat and food source(s): Prey includes many kinds of caterpillars and grubs, especially those with few hairs. They are known to prey on larvae of the fall armyworm and the Colorado potato beetle.

Literature: Slater and Baranowski 1978; Swan and Papp 1972.

Conchuela Stink Bug

Southern Green Stink Bug

ORDER HOMOPTERA

*Cicadas, Leafhoppers, Planthoppers, Treehoppers, Psyllids,
Whiteflies, Aphids, Mealybugs, and Scale Insects*

DESCRIPTION

- Homoptera may be winged or wingless as adults. When present, the 4 wings are usually held roof-like over the body.
- They have sucking mouthparts with a "beak" that arises from the hind part of the head.
- Immature stages often resemble adults, but lack fully developed wings. In some groups, e.g., scale insects and whiteflies, adult stages do not resemble immature stages.
- Homoptera come in many shapes and sizes.
- Most forms are small or microscopic, but cicadas are up to 3 inches in length.

LIFE CYCLE

- Metamorphosis is generally considered to be simple (egg, nymph, adults) but it is modified (intermediate) in whiteflies, scale insects, and some other groups.
- Some groups, e.g., aphids and some scales, give birth to living young and reproduce without mating (parthenogenesis).

PEST STATUS

- Feeding and egg-laying activities damage plants and some species transmit plant diseases.

HABITAT

- All species feed on plants. Depending on the species and life stage, they occur on fruit, branches, trunks, stems, or roots.
- Adult and immature stages may or may not be associated with the same habitat.

82, 83   DOG-DAY CICADAS

Homoptera: Cicadidae   *Tibicen* spp.

Description: Adults vary in size and color according to species. All have prominent bulging eyes and semi-transparent wings held roof-like over their large bodies. The larger species are about 1⅝ inches long and ½ inch wide with brown or green, black and white body markings. Nymphs resemble wingless adults, are brown and have strong front legs well developed for tunneling in the soil.

The smaller **periodical cicada,** *Magicicada septendecim* (Linnaeus), completes its life cycle in 17 years, and emerges in large numbers (broods) in large geographical areas. The periodical cicada species that do occur in Texas complete their life cycles in 13 years, although some emerge almost every year. Adults emerge from April through July, depending upon species and locality.

Life cycle: The common dog-day cicadas (sometimes called the annual cicada or locusts) appear in late summer and have life cycles of 2 to 5 years. Female cicadas insert clusters of eggs into the twigs and small branches using a saw-like egg laying structure (ovipositor). In 6 to 7 weeks, small nymphs hatch from the eggs and drop to the ground. They burrow into the soil, seeking tree roots. As they molt through several growth stages (instars), they may burrow several feet down. Fully developed nymphs burrow out of the ground at night, leaving a ½-inch hole behind them. Under some conditions, the exit hole is associated with a mud cone or chimney 3 to 4 inches high. The nymphs climb onto tree trunks, low plants, or other objects. Adult cicadas emerge from this last nymphal stage through a crack along the back, leaving the light brown cast skin behind (**83**). Adults can live for 5 to 6 weeks.

Pest status: Texas species are not considered to be plant pests.

Habitat and food source(s): Male cicadas rest on tree trunks and branches and "sing" to attract females, producing a periodic whine by means of two special vibrating membranes in the sides of the abdomen. Females do not sing. Adult cicadas do not feed on leaves, and may suck juices from tender twigs. Nymphs feed on the sap from tree roots.

Literature: Hamman and Neeb 1981; Johnson and Lyon 1988.

84, 85 THREECORNERED ALFALFA HOPPER

Homoptera: Membracidae   *Spissistilus festinus* Say

Description: Threecornered alfalfa hoppers are members of this family of insects often called **treehoppers** because they actively hop and fly when disturbed. Adults are green, about ¼ inch long, and are taller than wide due to an expanded segment (pronotum) behind the head that extends over the abdomen. Nymphs (**85**) are also green and wingless, lacking the enlarged pronotum. Each segment of the body is adorned with a pair of large filaments or spines.

This group contains other treehoppers, some of which mimic thorns in their appearance. The **twomarked treehopper**, *Enchenopa binotata* (Say); the **buffalo treehopper**, *Stictocephala bisonia* Kopp and Yonke; and the **whitemarked treehopper**, *Tricentrus albomaculatus* Distant, are other common species.

Life cycle: Winter is spent in the adult or egg stage. Eggs are inserted into plants by the females. Eggs hatch and develop through 5 stages (instars) before becoming winged adults. There are 3 to 4 generations per year.

Pest status: Adults and late stage (instar) nymphs "girdle" stems of soybeans and alfalfa with their feeding activities, causing stems to be brittle and plants to break at that site and fall over; nymphs feed on plant sap and may affect yield of a soybean crop when they occur in high numbers while pods are developing.

Habitat and food source(s): Threecornered alfalfa hoppers have a wide host range that includes alfalfa, clovers, cowpeas, grasses (Bermuda, Johnson grass), small grains (barley, oats, wheat), soybeans, sunflowers, tomatoes, vetch, and weeds.

Literature: Mueller 1980; Swan and Papp 1972.

86, 87   TWOLINED SPITTLEBUG

Homoptera: Cercopidae   *Prosapia bicincta* (Say)

Description: Adults are leafhopper-like but appear much wider, about ⅜ inch long, dark brown to black, and have two brilliant red-orange lines traversing the fore wings, which are held over the back of the body. Immatures residing within masses of spittle (**87**) are smaller, wingless, with white, yellow, or orangish bodies, brown heads, and red eyes.

There are several other spittlebug species common in Texas.

Life cycle: Winter is spent in the egg stage that hatches in the spring. Nymphs produce the spittle mass to prevent them from drying out, and develop through 4 stages (instars) within about one month. Eggs hatch in about 2 weeks. Two generations can occur per year.

Pest status: Most noticeable when immature stages, feeding on host plant, produce masses of frothy spittle that encircle the twigs and young leaves.

Habitat and food source(s): These spittlebugs feed on many plants, including grasses, ornamental plants, some crops, and weeds. Adults move about readily, often in tall weeds or grassy areas.

Literature: Brook et al. 1982.

88   LEAFHOPPERS

Homoptera: Cicadellidae   Many species

Description: Leafhopper adults are elongated, wedge-shaped, and somewhat triangular in cross-section. They jump and fly off readily. Depending on species, they range in size from ⅛ to ½ inch and their bodies are colored yellow, green, or gray, or they may be marked with color patterns. Nymphs resemble adults but are wingless. They can run rapidly, occasionally sideways, and hop.

Life cycle: Most species overwinter as eggs or adults. Eggs are inserted into leaf veins, shoots or stems of host plants. Wingless nymphs hatch from eggs in about 10 days and begin feeding on the tender new growth of their host plant. They develop through 5 stages (instars) over a period of 12 to 30 days, leaving shed skins in the feeding area. As nymphs grow larger, they develop wing pads. Most leafhoppers produce one generation per year, but some may develop up to six.

Pest status: Very common and various species feed on the juices of a wide variety of plants; occasionally damaging plants and transmitting plant dis-

Leafhopper

eases; medically harmless although adult leafhoppers are capable of biting, temporarily producing pain.

Habitat and food source(s): Species can be somewhat specific to certain host plants. As a group, they feed on leaves of a wide variety of plants including many types of grasses, flowers, vegetables, fruit trees, shrubs, deciduous trees, palms, and weeds. The **rose leafhopper,** *Edwardsiana rosae* (Linnaeus), feeds primarily on plants of the rose family, although foliage of other woody plants (blackberry, *Cornus,* oak, *Prunus, Populus,* raspberry, *Ulmus, Acer* and others) serve as food. The **potato leafhopper,** *Empoasca fabae* (Harris), feeds on legumes like alfalfa, as well as on apple, birch, chestnut, maple, and others. Species in the genus, *Erythroneura,* feed on sycamore leaves, but also on apple, grape and willow. The **aster** or **six-spotted leafhopper,** *Macrosteles quadrilineatus* Forbes, feeds on vegetables and annual flowers and spreads the aster yellows virus to woody plants like periwinkle and *Thunbergia* species. Nymphs and adults feed on the underside of leaves. Whitish cast skins from developing nymphs are commonly associated with an infestation. Removal of sap from the mesophyll or vascular tissues (phloem and xylem) and injection of toxic salivary secretions (e.g., proteinaceous fluid that clogs in the vascular tissues) during feeding activities cause leaves to develop yellow or clear stipples, spots or leaf portions that are visible on the upper leaf surface. Marginal yellowing (chlorosis) and browning (necrosis) of damaged leaves is often called "hopperburn" or "tipburn." Damaged leaves can fall prematurely. Some species cause terminal growth of damaged plants to become curled and stunted. Heavily damaged plant parts or plants can die. Egg-laying habits can also cause some plant injury. Some leafhoppers are readily attracted to lights.

Literature: Borror et al. 1989; Brook et al. 1982; Johnson and Lyon 1988.

89, 90   SHARPSHOOTERS

Homoptera: Cicadellidae   *Homalodisca* spp.,
                                        Graphocephala spp., etc.

Description: These species comprise a subgroup of the leafhoppers, the Cicindelinae. They are similar to leafhoppers and have forward-pointing heads, but are generally larger (about ⅜ inch) and outer margins (front edges) of fore wings at rest are more parallel-sided than wedge-shaped. Part of their hind legs (tibia) bear two rows of spines. The **blue-green sharp-**

shooter, *Graphocephala atropunctata* (Signoret), has green to bright blue wings, head and thorax, and yellow legs and abdomen as seen from underneath. The dark form of *Homalodisca triquetra* (Fabricius) has swollen white spots on the fore wings.

There are several families in the order, Homoptera (Superfamily Fulgoroidea), that are called "**planthoppers**" (**90**). They differ from leafhoppers (and sharpshooters) by having only a few large spines on the hind leg (tibia), and have antennae arising from below the compound eyes. Although rarely very numerous or damaging to host plants, immature stages (nymphs) are often noticeable in the spring. Immature Flatidae, such as those of *Metcalfa pruinosa* (Say) and *Ormenoides* spp., feed together (gregariously) on ornamental vines, shrubs and trees, producing masses of cottony-white waxy filaments on their bodies and terminal growth of plants. Adults are about ⁵⁄₁₆ inch long, wedge-shaped, and vary in color from whitish to pale green, to bluish-gray or brown.

Life cycle: Adults overwinter. Eggs are inserted into host plant tissue (a slit cut into the petiole). Nymphs are whitish yellow and develop through several stages (instars). Depending on species, several generations can occur per year.

Pest status: Often noticeable on garden plants like okra, resting along stalks and "hiding" from viewers by quickly walking sideways around to the other side; produce minimal plant damage to most crops, although they are capable of transmitting plant diseases such as Pierce's disease of commercial grape varieties.

Habitat and food source(s): The blue-green sharpshooter has a wide host range including many vines, shrubs, and trees. Damaged plant parts have sap and cell contents removed from leaves and may become speckled with yellowed (chlorotic) spots or become deformed, resulting in curled and cupped leaves. Cast skins of developing nymphal stages are often evident on the underside of damaged leaves. *Homalodisca triquetra* (Fabricius) is common on cotton, okra, *Prunus* sp., *Celtis* sp., some ornamental plants, weeds, and trees, although they seldom produce serious damage.

Literature: Borror et al. 1976; Johnson and Lyon 1988; Little 1963.

91   POTATO PSYLLID OR TOMATO PSYLLID

Homoptera: Psyllidae   *Paratrioza cockerelli* (Sulc)

Description: Adults, also called "jumping plant lice," resemble tiny cicadas. They are about ¹⁄₁₀ inch long, greenish to black, have a white fringe band around the first abdomen and clear wings held over the back when at rest. They jump and fly readily when disturbed.

Life cycle: This insect overwinters in southern Texas and New Mexico. Yellow-orange, bean-shaped eggs on short stalks are laid by mated females on the undersurface of leaves. Nymphs hatch from eggs in 4 to 15 days and have scale-like flattened, oval, yellowish-green to orangish bodies with red eyes and 3 pairs of short legs. Older nymphs are greenish and fringed with hairs. They develop through 5 stages (instars) in 2 to 3 weeks before becoming winged adults. Field populations are particularly abundant following cool, mild winters and occur during February and March in south Texas and then migrate north.

Pest status: This species can damage plants such as potato or tomato crops when they occur in high numbers; an outbreak occurred in the Winter Garden area around Uvalde in 1992.

Habitat and food source(s): This species occurs mainly on field grown potato and field or greenhouse grown tomato crops, but also attacks eggplant, pepper, and tomatillo. Wild host plants include wolfberry or matrimony vine (*Lycium* sp.), Chinese lantern, ground cherry and some other members of the nightshade or Solanaceae family of plants. Nymphs (not adults), sucking host plant juices, produce toxic effects (phytotoxemia, possibly by injecting a virus) on plant growth that includes retarded internode growth, upward cupping or rolling of leaves, and thickened nodes—resulting in a condition called "rosetting." Leaf margins, leaves, and other plant parts can become yellow (chlorotic) and reddish to purplish—symptoms called "psyllid yellows" and "purple-top." Potato tubers and fruits produced by discolored (chlorotic) plants are tiny, malformed, and unfit for commercial uses. Older leaves and heavily damaged plants may die.

Literature: Metcalf et al. 1962; Stewart 1993; Swan and Papp 1972; Westcott 1973.

92–94   HACKBERRY GALL PSYLLIDS

Homoptera: Psyllidae   *Pachypsylla* spp.

Description: Galls (92) appear as ⅛-to-¼-inch swellings of tissue on leaves or petioles. They can be carefully cut open to reveal the pale, developing psyllid inside. Adults (94) resemble tiny (³⁄₁₆-inch long) cicadas and they can become abundant in the fall when they are attracted to homes, often crawling through window screening, seeking overwintering habitat.

Hackberry trees also harbor several gall-forming midge species (Diptera: Cecidomyiidae) such as the species that produces the **thorn gall**, *Celticecis spiniformis* (Patton). Immature stages (93) of these gall midges, when carefully dissected out of galls, appear maggot or grub-like and have no legs or antennae as do psyllid immatures.

Life cycle: Common leaf-gall-forming species overwinter in the adult stage in bark cracks and crevices. Adults mate in the spring and females lay eggs on the underside of expanding leaves. Nymphs hatch from eggs in about 10 days and begin feeding, which causes leaf tissue to expand rapidly into a pouch or gall around the insect. They develop through several stages (instars) before emerging as adults in the fall (September), although the **hackberry bud gall maker**, *P. celtidisgemma* Riley, overwinters inside the gall as a last stage (5th instar) nymph to emerge as an adult in early summer. One generation occurs annually.

Pest status: They cause galls to form on the leaves and petioles; probably every hackberry tree is infested with one of the gall-forming psyllids; adults occasionally become a nuisance in and around the home in the fall.

Habitat and food source(s): Several *Pachypsylla* psyllid species occur on hackberry, *Celtis* spp., including the **hackberry nipplegall maker,** *P. celtidismamma* (Fletcher), the **hackberry blister gall maker,** *P. celtidisvesicula* Riley, and the **hackberry bud gall maker.** Galls formed by these species are unsightly and occasionally cause premature leaf drop, but they do not appear to harm the health of the trees.

Literature: Johnson and Lyon 1988.

95 YAUPON PSYLLID GALL

Homoptera: Psyllidae   *Gyropsylla ilicis* (Ashmead)

Description: The adult insect resembles a tiny (³⁄₁₆-inch) cicada. Galls produced by aphid-like immature stages appear as folded leaves on new, terminal growth. Immature yaupon psyllid nymphs are inside and are associated with a buildup of waxy filaments.

This is the only gall-making psyllid on yaupon. However, other psyllid species cause galls to form on the leaves of other plant species.

Life cycle: Adults are most active in late winter to early spring (late February to early March), when host plants flower and begin developing new leaves. Females lay clusters of eggs on opening leaf buds. First stage (instar) nymphs begin feeding on expanding leaves, which causes the leaf to deform by cupping upwards. Clusters of nymphs occurring together in deformed leaves develop through several stages for about 10 months before beginning to emerge as adults in November. There is one generation per year.

Pest status: Adults are tiny, rarely seen. Immature stages cause pocket-like galls that deform and stunt new growth of yaupon hollies.

Habitat and food source(s): This species attacks native yaupon hollies in landscapes. Dwarf yaupon is less affected. Inside leaf galls, along with several nymphs, is a white wax-covered fluid-filled ball slightly larger than a full-grown nymph that apparently is filled with honeydew excreted by the nymphs.

Literature: Mead 1983.

96 CITRUS BLACKFLY

Homoptera: Aleyrodidae   *Aleurocanthus woglumi*
                                               Ashby

Description: Adult stages have slate-blue wings with a white band across the center. The head and abdomen are bright red, and the antennae and legs are white.

Life cycle: Mated females lay yellowish-brown eggs in a spiral pattern on the underside of leaves. Tiny crawlers, which have 6 short legs and antennae, hatch from eggs. Their bodies are white to brown and flattened, oval in shape, with red eye spots and two long spines on their backs. Upon settling on the leaf surface, the crawler stage molts to a non-motile second stage (instar), which appears dull black with patches of yellow and spines on the upper body surface. Development continues to a larger, third larval stage and then to an oval, shiny black, spiny pupal stage marked with a fringe of white wax around the margin. Adults emerge from a T-shaped crack on the back of the pupa. Development from egg to adult occurs in 60 to 120 days, depending on temperature.

Pest status: Actually a species of whitefly, but called a "blackfly" because of its body color. It has been a pest of citrus, dooryard plants and nursery crops in south Texas since the 1950s. It should not be confused with black flies (Diptera: Simuliidae), which are true flies that suck blood.

Habitat and food source(s): Host plants include all species of citrus, mango, avocado, coffee, pear, plum, pomegranate, guava, and ash. Citrus blackfly adults and immatures feed on the underside of host plant leaves. They remove large quantities of sap which is excreted by immature stages as honeydew, which then serves as a substrate on which the black-colored sooty mold fungus, *Capnodium* sp., develops. Heavily infested trees become unsightly because of black-coated leaves and fruit. Photosynthesis and fruit production are reduced because light cannot penetrate the blackened fungus layer to the leaf surface. High numbers of flying adults associated with heavily infested host plants can be a nuisance.

Literature: French et al. 1989; Huffman 1996.

97, 98   SILVERLEAF WHITEFLY

Homoptera: Aleyrodidae   *Bemisia argentifolii* Bellows and Perring

Description: The silverleaf whitefly adult is tiny, about ($\frac{1}{25}$–$\frac{1}{20}$ inch) in length and holds its solid white wings roof-like over a pale yellow body while at rest. Eggs are pointed, oblong, and yellow, darkening at the apex just before hatching. The crawler stage or first instar settles down on the underside of leaves and molts into a sessile, flattened yellow oval larva. The last instar (**98**) or pupa has distinct eye spots. Pupae are teardrop shaped when viewed from the top, oval in cross-section, and bear two prominent hairs (setae) on the back end.

Several whitefly species are important plant pests in Texas.

Life cycle: The number of eggs produced is greater in warm weather, but typically ranges from 50 to 400 eggs per female. Eggs hatch into active, wingless, crawler stages, which soon settle into the sessile, scale-like second larval stage (instar). This stage molts into a third larval stage, which then becomes the pupa from which the adult emerges. The molt from the third larval stage to the pupa occurs internally and wings develop inside the puparium. The duration from egg to adult may be 18 days under warm temperatures, but may take as long as 2 months under cool conditions.

Pest status: Immature stages can infest and damage many host plants, occasionally transmitting plant diseases. It has become a widespread difficult-to-control pest of Texas greenhouse and nursery crops since 1987, particularly on cotton, vegetables, and ornamental plants, such as poinsettia and hibiscus.

Habitat and food source(s): Direct crop damage occurs when whiteflies feed on plant sap in high enough numbers, excreting honeydew, which promotes the sooty mold fungus and reduces plant quality. Yellowing, chlorosis, of leaves and/or bleaching of parts of plants has been associated with whitefly infestation. Silverleaf whitefly adults often concentrate on younger leaves where egg-laying is highest. Following the development of the plant, larger nymphs are typically more numerous on older leaves.

Literature: Borror et al. 1989; Drees 1994.

99   COTTON APHID OR MELON APHID

Homoptera: Aphididae   *Aphis gossypii* Glover

Description: Adult aphids are winged or wingless, soft-bodied yellow to dark green, 1/16 inch or less in size. Winged forms have a black head and thorax and hold their wings roof-like over the back of the body.

There are many aphid species and they can be identified by looking at specific structures such as the projections on the end of the abdomen called cornicles, and other features. Cotton and melon aphids are smaller and have shorter appendages than other common aphid species, such as the **green peach aphid,** *Myzus persicae* (Sulzer).

Life cycle: Wingless adults overwinter in protected areas such as in field debris and soil and feed on weed hosts. In the greenhouse, they can be active year-round. In spring winged females fly to suitable host plants and produce live young nymphs without mating through a process called parthenogenesis. Nymphs develop through several stages (instars) before becoming mostly wingless adults in 4 to 10 days depending on temperature. Winged adults are produced when certain environmental conditions such as overcrowding, host plant decline, or shortened day length occur. Adult aphids live for 3 to 4 weeks, each producing about 85 young. Many overlapping generations can occur annually. In greenhouses, up to 51 generations can be produced in one year.

Pest status: One of the most common aphids on a wide variety of agronomic and horticultural plants; heavily infested plants can be damaged or killed.

Habitat and food source(s): This species feeds on a wide variety of plants (members of 25 plant families!) including asparagus, beans, begonia, catalpa, citrus, clover, cucurbits, cotton, ground ivy, gardenia, hops, hydrangea, okra, spinach, strawberries, tomatoes, violets, and weeds. Feeding activities cause distorted growth, reduced growth, quality and yield. Excretion of the sugary fluid called honeydew by aphids is colonized by a black fungus called sooty mold, which causes plants to become unsightly and stressed by shielding mold-coated leaves from sunlight needed for photosynthesis. Numerous cast skins from aphid development are also unsightly. These aphids are also important vectors of some viral plant diseases.

Literature: Carter et al. 1980; Drees 1993.

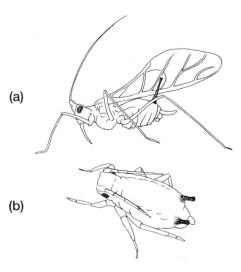

(a) Winged aphid; (b) wingless cotton/melon aphid

100   OLEANDER APHID

Homoptera: Aphididae

Aphis nerii Boyer de Fonscolombe

Description: This is a bright yellow aphid with black legs and cornicles (stalks on the back of the abdomen).

Life cycle: Aphids appear on new shoots, buds and foliage in the spring. Development is similar to other aphids. Large populations develop over the summer.

Pest status: This aphid infests oleander, butterfly weed, and milkweed, building up high populations on the terminal growth. It can be a nuisance on landscape plant specimens.

Habitat and food source(s): Host plants are restricted to oleander, butterfly weed, and milkweed. Aphids do not usually cause plant health to suffer, although their high numbers and accumulation of sooty mold associated with honeydew expelled can be a nuisance and be unsightly. In most cases, many of the oleander aphids become infested with a parasitic wasp, *Lysiphlebus testaceipes* (Cresson) (Hymenoptera: Braconidae). Infested aphids swell, turn brown, and die. The wasp cuts a hole in the back of the aphid's abdomen to emerge.

Literature: Johnson and Lyon 1988.

101 WOOLLY APPLE APHID

Homoptera: Aphididae

Eriosoma lanigerum
(Hausmann)

Description: Aphids are reddish-purplish, wingless or winged, and covered with woolly, bluish-white wax masses.

Aphids in several other genera, e.g., *Paraprociphilus, Eriosoma, Stegophylla,* produce large quantities of woolly wax filaments and infest leaves of alders, elms, and oaks. At certain times during the summer, infestations can become noticeable on host plants such as Arizona ash in central Texas. These aphids infest the undersides of leaves on terminal growth, causing leaves to turn pale green and curl.

Life cycle: Winter is spent in the egg or young nymphal stages underground in root galls, and as adult egg-laying females on the branches and trunks of host plants. Eggs are laid in bark cracks on elm in the fall and hatch in early spring. Wingless nymphs feed on new growth and twigs for two generations (May and June), producing winged forms that fly to other host plants (apple, hawthorn, and mountain ash). There, they feed on wounds on trunks and branches and move to the root zone. In summertime, females give birth to live young without mating (parthenogenesis). Wingless males are produced in the fall and mate with wingless females, each of which lay a single overwintering egg.

Pest status: Occurs on apples with susceptible rootstock or susceptible varieties and other plants.

Habitat and food source(s): Aphids become noticeable because of the woolly wax masses on wounds of the trunk and branches on apple, elm, hawthorn, mountain ash, pear and quince. Underground, aphids cause large knots on roots of apple trees. Heavily infested trees become stunted and may die. Rootstock of all but a few apple varieties is susceptible to attack. Woolly apple aphids have become a problem in areas of Texas where dwarf apple varieties have been planted using susceptible rootstock.

Literature: Johnson and Lyon 1988; Metcalf et al. 1962.

102 YELLOW PECAN APHID AND BLACKMARGINED APHID

Homoptera: Aphididae

Monelliopsis pecanis Bissel
Monellia caryella (Fitch)

Description: Both species are clear to yellow or pale green aphids that grow to be about ¹⁄₁₆ inch long. Adult blackmargined aphid, *Monellia caryella* (Fitch), have a black front margin on their fore wings and hold their wings flat over the back of the body. The yellow pecan aphid, *Monelliopsis pecan-*

is Bissel, has clear wings that are held roof-like over the back of the body. Immature stages (nymphs) are wingless and appear solid yellow.

The **black pecan aphid,** *Melanocallis caryaefoliae* (Davis), which also occurs on pecan, is a more solitary species, and most infested leaves will have only a few aphids. However, the aphid injects a toxic salivary secretion into the feeding site causing entire portions of the leaves between major leaf veins to turn yellow (yellow areas appear rectangular or quadrilateral) and ultimately brown. Heavily damaged leaves drop prematurely, which can negatively affect the current and following year's pecan production. The biology of this aphid is similar to the yellow pecan and blackmargined aphids.

Life cycle: The life cycle of these species is similar. Winter is spent in the egg stage in bark crevices and under loose bark. Wingless nymphs hatch in the spring after leaves develop and mostly move to the undersurface of leaves where they feed and develop through 4 stages (instars) over about 6 days. Winged and wingless adults that develop produce more young aphid nymphs without mating (through a process called parthenogenesis). Each adult can produce about 125 aphid nymphs over 18 to 33 days! Many (16 to 32) generations occur annually. When cooler weather arrives, eggs are produced for the winter.

Pest status: These aphids can build up in large numbers, resulting in an accumulation of sticky "honeydew" on surfaces underneath the infestation on which the black sooty mold fungus develops.

Habitat and food source(s): These aphids occur on pecan. Adults and nymphs remove sap from the leaves. Heavily infested trees have leaves that become coated with a sticky sugary film called honeydew. This energy-rich layer supports the development of a fungus called sooty mold. This black layer on leaves reduces the leaves' ability for photosynthesis. Severely infested trees prematurely drop their leaves. Although sap loss may affect the crop of pecans being produced during the season, the loss of energy from the tree can affect the production of pecans during the next year. High populations can develop on some varieties, particularly "Cheyenne."

Literature: Boethel and Bagnet; Tedders 1978.

103   GREEN PEACH APHID

Homoptera: Aphididae   *Myzus persicae* (Sulzer)

Description: Green peach aphids are small, usually less than ⅛ inch long. The body varies in color from pink to green with three darker stripes down the back, and the head supports long antennae and red eyes. Adult aphids may be winged (alate) or wingless (apterous). Winged forms are usually triggered by environmental changes (e.g., decreasing photoperiod or temperature, deterioration of the host plant or overcrowding). On the back of the fifth abdominal segment, a pair of tube-like structures, cornicles are present on most aphid species. These structures secrete a fluid when aphids become alarmed.

Life cycle: Most aphids reproduce sexually and develop through simple metamorphosis (overwintering diapause egg, nymphs and winged or wingless adults) but also through parthenogenesis, in which the production of offspring occurs without mating. In Texas and other southern states, green peach aphids develop only through parthenogenesis, and females can produce 3–6 fully formed young per day for several weeks. There may be 30 generations per year. In cooler areas, winter is passed as black shiny sexually-produced eggs on the bark of peach, plum, apricot, and cherry.

Pest status: This species damages plants by: (1) causing plant stress by directly removing plant juices (sap from phloem tissues); (2) reducing the aesthetic quality of infested plants by secreting a sugary liquid (excess plant sap called honeydew) on which a black-colored fungus called sooty mold grows, discoloring the foliage and further stressing the plant by preventing sunlight from reaching plant cells for photosynthesis; and (3) possibly transmitting plant diseases, particularly viruses.

Habitat and food source(s): Green peach aphid, also known as **tobacco** or **spinach aphid** has a wide range of host plants including lettuce, peach, potatoes, spinach, tomato, other vegetables and ornamental crops (flowering and bedding plants including chrysanthemums). They feed on all aboveground plant parts, and after some time, the cast whitish skins from the aphid's developmental stages will accumulate on infested plant parts.

Literature: Baker 1982; Johnson and Lyon 1988.

104–107   GREENBUG

Homoptera: Aphididae   *Schizaphis graminum*
                                         (Rodani)

Description: Mature female greenbugs are winged or wingless, pear-shaped, about ¹⁄₁₆ inch long, pale green, marked with a darker green stripe down the middle of the back. They have black tips on the legs and the two appendages (cornicles) on the back of the abdomen.

Several other aphid species are pests of small grains, corn and sorghum. The **yellow sugarcane aphid (105),** *Sipha flava* (Forbes), is most destructive to sorghum along the Texas coast but is also found on small grains, Johnson grass, and Dallis grass. These aphids feed on the underside of the lower leaves, causing damaged leaves to turn purple and eventually die from the injection of toxic saliva. The wingless form of the yellow sugarcane aphid is bright lemon-yellow with rows of bumps (tubercles) along the abdomen from which hairs (setae) project, has short cornicles (not longer than wide), and five segmented antennae. Introduced in 1986, the **Russian wheat aphid (106),** *Diuraphis noxia* (Mordvilko) damages wheat, barley, rye, triticale, and oats in the Texas Panhandle, and also infests some wild grasses. Damaged leaves develop curling, white to yellow streaking in warm weather or purple discoloration in cool weather and may die as a reaction to an injected toxin. The wingless Russian wheat aphid is darker green, also has short cornicles, but has six-segmented antennae, and a conspicuous elongated structure (caudal process) on the back end of the body, which gives it a "double tail" appearance when viewed from the side. The **corn leaf aphid (107)**, *Rhopalosiphum maidis* (Fitch), is common throughout Texas, especially in the leaf whorls of corn and sorghum, and to a lesser extent on small grains. It is not generally considered destructive because it does not inject a toxin when feeding and attracts natural enemies. The wingless form is bluish-green with black appendages and base of cornicles, which are longer than wide. The **English grain aphid**, *Sitobion avenae* (Fabricius), found on wheat, barley, rye, or oats, and the **bird cherry-oat aphid**, *Rhopalosiphum padi* (Linnaeus), found on small grains in western and northwestern Texas, are also rarely serious pests because they do not inject a toxic salivary secretion. The wingless English grain aphid is similar to the corn leaf aphid, but is grass-green (occasionally yellow or pink) with a brown head and has longer black legs and cornicles. The wingless bird cherry-oat aphid has an olive body with a reddish-orange spot on the back at the base of the cornicles and tips of antennae, legs and antennae are black.

Life cycle: Mature females produce live young nymphs without mating at a rate of 2 to 3 per day over a 20- to 30-day period. These nymphs develop into adults within 6 to 30 days, depending on temperature. Populations can increase quickly, about 5- to 6-fold per week under normal conditions. Many generations occur per year and they can be found year-round in Texas wherever host plants occur. Infestations spread by winged forms flying and being blown many miles by the wind.

Pest status: Greenbugs are pests of several cultivated and wild grasses. In wheat and sorghum crops, they can damage plants, transmit plant diseases, and reduce yields.

Habitat and food source(s): Greenbugs are found primarily on wheat during the winter months and sorghum during the spring and summer, but they also occur on Johnson grass, other wild grasses and occasionally on oats. Adults and nymphs occur on the underside of leaves, particularly on the lower, older leaves of host plants. They damage plants in three ways: (1) they remove sap, stressing plants by removing water and nutrients; (2) they inject a toxic salivary secretion that causes a yellowing or reddening discoloration and eventually death of infested tissues; and (3) they can transmit plant diseases such as the barley yellow dwarf virus in small grains and maize dwarf mosaic virus in sorghum. They infest plants of all growth stages and can kill young plants, reducing plant stand. Heavily damaged older plants have stunted growth, delayed growth, reduced kernel size, and quality. Several biotypes have evolved that have overcome plant resistance, tolerate temperature extremes, and infest new host plants.

Literature: Daniels 1981; Halbert et al.1988; Hoelscher et al. 1987.

Homoptera: Aphididae   *Tinocallis kahawaluokalani*
                                         (Kirkaldy)

Description: Adult aphids are ⅛ inch long, light green to yellow with black spots and body markings. The second abdominal segment has a double-pronged hump. Wings are clear with dark markings and they are held roof-like over the back of the body. Some adults are wingless. Nymphal stages are yellow and wingless.

Although several other aphid species have been reported to infest crape-myrtles, including **cotton aphids** or **melon aphids (99),** *Aphis gossypii* Glover, and **black citrus aphids,** *Toxoptera aurantii* Boyer de Fons-colombe, the crapemyrtle aphid is the most commonly encountered and can be distinguished from the other aphid species by the hump on the adult second abdominal segment.

Life cycle: Female aphids produce live young without mating (partheno-genesis), particularly during the summer months. Nymphal and adult stages can be found on host plants throughout the year, but appear to build up in higher numbers during the hot summer months.

Pest status: These aphids build up in high numbers on crapemyrtles, causing a buildup of honeydew and sooty mold, and making plants unsightly and unhealthy.

Habitat and food source(s): This aphid specifically infests crapemyrtles. Nymphal and adult stages suck plant juices from the underside of leaves they infest. Much of the sap withdrawn from the plant is directly eliminated as a sticky, sugary fluid called honeydew. Leaves coated with honeydew become infested with a fungus called sooty mold, *Capnodium* spp., which produces a dry-looking black coating on the leaf surface. Heavily discolored leaves drop prematurely. Severity of infestations varies from year-to-year, as populations are affected by environmental conditions and the presence of predaceous insects. Crapemyrtles were originally imported from Asia, and this aphid species was apparently imported with its host or introduced later. No parasitoids are known to attack this aphid in Texas.

Literature: Carter et al. 1980; Johnson and Lyon 1988.

GRAPE PHYLLOXERA

Homoptera: Phylloxeridae   *Daktulosphaira vitifoliae*
                                         (Fitch)

Description: Wingless adult forms are very small (1/25 inch long), oval-shaped, yellowish and live together inside root and leaf galls. There are four forms of adults, some of which have wings.

Life cycle: Winter is spent in the egg stage on canes (vines) and aphids in grape root galls. Eggs hatch in the spring and yellow aphids feed on the new growth, producing leaf galls. Upon maturing to adult females, live young are produced without mating (parthenogenesis). Some leaf-infesting aphids drop to the ground and begin producing root galls. Several parthenogenic generations develop through the summer. Winged forms are produced in the fall and migrate to vines where they lay eggs that hatch into males and sexual females. After mating, female aphids lay single eggs that overwinter. Five to eight generations occur per year.

Pest status: Causes galls on grape roots and can cause pea-sized galls on leaves.

Habitat and food source(s): Grape root stalk varieties susceptible to phylloxera galls decline when heavily infested. Leaves turn yellow and plants lose vigor before they slowly die. Native varieties are resistant to attack.

Literature: Metcalf et al. 1962; Swan and Papp 1972.

---

109 PECAN PHYLLOXERA

Homoptera: Phylloxeridae

Phylloxera devastatrix
Pergande

Description: Galls are produced by small, soft-bodied insects that are similar and closely related to aphids. They live inside hollow galls formed on new-growth twigs that may reach about 1 inch in diameter. Leaf galls remain green and fleshy until they have opened. Twig and stem galls are woody and may remain on the tree for several years.

Gall-forming aphids, *Pemphigus* species, also occur on petioles and twigs of cottonwood. They can be identified by the size and shape of the galls and characteristics of the exit holes produced when the galls split open.

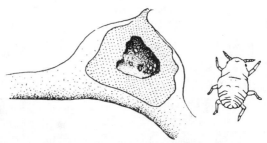

Pecan phylloxera, nymph and gall

Life cycle: Phylloxera overwinter in the egg stage in bark crevices. Eggs hatch around bud break in the spring and tiny nymphs begin to feed on tender young growth, releasing a substance that stimulates the plant tissue to develop galls. After developing into adults in 4 to 5 weeks, females deposit clutches of eggs inside the galls or on fresh, young growth. Nymphs hatching from these eggs develop inside galls. Within 3 weeks, the galls split open and release the phylloxera. However, this phylloxera has only one damaging generation per year.

Pest status: Four species cause galls on leaves, twigs, and nuts of pecan trees. Although unsightly, galls caused by the **pecan leaf phylloxera,** *Phylloxera notabilis* Pergande, are not particularly damaging although they cause infested leaves to drop early. Galls on twigs, caused by *P. devastatrix* Pergande, can lead to mid-season (July) defoliation and twigs breaking off during windy weather or excessive weight that results in reduced yield and misshapen trees.

Habitat and food source(s): These species occur on pecan. Other species of phylloxera cause galls on leaves and stems of hickory.

Literature: Holloway et al. 1984; Johnson and Lyon 1988.

110   "Wax" Scales

Homoptera: Coccidae   *Ceroplastes* spp.

Description: "Wax" scales are globular and coated with a heavy layer of wet beige, pinkish, whitish or grayish wax. From the top view, they appear rectangular, oval or lobed at the base, and they may grow to over ⅛ inch (**Florida wax scale,** *C. floridensis* Comstock) to almost ¼ inch (**barnacle scale,** *C. cirripediformis* Comstock) in diameter.

Other species of wax scales occur in the state. In addition, there are other scale insects in Texas. However, none resemble this group of species in shape or size.

Life cycle: The winter is spent as adult females. Males are very rare or unknown for some species. Eggs are oval and orangish, and fill the inside of the female scale insect. When removing scale insects in spring (April), hundreds of eggs pour out. Eggs hatch over a period of 2 to 3 weeks. First stage (instar) nymphs, called crawlers, hatch from eggs and crawl to and settle on leaves, twigs and stems of host plants. After settling, nymphs begin to secrete wax in tufts around the body that give these scale insects a star-like appearance. Nymphs of the barnacle scale migrate from leaves to the woody tissue soon after molting to the third stage (instar). There may be two or more generations per year.

Pest status: Also known as soft scales, wax scale species have recently become a widespread problem on landscape plants in many urban areas.

Habitat and food source(s): Wax scales infest ficus, gardenia, hawthorne, holly, ornamental pear, pyracantha, and other landscape trees and shrubs. They are a minor pest of citrus. Wax scales damage plants by removing large quantities of plant sap. Sticky "honeydew," secreted by these scale insects, is colonized by a fungus called sooty mold, causing infested plant parts to turn black and unsightly.

Literature: Johnson and Lyon 1988; Riley 1995.

111, 112   BROWN SOFT SCALE

Homoptera: Coccidae   *Coccus hesperidum* Linnaeus

Description: Adults are oval, flattened, slightly convex, reddish-brown scale insects. Immature scale insects (second instar) resemble adults but are smaller, except for the first instar, mobile crawler stage, which has three pairs of legs, is pinkish, oval in shape, and has two prominent hairs (setae) arising from the end of the abdomen. Adult males have only one pair of wings.

Members of the Coccidae family are also called "soft scales" or coccids, and include wax scales and tortoise scales. **Lecanium scales (112),** *Lecanium* spp., are common soft scales on a wide range of woody ornamental plants and fruit trees. The adult female scales are usually brownish, oval to round, and about ¼ inch in diameter.

Life cycle: Eggs are produced within the female and hatch into first stage nymphs, or crawlers. Crawlers disperse and find a suitable feeding site within a few days. After about a week, they molt into the second stage, passive nymph. Winged adult males emerge and female scales develop in about a month. Six to seven generations can occur per year indoors.

Pest status: Common and frustrating pest of house plants and indoor plantscapes; occasionally found outdoors.

Habitat and food source(s): This scale insect feeds on a wide variety of ornamental foliage and flowering plants, particularly ferns. Removal of sap from host plants causes plant stress, and the sweet liquid, called honeydew, coats the surfaces on infested host plants. A fungus called sooty mold colonizes the honeydew and causes the surface to turn black. As a result, heavily infested plants become unsightly and often loose their leaves. Shady new leaf and stem growth is preferred as sites for infestation.

Literature: Carter et al. 1982.

113   WHITE PEACH SCALE

Homoptera: Diaspididae   *Pseudaulacaspis pentagona*
                                       (Targioni-Tozzetti)

Description: Scales in this family are called "armored scales"; their scale covering can be removed because it is usually free from the body. Full-grown male scale insects are white, about ½2 inch long and elongate in shape. Adult males emerge as tiny two-winged insects. The female scale insect armor is irregular and roughly oval in shape, up to ¹⁄₁₆ inch in diameter and whitish with a yellowish or reddish spot. The female's body is underneath the armor. Nymphs resemble adult scale insects but are smaller and female nymphs lack the spot.

The **tea scale**, *Fiorionia theae* Green, is similar and occurs on the underside of leaves of certain ornamental shrubs.

Life cycle: Adult females overwinter and produce a clutch of eggs underneath their scales in the spring. Six-legged nymphs, called crawlers, hatch from eggs in about 4 days, but observations in Texas suggest that it may take 30-60 days. Crawlers settle in about 2 days and begin developing through several stages (instars), the first lasting 7 to 8 days. Adult females develop from the second nymphal stage in about 12 days, and winged males develop through this stage for about 5 days before emerging as winged adults 7 or 8 days later. Development from egg to adult can occur within 35 to 40 days. Males seek female scale insects and mate. Mated females begin laying eggs after about 16 days. Three generations occur annually.

Pest status: Often observed causing trunks and lower branches of peach trees to appear to turn white because of a buildup of high numbers of scale insects; can affect tree health.

Habitat and food source(s): In addition to peach and plum trees, this species also infests catalpa, chinaberry, French mulberry, lilac, persimmon, privet, and walnut. In severe cases, they appear as white, cottony masses encrusting the bark of the tree. These scale insects can also occur on leaves and fruit. Scale insect feeding activities can result in early leaf drop. Heavily infested trees can become stunted and parts or all of the tree can die.

Literature: Carter et al. 1980.

114   SAN JOSE SCALE

Homoptera: Diaspididae   *Quadraspidiotus*
                                          perniciosus (Comstock)

Description: Female scale insects are tiny, orange, sac-like insects beneath scale coverings which are ¹⁄₁₆ inch in diameter, circular, gray, waxy, and marked with concentric rings surrounding a central, raised nipple. Male scale insects have smaller, ¹⁄₂₅ inch long oval coverings with a circular, raised dot located near one end. The scale can be removed to reveal the body of the insect.

Life cycle: Mature females and immature (second nymphal instar) stages survive the winter. Rather than eggs, female scale insects produce tiny 6-legged, mobile, yellow-colored young, called "crawlers." This stage spreads the infestation to new areas on the host plant, including bark, leaves and fruit, and to new hosts. After inserting their thread-like mouthparts into the plant and feeding for 2 to 3 days, female crawlers secrete their initial scale coverings and never move from that spot. Males develop into 2-winged adults in 2 or 3 weeks and emerge from their scales to seek females and to mate. Up to 6 generations may be produced annually. All stages of development can occur throughout the year except during the winter.

Pest status: A major pest of citrus and stone fruits in Texas.

Habitat and food source(s): Host plants include apple, pear, peach, plums, Osage orange, shrubs, and shade trees. Populations of this scale insect can develop rapidly. The first signs of infestation include a decline of tree vigor, leaf drop and appearance of sparse yellow foliage, particularly on the terminal growth. Reddish spots on the underside of bark and around scales on leaves or fruit result from feeding of immature stages. In severe cases, the entire surface of bark can become covered with layers of overlapping grayish scales. Cracking and bleeding of limbs occur and heavily damaged trees may die.

Literature: Metcalf et al. 1962; Thomas et al. 1972.

115 EUONYMUS SCALE

Homoptera: Diaspididae   *Unaspis euonymi*
                                          (Comstock)

Description: Full-grown male scale insects are elongate, $\frac{1}{32}$ inch long and mostly white, with ridges along the tops of their bodies. Adult males emerge from these scales as tiny 2-winged insects. Female scale insects are larger, almost $\frac{1}{16}$ inch long, brown and shaped like an oyster shell. Also see **white peach scale.**

Life cycle: Winged adult males emerge and seek female scale insects and mate. Before dying, females produce a cluster of eggs underneath the scale shell. Six-legged, mobile yellow nymphal forms, called crawlers, hatch from the eggs and crawl to newly-formed foliage. Nymphs develop through several stages (instars) before reaching maturity. There are 2 or 3 generations per year, with eggs of the first generation hatching from April to June. However, all stages of development can be found during most of the year.

Pest status: Infests certain varieties of euonymus, causing leaf drop, plant stress and occasionally death of heavily infested plants.

Habitat and food source(s): Primarily found on evergreen euonymus (*Euonymus japonica* and *E. kiautschovica*), this species also infests celastrus, camellia, eugenia, hollies, pachysandra, and twinberry. Scale insects on leaves are predominantly the white males, occurring mainly on the underside of the leaf until they become numerous. Their feeding activity extracts juices from leaves and results in yellow spotting visible on the upper leaf surface. Yellow discoloration progresses until the leaf dies and drops from the plant. Brown female scale insects are more commonly found on the twigs and stems.

Literature: Carter et al. 1980; Whitcomb 1983.

COTTONY CUSHION SCALE

Homoptera: Margarodidiae   *Icerya purchasi* Maskell

Description: Adult female scale has fluted cottony egg sac secreted from the body of the scale.

Other Homoptera produce massive quantities of white wax, including some species of aphids, (see **woolly apple aphid, 101**), Flatidae (see **sharpshooters, 89**), mealybugs, whiteflies, and other scales. The **cottony camellia scale,** *Pulvinaria floccifera* (Westwood) is similar to the cottony cushion scale and occurs on camellia, English ivy, euonymus, holly, hydrangea, maple, mulberry, pittosporum, rhododendron, yew, and other ornamental plants. The **cochineal insect (117),** *Dactylopius coccus* Costa (Dactylophidae), a cottony scale that resembles a mealybug and occurs on prickly pears cacti, is known in Texas history as the scale used by native Americans to make a crimson dye that was used to paint missionary buildings, particularly in the San Antonio area, and exported by early settlers.

Life cycle: Cotton cushion scale eggs in the egg sac hatch into 6-legged crawler stages that move onto larger twigs and branches. They develop through several stages before becoming adults. They retain their legs and are able to move throughout their development.

Pest status: This is a large cottony scale of woody ornamental plants.

Habitat and food source(s): Host plants include apple, Boston ivy, boxwood, cypress, hackberry, locust, maple, oaks, peaches and plums (*Prunus*), pecan, pears, pine, pittosporum, pomegranate, quince, rose, verbena, walnut, willow, and other woody ornamentals. Developing stages suck sap from the host plants, resulting in reduced plant vigor, defoliation and reduction of twigs and branches. Adults are unsightly and produce large quantities of honeydew on which the sooty mold fungus grows, turning infested parts of plants black.

Literature: Borror et al. 1989; Johnson and Lyon 1988; Westcott 1973.

LONGTAILED MEALYBUG

Homoptera: Pseudococcidae   *Pseudococcus longispinus*
                                        (Tarioni-Tozzetti)

Description: Female and nymphal mealybugs are ⅛ inch or smaller, soft, oval, wingless insects covered with white fluffy wax, ringed with white wax tufts, and have long (⅛ to ³⁄₁₆ inch) tails. Males are tiny, gnat-like insects with one pair of wings.

The **citrus mealybug (118),** *Planococcus citri* (Risso), is another common species that occurs on a wide variety of greenhouse and nursery crops, feeding on above-ground portions of plants at shoot crotches and on foliage. Females lack long waxy tail filaments and produce masses (400 to 600) of tiny eggs that are covered by a "sack" (ovisac) of conspicuous dense, fluffy, white wax mass and are sometimes called "nests." Most mealybug species feed on foliage, flowers, fruits and stems, but some, such as **ground mealybugs**, *Rhizoecus* spp., feed on roots of holly, African violet, and other plants.

Life cycle: In warm climates, live longtailed mealybug young are believed to be produced without first producing eggs. Very young nymphs (crawlers) are flat, oval, and yellow. They develop through several stages (instars) over several weeks before reaching sexual maturity. Winged males emerge from a tiny fluffy cocoon and fly to the female mealybug to mate.

Pest status: Pests of numerous host plants.

Habitat and food source(s): New shoots and leaves of a wide range of greenhouse and outdoor plants are attacked, including apple, avocado, citrus, English ivy, ficus, gardenia, jasmine, oleander, persimmon, "pothos" (*Scindapsus* spp.), pittosporum, rhododendron. Plant damage is caused by loss of sap extracted by high numbers of mealybugs, resulting in wilted, distorted, and yellowed (chlorotic) leaves, premature leaf drop, stunted growth and occasionally death of infested plants or plant parts. The extracted sticky sugary sap excreted by mealybugs is called honeydew and falls on objects underneath the site of infestation. A black fungus, called sooty mold, colonizes the honeydew coated leaves causing them to look dark and unsightly.

Literature: Baker 1982; Baker 1988; Johnson and Lyon 1988.

RHODESGRASS MEALYBUG

Homoptera: Pseudococcidae   *Antonina graminis* (Maskell)

Description: Adult Rhodesgrass mealybugs are enclosed in a white to yellowish wax sack, lacking prominent features except for a long, hair-like excretory tube. The ¹⁄₁₆ by ⅛ inch body inside is purplish-brown, oval to circular and sack-like, lacking appendages. Crushed bodies of this mealybug produce a purplish stain, which is characteristic.

Ground pearls, *Margarodes* spp. (Margarodidae), are turf-infesting scale insects that are more common in western Texas. They are named for the nymphal stages that are covered with hard, spherical yellowish-purple shells that can grow to ⅛ inch in diameter. These "pearls" are not concentrated in the crown as are Rhodesgrass mealybugs, but rather are attached to roots where they suck plant juices.

Life cycle: No males are known and females bear live young 6-legged crawlers (first instar nymphs). The second and third nymphal stages are similar to adults but smaller. Development is completed in 60 to 70 days and 5 generations can occur per year.

Pest status: Uncommon to Texas now, the Rhodesgrass mealybug was a devastating pest of numerous grasses and forages. Mass release of the parasitic wasp, *Neodusmetia sangwawi* (Rao), decreased populations to levels that do not cause damage. It sometimes reaches pests status when the use of pesticides eliminates the parasite.

Habitat and food source(s): Host plants include a variety of grasses including Bermuda grass, Johnson grass, Rhodes grass, and St. Augustine grass. Later stage (instar) nymphs and adults occur at the base (crown) of the plants, beneath the leaf sheaths and the lower nodes, where they remove plant juices using their sucking mouthparts. Heavily infested plants become discolored, gradually turning brown and dying.

Literature: Brook et al. 1982; Neeb 1980; Schuster and Boling 1971.

ORDER THYSANOPTERA
Thrips

DESCRIPTION

- Thrips usually have two pairs of slender wings with few veins and fringed with long hairs.
- Some species and immatures are wingless, although some immature stages will have noticeable wing pads. Immature stages generally resemble the adults.
- Legs and antennae are short.
- Mouthparts are modified for rasping plant surfaces and sucking up the juices.
- Thysanoptera are tiny insects about ¹⁄₃₂ to over ⅛ of an inch long.

LIFE CYCLE

- Thrips have a simple metamorphosis (egg, nymph, adult). Some species have an intermediate or resting stage between larval development and emergence of adults.

PEST STATUS

- Most thrips feed on plants; others prey on small insects. Those that feed on plants are frequently injurious to greenhouse, vegetable or agricultural crops.
- They will also bite humans, but only cause momentary discomfort.

HABITAT

- Most commonly found on plants and in flowers.

Thrips

119　Western Flower Thrips

Thysanoptera: Thripidae

Frankliniella occidentalis
(Pergande)

Description: Adults are small, yellowish and have hair-fringed wings that are usually held across the back. Immature thrips are similar to adults lack fully developed wings.

Other common thrips species found in Texas include: **onion thrips (120)**, *Thrips tabaci* Lindeman; **citrus thrips,** *Scirtothrips citri* (Moulton); **greenhouse thrips,** *Heliothrips haemorrhoidalis* (Bouché); **gladiolus thrips,** *Thrips simplex* (Morison); and **tobacco thrips,** *Frankliniella fusca* (Hinds). Some thrips species are predaceous on other arthropods.

Life cycle: Adult female western flower thrips insert eggs into plant tissues. Just before hatching, the egg "squeezes" out of the tissue and hatches. Development progresses through 2 larval stages (instars), a pre-pupal non-feeding stage (with wing pads) that crawls down into the soil, and a pupal resting stage from which adults emerge. Development from egg to adult takes 8 to 20 days depending on temperature.

Pest status: Feeding damages developing and mature tissues of many plant parts including buds, leaves, flowers, and fruit. Thrips are capable of "biting" people by poking their single mandible into exposed skin. (This is often the case when people sit down in Texas' beautiful spring wild flower blooms to have their pictures taken. These wild flowers are filled with thrips!) They can also spread plant diseases such as tomato spotted wilt.

Habitat and food source(s): Western flower thrips feed on a wide variety of plants including chrysanthemums, gloxinia, impatiens, tomato, vegetables, and grasses. Some plant species, varieties and cultivars are more attractive to the thrips than others. Thrips are characterized by having a single mandible (jaw) used for rasping. This sword-like mandible is extruded when the mouth cone is compressed on plant tissue. The extruded mandible slashes open surface (epidermal) cells. The contents of the opened cells are then sucked in through the cone.

Literature: Drees and Cole 1990.

120　Onion Thrips

Thysanoptera: Thripidae

Thrips tabaci Lindeman

Description: Adult females have slender, yellowish, ⅕ inch-long bodies with hair-fringed wings held over their backs when at rest. Each leg ends in a small "bladder," not a claw. Nymphal stages are similar to adults but do not have fully-developed wings.

Life cycle: Adult females and nymphs occur throughout the year on and around host plants. Wingless males are rare. Females can reproduce without mating (parthenogenesis), thrusting bean-shaped eggs completely into leaf and stem tissue. Nymphs, hatching from eggs 5 to 10 days later, develop through 4 stages (instars) including two larval instars, a prepupal and a pupal stage, over a period of 15 to 30 days. The first 2 instars are spent on the host plant and the later non-feeding stages are spent in the soil. Up to 8 generations can occur annually.

Pest status: This is one of the more commonly encountered thrips in the home garden, particularly on onion leaves where feeding activities cause silver streaking. Adult and nymphal thrips can "bite" by piercing the skin with their sword-like mouthpart (mandible). Flying adults occasionally invade dwellings through screens or open windows, biting the occupants. Although irritating, bites are usually not serious and involve no venom.

Habitat and food source(s): Although this species is particularly common on onion leaves, they will feed on many other cultivated (vegetable and field crops) and wild (weed) plants. Adults and immature forms use their single sword-like mandible to rupture plant cells on the outer surface of leaves and other plant parts, and then suck out the contents by pressing their mouthparts onto the damaged surface. Feeding activities produce silverish or whitish streaks or blotches of empty cells on leaves. Damaged young, expanding leaves become distorted. Severely damaged leaves and plants may turn brown and die. Onion bulb growth can be distorted and diminished. Damage is most severe during dry seasons.

Literature: Metcalf et al. 1962.

CUBAN LAUREL THRIPS

Thysanoptera: Phlaeothripidae   *Gynailothrips ficorum*
                                                 (Marchal)

Description: This insect is usually first noticed because of the plant damage it produces. The adult Cuban laurel thrips is one of the larger thrips species, being up to ⅛ inch long, with bright red eyes and solid dark brown to black body. Adults are capable of flying but generally remain on the host plant.

Life cycle: All stages can be found in deformed host plant leaves. Adult females lay eggs on the upper surface of curled leaves. Immature stages are light yellow and wingless, and develop through several stages over 30 days or more before becoming adults. There may be up to 5 generations per year.

Pest status: These thrips can be a serious problem in interiorscapes or outdoors where Indian laurel is planted. They are capable of inadvertently biting people.

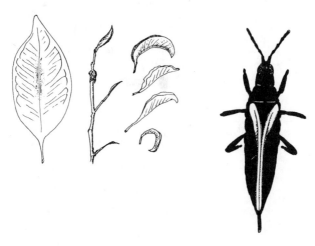

Cuban laurel thrip, and damage to ficus

Habitat and food source(s): Indian laurel is the preferred host of this species, although other *Ficus* species, *Viburnum* and *Citrus* species are occasionally attacked. Adults and immature stages feed on the upper surface of young tender leaves, causing sunken reddish feeding scars along the midribs. Leaves in the process of unfolding become deformed, becoming tightly curled and folded lengthwise, resulting in crescent-shaped leaves containing numerous adult and immature thrips. Damaged leaves first turn yellowish and then brown and hardened as they die and fall off the plant. Severely infested plants have slow growth or can be defoliated. Individuals can survive and develop inside dead, folded leaves.

Literature: Denmark 1967; Johnson and Lyons 1988; Reinert 1983.

ORDER NEUROPTERA

Alderflies, Dobsonflies, Fishflies, Snakeflies, Lacewings, Antlions, and Owlflies

DESCRIPTION

- Neuroptera are rather fragile insects with 2 pairs of many-veined wings of about the same size. Most hold their wings roof-like over the abdomen but some like dobsonflies overlap their wings.
- Antennae are long and threadlike or shorter and some are even clubbed.
- Adults and most immature stages (larvae) have chewing mouthparts. Although in lacewings, mouthparts (mandibles) are modified for grasping and sucking. Immature stages (larvae) of aquatic species have extensions on the sides of their bodies.
- They are ¼ of an inch to over 3 inches long.

LIFE CYCLE

- Metamorphosis is complete (egg, larva, pupa, adult).
- Adult green lacewings can be found throughout the year, but many species produce a single generation or less per year.

PEST STATUS

- Immature stages are predaceous.
- They are considered beneficial, because most feed on other insects.

HABITAT

- Lacewings and their immature forms, known as aphid lions, are the most common insects in this order, and both feed on aphids.
- Hellgrammites, the immature forms of dobsonflies, are found in well oxygenated sections of rivers and streams.

121–123   DOBSONFLIES AND FISHFLIES

Neuroptera: Corydalidae   *Corydalus* spp.

Description: Dobsonflies are large (can be over 2 inches long), and have long antennae. Their large, many veined fore wings are mottled. When at rest, wings are held flat over the back and extend beyond the abdomen. Males have long, extended curved mandibles that they use to grasp the female during mating. Aquatic immature stages, called hellgrammites (**121**), are elongate, dull-colored larvae with gill filaments and feathery gill clusters along the sides of the abdomen. They have two hooks on the end of the abdomen.

Alderflies (Sialidae) are similar to dobsonflies but smaller. Larvae of alderflies differ from hellgrammites in that they lack the two hooks at the end of the abdomen.

Life cycle: Immatures develop in water, especially well oxygenated and high quality water.

Pest status: Dobsonflies are noticed when attracted to lights at night; immatures are collected and used as fish bait; immatures are fierce biters, but they are considered beneficial.

Habitat and food source(s): The adults probably do not feed. The long mandibles of the males would make feeding very difficult. Hellgrammites are aggressive predators that attack other aquatic insects and other organisms in the water. They are found in flowing rivers and streams hidden among rocks.

Literature: Borror et al. 1989; McCafferty 1981.

124   MANTIDFLIES

Neuroptera: Mantispidae   *Climaciella*
                                                          brunnea (Say) and others

Description: This is one of the more unusual groups of insects. They have a long prothorax, forelegs modified for catching prey (raptorial), and a head more characteristic of praying mantis (Mantodea: Mantidae), but the wings are clear and delicately veined resembling those of lacewings, with a wingspread of nearly 1 inch. *Climaciella brunnea* actually appears wasp-like, mimicking *Polistes* (Hymenoptera: Vespidae), with a yellow and dark-brown banded abdomen and dark leading edges on the fore wings. There are about 10 species of mantispids in Texas.

Another unusual, closely-related group is the **snakeflies** (Raphidiidae), appearing somewhat similar to mantispids because of their elongated "neck" (prothorax), but they lack raptorial forelegs. These unusual and rare insects fly during April in the Hill Country among cedar groves.

Life cycle: Clusters of about 1,000 eggs, attached to short transparent stalks, are laid on leaves or other surfaces. Eggs hatch in 11 to 30 days. First stage (instar) larvae are small, dark brown with three pairs of functional legs behind the head. They spend much time standing vertically on the tips of their abdomens and actively crawl or leap, seeking a passing suitable host spider or insect (bee or wasp). When successful, they attach to the host and "hitch a ride" (are carried) to the nest or egg-laying site (i.e., they are phoretic). Two later stages are grub-like while feeding on their host's offspring. Fully grown larvae spin cocoons and pupate inside their last larval skin. Adults occur year-round, especially in summer and fall.

Pest status: Mantidflies are rather rare insects but occasionally become locally abundant and arouse curiosity; immature stages feed on spider egg masses or larvae of wasps and bees.

Habitat and food source(s): Adults are predaceous on other insects; considered beneficial. Later developmental stages are external parasites in spider egg sacs, and perhaps bee or wasp larvae. *C. brunnea* adults are active during the daytime and are attracted to flowers of thistle and other plants, feeding on insects (aphids, lygus bugs, lady beetles, stink bugs), sap and nectar (honey in captivity). They are also cannibalistic. Adults of some species are night active (nocturnal) and are often attracted to light.

Literature: Batra 1972; Borror et al. 1989; Redborg and Macleod 1983; Swan and Papp 1972.

125, 126 GREEN LACEWINGS

Neuroptera: Chrysopidae   *Chrysoperla* spp.

Description: Adults are light green with long slender antennae, golden eyes and long delicately-veined wings that are ½ to ¾ inch long. The common green lacewing, *Chrysoperla carnea* Stephens can be identified by the dark straight line on the side (genae or cheeks) of the head, which runs from the eye to the mouth. Its body is green with a wide pale stripe along the top of the body. *C. rufilabris* Burmeister has red "cheeks" (genae) and black cross veins. Larvae (**125**) grow to ½ inch long and have spindle-shaped bodies with prominent pincher-like mouthparts, resembling tiny alligators. Larvae of both common species have two stripes on the head, but they are straight-sided on *C. rufilabris* while those of *C. carnea* widen towards the back of the head.

Another common Texas species is the **goldeneyed lacewing,** *Chrysoperla oculata* Say, in which adults arc distinctively marked with a black band on the front of the head that runs underneath the antennal sockets, and a red "Y" between and above the sockets, and red encircling the second segment of each antenna. Larvae appear speckled with white and dark body spots.

Life cycle: Mated and fed females lay groups of white eggs on ¼ inch thread-like stalks, which help keep young larvae from eating each other after they hatch. Larvae grow through three stages (instars) for 2 to 3 weeks before each spins a spherical white silken cocoon. The adult emerges in about 5 days. Winter is spent in the cocoon or adult stage, depending on species. Adults disperse widely after emerging before mating and laying eggs. *C. rufilabris* adults can be found throughout the year in central Texas, but they are most abundant in the fall. *C. carnea* is more abundant in the spring, and in the fall their bodies become reddish-brown as they prepare to overwinter. Some species have several generations per year while others have one.

Pest status: Lacewings are considered to be a beneficial insect/natural enemy, being predatory as larvae and adults. Fifteen species of green lacewings (Chrysopidae) in three genera occur in east Texas. The common

Green lacewing

green lacewing, is adapted to live in fields and gardens while C. *rufilabris* Burmeister is more adapted for living in trees.

Habitat and food source(s): Larvae have sickle-shaped jaws (mandibles) with which they pierce prey and suck out body juices. The larvae, called "aphid lions," are extremely carnivorous and predaceous on many soft-bodied insects and mites, including insect eggs, thrips, mealybugs, immature whiteflies, and small caterpillars. They can consume over 200 aphids or other prey per week. Adults have chewing mouthparts. Adults are poor fliers, active at night, and feed on pollen, nectar, and "honeydew" (the exudate of aphids and other sucking insects). Some species are predaceous as adults to a limited extent.

Literature: Agnew et al. 1981; Henn and Weinzeri 1990; Mahr 1994.

127, 128 ANTLIONS OR DOODLEBUGS

Neuroptera: Myrmeleonidae   *Myrmeleon* spp.

Description: Most people know this insect because of the funnel-shaped pit, up to 2 inches in diameter and depth, produced by the larval stages of this insect to trap ants. Larvae (**128**) have globular abdomens and narrower, flattened heads bearing sickle-shaped jaws. Adults superficially resemble drab-colored, 1½-inch-long damselflies (Odonata) with four long, narrow, net-veined wings held roof-like over a long, skinny abdomen when at rest. Unlike damselflies, however, adult antlion antennae are prominent and clubbed at the end.

The **owlflies** (Ascalaphidae) also belong to the superfamily Myrmeleontoidea. Adults appear dragonfly-like (Odonata) but have long clubbed antennae.

Life cycle: Antlion adults fly infrequently and lay eggs in the sand. The larva develops through several stages (instars), digging many pits, before pupating in a spherical, sand-covered cocoon in the spring or summer. Development may occur over two years.

Pest status: Larvae feed in pits on ants; considered beneficial.

Habitat and food source(s): Larvae have piercing jaws (mandibles) used to pierce ant bodies and suck out body fluids. Larvae produce traps by burrowing into the sand backwards and then while going in a circle, they fling up sand to one side using upward jerks of their heads. When complete, larvae remain buried at the bottom of the pit trap with only their jaws exposed. Ants and other small insects falling in the trap are prevented from leaving by the larva constantly throwing more sand up onto the sides of the trap.

Literature: Borror et al. 1989; Metcalf et al.1962; Swan and Papp 1972.

ORDER COLEOPTERA

Beetles

DESCRIPTION

- Coleoptera is the largest order of insects, including about ¼ of all known insects species.
- Coleoptera usually have two pairs of wings, when present. The front pair of wings (elytra) are thick and form a hard shell over all (or part) of the abdomen and meet in a straight line down the middle of the back. The hind wings are membranous and are folded under the front wings when at rest.
- Mouthparts are formed for chewing in adult beetles and immatures (larvae), but some are modified considerably for piercing or pollen feeding. One group, the weevils, have an elongated "snout" which gives them the appearance of having sucking mouthparts, but mandibles are at the end of the snout.
- Immatures (larvae) can have six or fewer legs or be legless and almost maggot-like. Larvae, generally called grubs, come in many sizes and shapes and generally have short antennae, and a distant head capsule. There may be extensions or hooks on the end of the abdomen.
- They are microscopic to over 4 inches long.

LIFE CYCLE

- Beetles have complete metamorphosis (egg, larva, pupa, adult). Some groups produce young without mating (parthenogenesis) or change form and habitat during development (hypermetamorphosis).

PEST STATUS

- This order includes some of the best known and most important of our insect pests and beneficial species. Perhaps the most famous members of this group are lady beetles, June beetles, and the cotton boll weevil. Most pest species damage ornamental and crop plants, although some occur in stored products or are associated with animal remains or excrement.

HABITAT

- Food habits are highly varied. Some feed on living plants; some are predaceous; some are scavengers; and others bore in wood.
- Most of the members are terrestrial, although certain groups are aquatic.
- Immature stages are not necessarily associated with the same habitat(s) as the adults.

TIGER BEETLES

Coleoptera: Cicindelidae   *Cicindela* spp.

Description: Adult beetles are about ½ inch long and have long antennae and legs. Tiger beetles differ from ground beetles in that the head is wider than the thorax. Common species are grayish brown to black often with white spots and markings on the wing covers (elytra), although they may show considerable variation in coloration and markings. Some species have metallic or iridescent blue, green, and bronze coloration. Adults of species are identified by distinguishing characters that include presence of hairs on the face of the head as well as the pattern and texture of the wing covers. Cicindelidae are occasionally included in the ground beetle family, Carabidae.

Life cycle: Adults and partially-developed larvae overwinter in burrows in the soil. Eggs are laid in individual burrows by females. Larvae hatching from eggs dig burrows that are enlarged as they develop through 3 larval stages (instars). Burrows may be over a foot deep in hard-packed sand. Larvae are flat-headed with powerful jaws and S-shaped with recurved hooks on their fifth abdominal segments that they use to anchor themselves in burrows in the soil.

Pest status: Considered beneficial insects, both adult and larval stages are predaceous on other insects. Larvae and adults can bite if handled improperly.

Habitat and food source(s): Most tiger beetles are active during sunny days and are frequently seen in sandy areas such as along the shores of rivers and streams, resting on the surface and then running or flying quickly away when approached. Some are active at dusk or are nocturnal. Larvae wait in burrows for passing prey like a trap with open sickle-like jaws. Both adult and larval stages of tiger beetles feed on a wide variety of insects.

Literature: Frank and Slosser 1991; Swan and Papp 1972.

130–132   GROUND BEETLES

Coleoptera: Carabidae   Many species

Description: This group of beetles varies greatly in size (⅛ to 1 inch), shape, and color. Most are flattened, dark brown, hard-bodied beetles with many fine lengthwise ridges on their wing covers (elytra). The width of the segment just behind the head (pronotum) is usually narrower than the abdomen. The head is narrower than the prothorax, bearing sickle-like jaws (mandibles) and 11-segmented antennae. Some ground beetles are metallic green or blue or are marked with spots of metallic red or gold. One of the most striking ground beetles is the **caterpillar hunter (130)**, *Calosoma scrutator* (Fabricius). This beetle is about 1 inch long and brilliant metallic green. Ground beetle larvae are ⅜ to 1¾ inch long, slightly flattened, cream to brown in color, and slightly tapered at each end. They have three pairs of well-developed legs and run quickly. The heads bear sickle-shaped jaws (mandibles) that are pointed forward.

One ground beetle species, *Scarites subterraneus* (Fabricius) (**131**), is unusual because it has a wide, flat head and prothorax, and a narrow, articulated "waist" between the prothorax and abdomen. The **seedcorn beetle,** *Stenolophus lecontei* (Chaudoir), is a smaller (⅓ inch long) dark brown, striped species that occasionally feeds on corn seeds and seedlings.

Life cycle: Winter is spent in the larval or adult stage. Adults emerge to mate and disperse. Eggs are laid singly in soil. Larvae hatch from eggs and develop through several stages (instars) before pupating. Development is usually complete in one year.

Pest status: Species in this highly variable group of beetles are predominantly predators of other arthropods, both as adults and larvae; some species occasionally become a nuisance when they occur locally in high numbers. They are considered beneficial, although they are capable of biting.

Habitat and food source(s): Ground beetles are commonly encountered under stones, bark, logs and other debris laying on the ground. When disturbed, they run rapidly. At night larvae and adults seek prey, feeding on insects and other organisms.

Literature: Borror et al. 1989; Brook et al. 1982.

133   PREDACEOUS DIVING BEETLES

Coleoptera: Dytiscidae   Several species

Description: Adult beetles have streamlined, oval or football-shaped flattened bodies that are usually ⅛ to 1 inch long. Most species are brown to black but some have distinctive patterns of spots, lines or mottling on the wing covers (elytra). They have elongate hairlike (filiform) antennae. Larvae, which have a long thorax and long legs, are not frequently seen. The head bears conspicuous large sickle-shaped mandibles without teeth.

Predaceous diving beetles are easily confused with **water scavenger beetles** (Hydrophilidae). The later surface for air head first and have a ridge or keel on the underside that runs down the thorax and extends into a point.

Life cycle: Adults and larvae are found in water. Larval development time is not known for many species in this large family. Some species that inhabit vernal ponds develop into adults in a few months.

Pest status: This is a beneficial insect, being predaceous on other insects. Immature stages (larvae) are sometimes called "water tigers" and are capable of biting. When numerous in fish hatcheries, they may reduce numbers of fry.

Habitat and food source(s): These predaceous insects may be found in nearly any body of water, where they feed on a variety of aquatic organisms, including small fish. Adults frequently surface for air, holding the tip of the abdomen to the surface to obtain air, which is stored under the wing covers (elytra) to breath. They are good swimmers and use their legs in unison to propel themselves in a straight line but in a jerky fashion. Males of some species have an enlarged portion on the front leg that is used as a suction disc to hold the female while mating.

Literature: McCafferty 1981.

Coleoptera: Gyrinidae

Dineutus and *Gyrinus* spp.

Description: Whirligig beetles are black or nearly so and ⅛ to 1⅜ inches long. They are flattened (dosoventrally) and streamlined for aquatic life. The eyes are each divided into upper and lower compound eye portions allowing them to see above and below the water surface. The forelegs are relatively long and often held forward. They are easily recognized by the erratic swimming behavior on the surface of the water. Larvae are elongate and often have sideways (lateral) extensions on the abdomen, up to 1 inch long and have 4 terminal hooks on the very tip of the abdomen.

Several aquatic beetles have the same general body shape. The separated eyes of Gyrinidae are characteristic of adults.

Life cycle: Larvae are seldom seen. Developmental times are unknown.

Pest status: These beetles are beneficial. Larvae are predaceous.

Habitat and food source(s): These beetles often congregate in both flowing and still water, especially streams and ponds. Adults feed on organisms on the surface of the water or scavenge debris. They spend much of their life on the surface of water. Some *Dineutus* species can secrete a milky substance that emits an odor that resembles ripe apples, while *Gyrinus* species emit an unpleasant odor. They can swim rapidly. Larvae are predators on aquatic organisms and are seldom seen but are found on the bottom of streams and ponds. Adults are sometimes attracted to lights.

Literature: McCafferty 1981.

CARRION BEETLES

Coleoptera: Silphidae

Nicrophorus and *Silpha* species

Description: Adult beetles of common species are from ⅜ to about 1 inch long, have clubbed antennae and the head is narrower than the first thoracic segment (pronotum). They are flattened soft-bodied beetles and coloration varies with species from all black to black with orange, red or yellowish markings. Wing covers (elytra) are shiny-smooth to leathery, and in *Nicrophorus* species they are squared off (truncated) and do not reach the end of the narrower abdomen.

Life cycle: Adult females are attracted to dead animals and lay eggs on the decomposing bodies. Eggs hatch and larvae develop through several stages before pupating in the ground.

Pest status: They are considered to be beneficial because they help decompose dead animal matter; some species are called "burying beetles" because of their habit of excavating beneath bodies of small dead animals such as mice or snakes and burying them as food for their young.

Habitat and food source(s): Adults and larvae occur underneath carcasses of dead animals and feed on carrion. Some species are predaceous and feed on fly maggots in carrion, while others feed on decaying vegetable matter or fungi.

Literature: Borror et al. 1989; Swan and Papp 1972.

135 WATER SCAVENGER BEETLES

Coleoptera: Hydrophilidae   Several genera

Description: Adults have short, clubbed antennae that are sometimes hidden beneath the head. Their mouthparts (maxillary palpi) are elongated and hairlike (filiform) and may be mistaken for antennae. Most species have a conspicuous keel or ridge between the legs that extends backward into a point. The hind legs have long hairs that aid in swimming. Their bodies are usually not as flattened as **predaceous diving beetles** (Dytiscidae) with which they can be confused. They "row" by alternating the hind legs, producing a wiggle from side to side as they swim. They range in size up to 1½ inch. Larvae may be up to 2⅜ inches long. Their jaws (mandibles) are usually toothed. The abdomen often has a wrinkled appearance and long filaments extending from the sides (some predaceous diving beetles also have filaments). The tail filaments are usually short.

Life cycle: Egg-laying (oviposition) sites vary, although females of a few species carry eggs on their bodies. Some species of males stridulate or chirp to locate mates. Pupation is generally terrestrial.

Pest status: Water scavenger beetles are not pests but the large species may be noticed.

Habitat and food source(s): They are usually found in ponds, shallow lakes, and along the shoreline of flowing water, although one subfamily is found in dung. Adults are general feeders or feed on decaying organic matter (omnivorous or detritus feeding) but a few are predaceous. Most larvae are predaceous, although some feed on plants. Adults may be found at lights.

Literature: McCafferty 1981.

136, 137 STAG BEETLES

Coleoptera: Lucanidae   *Lucanus placidus* Say

Description: Stag beetles are large, robust beetles typically dark brown in color. They have the club of the antennae with the segments separated rather than compact like scarab beetles. Males have elongated mandibles that are used to joust with rival males. Females have more normal jaws. Size is variable and ranges from 1 to 1½ inches. Larvae are similar in shape to white grubs of Scarabeidae but larger. There are relatively few species of stag beetles in Texas. The **giant stag beetle**, *Lucanus elephas* Fabricius (**136**), has males with more elaborately branched and extended mandibles. Some tropical forms have very elongated mandibles in the males.

Life cycle: Larvae take a year or perhaps multiple years to develop. Adult emergence peaks in late May and June (spring or summer).

Pest status: Texas' species are not common enough to be considered pests. Adults may bite if handled.

Habitat and food source(s): Larvae develop in damp decaying wood. Adults are sometimes attracted to lights. Adults can also be found near stumps or rotting logs.

Literature: Dillon and Dillon 1972.

138   BESS BEETLES

Coleoptera: Passalidae   *Odontotaenius* sp.

Description: Adult beetles are up to 1⅜ inches long, shiny black with a series of grooves running the length of the wing covers (elytra) and a short horn on the front of the head between the eyes. Immature beetles are similar to white grubs (Scarabeidae). However, larvae have only two pairs of true legs and grow to about 1½ inches long.

Life cycle: Adults and C-shaped grubs occur together in decomposing logs. Larvae probably take at least 1 year to develop.

Pest status: Occurs in decaying logs, often in large numbers; considered beneficial in its activities to decompose dead wood.

Habitat and food source(s): Wood infested by these beetles is usually well decomposed and falls apart readily. Bess beetles are somewhat social insects, with colonies living in galleries (tunnels) in decaying logs and stumps. Adults tend and feed larvae, preparing food with salivary secretions. Food consists of decaying plant matter. When disturbed, adults produce a squeaking sound by rubbing their wings on the abdomen. This is apparently used for communication between members of the colony. Adult beetles are often covered by mites.

Literature: Borror et al. 1989.

139–141   WHITE GRUBS, MAY AND JUNE BEETLES

Coleoptera: Scarabaeidae   *Phyllophaga crinita*
                                                                    (Burmeister) and others

Description: Adult beetles, commonly referred to as May beetles or June-bugs are ½ to ⅝ inch long, and reddish brown. White grubs (**141**) are C-shaped larvae, up to 1 inch long, with cream-colored bodies and brown head capsules. They have three pairs of true legs, one on each of the first three segments behind the head.

There are more than 100 species of scarab beetles from several genera (*Cyclocephala, Phyllophaga,* and others) in Texas that are considered to be white grubs. However, the most common is *Phyllophaga crinita.* Their biologies are similar, but species differ in distribution, habitat preference, length of life cycle and seasonal occurrence. Other common species include the **southern masked chafer (140)**, *Cyclocephala lurida* Bland. One notable member of the family Scarabaeidae, the **Japanese beetle,** *Popillia japonica* Newman, introduced into the northeastern United States and migrating west and south, has recently (1997) been detected in Texas.

Life cycle: Adults begin to emerge in spring. During adult flights large numbers of beetles can be attracted to lights. Peak flights occur in mid to late June in central Texas. Females, less attracted to lights, tunnel 2 to 5 inches into the soil and deposit eggs. In 3 to 4 weeks, small grubs (larvae) hatch from eggs and develop through 3 stages (instars), with the first 2 stages lasting about 3 weeks. The last larval stage remains in the soil from the fall through spring. In spring and early summer, white grubs pupate 3 to 6 inches deep in the soil. Adults emerge from pupae in about 3 weeks. There is one generation per year, but in north Texas, development may take 2 years.

Pest status: Larval stages eat roots of grasses, vegetable and ornamental plants; adults can be a nuisance around lights at night in early summer.

Habitat and food source(s): *Phyllophaga crinita* is common in Texas turf grass, particularly Bermuda grass, St. Augustine grass, and tall fescue. Feeding by large numbers of grubs causes lawns to turn yellow and die. Severely damaged grass can be "rolled up" like a carpet. Grubs also feed on the roots of weeds, vegetable transplants, and ornamental plants. In agriculture, they are important pests of forage, corn, sorghum, and sugarcane. Most severe injury to plants is caused by large (third stage or instar) grubs feeding on roots in the fall and spring. White grubs are frequently encountered by tilling garden soil or by sifting through soil underneath damaged turf grass. Adults can be abundant around lights in early summer.

Literature: Drees et al. 1994; Hamman et al. 1985.

142 GREEN JUNE BEETLE

Coleoptera: Scarabaeidae   *Cotinis nitida* (Linnaeus)

Description: Beetles are about 1 inch long, ½ inch wide, colored dull velvety-green on the top, with the sides of the shield behind the head (pronotum) and margins of the flattened wing covers (elytra) a browish-yellow and underside a bright metallic green with orange-yellow areas. Eggs are oval and grayish. Larvae are creamy white C-shaped grubs, with a dark brown head, well-developed legs like June beetle larvae and grow up to 2 inches long.

C. mutabilis (Gory and Percheron) is a similar species found in Texas. Other colorful and attractive scarab species are found on prickly pear and other flowers (**143**).

Life cycle: Female beetles lay eggs in the soil. Larvae hatching from eggs feed and develop through several stages (instars) before spending the winter deep in the soil. They pupate in earthen cells in the spring and adults emerge in June or July. There is one generation per year.

Pest status: Adult beetles are attracted to decaying or ripe fruit and feed on such; larvae are infrequent pests in lawns and feed on roots of other plants.

Habitat and food source(s): Larvae feed in the soil on turf grasses, corn, oats, sorghum, alfalfa, vegetables, and ornamental plants. They feed on humus, decaying plants, roots and manure. Larvae have a peculiar habit of "crawling" on their backs when migrating on the soil surface. Adults feed on over-ripe fruit like peaches and sometimes on peach leaves. Adults can be found flying in the air or can be attracted to fermented, over-ripe fruits and some flowers.

Literature: Metcalf et al. 1962; Swan and Papp 1972.

144, 145   EASTERN HERCULES BEETLE

Coleoptera: Scarabaeidae   *Dynastes tityus* (Linnaeus)

Description: Beetles are about 1½ to 2½ inches long and colored yellowish or greenish-gray with brown to black spots, rarely are they reddish-brown. Males have three projections on the shield behind the head (pronotum) with the central one the longest and nearly meeting an additional projection on the head. Females have only small raised areas (tubercles) in place of the horns. Larvae are large C-shaped grubs like huge white grubs.

There are many other species of scarab beetles in Texas. The name **rhinoceros beetle** has been used for this species as well as the close relatives. However, that name now appropriately is applied to *Xyloryctes jamaicensis* (Drury), which is a dark brown species about 1 inch long having a single long upright horn on the head of the males. Females have a small tubercle instead of a horn. Larvae feed on roots of ash trees.

The **ox** or **elephant beetles (145)**, *Strategus* spp., are large (up to 2 inches long), and brown. Males have three horns behind the head (on the pronotum). Immature stages look like very large white grubs and can be found in compost heaps or occasionally in potting media.

Life cycle: Larvae take most of the year to develop and spend the winter. Adult beetles are active in the summer. These beetles have one generation every year or two.

Pest status: Although not frequently encountered, this species is notable because of the large size and appearance.

Habitat and food source(s): Larvae live in rotten logs or high organic matter conditions. Adults do not seem to feed much but may eat leaves.

Literature: Borror et al. 1989; Swan and Papp 1972; Zim and Cottam 1956.

CARROT BEETLE

Coleoptera: Scarabaeidae   *Ligyrus gibbosus*
                                            (De Geer)

Description: Adults are ½ inch long, reddish-brown to black and similar in shape to a June beetle but a little stouter. Wing covers (elytra) are textured with stripes (striated) and indentions (punctate). Larvae are similar to turf-feeding white grubs, over 1 inch in length when fully grown, with a bluish tinge and a reddish-brown head.

Life cycle: Female beetles lay eggs in spring in the soil. Larvae hatch from eggs in a few weeks and grow through several stages (instars) throughout the summer before pupating. Adults emerge later in the year and spend the winter in the soil. There is one generation per year.

Pest status: Adult beetles and larvae (grubs) feed below the surface of the soil on a variety of plants; adults become conspicuous when they congregate and chew on tar in shingles or in cement seams.

Habitat and food source(s): Larvae and adults can be found in the soil where they feed on roots. Larvae feed on roots of cereals, grasses and pigweed. Adults feed on carrots, celery, parsnips, potatoes, beets, corn, cotton, dahlias, elm, and oak. This is the most commonly reported species that attacks tar substances as an adult, an unusual behavior that has not been explained although there must be some chemical attraction to these substances. Adults can be found in the soil and are attracted to lights.

Literature: Metcalf et al. 1962; Swan and Papp 1972.

146, 147   "RAINBOW SCARAB," DUNG BEETLE

Coleoptera: Scarabaeidae   *Phanaeus vindex*
MacLeay

Description: Male and female beetles are between ½ and 1 inch long and overall metallic bluish-green and copperish. The front of the head is flattened and golden-bronze. The male has a long, curved horn extending from the front of the head (clypeus) while the slightly larger female has a tubercle. The front legs are modified for digging.

There are several dung beetles or "tumblebugs" in the subfamily Scarabaeinae (*Canthon, Copris, Deltochilum,* and *Dichotomius,* and others) that are important in recycling animal feces. Some are small, dark, dung-feeding scarab species (e.g., *Ataenius* and *Aphodius* species). One species, *Onthophagus gazella* Fabricius (**147**), was introduced in the 1970s and is now common throughout the state. In parts of Texas, they remove 80% of the cattle droppings. Most species are dull to shiny black and 1⅜ inch or less in length with wing covers (elytra) that may have ridges (striae). They are often attracted to lights at night. These beetles are related to the sacred scarab of ancient Egypt, *Scarabaeus sacer* Linnaeus.

Life cycle: Adult males and females, working in pairs, dig deep burrows underneath animal excrement in which they bury portions of the droppings. Eggs, deposited in the excrement, hatch and C-shaped grubs (larvae) feed on the dung. The grubs develop through several stages (instars) before pupating within cells in the remains of the excrement.

Pest status: This species, along with other dung beetles, plays an important role in nature by reducing fecal material and thereby reducing the habitat for filth-breeding flies; considered beneficial.

Habitat and food source(s): Larvae feed on animal excrement buried by the adults. These beetles are rarely encountered unless an effort is made to examine fresh potential larval habitats! Animal excrement is rich in insect fauna and can yield these strikingly beautiful beetles.

Literature: Borror et al. 1989; Swan and Papp 1972.

148–150   FLAT-HEADED BORERS OR METALLIC WOOD BORERS

Coleoptera: Buprestidae

Chalcophora, Chrysobothris, Agrilus, and other genera

Description: Adult beetles are elongate or oval with short antennae in most genera, with the leaf-mining genera being nearly circular in appearance. Nearly all adults have some metallic coloration on their bodies, often with the brightest coloration under the wings or on the underside. *Chalcophora virginiensis* (Drury) (**148**) is a large black species with a sculptured appearance on the back. *Buprestis lineata* (Fabricius) has broad red lines on the elytra and a metallic pronotum. These two species often emerge from pine in log homes. *Chrysobothris* are intermediate in size with a sculptured back. Several species attack pines and broad-leaved trees. *Acmaeodera* are most commonly seen on flowers as adults and the irregular bright yellow to orange mixed with blue-black colors let them blend with the flowers. These adults have the wing covers (elytra) united along the back but they can still pull out the wings below and fly well.

Agrilus is considered the world's largest genus with over 8,000 species. *Agrilus* are elongate and attack twigs or, less commonly, larger portions of trees. Larvae (**150**) are elongate grubs with the segments just behind the head (thorax) enlarged (widened) and flattened. They are usually white to cream colored with a darker plate on the thorax. The head is actually mostly hidden and fleshy.

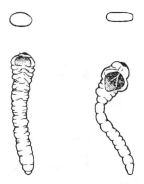

Larvae of round-headed borer (left) and flat-headed borer (right) with cross sections of tunnels

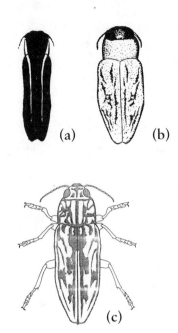

Metallic wood-boring beetles (a) Agrilus, (b) Chrysobothris, and (c) Chalcophora

There are many other beetle groups that have wood-boring species. Larvae can easily be confused with **long-horned wood borers (171–175)**, but the adults are much different.

Life cycle: Adult beetles are usually short-lived, surviving for a few weeks. Adults emerge in the spring and summer depending on the species. Eggs are laid in crevices in the bark for wood-boring species. Larvae develop inside the plant primarily just under the bark for wood borers or inside stems or roots. Leaf-mining species may have several generations per year. However, most species have one generation per year or take multiple years to develop. There are a few records of development over 8 years. Pupation occurs inside the plant.

Pest status: Larvae of most species feed in trunks, branches, or twigs of woody plants, usually when the plant is dead or dying; some species remain in wood after it is used as building materials and adults emerge up to several years later.

Habitat and food source(s): Knowing the host plant for a particular species of metallic wood borers often helps with identification. Some of the larger species feed on pines, although most woody plants have at least one species that feeds on it. Larvae usually tunnel just under the bark surface but may go into the heartwood. Tunnels are oval in cross-section and often have a zig-zag pattern that increases in width as the larvae grow. Emergence holes of adults are most likely to have a semicircular shape or at least one relatively flat side. Leaf-mining species are present on oaks and a few small herbaceous plants where they form short broad leaf mines. Adults of some groups, especially *Acmaeodera,* are found on flowers where they probably feed on pollen. In a few species, adults feed on leaves.

Literature: Baker 1972; Swan and Papp 1972.

151, 152   CLICK BEETLES AND WIREWORMS

Coleoptera: Elateridae   Many species

Description: Click beetles are elongated, parallel-sided, and usually have backward projections on the side corners of the shield behind the head (pronotum). They are somewhat flattened and range in size and color by species. Smaller species are about ¼ inch long. Most species are brown to black in color, although some have reddish and yellowish colors and patterns. The **eyed click beetle** (**151**), *Alaus oculatus* (Linnaeus), reaches 1½ inches in length and is beautifully marked with prominent oval eye spots on the pronotum and mottled gray wing covers. When placed on their backs, these beetles characteristically "click," snapping their thoracic segments (prothorax and mesothorax) to cause their bodies to flip in the air to right themselves. Larvae, called "**wireworms**" (**152**) are usually hard-bodied, brownish, ½ to 2½ inches long and cylindrical, with three pairs of tiny true legs behind the head, and an ornamented shield-like segment on the tail end of the body.

The **false click beetles** (Eucnemidae) are similar to click beetles, and some species can even "click." They are less common and usually occur in wood just beginning to decay. The **Texas beetle,** *Brachypsectra fulva* LeConte (Brachypsectridae) somewhat resembles a ³⁄₁₆-inch-long click beetle without the clicking mechanism. There is only one species in this family.

Life cycle: Biology varies by species. In general, adults and larvae overwinter in the ground, becoming active in the spring. Adult females dig burrows and lay eggs around the base of host plants. Eggs hatch within a few weeks and larvae develop through several molts over a period of time from several months to over 4 years. They pupate in the cells within the soil in late summer or fall, and emerge as adults a few weeks thereafter. Generations can greatly overlap.

Pest status: Larvae of some species damage seeds and underground parts of crop plants.

Habitat and food source(s): Larval stages (wireworms) damage seeds and seedlings of a wide variety of crops including alfalfa, beans, beets, clovers, corn, grasses, small grains (wheat, oats, etc.), many vegetable and bedding plants. They also tunnel into potato and sweetpotato tubers. Larvae of some species, such as the **eyed click beetle,** occur in dead trees and rotting stumps and logs. Adults of *Deilelater* have two light-producing spots on the thorax and one on the abdomen, somewhat similar to that of lightningbugs (Lampyridae).

Literature: Arnett 1985; Borror et al. 1989; Metcalf et al. 1962; Swan and Papp 1972.

Coleoptera: Lampyridae   Several species

Description: These insects are more accurately called "lightning beetles" because they are neither flies (Diptera) or true bugs (Hemiptera). Adults of the **woods firefly,** *Photuris pennsylvanicus* (De Geer), common in Texas, are long and narrow, about ½ inch long with a black head, a reddish section behind the head with dark middle markings (pronotum) and flexible dark brown wing covers (elytra) edged with yellow. Their most notable feature is the underside of the abdomen with the last number of segments colored greenish-yellow, forming a "tail light" capable of producing flashes of light. The light produced by lightning beetles gives off no heat and is produced by the reaction of two substances (luciferin and the enzyme, luciferase). Larvae are flattened, spindle-shaped and have shield-like segments. Females of some species are wingless and appear similar to larvae. Wingless females and many larvae also have structures that produce light and are called "glowworms."

Few other insects can be confused with lightningbugs because no other insect possesses the light-producing structures on their abdomens, although some click beetles (Elateridae) also have light-producing structures elsewhere on their bodies. However, some of the **soldier beetles** such as *Chaulognathus pennsylvanicus* (De Geer) (Cantharidae) superficially resemble lightningbugs in body shape. These beetles are ½ inch long , yellow with a black marking on each wing cover (elytra).

Life cycle: Winter is spent in the larval stage in chambers formed in the soil. They pupate in the spring and emerge in early summer. After mating females lay spherical eggs singly or in groups in damp soil. Larvae hatch from eggs in about 4 weeks and larvae develop through several stages (instars) before pupating. The life cycle of most species takes 2 years.

Pest status: Lightningbugs have predatory larvae and are considered beneficial.

Habitat and food source(s): Immature stages of lightning beetles are predatory on other small insects, earthworms, slugs, and snails. Adults of some species are also predatory. Larvae and adults are active at night (they are nocturnal), and immobilize their prey by injecting them with toxic digestive enzymes before sucking out the liquefied body contents. Adults produce light to find mates and some species use light to attract other species of lightningbugs as prey. Adults of some species apparently do not feed. They are common in open areas near woods in early summer (late May) beginning at dusk when they illuminate.

Literature: Borror et al. 1989; Metcalf et al. 1962; Swan and Papp 1972.

DERMESTID BEETLES: LARDER BEETLES AND CARPET BEETLES

Coleoptera: Dermestidae   *Dermestes, Attagenus* and *Anthrenus* spp.

Description: Symptoms of dermestid beetle infestations include damaged articles, the appearance of larvae migrating in the vicinity of infested materials or the appearance of adult beetles around sources of light such as in window sills. Larval food sources are many and often difficult to locate, but are usually in dark, undisturbed locations. Larvae (**154**) are brown and hairy, usually with longer tufts of hair (setae) on the back end. Size and shape depends on species, but they are usually less than ½ inch long. Adults are somewhat characteristic in size and color patterns: The **larder beetle,** *Dermestes lardarius* Linnaeus, is ⁵⁄₁₆ inch long, dark brown, with each wing cover (elytra) marked with a wide, yellow band and three black spots. The body is covered with fine yellow hairs. The **black larder beetle,** *D. ater* De Geer, is similar but black and lacking the dull yellow band on the wing covers. The **hide beetle,** *D. maculatus* De Geer, has elytra that are uniformly dark. The under surface is white and the ends pointed sharply. The **black carpet beetle,** *Attagenus unicolor* (Brahm), is less than ³⁄₁₆ inch long and black to dark brown. The **varied carpet beetle,** *Anthrenus verbasci* (Linnaeus), is less than ⅛ inch long and has a color pattern of white, brownish and yellowish scales on the back. The **furniture carpet beetle,** *A. flavipes* LeConte, is similar to the varied carpet beetle, but the elytra terminate in a cleft.

There are several other species of dermestid beetles. One of the worst stored-product pests in the world is the **khapra beetle,** *Trogoderma granarium* Everts. It prefers stored dried vegetable products (grains, seeds,

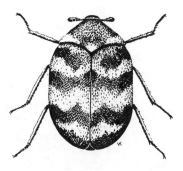

Carpet beetle

flour, cereal, hay, straw) but will also attack animal products. Originally from India, it was introduced into the western United States during the 1940s and has been under federal quarantine. It is periodically detected in grain shipments entering U.S. ports.

Life cycle: Adult carpet beetles overwinter in cracks and crevices, entering buildings in spring and early summer seeking food sources. The female larder beetle lays eggs that hatch in 12 days or less. Larvae develop through 5 to 6 stages (instars) before pupating. Cast skins from larvae often accumulate around the food source. Carpet beetles pupate in their last larval skin and may remain there for several weeks. The black larder beetle develops from egg to adult in about 6 weeks, while the varied carpet beetle can take almost a year to develop (egg - 17 to 18 days; larvae - 222 to 323 days through as many as 16 instars; pupae - 10 to 13 days).

Pest status: Larvae are important pests of stored products; larder beetles are occasionally cultured and used by museum personnel to remove hair and tissues from the skeletons of delicate animal specimens.

Habitat and food source(s): Adult carpet beetles feed on pollen and nectar in the spring. Larvae of the larder beetle, the black larder beetle, and the hide beetle feed on animal products, including meats, cheeses, animal skins, feathers and horns. Black and varied carpet beetle larvae feed on fabrics containing wool and other animal hair in clothing, furniture, and other household materials. Larvae are capable of digesting keratin, the protein in animal hair and feathers. They may also damage materials of plant origin (cotton, linen, silk) and synthetic materials containing nutritious contaminants. The varied carpet beetle is often found in collections of dead, dried insects, and other arthropods kept in unprotected, loosely-fitting, dark storage boxes.

Literature: Ebeling 1978; Metcalf et al. 1962.

155   "RED CROSS" BEETLE

Coleoptera: Melandryidae   *Collops balteatus* LeConte

Description: This soft-bodied beetle is most easily recognized by the red markings on the wing covers, elytra, which are in the form of a cross. The remainder of the elytra has four bluish-black spots. The head, abdomen, and legs are black to brownish black. The pronotum is red with a one or two bluish-black spots on the center of the pronotum. Length is about ¼ inch.

Several related species are similar in general appearance but with different markings. *Collops quinquemaculatus* (Fabricius) is very similar in appearance but is smaller and the pronotum is red.

Life cycle: Not much is known about the life cycle of this species.

Pest status: These beetles are considered beneficial because they are predators.

Habitat and food source(s): Adults can be found on flowers where they probably feed on pollen. They also feed on insects and insect eggs such as leafhoppers and eggs of the chinch bug. They are common in cotton and other agricultural commodities.

Literature: Frank and Slosser 1991; Swan and Papp 1972.

156 SAP BEETLES

Coleoptera: Nitidulidae   *Carpophilus* and several
                                            genera

Description: Sap beetles are minute to small. They are broad, flattened with large head and eyes. The antennae are short and the last three segments are clubbed. Several species have short wing covers, (elytra) leaving the last few segments of the abdomen exposed. Many are brightly colored with red or yellow spots or bands on black elytra. Others are more dull brown. Larvae are elongate, usually white, with short setae and spines.

Life cycle: They pupate in the soil and spend the winter as adults.

Pest status: They can be a nuisance when abundant on overripe fruit. Others are pests of dried fruit. This group of beetles has recently become important because they transmit the oak wilt disease when adults are attracted to the fungal mats that develop on the trunks of infected trees under the bark.

Habitat and food source(s): Adults of some species can be found abundantly in flowers especially cactus. They are attracted to decaying vegetable matter, fermenting fruit, and sap. Some are found under bark.

Literature: Swan and Papp 1972.

SOUTHERN LYCTUS BEETLE

Coleoptera: Lyctidae   *Lyctus planicollis* LeConte

Description: Adults are elongate, brown to nearly black beetles about ¼ inch long. They have short yellowish-white hairs on the surface, are nearly cylindrical in shape, but somewhat compressed on top. The large head is exposed and the antennae have a 2-segmented club. Larvae are similar to small white grubs that may appear C-shaped when removed from the tunnel.

There are several other species in this family. **Bostrichid beetles** (Bostrichidae) and **anobiid beetles** (Anobiidae) may also tunnel in wood and have a similar elongate and cylindrical appearance. However, they are not associated with fine sawdust.

Life cycle: Eggs are laid in pores or cracks in wood. Larvae feed in the wood burrowing in all directions below the surface. Active infestations can be found by the powdery wood fibers that are extruded from the circular hole on the surface. The talcum-like fine, dry powder found in the galleries, which forms piles under infested wood as beetles push it out of exit holes, gives this family of beetles the common name **powder post beetles.** Larvae can withstand very dry conditions and may take a few years to develop. Larvae pupate in the tunnels.

Pest status: This beetle is widespread and can infest lumber. It can be found in old buildings and in wood used to build new homes.

Habitat and food source(s): They tunnel in hardwoods including ash, hickory, and oak. Ash paneling in new homes is frequently infested with this beetle.

Literature: Ebeling 1978; Swan and Papp 1972.

CIGARETTE BEETLE

Coleoptera: Anobiidae

Lasioderma serricorne (Fabricius)

Description: A small beetle (⅒ inch) with the head tucked somewhat under the thorax (pronotum) giving it a rounded appearance from the side. The color is dull generally brownish red or reddish yellow. The legs are short and can be retracted into cavities in the body. Antennae are saw-toothed (serrate) and the wing covers, (elytra) are not quite smooth.

The larvae are nearly cylindrical with short legs and short hairs (setae) on the body. They are somewhat C-shaped especially when mature with distinct head capsules. Larvae are about ⅛ inch.

The **drugstore beetle,** *Stegobium paniceum* (Linnaeus), is very similar in appearance and may be found in many of the same habitats. The last three segments of the antennae are clubbed in this species and the elytra have longitudinal furrows (striae).

Life cycle: Eggs are laid on the food source. Developmental time is highly variable depending on conditions, but is typically 30–50 days. There are commonly 3 to 6 generations per year. Young larvae are active and may move around seeking new food sources.

Pest status: Cigarette beetles are found in nearly all temperate to tropical regions. Moreover, they are transported in tobacco and various food products.

Habitat and food source(s): They feed on tobacco, seeds, spices, dried plant material, drugs, and even upholstery.

Literature: Ebeling 1978; Swan and Papp 1972.

157 SAWTOOTHED GRAIN BEETLE

Coleoptera: Cucujidae

Oryzaephilus surinamensis (Linnaeus)

Description: The adult beetle is small (⅒ inch), very flattened, and brown with the segment just behind the head (pronotum) having characteristic "sawtoothed" outer margins, bearing 6 "teeth" on each side.

A closely related species, the **merchant grain beetle,** *Oryzaephilus mercator* (Fauvel), is very similar but differs in the dimensions of the head capsule (i.e., the region just behind the eyes is shorter, less than the vertical diameter of the eye for the merchant grain beetle, being longer for the saw-toothed grain beetle).

Life cycle: Fertilized females lay numerous shiny white eggs, singly or in clusters, in foodstuffs and packaging. Larvae hatch from eggs in 3 to 17 days depending on temperature. Yellowish-white, deeply segmented larvae develop through several (2 to 4) stages (instars) while growing to about ⅛ inch long. Pupation often occurs in cells made of food particles cemented together, usually onto a solid object. Development from egg to egg occurs in 27 to 375 days. Four to six generations can occur annually.

Pest status: These beetles infest stored dry goods in the pantry or the kitchen and can be a nuisance.

Habitat and food source(s): Adults find their way into stored grains, flour, sugar, nuts, and other dry material of plant origin through cracks and crevices of imperfectly sealed containers. They are incapable of attacking sound grain kernels and often occur in food previously infested by other stored product pests.

Literature: Ebeling 1978; Swan and Papp 1972.

158–160 CONVERGENT LADY BEETLE

Coleoptera: Coccinellidae *Hippodamia convergens* Guérin-Méneville

Description: Lady beetles are also called "ladybugs" or "ladybird beetles." The adult beetle is orange with 6 small dark spots on each wing cover (elytra). The segment behind the head (pronotum) is black with a white margin and marked with two convergent white dashes (appearing like \ / with the head at the top). The larva (**159**) is soft-bodied, with gray and orange markings, and covered with rows of raised black spots.

There are several naturally occurring and introduced lady beetle species (see **multicolored Asia lady beetle, 158**). The **spotted lady beetle,** *Coleomegilla maculata* (De Geer), is dark pink rather than orange-red, and has large black spots on the wing covers (elytra) and no white markings on the shield just behind the head (pronotum). Other commonly occurring lady beetles include the **twicestabbed lady beetles,** *Chilocorus stigma* (Say) and *Olla v-*

Convergent lady beetle

nigrum (Mulsant).These species are all black except for two red spots on the elytra. The twice-stabbed form of *Olla* (**160**) has white markings on the side of the pronotum. *C. cacti* feeds predominantly on scale insects. One of the smaller lady beetle species is *Scymnus loewii* Mulsant, being only ¹⁄₁₆ inch long. Adult beetles are dull orange on the sides with a black "V" pattern on the wing covers. Larvae of this species secrete wax filaments on their bodies, which make them look much like mealybugs (Homoptera: Pseudococcidae).

Life cycle: Adult female beetles lay yellow oval-shaped eggs in clusters or singly near infestations of aphids or other pests. Larvae hatch from eggs and develop through several stages (instars) before they pupate. Development from egg to adult takes 2 to 3 weeks.

Pest status: Lady beetle are beneficial, being natural enemy of small insect pests. Adults and larvae are predaceous.

Habitat and food source(s): Larvae and adults feed primarily on aphids, but they will also feed on scales, eggs of caterpillars, and other soft-bodied insects and mites. Adults occasionally feed on nectar, pollen, and "honey-dew" (exudate of aphids and other sucking insects). Adults disperse seeking feeding and reproduction sites.

Literature cited: Frank and Slosser 1991; Henn and Weinzieri 1990.

158, 161   MULTICOLORED ASIAN LADY BEETLE

Coleoptera: Coccinellidae   *Harmonia axyridis* Pallas

Description: Adult beetles are ¼ to ⅜ inch long, bright yellowish- to reddish-orange, and marked with from zero to 20 small-to-prominent spots on the wing covers (elytra). The distinguishing markings occur on the thoracic shield-like plate just behind the head (pronotum), which has 2 prominent white areas or marginal spots (that appear like cheeks or "glasses") on each side. A black M-shaped mark or a solid black trapezoid mark in the center of the pronotum is unique to this species. Mature larvae (**161**) are black with a reddish-orange "blaze" stripe or sawtooth-edged band on each side of the abdomen.

Several other lady beetle species superficially resemble the harmonia lady beetle, including another imported species called the **seven-spotted lady beetle,** *Coccinella septempunctata* (Linnaeus), which occurs in the Texas panhandle and north central areas in field crops where it feeds on aphids. This species, often called "C7," has orange-red wing covers (elytra) marked with 7 black spots, a black head and a white area on the front part of the outer margins of the black pronotum. Another large species, *Cycloneda munda* (Say), has no spots on the orange-red elytra and a pronotum margined in white. The **ash-gray lady beetle (161),** *Olla v-nigrum* (Mulsant), *abdominalis* form, is overall tan-gray and has a small black spot near each side margins of the pronotum.

Life cycle: Adult beetles spend the winter congregated in protected spaces and become active in the spring (February and March). Females lay football-shaped yellow eggs singly or in clusters. Larvae hatch from eggs in about 4 days and develop over a period of 2 weeks before pupating. Adults emerge in about 6 days. Development time from egg to adult is about 36 days but varies with temperature. Several generations can occur annually. They leave their feeding sites in search of overwintering habitats in November.

Pest status: An introduced lady beetle species, the multicolored Asian lady beetle is considered to be a successfully introduced natural enemy of some important insect pests of shrubs and trees. However, high numbers of adults congregate in wall voids, chimneys, unheated attics, and similar harborage areas during the fall and winter months, becoming a nuisance. It was imported repeatedly into the United States, beginning in 1916, from southeastern Asia (China, Japan, and southern Siberia), but was not found in Texas until 1992. It has since become a common and abundant lady beetle species, particularly in the eastern and central part of the state.

Habitat and food source(s): Larval and adult stages feed on aphids and scale insects and on plants such as pecan, crape myrtles, Virginia pines, roses and aphid-infested crops such as wheat, sorghum, and cotton. In pecan orchards, the multicolored Asian lady beetle feeds on two species of yellow pecan aphids more so than on the black pecan aphid. They also eat pecan stem phylloxera emerging from opening galls.

Literature: Frank and Slosser 1991; Knutson et al. 1994; Anon. 1986.

162   TUMBLING FLOWER BEETLES

Coleoptera: Mordellidae   *Mordella atrata* Melsheimer
                                        and *M. marginata*
                                        Melsheimer

Description: These beetles are basically black and about ¼ inch long. They are wedge-shaped with the tail coming to a point. *M. atrata* is almost solid black except for the base of the tail which shows silvery pubescense. *M. marginata* is very similar but shows a variety of irregular silvery pubescent patterns on the pronotum and elytra. The hind legs are flattened and have an enlarged leg segment, femur, which they use to kick when they are on a hard surface. This kicking gives them the name of tumbling flower beetles because they bounce erratically when disturbed. There are several other members of the genus *Mordella*.

The largest genus in the family is *Mordellistena*, which are generally smaller and seldom as common. They may be patterned or plain and come in a variety of colors from black, yellow, brown, and reddish.

Life cycle: Adults are common on flowers where they can be abundant in some situations. Larvae of *Mordella* species are recorded from dead and decaying logs. Larvae of *Mordellistena* are primarily stem borers in pithy stems of plants especially composites and grasses. There is apparently one generation per year.

Pest status: Mordellids are not known to be a pest, although the larvae infest stems of sunflowers and other herbaceous plants.

Habitat and food source(s): Adults apparently feed on pollen of many flowers. They are often found on umbelliferous flowers and composites and can be abundant in some circumstances. The adults are most often seen in the spring. Several species may occur together.

Literature: Jackman and Nelson 1995; Liljeblad 1945.

163–166   CONFUSED FLOUR BEETLE

Coleoptera: Tenebrionidae   *Tribolium confusum*
                                             Jacquelin duVal

Description: This ⅛ inch long, flattened, reddish-brown beetle may appear somewhat shiny. The shield behind the head (pronotum) has minute punctures and the wing covers (elytra) are grooved (striate) with sparse punctures.

A close relative, the **red flour beetle,** *Tribolium castaneum* (Herbst), is similar and the two species may occur together in stored food. This beetle has the last 3 antennal segments enlarged abruptly and of equal size, but it lacks the notched expansion of the head behind the eyes and has the eyes farther apart than in the confused flour beetle. The **yellow mealworm (164),** *Tenebrio molitor* Linnaeus, and **dark mealworm,** *T. obscurus* Fabricius, are also occasional stored-product pests, with adults almost ½ inch long. They are probably better known because they are cultured and sold commercially as fish bait and pet food for reptiles, amphibians, and other insect feeders. Larvae are cylindrical, hardened, shiny, yellow- or brown-colored (color is characteristic for the species).

Life cycle: Adult beetles are active and move about irregularly, hence the name. They can live for over a year. Eggs laid by females hatch in 5 to 12 days. Larvae are white, tinged with yellow, slender, and cylindrical. They develop through 5 to 12 stages (instars) and grow to about 3/16 inch long over as few as 30 days. They have two short appendages on the end of the last abdominal segment. There may be 5 generations per year.

Pest status: This species is found worldwide infesting stored food. Infestation may affect flavor of product.

Habitat and food source(s): They are found in stored-food products like flour, cereals, and other products (e.g., dried beans, peas, peppers and fruits, shelled nuts, spices, chocolate, snuff, museum specimens, and some drugs). Adults and larvae feed throughout stored food primarily in milled or prepared products. They are perhaps the most common pest of processed flour. This species is often used as a test animal in laboratory experiments because it is easy to keep in culture.

Adults of the genus Lobopoda (**165**) frequently enter homes, but are harmless. Other tenebrionid beetles can be found under stones and bark (**166**) and are adapted for living in dry conditions.

Literature: Ebeling 1978; Metcalf et al. 1962; Swan and Papp 1972.

Coleoptera: Meloidae   *Epicauta* spp. and others

Description: Blister beetles vary by species in shape, size (⅜ to 1 inch long) and color (solid gray to black or with paler wing margins, metallic, yellowish striped or spotted). Most are long, cylindrical narrow-bodied beetles that have heads that are wider than the first thoracic segment (pronotum). The wing covers (elytra) are usually soft and pliable. Although over 100 species occur in Texas, common blister beetles include the **black blister beetle (168)**, *Epicauta pennsylvanica* (De Geer), *E. occidentalis* (east and central Texas), and *E. temexa* (south Texas), which are mostly orangish-yellow with three black stripes on each of the wing covers (elytra). A west Texas species, *Cysteodemus armatus* LeConte, has wing covers that are broadly oval and convex, colored black with bluish or purplish highlights.

Life cycle: Hypermetamorphosis is characteristic of this family. Winter is spent in later larval stages and pupation occurs in the spring. The pupal stage lasts about 2 weeks and adults appear in early summer. Female beetles lay clusters of eggs in the soil. The first stage (instar) larva hatching from the egg (triungulin) is a tiny, active, long-legged larva that seeks the appropriate host. Once there, the larva develops through several stages, each with progressively reduced appendages and increasingly grub-like appearance. The first larval stages develop within about a month, but the second to the last (pseudopupa) can remain for about 230 days before molting into the last (sixth) larval stage in the spring. Generally, one generation occurs per year although some develop in 35 to 50 days and others develop in 3 years.

Pest status: Adults usually occur in loose groups or swarms that feed on leaves of certain plants, especially legumes. Their bodies contain a toxin (cantharidin) that can cause blisters to form on the skin. Animals, particularly horses, ingesting beetle contaminated feed become extremely ill and may die. Handling blister beetles can cause blisters on the skin as a reaction to cantharadin. Larval stages feed on grasshopper eggs or are predaceous and are thus considered to be beneficial, although a few species feed in nests of solitary bees.

Blister beetle

Habitat and food source(s): Blister beetle species feed on flowers and foliage of a wide variety of crops including alfalfa, ornamental plants, potatoes, soybeans, garden vegetables, and other plants. Immature stages feed on grasshopper eggs, live in solitary bee hives or are predaceous, depending on species.

Literature: Adams and Selander 1979; Borror et al. 1989; Dillon 1952; James and Harwood 1969; Metcalf et al. 1962; Swan and Papp 1972.

170 "Ironclad" Beetle

Coleoptera: Zopheridae

Zopherus nodulosus haldemani Horn

Description: The adult beetle is ⅝ to 1³⁄₁₆ inch long and notable in appearance. The body is adorned by a black and creamy white blotchy color pattern and its exoskeleton (integument) is extremely hard. Although the color pattern is quite striking when the beetle is held, it effectively blends with bark on tree trunks.

Other species of the genus *Zopherus*, which contains 19 species, are known from western Texas. This beetle family (Zopheridae) is closely related to Tenebrionidae.

Life cycle: Development progresses through egg, larvae, pupal, and adult stages. Little is known about the biology of this species.

Pest status: Found in the central portion of Texas and south into Mexico, the beetles are not known to damage live plants. True ironclad beetle species occur in California.

Habitat and food source(s): Larval and pupal stages of this insect have been collected from the dead wood of pecan, which apparently serves as the developmental site for this species. Adult beetles have been collected from trunks of oak trees in the College Station area. Adult beetles are thought to feed on lichens growing on trunks of these trees. This beetle can be found clinging onto the trunks of trees or outer walls of homes in wooded areas.

Literature: Burke 1976.

171–175 Locust Borer

Coleoptera: Cerambycidae

Megacyllene robiniae (Forster)

Description: Adults are medium sized (¾ inch long) long-horned brown to black beetles with distinctive gold-yellow markings. This is one of many species of a family of beetles called **long-horned beetles (171–175)**. Whitish larvae have three pairs of small legs of the first three body segments behind the head capsule. Underneath the bark and in the heartwood, larvae

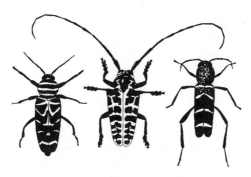

Long-horned beetles or round-headed borer: locust borer (left); cottonwood borer (center); and redheaded ash borer (right)

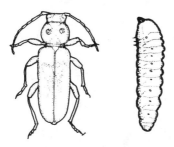

Old house borer and larva

(175) produce tunnels that are oval to almost round in cross section because of the shape of the larvae. Larvae in this group of beetles are also called **round-headed borers (175)**. (See also Buprestidae.)

Adults of the **redheaded ash borer,** *Neoclytus acuminatus* (Fabricius), have a narrow body with a reddish thorax and light brown wing covers (elytra) marked with 4 yellow lines on each. The yellow lines are slanted downward toward the middle, giving the appearance of chevrons across the back. The antennae are rather short and the long legs are thin and fragile. Redheaded ash borers feed in many species of tree trunks and branches including those of oak, ash, elm, and even grapes. The **painted hickory borer,** *M. caryae* (Gahan) and *Placosternus difficilis* (Chevrolat) (**172**) commonly infest mesquite. None of these species will attack cured structural timbers in the home. However, the **old house borer,** *Hylotrupes bajulus* (Linnaeus), does feed on structural timbers. It produces oval to round exit holes about ¼ inch in diameter. Adults are ½ to 1 inch long, grayish-black to dark brown with yellow-gray hairs on the front part of the body and elevated shiny black areas in the shield behind the head (pronotum). The wing covers (elytra) are marked with two grayish markings, which may be rubbed off in some specimens.

Life cycle: Larvae of the locust borer hatch from eggs laid in bark crevices. Visible symptoms of larval infestation are wet spots and frass on the bark of living black locusts. Later, larvae tunnel into the inner bark and construct cells in which they spend the winter months. In a year the larvae are fully grown and are about 1 inch in length. Adults typically emerge late in the summer or in the fall.

Pest status: Larvae can damage trunks and branches of locust trees; occasionally, adults emerge indoors from firewood stored in the home; distribution of this species is limited to east Texas.

Habitat and food source(s): Immature stages occur in black locust tree trunks and branches. Adult beetles are frequently found feeding on goldenrod or other flowers in the fall.

Literature: Baker 1972.

176   TWIG GIRDLER

Coleoptera: Cerambycidae   *Oncideres cingulata* (Say)

Description: These beetles are ½ to ¾ inch long, light to dark brown with a wide gray band across the wing covers (elytra) and a dense sprinkling of pink, orange or dark yellow spots. They have long antennae.

Mesquite twig girdlers, *Oncideres rhodosticta* Bates, are similar in appearance to pecan twig girdlers, but can be distinguished by the presence of three shiny, black dots immediately behind the head. The **huisache girdler**, *O. pustulatus* LeConte, is about 1 inch long, brown with a light brown band across the middle of the upper surface of the body and peppered with small, shiny black dots.

Life cycle: Adults appear from late August through October. After mating, females select a host plant, chewing a clean-cut "V"-shaped groove around a branch. Thereafter, they crawl above the girdled site and insert cream-colored oval eggs singly into notches chewed into the bark. Larvae hatch from eggs in about 7 days and begin tunneling underneath the bark. Larvae grow through several stages (instars) during the year before transforming into pupae the following summer. A few of the larvae do not complete development until May or June of the second year, which accounts for a small amount of girdling damage occurring in the spring.

Pest status: Females chew a groove around the circumference of small branches, "girdling" them, thereby killing damaged parts of trees; damaged branches eventually fall from the tree; larvae feed inside the fallen tree part and are not a threat to tree health.

Habitat and food source(s): The twig girdler occurs throughout Texas except in the Trans-Pecos area. They attack citrus, elm, hackberry, hickory,

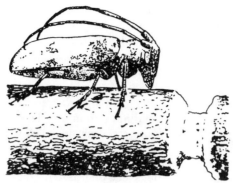

Twig girdler

huisache, mimosa, pecan, persimmon, red oak, retama, tepehuaje, Texas ebony, walnut, and various fruit trees. Twigs selected by female beetles to girdle range in diameter from ⅓–½ inch. Severe girdling can disfigure trees. Damage appears mainly in late summer and fall when adult beetles are active. Leaves on the girdled branches turn brown, die, and fall; the branches often fall from the tree during high winds and storms. Beetles are not commonly encountered on trees. They are attracted to lights.

Literature: Rice 1989; Rice and Drees 1990; Rice 1995.

177   COTTONWOOD BORER

Coleoptera: Cerambycidae   *Plectrodera scalator*
                                            (Fabricius)

Description: Adult beetles are large (1¼ inch long), robust longhorned beetles with black antennae as long or longer than the body. The body is beautifully marked with a bold pattern of black rectangular areas on a creamy-white to yellow background. Larvae are legless, cylindrical (oval in cross section), creamy-white bodies and brown to black headed, growing to 1½ inch long.

There are many cerambycid beetles that attack trees and other plants, but few have larval stages that feed on roots or are larger than the cottonwood borer. Larvae of the **tilehorned prionus,** *Prionus imbricornis* (Linnaeus), feed in the crown and larger roots of certain trees, developing over a period of 3 to 5 years. Adult beetles are dark brown, over 1½ inches long and their antennae are not as long as the body.

Life cycle: Adult cottonwood borers emerge from mid-May through early-July. Mated females dig burrows at the base of the tree and lay yellowish-white elliptical eggs in niches of chewed, shredded bark around the crown and buttress roots. Development requires 1–2 years before larvae pupate within larval galleries.

Pest status: Adults are commonly encountered on trunks and branches of host trees. Infested mature trees are usually not seriously damaged. Heavily infested young trees may be killed or fall over.

Habitat and food source(s): Cottonwood borers primarily infest cottonwood, but also occur on poplars and willows. Larvae (grubs) tunnel around the crown and buttress roots. Galleries, at and below the soil line, vary in length and form tunnels up to 8-inches long to 2- to 3-inch diameter oval areas, depending on tree size and infestation site. They are often packed with wood shavings (frass). Young trees may be killed when larvae tunnel under the bark (through the xylem tissue) all the way around the base of the tree, girdling it. More commonly, they structurally weaken the tree causing it to fall over in high winds. Adults feed on leaf stems (petioles) and bark of tender shoots, occasionally causing shoots to break, wilt, and die, a symptom called "flagging."

Literature: Johnson and Lyon 1988.

178   SOYBEAN STEM BORER

Coleoptera: Cerambycidae   *Dectes texanus* LeConte

Description: Larvae (grubs) are creamy white, cylindrical but corrugated and legless, growing up to ⅝ inch long. Adults are roughly ½ inch long, charcoal gray, and have antennae that are longer than the body.

Larvae of the **lesser cornstalk borer,** *Elasmopalpus lignosellus* (Zeller) (Lepidoptera: Pyralidae), also tunnel into the stalks of soybeans and other plants. These active, bluish-green caterpillars have three pairs of true legs behind the head and a series of "false" legs (prolegs) on the abdomen. They are more common in sandier soils along the Texas coast.

Life cycle: Winter is spent in the larval stage in the stubble of soybeans and other host plants. They pupate in late spring and adults emerge in early summer. Mated females chew crevices along leaf petioles in which they lay eggs. Larvae develop through 4 stages (instars) in stems of host plants until cold weather begins. There is only one generation per year.

Pest status: Larvae tunnel through the stalks of soybeans grown in the Texas Panhandle, causing damaged plants to fall over (lodge), potentially reducing yield.

Habitat and food source(s): In addition to soybeans, soybean stem borers' host plants include cocklebur, ragweed, and other weeds. Larvae tunnel through the stem and feed on inner (pith) tissues during July and August, eventually cutting off plants at the base. These plants may fall over (lodge) and become difficult to harvest. This is a particular problem late (September and October) in the growing season. Larvae are apparently cannibalistic, as only one larva develops per stem. Adults can be found in the spring using a sweep net or lights at night.

Literature: Carter et al. 1982; Drees and Way 1988; Little 1963.

1   **Springtail** (Collembola)

2   **Silverfish,** *Lespisma sacchrina*

3   **Mayfly** (Ephemeroptera)

4   **Mayfly,** nymph

5   **Common skimmer,**
     Libellula luctusa, male

6   **Dragonfly,** nymph

7 **Damselfly**

8 **Damselfly,** nymph (Calopterygidae)

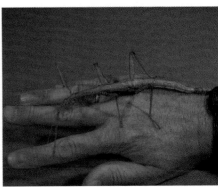

9 **Walkingsticks,** *Anisomorpha* sp., mating

10 **Walkingstick,** *Megaphasma dentricus*, female

11 **Differential grasshopper,** *Melanoplus differentialis*

12 **Banded-winged grasshopper,** *Arphia* sp.

13 Lubber grasshopper,
Brachystola magna

14 "Rainbow" or "pictured"
grasshopper, *Dactylotum* sp.

15 "False" katydid, *Scudderia* sp.

16 Tree cricket, *Oecanthus* sp.,
nymph

17 Field cricket, *Gryllus* sp.

18 Cave or camel cricket,
Ceuthophilus sp.

19 Southern mole cricket,
    Scapteriscus borellia

20 Praying mantid,
    Stagmomantis sp. (right)

21 Praying mantid, egg mass (left)

22 American cockroach, *Periplaneta
    americana*, adults and nymphs

23 Smokybrown cockroach,
    Periplaneta fuliginosa

24 Pale-bordered field cockroach,
    Pseudomops sp.

25 German cockroach,
   Blattella germanica

26 Drywood versus subterranean
   termites

27 Subterranean termites,
   Reticulitermes sp.

28 Subterranean termite,
   Reticulitermes sp., queen

29 Subterranean termite,
   Reticulitermes sp., winged
   reproductive

30 **Desert termite,** *Gnathamitermes*
   tubiformans, **castings around**
   plant stems (right)

31 **Ringlegged earwig,**
Euborellia annulipes

32 **Stonefly** (Plecoptera)

33 **Stonefly (Plecoptera),** nymph

34 **Barklice,** *Archipsocus nomas,*
silk-wrapped tree trunk (right)

35 **Barklice,** *Cerastipsocus venosus* (left)

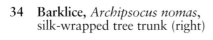

36 **Chicken head louse,**
Cuclotogaster heterographus

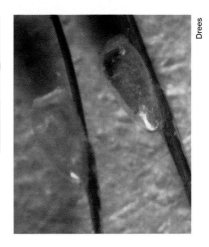

37 **Head louse,**
Pediculus humanus capitus

38 **Lice eggs** or **"nits"** (right)

39 **Giant water bug,** *Lethocerus* sp. (left)

40 **Water boatman,** *Corixa* sp.

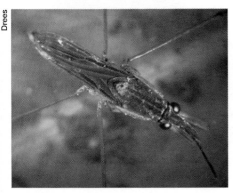

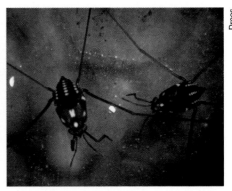

41 **Water strider,** *Gerris* sp.

42 **Water strider,** *Gerris* sp., nymph

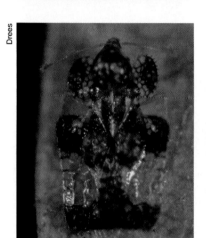

Drees

43 **Azalea lace bug,** *Stephanitis pyriodes* (left)

Drees

44 **Sycamore lace bug,** *Corythuca ciliata*

45 **Hawthorn lace bug,** *C. cydoniae* (left)

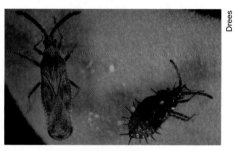

Drees

46 **Lantana lace bug,** *Teleonemia scrupulosa*

Drees

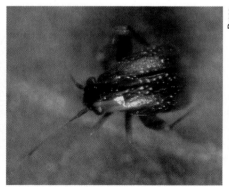

Drees

47 **Tarnished plant bug,** *Lygus lineolaris*

48 **Garden fleahopper,** *Halticus bractatus*

49 Damsel bug, *Nabis* sp.

50 Minute pirate bug, *Orius* sp.,
attacking cotton bollworm

51 Assassin bug, *Zelus renardii,*
preying on a cotton bollworm

52 Assassin bug, *Microtomus purcis*
(right)

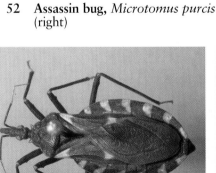

53 Bloodsucking conenose or
"kissing bug," *Triatoma* sp.

54 Wheel bug, *Arilus cristatus,*
preying on a squash bug

55 **Chinch bug,** *Blissus* sp., nymphs and adults

56 **Large milkweed bug,** *Oncopeltus fasciatus*

57 **Lygaeid,** *Lygaeus* sp.

58 **Bigeyed bug,** *Geocoris* sp.

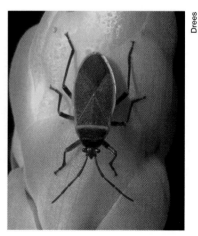

59 **Bigeyed bug,** *Geocoris* sp., nymph

60 **Largus bug,** *Largus succinctus* (right)

61   Squash bug, *Anasa tristis*

62   Squash bug, *Anasa tristis*,
     nymphs on squash (right)

63   Coreid, *Phthia picta*

64   Coreid, *Hypselonotus* sp.

65   Leaffooted bug,
     Leptoglossus phyllopus (left)

66   Leaffooted bug, *Narnia* sp.,
     on prickly pear cactus

67 **Coreid bug,** *Acanthocephala declivis* (left)

68 **Broad-headed bug,** *Alydus* sp., nymph on althea

69 **Redshouldered bug,** *Jadera haematoloma* (left)

70 **Burrower bug,** *Pangaeus* sp.

71 **Thyreocorid bug,** *Corimelaena* sp.

72 **Shield bug** (Scutellaridae)

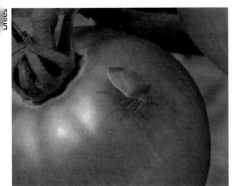

73 **Southern green stink bug,**
   Nezara viridula

74 **Southern green stink bug,**
   Nezara viridula, nymph

75 **Southern green stink bug,** *Nezara viridula*, nymph hatching from eggs

76 **Brown stink bug,** *Euschstus servus*

77 **Harlequin bug,**
   Murgantia histrionica

78 **"Rough" or "tree" stink bug,**
   Brochymena sp., nymph

79   Rice stink bug, *Oebalus pugnax* (left)

80   Spined soldier bug, *Podisus maculiventris*, preying on cotton bollworm

81   Spined soldier bug, *P. maculiventris*, nymph preying on cotton square borer

82   Dog-day cicada, *Tibicen* sp.

83   Cast skins of cicada, nymphs (Cicadidae)

84   Threecornered alfalfa hopper, *Spissistilus festinus*

Drees

Drees

85 **Threecornered alfalfa hopper,**
    Spissistilus festinus, nymph

86 **Twolined spittlebug,**
    Prosapia bicincta

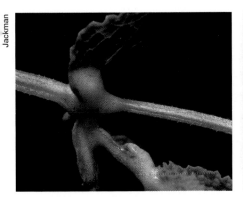

Jackman

C. L. Barr

87 **Spittlebug,** spittle and nymph
    (Cercopidae)

88 **Leafhopper,** *Graphocephala* sp.

Drees

Drees

89 **Sharpshooter,** *Oncometopia* sp.

90 **Planthoppers,** *Ormenoides*
    venusta (right)

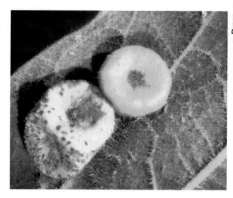

91 **Potato** or **tomato psyllids,**
Paratrioza cockerelli

92 **Hackberry gall psyllid,**
Pachypsylla sp., galls

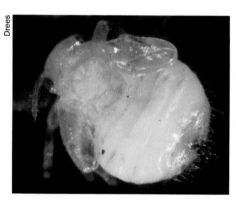

93 **Hackberry gall psyllid,**
Pachypsylla sp., nymph

94 **Hackberry gall psyllid,**
Pachypsylla sp.

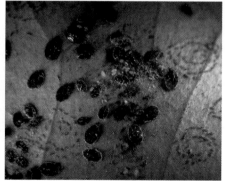

95 **Yaupon psyllid gall,**
Gyropsylla ilicis

96 **Citrus blackfly,** *Aleurocanthus woglumi*, larvae and eggs

97 **Silverleaf whitefly,** *Bemisia argentifolii,* and pupal skin (left)

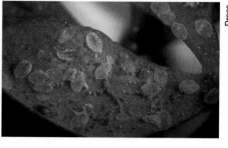

98 **Silverleaf whitefly,** *Bemisia argentifolii,* eggs and larvae

99 **Cotton** or **melon aphid,** *Aphis gossypii*

100 **Oleander aphids,** *Aphis nerii* (right)

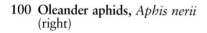

101 **Woolly apple aphid,** *Eriosoma lanigerum,* damage to apple roots

102 **Blackmargined aphids,** *Monellia caryella*

103 Green peach aphid,
   Myzus pericae

104 Greenbug, *Schizaphis graminum*

105 Yellow sugarcane aphid,
   Sipha flava

106 Russian wheat aphid,
   Diuraphis noxia

107 Corn leaf aphid,
   Rhopalosiphum maidis

108 Crapemyrtle aphids, *Tinocallis
   kahawaluokalani*, infesting leaf

109 Pecan phylloxera,
Phylloxera devastatrix

110 "Wax" scales, *Ceroplastes* spp.

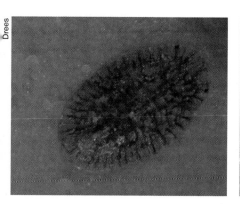

111 Brown soft scale,
Coccus hesperidum

112 Lecanium scale,
Lecanium sp. (Coccidae), on elm

113 White peach scale,
Pseudaulacaspis pentagona

114 San Jose scale,
Quadraspidiotus perniciosus

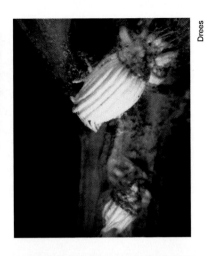

115 **Euonymous scale,**
Unaspis euonymi

116 **Cottony cushion scale,**
Icerya purchasi (right)

117 **Cochineal insect (scale),**
Dactylopius coccus, on prickly
pear

118 **Citrus mealybug,** *Planococcus citri,* on New Guinea impatiens

119 **Thrips** (Thripidae) (left)

120 **Onion thrips,** *Thrips tabaci,* nymph

121 **Hellgrammite,** *Corydalus* sp.

122 **Dobsonfly,** *Corydalus* sp., male (right)

123 **Dobsonfly,** *Corydalus* sp., female

124 **Mantidfly,** *Mantispa* sp.

125 **Green lacewing,** *Chrysoperla* sp., larva

126 **Green lacewing,** *Chrysoperla* sp.

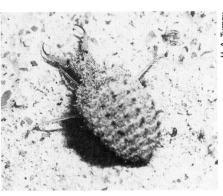

127 Antlion, *Myrmeleon* sp.

128 Antlion, *Myrmeleon* sp., larva

129 Tiger beetle,
  Cicindela ocellata rectilatera

130 Caterpillar hunter,
  Calosoma scrutator

131 Ground beetle,
  Scarites subterraneus

132 Ground beetle, *Pasimachus* sp.

133 Predaceous diving beetle, *Thermonectus* sp.

134 Whirligig beetle, *Gyrinus* sp. (right)

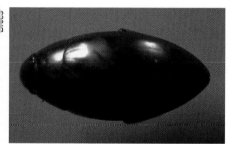

135 Water scavenger beetle *Hydrophilus* sp.

136 Stag beetle, *Lucanus elaphus*, male

137 Stag beetle, *Lucanus placidus*, female

138 Bess beetle, *Odontotaenius disjunctus*

143

139 June beetle, *Phyllophaga* sp., adult

140 Masked chafer, *Cyclocephala* sp., adult

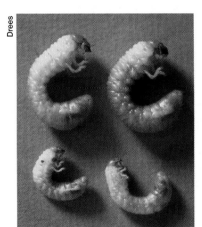

141 White grubs, June beetle larvae (left)

142 Green June beetle, *Cotinis nitida*

143 Flower-feeding scarab, *Euphoria kerni*

144 Eastern Hercules beetle, *Dynastes tityus*, male

G. McIlveen, Jr.

Drees

Drees

Drees

145 Elephant or ox beetle, *Strategus aloeus*, grubs

146 "Rainbow scarab," *Phanaeus vindex*, male (horned) and female

147 Introduced dung beetle, *Onthophagus gazella*

148 Metallic wood borer, *Chalcophora virginiensis*

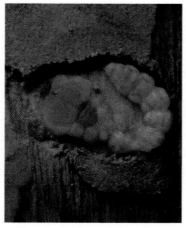

149 Metallic wood borer, *Psiloptera drummandi*

150 Flat-headed wood boring beetle, larva

151 Eyed click beetle, *Alaus oculatus*

152 Wireworm or click beetle, larva

153 Firefly, *Photinus* sp.

154 Dermestid beetle, larva (right)

155 Red cross beetle,
Collops balteatus, female

156 Sap beetle, *Carpophilus* sp.

157 Sawtoothed grain beetle,
Oryzaephilus surinamensis (left)

158 Lady beetles, (from top, clockwise)
seven-spotted, twice-stabbed, multicolored Asian, *Scymnus*, and convergent

159 Convergent lady beetle,
Hippodamia convergens, larva

160 Ash-gray lady beetle, *Olla* sp.,
Two-spotted color form adult
feeding on aphid

161 Multicolored Asian lady beetle, larvae
(left)

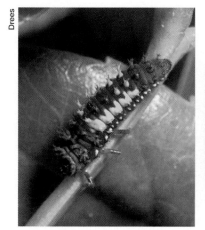

162 Tumbling flower beetle, *Mordella* sp.

147

163 Confused flour beetle,
Tribolium confusum

164 Yellow mealworm,
Tenebrio molitor

165 Tenebrionid, *Lobopoda* sp.

166 Tenebrionid, *Eleodes* sp.

167 Blister beetles, *Epicauta* sp.,
mating

168 Black blister beetle, *Epicauta
pennsylvanica*, on goldenrod flower

169 Striped blister beetle,
Epicauta sp.

170 "Ironclad" beetle,
Zopherus nodulosus haldemani

171 Long-horned beetle,
Placosternus difficilis

172 Long-horned beetle,
Aethecerinus wilsoni

173 Pine sawyer, *Monochamus* sp. (left)

174 Long-horned beetle,
Strangalia luteicornis

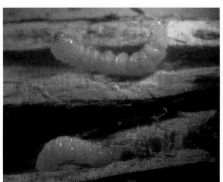

175 Round-headed borer,
larva of a long-horned beetle

176 Twig girdler, *Oncideres pustulatus,*
female (right)

177 Cottonwood borer,
Plectrodera scalator

178 Soybean stem borer,
Dectes texanus, larva

179 Cowpea weevils,
Callosobruchus maculatus

180 Flea beetle, *Disonycha fumata*
(right)

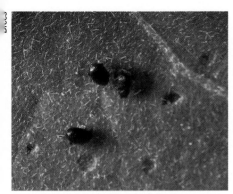

181 Flea beetles, *Epitrix* sp.

182 Southern corn rootworm or spotted cucumber beetle, *Diabrotica u. howardi*

183 Southern corn rootworm or spotted cucumber beetle, *Diabrotica u. howardi*, larva

184 Mexican corn rootworm, *D. virgifera zeae* (right)

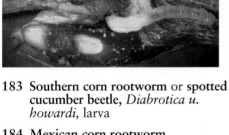

185 Banded cucumber beetle, *D. balteata*

186 Elm leaf beetle, *Pyrrhalta luteola*, larvae and eggs

187 **Leaf beetle,** *Derospidea brevicollis*, larva on prickly ash and Hercules club

188 **Leaf beetle,** *Trirhabda baccharidis*, common on baccharis (right)

189 Cottonwood leaf beetle, *Chrysomela texana*

190 Cottonwood leaf beetle, *Chrysomela scripta*, larvae

191 Colorado potato beetle, *Leptinotarsa decemlineata*

192 Colorado potato beetle, *L. decemlineata*, larvae (right)

193 Yellowmargined leaf beetle,
   Microtheca ochroloma

194 Yellowmargined leaf beetle,
   Microtheca ochroloma, larvae

195 Golden tortoise beetle,
   Charidotella sexpunctata bicolor

196 Tortoise beetle, *Chelymorpha* sp.,
   larvae

197 **Alfalfa weevil,** *Hypera postica*
   (left)

198 **Boll weevil,** *Anthonomus grandis*

200 Pecan weevil, *Curculio caryae*

199 Plum gouger, *Coccotorus scutellaris*

201 Pecan weevil, *Curculio caryae,*
larvae in pecan

202 Acorn weevils, *Curculio* sp.

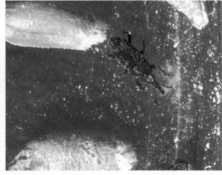

203 "Goldenheaded weevil,"
Compsus auricephalus

204 Rice weevil, *Sitophilus oryzae*

205 Rice water weevil, *Lissorhoptrus oryzophilus*, and leaf scar

206 "Sesbania clown weevil," *Eudiagogus pulcher*

207 Sweetpotato weevil, *Cyclas formicarius elegantulus*

208 Southern pine beetle, *Dendroctonus frontalis*, pitch tubes (right)

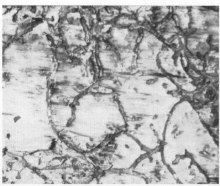

209 Southern pine beetle, *Dendroctonus frontalis*, galleries

210 Bark beetle, *Ips* sp.

155

211 Asian ambrosia beetle, *Xylosandrus crassiusculus*, frass tubes

212 Scorpionfly, *Panorpa nuptialis*, female

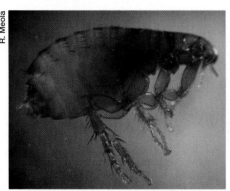

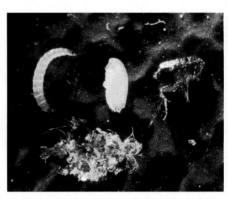

213 Cat flea, *Ctenocephalides felis*

214 Cat flea, *Ctenocephalides felis*, larva, pupa, adult, and pupa case (bottom of photo)

215 Crane fly (Tipulidae)

216 Lovebugs, *Plecia nearctica*

217 **Hessian fly,** *Mayetiola destructor,*
adult laying eggs

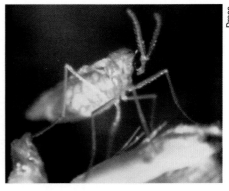

218 **Sorghum midge,**
Contarinia sorghicola

219 **Moth fly** (Psychodidae)

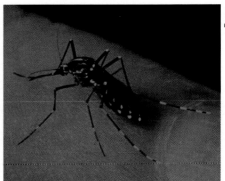

220 **Asian tiger mosquito,**
Aedes albopictus

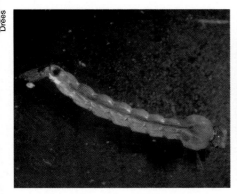

221 **Mosquito larva** (Culicidae)

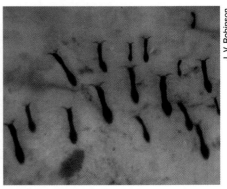

222 **Black fly,** *Simulium* sp., larvae

223 Midge (Chironomidae)

224 Horse fly, *Tabanus* sp., female

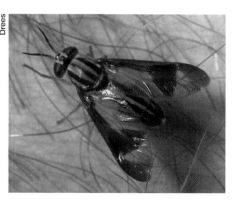

225 Deer fly, *Chrysops* sp., female

226 Black soldier fly, *Hermetia illucens*

227 Black soldier fly, *H. illucens*, larvae

228 Robber fly (Asilidae)

229 Robber fly, *Laphria* sp.

230 Bee fly (Bombyliidae)

231 Longlegged fly (Dolichopididae)

232 Syrphid fly (Syrphidae)

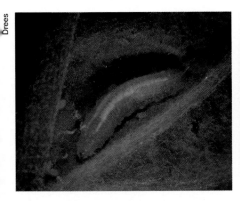

233 Syrphid fly, maggot preying on yellow pecan aphid

234 Serpentine leafminer, adult "stippling" damage to chrysanthemum

235 Small flies (left), (Diptera): **fungus gnats** (Sciaridae) (top); **leafminer fly** (Agromyzidae) (middle left); **shore fly** (Ephydridae) (middle right); **fruit fly** (Drosophila) (bottom)

236 Eye gnats, *Hippelates* sp.

237 House flies, *Musca domestica*, mating

238 Stable fly, *Stomoxys calcitrans*

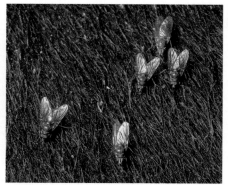

239 Blow fly, *Calliphora* sp.

240 Horn fly, *Haematobia irritans*

241 Horse bot fly,
Gasterophilis intestinalis, maggots

242 Common cattle grub,
Hypoderma lineatum

243 Parasitic fly, *Archytas* sp.,
caterpillar is parasite

244 Flesh fly (Sarcophagidae)

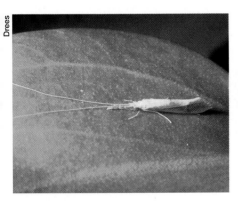

245 Caddisfly (Trishoptera)

246 Casemaking clothes moth,
Tinea pellionella, larval cases

247 Bagworm, *Thyridopteryx ephemerae-formis,* larval "bag" on arbovitae (left)

248 Tomato pinworm, *Keiferia lycopersicel* blotch-type mines and leaf-folding

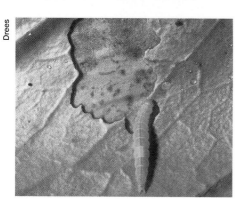

249 Diamondback moth,
Plutella xylostella, larva

250 Ermine moth, ailanthus webworm,
Atteva punctella

251 Southwestern squash vine borer,
Melittia calabaza

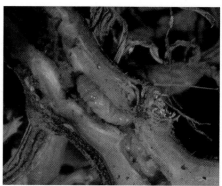

252 Squash vine borer,
Melittia cucurbitae, larva

254 Nantucket pine tip moth,
Rhyacionia frustrana

253 Great leopard moth, *Hypercompe
scribonia* (Stoll)

255 Nantucket pine tip moth,
Rhyacionia fustrana, caterpillar

256 Puss caterpillar or "asp,"
Megalopyge opercularis (right)

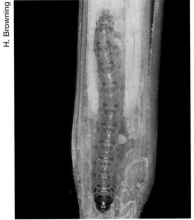

257 Sugarcane borer, *Diatraea sacchari*,
caterpillar (left)

258 Greater wax moth,
Galleria mellonella, larva

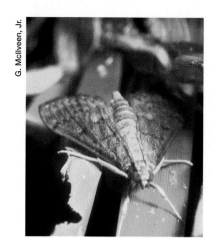

259 Tropical sod webworm,
Herpetogramma phaeopteralis (left)

260 Tropical sod webworm,
H. phaeopteralis, caterpillar

261 Genista caterpillar,
Uresiphita reversalis, caterpillar

262 Lesser canna leafroller,
Geshna cannalis

263 Indian meal moth,
Plodia interpunctata (left)

264 Larger canna leafroller, *Calpodes ethius*
pupa and caterpillar

265 Skipper, *Wallengrenia otho*

266 Black swallowtail,
       Papilio polyxenes asterius

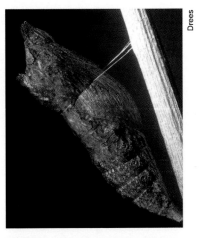

267 Black swallowtail,
       P. p. asterius, caterpillar

268 Black swallowtail, *P. p. asterius*,
       chrysalis (right)

269 Pipevine swallowtail,
       Battus philenor

270 Spicebush swallowtail,
       Pterourus troilus, caterpillar

271 Swallowtail butterflies: palamedes swallowtail (top, left); three-tailed swallowtail (top, right); tiger swallowtail (middle); spicebush swallowtail (bottom)

272 Giant swallowtail or orange dog, *Heraclides cresphontes* Cramer

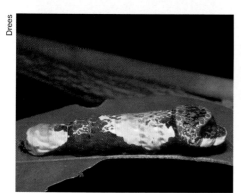

273 Giant swallowtail or orange dog, *H. cresphontes*, caterpillar

274 Cloudless sulfur, *Phoebis sennae eubule*

275 Alfalfa caterpillar, *Colias eurytheme*

276 Cotton square borer, *Strymon melinus*, or gray hairstreak

J. Lee

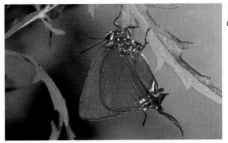

Drees

277 Mating blues (Lycaenidae)

278 Great purple hairstreak,
Atlides halesus

279 Snout butterfly, *Libytheana* sp.

Drees

Drees

280 Buckeye, *Junonia coenia* (Hübner)

Drees

281 Brushfooted butterflies: (top)
California sister, red admiral;
(second row) **red spotted purple,
mourning cloak;** (third row)
**variegated fritillary, American
painted lady;** (bottom) **monarch
butterfly and viceroy**

Drees

282 Red admiral, *Vanessa atalanta*, larva

283 Silvery checkerspot,
   Charidryas nycteis

284 Hackberry butterfly,
   Asterocampa celtis

285 Goatweed butterfly, *Anaea aidea*

286 Gulf fritillary, *Agraulis vanillae
   incarnata*, (right)

287 Gulf fritillary,
   A. v. incarnata, caterpillar

288 Zebra longwing,
   Heliconius charitonius vazquezae

289 Hermes satyr,
Hermeuptychia hermes

290 Monarch butterfly,
Danaus plexippus

291 Monarch butterfly, *D. plexippus*,
caterpillar

292 Monarch butterfly, *D. plexippus*,
pupa or chrysalis (right)

293 Spring cankerworm,
Paleacrata vernata

294 Eastern tent caterpillar,
Malacosoma americanum, tent

G. McIlveen, Jr.

295 Forest tent caterpillars,
Malacosoma disstria (left)

Drees

296 Luna moth, *Actias luna*

297 Luna moth, *Actias luna*,
caterpillar (left)

Drees

Jackman

298 Imperial moth, *Eacles imperialis*

299 Imperial moth, *Eacles imperialis*,
caterpillar (left)

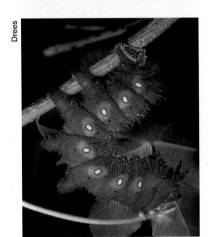

Drees

Drees

300 Cecropia moth, *Hyalophora cecropia*

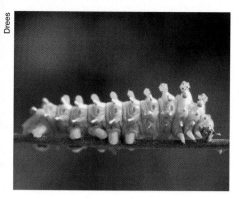

302 Io moth, *Automeris io*

301 Cecropia moth,
Hyalophora cecropia, caterpillar

304 Polyphemus moth,
Antheraea polyphemus

303 Io moth, *Automeris io*, caterpillar

305 Catalpa sphinx,
Ceratomia catalpae, caterpillar

306 White-lined sphinx, *Hyles lineata*

308 Tomato hornworm, *Manduca quinquemaculata*, caterpillar

307 Walnut sphinx, *Laothoe juglandis*

309 Tomato hornworm, *Manduca quinquemaculata* (left)

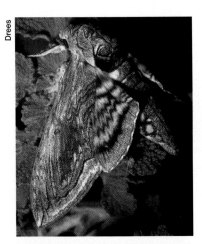

310 Walnut caterpillars, *Datana ministra*, early stage (instar) caterpillars

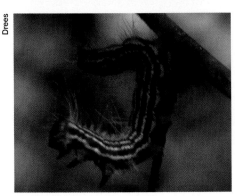

311 Yellownecked caterpillar, *Datana ministra*

312 Unicorn caterpillar, *Schizura unicornis*

313 **Whitemarked tussock moth,**
Orgyia leucostigma, caterpillar

314 **Fall webworm,**
Hyphantria cunea, caterpillar

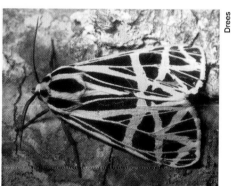

315 **Fall webworm,** *Hyphantria
cunea,* web on pecan

316 **A tiger moth,**
Grammia parthenice intermedia

317 **Yellowcollared scape moth,**
Cisseps fulvicollus

318 **Cutworm** (Noctuidae)

319 Corn earworm, *Helicoverpa zea* (left)

G. McIlveen, Jr.

A. Knutson

320 Beet armyworm, *Spodoptera exigua*, caterpillar in cotton boll

Drees

321 Fall armyworm, *Spodoptera frugiperda*, caterpillar

322 Noctuid moth, *Melipotis indomita*

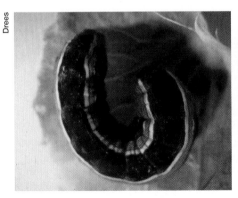

Drees

323 Yellowstriped armyworm, *Spodoptera ornithogalli*, caterpillar

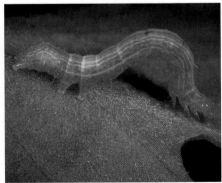

324 Cabbage looper, *Trichoplusia ni*

325 **Sawfly,** larvae

326 **Pigeon tremex,** *Tremex columba*

327 **Ichneumon wasp,**
   Megarhyssa macrurus, parasitic
   on pigeon tremex, *T. columba*

328 **Ichneumon wasp**

329 **Parasitic wasp** (Braconidae),
   pupae on a hornworm

330 **Cynipid wasp**
   (Cynipidae), gall on oak

331 Cicada killer, *Sphecius speciosus*

332 Sand wasp, *Bembix* sp.

333 Tarantula hawk, *Pepsis* sp.

334 Blue mud dauber,
   Chalybion californicum

335 Mud dauber,
   Chalybion caementarium

336 Potter wasp, *Eumenes*, nest

337 Cuckoo wasp, parasitic on mud dauber wasps and ground-nesting bees

338 Leafcutting bee, *Megachile* sp.

339 Carpenter bee, *Xylocopa* spp., and nest opening

340 Bumble bee, *Bombus* spp., and nesting opening

341 Honey bee, *Apis mellifera,* worker

342 Honey bee, *A. mellifera,* nest in wall void (right)

343 **Honey bee,** *A. mellifera*, colony with queen

344 **Red velvet-ant** or **"cow killer,"** *Dasymutilla occidentalis*

345 **Tiphiid wasp,** *Myzinum* sp., male, parasitic on white grubs

346 **Baldfaced hornet,** *Dolichovespula maculata*

347 **Baldfaced hornet,** *D. maculata*, nest

348 **Paper wasp,** *Polistes exclamans*, nest

349 Paper wasp, *Polistes carolina*

350 Paper wasp, *Polistes metricus*

351 Southern yellowjackets, *Vespula squamosa*, at nest entrance

352 Southern yellowjackets, *V. squamosa*, developmental stages; larval stages, pupae, adult

353 Texas leafcutting ant, *Atta texana*, winged male reproductive

354 Texas leafcutting ant, *A. texana*, worker carrying leaves

355 Texas leafcutting ant, *Atta texana*, mounds (left)

356 Carpenter ant, *Camponotus* sp., workers

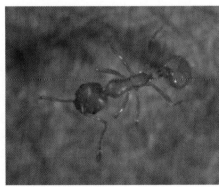

357 Black carpenter ant, *Camponotus pennsylvanicus*, worker

358 Pharoah ant, *Monomorium pharaonis*, worker

359 Crazy ant, *Paratrechina longicornis*

360 Pyramid ant, *Dorymyrmex insana*, nest

361 Red harvester ant, *Pogonomyrmex barbatus*, workers at nest entrance

362 Red imported fire ant, *Solenopsis invicta*, workers attacking pink bollworm

363 Red imported fire ant, *Solenopsis invicta*, mound

364 Striped bark scorpion, *Centruroides vittatus*

365 "Vinegaroon," *Mastigoproctus giganteus*

366 Tarantula, *Aphonopelma* spp.

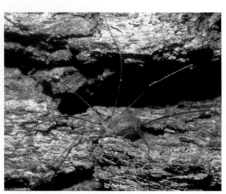

367 Brown recluse spider,
Loxosceles reclusa, female

368 Southern black widow spider,
Latrodectus mactans

369 Harvestman (Opiliones)

370 Lone star tick,
Amblyomma americanum

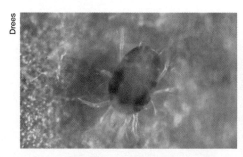

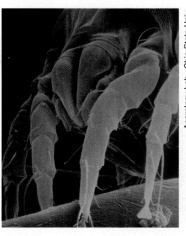

371 Twospotted spider mite,
Tetranychus urticae

372 House dust mite,
Dermatophagoides spp. (right)

Jackman

Drees

Drees

Acarology Lab., Ohio State Univ.

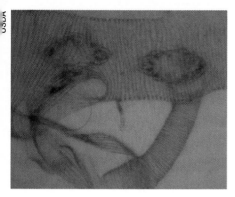

373 Honey bee mite

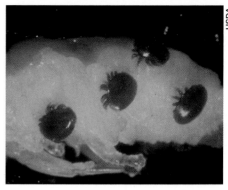

374 Varroa mites on honey bees

375 Pseudoscorpion (left)

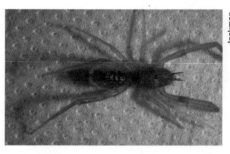

376 Windscorpion or solfugid

377 Sowbugs and pillbugs

378 Amphipod or "scud"

379 Centipede, *Scolopendra* sp.

380 Millipede (Diplopoda)

381 Millipede (5 inches long), *Narceus americanus*

179 COWPEA WEEVIL

Coleoptera: Bruchidae   *Callosobruchus maculatus*
                                            (Fabricius)

Description: Adult weevils are ⅛ inch long, reddish-brown slightly elongate beetles compared to the typical rounded appearance of other members of this family. Although weevil-like they are not true weevils (Curculionidae) and do not have heads prolonged into a long, narrow "snout." Wing covers (elytra) are marked with black and gray and there are 2 black spots near the middle. The wing covers (elytra) are short, leaving the last segment of the abdomen exposed. This last abdominal segment also has 2 visible spots. The larva is whitish and somewhat C-shaped with a small head.

There are several other bruchid species including stored-product pests; the **pea weevil**, *Bruchus pisorum* (Linnaeus), the **broadbean weevil**, *B. rufimanus* Boheman, and the **bean weevil**, *Acanthoscelides obtectus* (Say).

Life cycle: Eggs laid by females hatch in 5 to 20 days. Larvae typically take from 2 weeks to 6 months to develop before pupating. Six or seven generations may occur per year.

Pest status: Adults and larvae infest stored seeds.

Habitat and food source(s): They prefer dried cowpeas but will attack other beans and peas in storage. Adults move about readily and can infest seeds in the field, but can also breed continuously in stored dry cowpeas. Larvae develop inside the dried peas. Damage appears as round holes in the peas, although larvae chew near the surface and leave a thin covering uneaten which appears as a window. Later the adult emerges from the "window." Adults may be found outdoors in flowers in early spring.

Literature: Ebeling 1978; Metcalf et al. 1962; Swan and Papp 1972.

180, 181 FLEA BEETLES

Coleoptera: Chrysomelidae   *Epitrix* spp., *Phyllotreta* spp.
                                             and others

Description: Adult flea beetles are small (¼ inch or smaller, often ¹⁄₁₆ inch long) leaf-feeding beetles with a segment (femora) of the hind legs enlarged for jumping, which they do when disturbed. Body color varies by species. The **potato flea beetle**, *Epitrix cucumeris* (Harris), and the **eggplant flea beetle**, *Epitrix fuscula* Crotch, are black. However, some species are brownish or metallic. Other species have white stripes on their wing covers (elytra), such as the **striped flea beetle**, *Phyllotreta striolata* (Fabricius).

There are many other species of flea beetles.

Life cycle: Development varies with species, but in general adult beetles spend the winter in leaf litter and become active in spring, feeding on leaves of weeds and other plants. They migrate to gardens and lay eggs singly or in clusters in the soil, in plant stems or on leaves, depending on species. Eggs hatch in about 10 days. Larval stages are whitish, up to ¼ inch long, and have tiny legs behind a dark-colored head capsule. After feeding for 3 to 4 weeks and developing through several stages (instars), they pupate and emerge in 7 to 10 days. Several generations can occur per year.

Pest status: They damage leaves of plants as adults, and plant roots, stems, or leaves as larvae; adults can transmit some plant diseases through their feeding activities.

Habitat and food source(s): Adult beetles feed on the leaves of a variety of wild, ornamental, and vegetable plants, particularly cucumbers, okra, peppers, tomatoes, and eggplant. One bluish-black species, *Altica litigata* Fall, feeds on plants in the primrose family (Onagraceae) in high numbers. Adult beetles chew small round or irregularly-shaped holes in plant leaves. Damage appears as if someone shot leaves with buckshot. Larval stages mainly feed on the roots and tubers of plants. Larvae of some species feed on or in foliage or tunnel into plant stems.

Literature: Metcalf et al. 1962.

182–185 SOUTHERN CORN ROOTWORM OR SPOTTED CUCUMBER BEETLE

Coleoptera: Chrysomelidae

Diabrotica undecimpunctata howardi Barber

Description: This is one of the most common beetles found in the home garden and flower beds. The adult is about ¼ inch long, yellow-green with a black head and antennae. There are 12 black spots on the wing covers (elytra). The larva (rootworm) (**183**) is cream colored and about ¾ inch long when fully developed, with a brown head capsule and bearing 3 pairs of short legs.

There are several other common *Diabrotica* species in Texas: the **western corn rootworm**, *D. virgifera virgifera* LeConte, a pest of corn in the high plains that can be recognized by adult beetles having a solid pale green or striped elytra and with no dark edge on the upper part (femur) of the hind leg; the **Mexican corn rootworm (184)**, *D. virgifera zeae* Krysan and Smith, a pest of corn in central and south Texas with adults having a solid pale green elytra that may be marked with faint stripes, and with a dark edge on the hind femur; and, the **banded cucumber beetle (185)**, *D. balteata* LeConte, common in soybeans (larvae feed on soybean roots) and some vegetables with

Spotted cucumber beetle

the elytra of adults being bright green with transverse yellow bands; and the **northern corn rootworm,** *D. barberi* Smith and Lawrence, which occurs in the Texas Panhandle.

Life cycle: Adult spotted cucumber beetles overwinter and become active in the spring, feeding on a wide variety of host plants including weeds and grasses. They enter corn and sorghum fields soon after plants emerge and lay eggs in the soil. Eggs hatch in 5 to 11 days and young larvae crawl through the soil and feed on roots of host plants. Larvae develop through 3 stages (instars) in 10 to 16 days before pupating and then emerge as adults after 5 to 12 days. Thus, the development takes 20 to 39 days, depending on soil temperature.

Pest status: Adult beetles feed on leaves and flowers of some plants and larvae feed on roots of certain crops, causing stand loss and yield reduction.

Habitat and food source(s): Damage to corn, peanuts, and sorghum occurs in the seedling (6- to 9-leaf) stage of plant development. Larvae chew along roots, excavating grooves and tunnels. Often, the larvae tunnel directly into the base of the stalk, stunting plant growth or killing entire plants. Adult beetles feed on a wide variety of plants including leaves and flowers of vegetables (beans, cucurbits) and ornamentals. Adults can be found on wild flowers or legumes.

Literature: Drees, *in press.*

186–190   ELM LEAF BEETLE

Coleoptera: Chrysomelidae   *Xanthogaleruca luteola*
                                          (Muller)

Description: Adult beetles are about ¼ inch long, overall yellow to brownish-green in body color, and marked with black spots on the head and thorax, and broad black stripes following the outer wing cover (elytra) margins. Larvae (**186**) grow to about ½ inch and are yellowish with black spots and broad stripes along the sides. Pupae are ¼ inch long and are bright orange-yellow with scattered black bristles.

Adult and larval **cottonwood leaf beetles,** *Chrysomela texana* Brown and *C. scripta* Fabricius (**189, 190**), feed on cottonwood leaves.

Elm leaf beetle

Life cycle: Adult beetles spend the winter in protected sites, occasionally in homes. Beetles fly to elm trees in the spring, feed on newly-emerged foliage and deposit clusters of 5 to 25 lemon-shaped yellow eggs in 2 or 3 rows on the underside of leaves. In about 7 days, small black larvae hatch and feed on the underside of leaves. Larvae develop through several stages (instars) for about 21 days. Mature larvae crawl down the tree trunk and pupate in the soil at the base of the tree. Adult beetles emerge from pupae in about 14 days. Three or more generations can occur per year.

Pest status: Larvae and adults feed on leaves of elm trees causing unsightly damage and premature defoliation.

Habitat and food source(s): This is an introduced species that feeds on elm leaves, especially on Siberian and European elms. Cedar elm, American elm, and winged elm are less susceptible when other hosts are available. Larvae skeletonize foliage by removing the parts of the leaves between the leaf veins, leaving the upper leaf surface intact. Damaged portions of leaves soon turn rusty, reddish-brown, and dry skeletonized leaves fall to the ground. Adults eat roughly circular holes in leaves.

Literature: Johnson and Lyon 1988; Turney and Crocker 1980.

191, 192 COLORADO POTATO BEETLE

Coleoptera: Chrysomelidae   *Leptinotarsa decemlineata* (Say)

Description: Adult beetles are convex in shape, ⅜ inch long and colored yellow with black stripes on the wing covers (elytra) and black spots on the shield behind the head (pronotum). Larvae (**192**) appear hump-backed and are red with black spots on the sides of each body segment. They have a black head and 3 pairs of legs, and reach ½ inch long when fully grown. Eggs are orange-yellow, oblong and deposited in clusters on the underside of leaves.

A closely related species, *L. texana* (Schaeffer), may be confused with this species and feeds on silverleaf nightshade.

Life cycle: Adult beetles overwinter in the soil, emerging in the spring. Females lay clusters of eggs, which hatch in 4 to 9 days. Larvae hatching from eggs develop over 2 to 3 weeks through 4 stages (instars), shedding their skins (exoskeletons) between each stage, before pupating in cells in the soil. Pupae are yellowish. Adults emerge in 5 to 10 days. Two to three generations are produced per year.

Colorado potato beetle

Pest status: Sometimes called "potatobugs," larvae and adults are common locally in vegetable gardens where they feed on leaves and terminal growth of host plants.

Habitat and food source(s): Larvae and adults feed on leaves of potatoes and eggplant, but they occasionally feed on some other plants in the nightshade family (*Solanum* spp.).

Literature: Metcalf et al. 1962; Westcott 1973.

193, 194   YELLOWMARGINED LEAF BEETLE

Coleoptera: Chrysomelidae   *Microtheca ochroloma* Stål

Description: Adult beetles are ⅜ inch long and dark brown to black. The wing covers (elytra) are textured with rows of pits and light cream-colored margins along the outer edges. Larvae (**194**) are ⅜ inch long, grub-like, dark brown to black, and have 3 pairs of short legs behind the head.

This beetle has been confused with flea beetles. However, the hind legs of the yellowmargined leaf beetle are not enlarged for jumping as in flea beetles.

Life cycle: Adult beetles overwinter and mate soon after emerging from the pupa. Larvae hatch from eggs and develop through several stages before pupating. Development from egg to adult occurs over about 23 days. Adults leave the host plant and enter a resting stage (estivation) about mid-June and remain there until October.

Pest status: Adult and larval stages feed on foliage of certain leafy vegetables.

Habitat and food source(s): This species was accidentally introduced from South America and was first detected in New Orleans in 1945 on grapes from Argentina. Since then, it has spread to other southeastern states and into eastern Texas during the 1970s. Leaves of mustard greens, turnip greens, collard greens, Chinese cabbage, bok choy, radish, Irish potato, watercress, and roses are consumed by adults and larvae, giving them a tattered appearance with many irregular-shaped holes. Populations increase and damage is more severe in spring and fall.

Literature: Drees 1990a.

195, 196   TORTOISE BEETLES

Coleoptera: Chrysomelidae   *Psalidonota texana*
                                             Schaeffer and others

Description: Adults are broadly oval to round and nearly convex in shape with some sculpturing of the surface and the edges broadly expanded. They are green-gold with purple mottling and about ¼ inch long.

A few related species have similar metallic appearance and may feed on different host plants. The (**195**) **golden tortoise beetle** (**195**), *Charidotella sexpunctata bicolor* (Fabricius), is brilliant brassy or greenish-gold in life. When disturbed, the color becomes orange with black spots. The metallic coloration is lost completely in dead specimens, leaving them a dull reddish yellow color. They also are about ¼ inch long.

Larvae of both species are spiny along the sides and have hooks on the end of the abdomen. Larvae may carry fecal material on their back, which helps camouflage them and deter predators and parasites.

Life cycle: As is characteristic of the family, the larvae and adults may be found on the same host plant. There are multiple generations per year.

Pest status: Although the tortoise beetle is not considered a pest, the golden tortoise beetle occasionally may be a pest on sweet potatoes.

Habitat and food source(s): This beetle and the larvae feeds on foliage of anacua in south Texas; while other tortoise beetles feed on sweet potato and related plants.

Literature: Dillon and Dillon 1972.

197 ALFALFA WEEVIL

Coleoptera: Curculionidae   *Hypera postica* (Gyllenhal)

Description: Adult beetle is a brown weevil, about ⅒–⅕ inch long, with a downward-projecting beak and a wide darker stripe down the middle of the back. The color may vary from almost uniform brown to nearly black. Larvae are legless, plump-bodied, and yellowish when young, turning to pale green as they get larger with a white stripe down the center of the back and thinner white stripes closer to the sides. The head is a dark brown to black. Larvae are up to ⅖ inch long.

This is the most common weevil on alfalfa. A few other species of snout beetles (Curculionidae) may show up on alfalfa but they are less likely to be of economic importance.

Life cycle: The eastern form spends the winter as eggs and the western form spends the winter as adults. Females lay clusters of yellowish eggs in cavities in the stems of alfalfa. Larvae develop in the spring through 3 or 4 stages (instars) over 29 to 58 days. They pupate in cocoons in the soil and adult weevils emerge in about 10 days. There is one generation per year with adults living 10 to 14 months. Adults readily fly and migrate to new fields.

Pest status: The most important pest of alfalfa nearly anywhere in the United States; can reduce the alfalfa stand, often causing the loss of one cutting of alfalfa; introduced from southern Europe sometime around 1900.

Habitat and food source(s): Alfalfa is the primary host plant, but they can also be found feeding on bur clover, sweet yellow clover, vetch, and sometimes on other clovers. Both adults and larvae feed on foliage or buds. Feeding causes leaves to appear shredded (skeletonized). High population densities can completely defoliate spots in the field, resulting in sections appearing whitish. Damaged plants are stunted when the bud is removed by feeding.

Literature: Metcalf et al. 1962; Swan and Papp 1972.

BOLL WEEVIL

Coleoptera: Curculionidae   *Anthonomus grandis*
                                                             Boheman

Description: The adults are brown to grayish-brown, fuzzy beetles with prominent snouts (or bills) bearing the mouthparts, and varying in size from ⅛ to almost ½ inch long. Larval stages, found inside cotton squares and bolls, are legless grubs with brown heads that grow to about ½ inch long before forming a pupa that resembles the adult features but appears mummy-like.

Life cycle: Adults overwinter, or "diapause," in leaf litter and fly to cotton fields in the spring. After feeding for 3 to 7 days, weevils mate and females lay eggs in cotton squares (flower buds) or bolls (fruit) that are ¼ inch or more in diameter. Larvae hatch in 2½ to 5 days, and larvae feed for 7 to 14 days and develop through several stages (instars) before pupating. Adults emerge in 4 to 6 days and chew their way out of the cotton square or boll in which they developed. Development from egg to adult can be completed in 16 to 18 days. Six or seven generations can be produced each year.

Pest status: Caused major changes in cotton production practices since it migrated from Mexico into and across Texas and the southern states (1892-1920s); larvae feed in cotton squares and bolls.

Habitat and food source(s): This insect feeds and develops only in cotton and closely related tropical (malvaceous) plants. Adult weevils feed on tender cotton terminals in the spring, pollen in cotton squares (flower buds), and bolls (fruit). Weevils drill holes into the squares or bolls with their chewing mouthparts at the tip of their "snout" (rostrum). Females lay eggs in some of these feeding sites. After inserting the egg into the feeding puncture, she secretes a sticky substance that covers the cavity and hardens into a wart-like blemish. Feeding punctures do not have this wart-like blemish. Infested cotton squares or bolls turn yellow and fall off the plant. Larger infested bolls may not drop, but cotton lint developing in these bolls is damaged. Heavily infested cotton may produce much foliage but few mature bolls. The **pink bollworm,** *Pectinophora gossypiella* (Saunders) (Lepidoptera: Gelechiidae) also has larva found in cotton bolls. These caterpillars can be distinguished by their color and the presence of legs.

Literature: Bohmfalk et al. 1982; Metcalf et al. 1962.

199 **PLUM CURCULIO**

Coleoptera: Curculionidae   *Conotrachelus nenuphar*
                                                             (Herbst)

Description: Although the insects are rarely observed, the fruit damage is common and characteristic. Egg-laying scars are crescent-shaped depressions (indentations) in fruit with a puncture mark in the center. Adult weevils are ¼ inch long, gray to black with light gray and brown mottling. The wing covers (elytra) appear roughened and bumpy. Larvae develop inside fruit and appear as white legless grubs with brown heads, growing up to ⅜ inch long.

A related species is the **plum gouger (199)**, *Coccotorus scutellaris* LeConte. It primarily attacks native plums, although adults may also feed on buds and blossoms of peaches and plums. Damaged fruit becomes gnarled and distorted from adult feeding and egg-laying punctures, and the larvae feed on the kernels of the pits. Adult plum gouger weevils have smooth, dark brown wing covers and yellow-brown heads and legs.

Life cycle: Adult plum curculios overwinter in leaf litter and ground debris in woods and along fence rows. In the spring, they become active before wild plum trees bloom, where they feed on foliage and flowers until fruit begins to develop. Females insert eggs in developing fruit for about one month, beginning just after shuck split. Larvae (grubs) hatching from eggs develop for 2 to 4 weeks before crawling out of the fruit into the soil where they burrow 1 to 3 inches deep to construct a cell in which they pupate. Development from egg to adult requires 5 to 8 weeks. Second generation adults appear in July and August and, together with first generation adults, feed on foliage until fall when they leave host plants for overwintering habitats.

Pest status: Female weevils produce egg-laying scars on developing peaches, plums, pears, apples, mayhaws, and some small berries; infested fruit drops from the tree, reducing yield.

Habitat and food source(s): Plums and nectarines are damaged more than peach varieties by females surviving the winter, although peaches maturing in late May and June are also attacked. Second generation larvae occur in peaches at harvest time. Apples are occasionally blemished by egg-laying scars, but larvae fail to develop in the fruit. Larvae feed inside the fruit, particularly around the pit. Mayhaws are attacked in southeast Texas.

Literature: Thomas et al. 1972.

200–203 PECAN WEEVIL

Coleoptera: Curculionidae   *Curculio caryae* (Horn)

Description: Adult pecan weevils are ⅜ inch long, brownish beetles with snouts as long as the body. Larvae or grubs (**201**) are legless, creamy white, and have reddish-brown heads that grow to ⅗ inch long. No other insects develop in pecan kernels in the field. Acorns of live oaks in urban areas of north-central Texas are sometimes 100% infested by larvae of **acorn weevils (202)**. Several species occur, but the most common is *Curculio fulvus* Chittenden. Adult (**202**) and larval acorn weevils are similar in appearance to pecan weevils and often occur around homes surrounded by oak trees. Larvae and pupae become common in flower beds and gardens in which acorns have fallen.

Several weevil species, such as the **goldenheaded weevil,** *Compsus auricephalus* (Say) (**203**), may occasionally be found in pecan orchards. This weevil has larvae that feed on the roots of legumes such as alfalfa and are not likely to damage pecans.

Life cycle: Adult weevils and full-grown larvae spend the winter in cells, 4 to 12 inches deep in the soil. Larvae pupate in late summer or fall. Adult weevils become active in August and early September. Mated females chew a hole in the pecan shell and deposit eggs inside. Larvae feed inside the nuts from late summer through the fall, growing and developing through several stages (instars). In late fall and early winter, about 42 days after eggs are laid, full-grown larvae chew a ⅛ diameter hole in the shell and drop to the ground. They burrow into the soil and construct a cell where they remain for 8 to 10 months before pupating and transform to adults, although some larvae do not pupate and transform to adults until the following year. Adults remain in cells and emerge from the soil a year later. The entire life cycle takes 2 or 3 years.

Pest status: Larvae feed in developing pecan nuts, causing yield loss. It occurs only in north-central Texas and is absent from Waco toward the Gulf coast.

Habitat and food source(s): Adult weevils feed and lay eggs on developing (water stage) pecan nuts, causing them to drop from the tree. Larval stages develop in more developed nuts (dough stage), destroying the kernels. In most years, larval damage results in the most yield loss.

Literature: Crocker et al. 1987; Holloway 1980; Holloway et al. 1984.

204 RICE WEEVIL

Coleoptera: Curculionidae

Sitophilus oryzae
(Linnaeus)

Description: Adults are about ¹⁄₁₀ inch long, reddish-brown to black with four reddish or yellowish spots on the wing covers (elytra). The head bears a slender snout and the shield behind the head (pronotum) has coarse round punctures. The elytra have deep lines (striae) and coarse punctures. Larvae are legless, white with a distinct head capsule.

The **granary weevil**, *Sitophilus granarius* (Linnaeus), and the **maize weevil**, *Sitophilus zeamais* Motschulsky, are other curculionid species that occur in stored-food products. The granary weevil has elongated punctures on the pronotum and is flightless.

Life cycle: Adult rice weevils are good fliers and easily disperse. Adults chew into the grain kernels from the outside and also to lay eggs. Females can lay 300 to 400 eggs, typically one per cavity. Larvae develop through several stages (instars) and pupate inside the kernel. They may complete a generation in a month in warm conditions. Adults live for 7 to 8 months but are recorded living for over 2 years.

Pest status: The rice weevil is a cosmopolitan pest in stored-grain products.

Habitat and food source(s): This insect infests stored grains of all types, including wheat, corn, oats, barley, sorghum, macaroni, and other grain products. They may also infest grain in the field. Larvae hollow out kernels of grain and usually attack whole kernels. Holes in the side of the grain are made by adults and by the emerging adults.

Literature: Metcalf et al. 1962; Swan and Papp 1972.

Coleoptera: Curculionidae   *Lissorhoptrus oryzophilus*
                                             Kuschel

Description: Adult weevils are small (⅛ inch), grayish-black snout beetles, which may have a darker brown V-shaped area on their backs.

Life cycle: Adults spend winter hibernating (diapausing) in clump grasses, field trash, and Spanish moss. Female weevils insert white eggs into leaf sheaths under water. In 4 to 9 days, tiny (½₂ inch), white, slender, legless, C-shaped larvae or grubs hatch from eggs and develop through 4 stages (instars) for about 27 days until they are about ⅓ inch long. They then pupate within a water-tight, oval mud cell attached to the roots and emerge 5 to 7 days later. Adults emerge throughout the reproductive stage of rice development and feed on leaves before leaving the field in late summer and fall. Development from egg to adult normally occurs within 35 days. Two generations and possibly a partial third can occur annually.

Pest status: Larval stages feed on roots of developing rice plants, causing yield reduction when they occur in large numbers.

Habitat and food source(s): In spring (April through May), when rice plants have emerged and are being flooded, they fly into rice fields and feed on the upper layer of cells (epidermis) of leaves, producing long, narrow window-like (skeletonized) slits along the leaf called feeding "scars." Upon reaching host plants, flight muscles of adults degenerate. Larvae chew on roots of developing rice and obtain oxygen from the host plant by means of paired hooks on the upper surface of their second through seventh abdominal segments. Adults are most active during the evening and night. Alternate host plants include aquatic grasses and sedges that occur in and around rice fields.

Literature: Cave and Smith 1982; Drees et al. 1996; Peairs and Davidson 1956; Smith et al. 1986; Smith 1983.

Coleoptera: Curculionidae   *Eudiagogus pulcher* Fahraeus
                                             E. rosenschoeldi Fahraeus

Description: These species represent members of a genus of broad-nosed weevils. Adults are about ⁵⁄₁₆ inch long, and have slate-black bodies marked with a metallic rosy-white pattern. Markings on *Eudiagogus pulcer* appear as smooth-edged lines and rectangles, while those of *E. rosenschoeldi* are rough-edged and mottled. Although capable of flight at certain times of the year, adults collected from host plants rarely fly.

Life cycle: Mated females lay eggs on the stems, lower plant surfaces, and exposed roots of host plants. Eggs hatch in about 7 days. Larvae develop in the soil through 5 stages (instars) over a period of about 22 days before pupating in close proximity to the roots of the host plants. Adult weevils emerge in about 7 days. Several generations occur annually. Females mate before entering their winter resting stage (diapause) and overwinter under the bark of trees.

Pest status: These colorful weevils are common on *Sesbania* weeds where adults feed on leaves, and larvae on root nodules; not a pest.

Habitat and food source(s): In central Texas, these species occur on several species of *Sesbania* weeds (*S. vesicaria*, *S. macrocarpa*, and *S. drummondii*), also called rattlepods, which are common along edges of lakes, ponds and streams. They have also been reported to feed on *Cassia* and *Xanthoxylum* species. Adults feed on leaflets, producing semicircular notches along the leaflet edges, and are common through the warmer months of the year (March through November). Larvae feed on the nitrogen-fixing root nodules of these legumes.

Literature: Kovarik and Burke 1989.

207   SWEETPOTATO WEEVIL

Coleoptera: Curculionidae   *Cyclas formicarius*
                                   elegantulus (Summers)

Description: The adult is about ¼ inch long, shiny and slender-bodied for a weevil, appearing almost ant-like. The middle of the body (prothorax) and the legs are red and the rest of the body is blue-black. Larvae are elongate but slightly C-shaped in appearance, legless and dirty white to gray in color with a distinct head capsule that is yellow-brown in color.

Life cycle: The life cycle can continue throughout the year in stored sweet potatoes. All stages may be found almost anytime. Eggs are deposited singly in a small cavity that the female eats in stems of sweet potatoes or in cracks or crevices. Larvae hatch in about a week and take 2 to 3 weeks to develop through several stages (instars) in good conditions. A generation takes about one month to 6 weeks. Adults can fly well with reports of over a mile and they may live up to 8 months.

Pest status: This is a pest of sweet potatoes because the larvae tunnel into tubers; damaged tubers develop a bitter taste and a bad odor. This weevil is primarily found in east Texas.

Habitat and food source(s): Found on sweet potatoes in the field and in storage. Larvae tunnel into tubers and stems. They may also feed on related plants like morning glory.

Literature: Metcalf et al. 1962; Peterson 1951.

208–210   SOUTHERN PINE BEETLE

Coleoptera: Scolytidae   *Dendroctonus frontalis*
                                Zimmermann

Description: The usual method of detecting this insect is by observing masses of pitch on the bark of dying pine trees (**208**). Adult beetles are tiny, being ¹⁄₁₆ to ³⁄₁₆ inch long, dark brown to black cylindrical beetles. Diagnosis of dead trees is made by the appearance of the pattern of galleries (**209**) that appear S-shaped underneath the bark and outside of the heartwood (in the phloem-cambium layer).

Other bark beetles that attack pine trees include the **black turpentine beetle**, *Dendroctonus terebrans* (Olivier), and **engraver beetles** (*Ips* spp.) (**210**). These beetles produce superficially similar symptoms to those caused by southern pine beetles on the trunk, but infestations may not result in rapid decline and death of infested trees. The gallery patterns of these beetles are not S-shaped patterns.

Life cycle: Adults emerge from a host tree and fly to a new host tree where they begin burrowing into the bark to construct galleries. They release an attractant chemical (pheromone) that attracts more beetles and mate. In galleries, adult females deposit eggs that hatch in 3 to 34 days, depending upon temperature, into cream-colored, legless grub-like larvae with brown heads. Larvae develop through 4 stages (instars) until they reach about ¼ inch in length over a period of 15 to 40 days before pupating. Adults hatch within 17 days. A generation from egg to adult can be completed in 26 to 54 days, and 7 to 9 generations (many overlapping) can occur annually in Texas.

Pest status: Occurs in east Texas where they colonize susceptible pine trees in high numbers, causing rapid decline and death of infested trees.

Habitat and food source(s): Southern pine beetles attack mainly densely stocked, slow growing pine stands with a high percentage of over-mature timber. Some pine tree species are more susceptible than others. Trees damaged by lightning and other natural events or by nearby construction are more likely to be infested. Needles on infested pines first turn yellow and then red, before dropping. Masses of resin (pitch) develop on the bark surface and fine brown to white boring dust accumulates in bark crevices, underneath sites of infestation, and at the base of the trunk. Infested trees die quickly due to girdling action of galleries and a blue stain fungus. Beetles disperse in the fall and develop in scattered host trees. From March through May, beetles emerge and colonize new host trees. Damaged trees decline rapidly during summer months, and infestations may spread from tree to tree as additional beetles are attracted to the site of infestation.

Literature: Anon. 1982; Thatcher et al. 1980.

211   ASIAN AMBROSIA BEETLE

Coleoptera: Scolytidae   *Xylosandrus crassiusculus*
                                          (Motschulsky)

Description: The Asian ambrosia beetle is about ¹⁄₁₆ inch long, stout bodied and reddish-brown. The males are much smaller, have a more hunchbacked appearance and are flightless.

Unlike the shothole borer, where each individual emerges from a separate hole, Asian ambrosia beetles emerge from the tree via the parental entrance hole. The **shothole borer**, *Scolytus rugulosus* (Müller) and the **peach bark beetle**, *Phloeotribus liminaris* (Harris) also leaves bark appearing as if it had been shot with a shot gun. These beetles attack a wide variety of weakened and dying fruit and ornamental trees. The galleries produced by these beetles are produced just underneath the bark. The shot-hole effect is produced when newly emerged beetles leave the host plant.

Life cycle: Female beetles excavate galleries deep into the wood of twigs and branches, pushing out strings of boring dust that resembles tooth picks (**211**). These protrusions can be up to an inch in length, often with several hundred on an individual tree. Afterwards, the beetles cultivate an ambrosia fungus that has been carried into the gallery by the adult. Females then lay eggs that hatch into legless larvae and develop through several stages (instars) before pupating. Both the adults and the larvae feed on the fungus rather than the host plant. Female beetles remain with their brood until they mature. Newly emerged adult beetles mate with their offspring before leaving the gallery. Flight activity apparently occurs throughout the year, with higher activity in March.

Pest status: A minute beetle that has been attacking pecans and ornamentals in east Texas since the mid 1980s.

Habitat and food source(s): This beetle attacks 126 plant species including pecan, peach, plum, cherry, persimmon, golden rain tree, sweet gum, Shumard oak, Chinese elm, sweet potato, and magnolia. Infestations start with a female beetle boring into a twig, branch, or trunk of a host plant. Host material can range from approximately 1 inch to 1 foot in diameter. This beetle will attack seemingly healthy trees. Attacks generally occur on the trunk of the host plant.

Literature: Johnson and Lyon 1988; Ree 1994.

ORDER MECOPTERA
Scorpionflies

DESCRIPTION

- Mecoptera are small to medium-sized insects with the spindly legs and 4 long, narrow wings and long antennae.
- Scorpionflies are so named because males of some species have the end of the abdomen enlarged, which makes it look like the "stinger" of a scorpion.
- They have chewing mouthparts located at the end of a pointed snout; which is 2–3 times as long as the head is wide.
- Immature stages (larvae) resemble caterpillars and live in damp soil.
- Larvae and adults are up to 1 inch long.

LIFE CYCLE

- Metamorphosis is complete (egg, larva, pupa, adult).
- Scorpionflies are not common, but may be locally abundant.

PEST STATUS

- Adult males cannot sting.
- Adults feed on insects, usually after they are dead, although some species capture live insects.

HABITAT

- These insects are found resting on plants that grow along the banks of streams and in damp woods at certain times of the year.
- Larvae feed on organic matter and are seldom seen.

212 SCORPIONFLIES

Mecoptera: Panorpidae   *Panorpa* spp.

Description: These unusual insects have 4 similar long, narrow, membranous yellow wings with dark brown marking banded patterns. The head bears long, thread-like antennae and the mouthparts are at the end of an elongated "snout." The body is up to 1 inch long. Males have abdomens with an elongated end that resembles that of a scorpion.

Life cycle: Winter is spent in the last larval stage. They pupate in cells in the soil before emerging as adults. Eggs are deposited in the soil. Larvae are caterpillar-like in appearance and live on the soil surface. One generation occurs per year.

Pest status: Locally common in the fall in marshy areas; not a pest.

Habitat and food source(s): Scorpionflies occur in wooded areas and ravines with dense vegetation. Adults feed on mainly dead insects and larvae feed on dead insects, other animal matter and may be predaceous. Courtship behavior involves males vibrating their wings rapidly in front of the female and presenting her with small pellets of saliva, which the females eat.

Literature: Borror et al. 1989; Swan and Papp 1972.

ORDER SIPHONAPTERA
Fleas

DESCRIPTION

- Siphonaptera are small, wingless insects with the body flattened laterally (from side to side).
- All the spines on the body point to the rear of the insect, which allows them to run through the hair of an animal easily.
- The immature stages (larvae) are elongate and worm-like, quite different from the adults.
- Mouthparts are formed for piercing and sucking.
- Most fleas are under ⅛ of an inch in length.

LIFE CYCLE

- Metamorphosis is complete (egg, larva, pupa, adult).

PEST STATUS

- Fleas are well known as pests of domestic animals and man. One species transmits the bacterium that causes plague, which has killed millions of people over the past 3,000 years.
- Adults are blood-feeders and usually feed on animals but will attack humans.

HABITAT

- Larvae are seldom seen and feed on dried blood, adult flea feces, and other organic debris.
- They live in the nests of various animals, in carpets in the home or in the soil in areas where their host animals frequent.

213, 214   CAT FLEA

Siphonaptera: Pulicidae   *Ctenocephalides felis*
                                           (Bouché)

Description: Adults are small (⅛ inch), dark brown, wingless insects with a flattened body and hind legs modified for jumping. Larvae are whitish, legless and worm-like and grow to almost ¼ inch. Eggs are white and round.

There are several flea species in Texas, including the **dog flea**, *Ctenocephalides canis* (Curtis), and the **oriental rat flea**, *Xenopsylla cheopis* (Rothschild). One unusual flea, the **sticktight flea (214)**, *Echinophaga gallinacea* (Westwood), is found in south Texas; it burrows into the skin of its hosts, particularly birds.

Life cycle: Mated female fleas lay eggs after consuming host blood. Eggs fall to the ground in the near vicinity where hosts spend time and rest. Whitish larvae hatch from eggs within 2 to 3 weeks. Larvae can develop over 9 to 15 days under optimum conditions, but depending on the temperature may take up to 200 days. Fully developed larvae spin cocoons of silk that become encrusted with soil particles and debris, making them hard to detect. The pupal stage lasts from 7 days to a year before adults emerge. Under optimum temperature and humidity conditions development can be completed in 30 to 75 days.

Pest status: Adult fleas bite pets and humans; bites are irritating and can potentially transmit diseases; consumption of fleas can also result in the transmission of tapeworms; constant scratching of itchy flea bites can result in other skin problems and allergic reactions.

Habitat and food source(s): Adult mouthparts are modified for piercing and sucking blood, larvae have chewing mouthparts. Adult fleas move around freely on the host and from host to host, and can bite repeatedly. Although cat fleas prefer cats as hosts, they are capable of surviving on dogs and other wild or domestic animals. Adults suck blood for survival and egg development, with partially digested blood expelled as feces serving as food for larvae. Newly emerged, unfed adults can survive for weeks off of the host.

Literature: Ebeling 1978; Patrick and Hamman 1980.

Sticktight flea

ORDER DIPTERA
Flies, Mosquitoes, Gnats, Midges

DESCRIPTION

- Diptera or true flies vary greatly in shape and size.
- Diptera are usually winged, but have only one pair of wings with relatively few veins. Hind wings are represented only by a pair of slender, knobbed structures called halteres. A few forms, primarily parasites, are wingless as adults.
- Immature stages (larvae), often called maggots, differ from adults and are usually found in different habitats. Those of some groups, including midges and mosquitoes, have head capsules but others have poorly formed heads. Larvae may be thin and elongate or thin and wide and some are elaborately ornamented.
- Mouthparts of adults and larvae are formed for piercing, sucking, rasping, and/or lapping. A few flies lack conventional mouthparts.
- Flies can be very small to over 1 inch in length.

LIFE CYCLE

- Flies have complete metamorphosis (egg, larva, pupa, adult).

PEST STATUS

- Some members of the order cause a great amount of damage to crops, become a nuisance when locally abundant and spread diseases of animals and plants. Some groups are considered beneficial because they prey on or parasitize insect pests.
- This is one of the most important orders from the standpoint of human health because of the species that transmit diseases.
- Mosquitoes can transmit yellow fever and malaria, and have been responsible for millions of human deaths.

HABITAT

- Many fly larvae are associated with aquatic or semi-aquatic habitats or very moist areas with organic matter.
- Some are internal parasites of mammals.
- The order includes forms that are parasitic, predaceous and others that live on either living or dead plant or animal material.

Diptera: Tipulidae   Many species

Description: Some people think these flies look like Texas-sized mosqui-toes, and they have wrongly been called "mosquito hawks." Crane flies are large tan-colored fragile flies with long legs. Adults and larvae do not feed on mosquitoes. Larval forms of crane flies are gray-brown cylindrical larvae that may bear fleshy lobes on the (posterior) end. Occasionally, the segments toward the end of the body can be greatly expanded.

There are many species of these flies that occur in Texas. The term "mosquito hawk" generally refers to dragonflies (Odonata).

Life cycle: Larvae develop in wet locations throughout the year. Many adults emerge in February and March.

Pest status: Large numbers of adult crane flies can be a nuisance indoors.

Habitat and food source(s): Crane fly larvae feed primarily on decomposing organic matter. Adults do not feed. Larvae occur in moist environments such as woodlands, streams, and flood plains, although some species inhabit open fields, dry rangeland, and even desert environments. In compost piles, they often occur on the soil surface below the pile of decaying vegetation. Some species have been reported to feed on roots of forage crops, turf grasses, and seedling field crops. Usually their presence causes little concern because they are assisting in the process of decomposition.

Literature: Byers 1984; James and Harwood 1969.

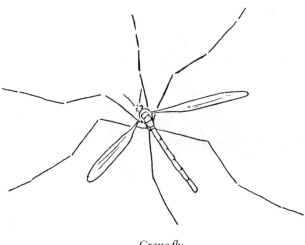

Crane fly

Diptera: Bibionidae   *Plecia nearctica* Hardy

Description: They are about ½ inch long, black with a reddish-orange area on the top of the thorax, and a pair of smokey-colored wings.

There are many other species of Bibionidae called **march flies.** Other Texas species are generally black with clear wings and become abundant in certain periods of the year. They are all weak fliers.

Life cycle: Large numbers of adults emerge primarily in the spring (May) and fall (September). Males and females fly and couple in open areas along roadways, appearing to swarm in weak flight. Although females live for only a week or so, adult flight activity lasts for a period of about 4 weeks. Eggs are deposited in swampy areas and ditches. Larvae develop through several stages (instars), becoming about ⅜ inch long and slate-gray with dark heads. Thereafter, they pupate in the soil and emerge as adults in about 8 days.

Pest status: High numbers in flight over roadways can be annoying, causing bug-splattered windows and radiator grills that can lead to obscured vision and engine overheating.

Habitat and food source(s): Larvae have chewing mouthparts. Adults fly mainly during daylight hours and feed on nectar and other moisture sources. They are naturally attracted to open areas such as roadways through wooded areas. Larvae feed on decomposing organic matter, plant roots, and even lawns with thick thatch.

Literature: Drees 1990.

Lovebugs

DARKWINGED FUNGUS GNATS

Diptera: Sciaridae   *Bradysia* spp.

Description: Adult fungus gnats are small (⅛ inch long), fragile, grayish to black flies with long, slender legs and thread-like antennae (**235**). Their wings are clear or smokey-colored with no pattern and few distinct veins. Larvae are clear to creamy-white and can grow to about ¼ inch long. They have shiny black head capsules.

Shore flies (Ephydridae) are also commonly encountered in the greenhouse. They appear more like small house flies in body structure, and have smokey wings with small whitish-appearing clear spotted patterns. Larvae of shore flies feed on algae.

Life cycle: Fungus gnats develop through egg, larva, pupa, and adult in 2 to 4 weeks. Fungus gnats normally follow a predictable cycle of population development: The first two generations are the largest, followed by a leveling off or decline in numbers.

Pest status: Adults are a nuisance indoors to greenhouse operators and homeowners with infested houseplants; larvae can damage roots of tender potted plants.

Habitat and food source(s): Larvae have chewing mouthparts and feed primarily on fungi, decaying organic matter and plant roots, particularly in very moist environments. The larval stages can damage healthy roots, stunting or killing young plants even where there is no fungal food source. Fungus gnat larvae may also aid in the introduction and spread of plant diseases. Larval and pupal stages can survive periods of drought.

Literature: Cole 1985; Lindquist 1994.

217 HESSIAN FLY

Diptera: Cecidomyiidae   *Mayetiola destructor* (Say)

Description: Eggs, although rarely seen, are thin, and cylindrical and laid along the veins of leaf sheaths. They are uniform glossy red when deposited, and turn a darker red at one end and opaque white at the other just before hatching. Spindle-shaped, legless larvae with no head capsules (maggots) are red for 4 to 5 days after hatching from the egg, and gradually turn white with a translucent green stripe down the back as they grow to ³⁄₁₆ inch long. Puparia, most readily observed when dissecting infested plants, are ⅜ inch long, dark brown, and spindle-shaped, often called "flaxseed," and contain the pupae. Adults are small (⅛ to ³⁄₁₆ inch long), dark or red-tinged, gnat-like flies with long legs and antennae.

Life cycle: Winter is spent in the pupal stage inside the puparium, just below the soil surface in the crown of the host plant. Adult flies emerge in spring and lay eggs on host plants. Larvae (maggots) hatch from eggs in 3 to 7 days, and develop through 3 stages (instars) over a period of 25 to 30 days before forming a puparium (by inflating the last larval skin). Summer is spent in field stubble. They are mainly active in the spring and fall, although there may be up to 6 generations per year.

Pest status: Larvae (maggots) burrow between leaf sheaths and remove plant sap from stems of small grain crops, causing damaged plants to die, thereby reducing yield; occur from north central to central Texas.

Habitat and food source(s): Larvae secrete enzymes that cause stems to exude sap on which the larvae feed. Hessian flies attack small grains, including wheat, rye, barley, and some wild grasses. Larvae in leaf sheath tissue at the crown or joints along the stem, rupture plant cells and feed on sap. Damaged plants are stunted and may die or fall over (lodge) before harvest.

Literature: Cameron et al. 1982.

218 SORGHUM MIDGE

Diptera: Cecidomyiidae   *Contarinia sorghicola*
                                       (Coquillett)

Description: Adults are tiny, ⅟₁₆ inch long, with reddish-orange abdomens.

Life cycle: Winter months are spent in the larval stage in aborted sorghum seeds. In the spring, adults emerge and are attracted to flowering host plants. They deposit white, cylindrical eggs on stalks in the spikelets of flowers. Colorless spindle-shaped larvae hatch from eggs in 2 to 3 days and develop through several stages (instars), gradually changing color from pink to reddish-orange. Pupae are dark orange and become darker as adults develop inside. The development from egg to adult is complete in 14 to 16 days. Several generations are completed in Johnson grass seed before the generation appears that damages sorghum seed.

Pest status: Immature stages damage developing sorghum seeds and are one of the most important pests of this crop.

Habitat and food source(s): Johnson grass and sorghum are the primary hosts, although they can develop on some other grasses. Larvae feed on the developing ovary of sorghum seeds, preventing normal development. Damage results in sorghum heads with small or malformed seeds that appear blighted or "blasted."

Literature: Carter et al. 1982.

219 MOTH FLIES

Diptera: Psychodidae   Numerous species

Description: Adults are small and very hairy, with a pair of pointed wings. They resemble small moths because they hold their wings roof-like over the body when at rest. They are weak fliers and appear to hop or jump.

Life cycle: Eggs laid by females hatch into pale-colored larvae. Following a feeding and development period, larvae pupate and soon emerge as adult flies. Adults live only 3 to 4 days without food, but they can survive for weeks if nectar or other liquid food sources are available.

Pest status: Moth flies are a nuisance when numerous in and around homes and structures in the close vicinity of breeding habitats. Larvae are considered beneficial, an essential part of the cycle that breaks down waste into water-soluble compounds.

Habitat and food source(s): Moth flies are common around sink drains, sewage treatment facilities, storm drains, dung, and rotten vegetation. They are sometimes called "drain flies." Larvae are aquatic or semi-aquatic, feeding on bacteria, fungi, algae, and other microorganisms present in decaying organic matter. They often feed in the liquid or slime layers that develop around debris in drains, sewage treatment beds, and standing water. However, when food is scarce they may become cannibalistic. Larvae are capable of surviving temperature extremes and habitats low in oxygen.

Literature: Drees and Owens 1982.

220, 221 MOSQUITOES

Diptera: Culicidae   *Aedes* spp., *Culex* spp., and others

Description: Adults are about ¼ inch long, with long legs, a pair of clear wings, and a slender body. The body and wing veins are covered with scales. The head bears compound eyes, thread-like antennae, and long, slender sucking mouthparts. Non-biting males can be distinguished from females because they bear very hairy "feathery" antennae they use as hearing structures to locate females. The **Asian tiger mosquito (220)**, *Aedes albopictus* (Skuse), was first detected in Texas in 1985 and is now a wide-spread and common species. It is distinctly black with white markings on the body and legs. The thorax is marked with a single white stripe down the middle. In contrast, the thorax of the **yellowfever mosquito**, *Aedes aegypti* (Linnaeus), has two curved ("lyre-shaped") stripes.

Aquatic larvae **(221)** "swim" upside down, wriggling their segmented abdomen that bears "gills" and a breathing siphon at the end. The thorax and head are globular and each body segment bears tufts of hairs (setae). When at rest, they usually hang diagonally from the siphon tube, which pierces the water surface tension to breathe, although some mosquitoes, e.g., *Anopheles*, rest horizontally. Aquatic pupae are C-shaped with the top enlarged to contain the developing head, thorax, wings, and legs. They can also "swim" by wriggling their abdomens, and at rest they "float" with their backs (which bear "trumpet"-like breathing structures) to the surface.

This family (Culicidae) also includes subfamilies of **phantom midges** (Chaoborinae) and **dixid midges** (Dixinae). A number of other midges and gnats are often mistaken for mosquitoes (see Midges and Bloodworms).

Life cycle: Females of "standing-water" mosquito species (*Anopheles, Coquilettidia, Culiseta, Culex*) deposit masses of eggs in "rafts" on the water surface, while "floodwater" species (*Aedes, Psorophora*) lay eggs either on plants on or below a still water surface or in moist soil depressions that will be subject to later flooding. Time for eggs to hatch varies with species from 16 to 24 hours to more than 2 years for floodwater mosquitoes. Larvae develop through 3 molts (4 instars) over a period of about one week before pupating. Adults emerge from the back of the pupa after 2 to 3 days. Adults live for 2 or more weeks, although standing-water species overwinter as mated, engorged females.

Pest status: Adult females bite and may transmit diseases—malaria, filariasis, arthropod-borne viruses such as yellow fever, dengue, and encephalitis. Saliva, injected by females while engorging on blood, causes itching. There are about 55 species of mosquitoes in Texas (170 species nationally).

Habitat and food source(s): Blood-feeding females have piercing-sucking mouthparts and usually must ingest a blood meal to develop eggs. Males, as well as females, sip nectar, honeydew, and fruit juices. Larvae are filter feeders, consuming aquatic bacteria and other microorganisms. A few species have larvae that are predaceous on other mosquito larvae. Mosquito species vary in aquatic larval habitats, ranging from ponds, puddles, containers, and tree holes to other sources of standing, slow-moving, fresh, or salty water. Large numbers of mosquitoes can develop in swamps, tidal marshes, flood water, and rice fields. Male mosquitoes swarm in "clouds" to attract females. Mosquitoes can fly and disperse with the wind.

Literature: Ebeling 1978; Olson 1996.

222   BLACK FLIES, BUFFALO GNATS, OR TURKEY GNATS

Diptera: Simuliidae   *Simulium* spp. and others

Description: Adult flies are small (⅟₂₅–⅛ inch) and vary in color by species, usually being black or gray, light tan or yellow. Adults are typically robust with a characteristic arched or humped back (prothorax) giving rise to the common name "buffalo gnat." Black fly species are common along fast-moving rivers at certain times of the year, particularly in northeast Texas. There, various confined birds have been killed because of attacks by large numbers of black flies.

Black fly or turkey gnat

Another group of tiny biting flies is the biting midges also called "punkies" or "no-see-ums" (Ceratopogonidae). Usually less than ¹⁄₁₆ inch long, these midges are often mistaken for black flies. However, they can be distinguished by the difference in antennae (black fly antennae are short and stout whereas the ceratopoginid antennae are longer and hair-like) and wing venation (black flies have strong distinct veins toward the front edge of the wing whereas ceratopogonids do not).

Life cycle: Female black flies deposit 150–500 creamy-white eggs that darken until they are almost black just prior to hatching. The eggs usually are deposited singly or in masses in moving water or on some convenient object near the water's edge. The water may be a slow-moving stream, but most species prefer rapidly flowing water. In rare cases, breeding may occur in marshy areas. The time required for hatching varies with the species and may be 3–5 days or as long as 30 days at low temperatures. Larvae most often are found just beneath the surface of rapidly flowing water. They do not come to the surface to breath like mosquito larvae because the gill filaments of larvae extract oxygen directly from the water. Duration of larval development, like the egg stage, varies with species and temperature and ranges from 10–14 days to 7–10 weeks. Some species overwinter as larvae, although in northern areas, winter is usually passed in the egg stage. The last larval instar spins a reddish-brown, basket-like cocoon in which pupation occurs. These cocoons are attached to slightly submerged objects such as rocks, logs, roots, and other debris. Pupae also possess respiratory filaments with which they remove dissolved oxygen from the water. The pupal period varies from 4–5 days to as long as 3–5 weeks, depending on water temperature and species. Adults emerge from the pupal case, rise to the water surface, unfold their wings and fly away. Mating usually occurs shortly after the initial flight. The complete life cycle, from egg to adult, varies from 6–15 weeks and the number of generations per year ranges from 1 to 6, depending on species and climatic conditions.

Pest status: Adult females produce a painful bite that can cause localized swelling and in extreme cases anaphylactic shock.

Habitat and food source(s): Larvae are filter feeders usually in flowing water and adult females have mouthparts modified for biting and blood feeding. Larvae of most species feed on small animals, such as protozoa and crustaceans, or plants such as algae, by straining particulate matter from water flowing by them with the aid of mouth brushes; some species feed in the silt or on submerged surfaces. Adults feed on the nectar of flowers; only the female requires a blood meal for egg development. Although a given species may prefer a particular animal host, most will readily feed upon other host species as well. Black flies attack man and a wide variety of domestic and wild animals and birds; others feed only on cold-blooded animals.

Literature: Bay and Harris 1988; James and Harwood 1969.

Diptera: Chironomidae   Many species

Description: Adults superficially resemble mosquitoes, but do not bear mouthparts modified for piercing and sucking. Antennae of males are hairy, and wings are bare or hairy (mosquito wings bear scales). Species vary in size (³⁄₁₆ to ⅜ inch long), body color, and markings. Aquatic, red-colored larvae of the genus, *Chironomus,* are called "bloodworms."

Life cycle: Females lay eggs in water. Larvae develop under water through several stages (instars) before pupating.

Pest status: Adults can swarm and be locally abundant, becoming a nuisance. When very abundant they may get into eyes or ears or can be inhaled. Immature stages are important as food for small fish. Bloodworms are sold in the pet trade for fish food.

Habitat and food source(s): Larvae have chewing mouthparts and are common in standing or flowing water where they are bottom-dwelling scavengers, feeding on organic matter such as algae and decaying plants. They are more abundant in polluted water with excessive algal growth. Some midges, e.g., *Chironomus,* construct mud tubes in which they live. Massive emergence of adults can occur at certain times. Adults rest on vegetation during the day and swarm at dusk and dawn (crepuscular behavior), often around lights.

Literature: Ebeling 1978; James and Harwood 1969.

224, 225   HORSE FLIES AND DEER FLIES

Diptera: Tabanidae   *Tabanus, Chrysops,* and
                                       others spp.

Description: There are over 100 species of horse (**224**) and deer flies (**225**) known to occur in Texas. Eyes of live specimens are often beautifully colored with iridescent and metallic color patterns. Deer flies (*Chrysops* spp., 33 species) range from ¼ to ½ inch long, and are black to brown in col-

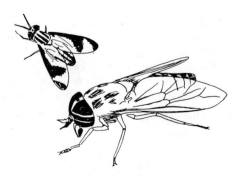

Horse fly or deer fly

oration, often with yellowish markings. They characteristically have clear wings with black or brown patterns, making wings appear to be banded. Horse flies (*Tabanus,* 52 species, and other genera) range from ⅜ to just over 1 inch long and vary in coloration by species. Some are all black, while many have colored patterns on their abdomens and wings.

Life cycle: Winter is spent as partially grown larvae that pupate in spring. Adults begin emerging in late spring and summer, varying by species. Females often lay eggs in specific locations, such as on vegetation overhanging water. Eggs are laid in masses that darken to brown or black before larvae hatch out and drop to the ground or into water. Larvae are generally whitish, spindle-shaped and develop through 6 to 13 stages (instars) over one or more years before pupating. One generation per year occurs for most species.

Pest status: Adults bite animals and man. Bites can be very painful and remain swollen for several days. Incessant attacks on livestock can reduce weight gain. They are capable of mechanically transmitting some animal diseases (e.g., anaplasmosis).

Habitat and food source(s): Larvae have chewing or teasing mouthparts; adult female mouthparts are modified for piercing and sucking blood. Adult females of many horse and deer fly species are attracted to man and animals in search of a blood meal, although a blood meal may not be necessary for them to produce the first cluster of eggs. Males are nectar feeders and often hover at certain times of the day, presumably to attract females and maintain a territory. Species are often locally abundant near breeding habitats, and the various species have distinctive adult activity periods during the year and/or during the day. Larvae live in species-specific habitats, although most are aquatic or semi-aquatic; some are terrestrial. They are generally predaceous and cannibalistic, feeding on other insect larvae and earthworms, although some (particularly deer fly larvae) may feed on plant matter.

Literature: Goodwin and Drees 1996; James and Harwood 1969.

226, 227 BLACK SOLDIER FLY

Diptera: Stratiomyidae   *Hermetia illucens* (Linnaeus)

Description: Adult flies are robust, ⅝ inch long, black flies with smokey-black wings. Wings are held over the back when at rest. The first abdominal segment has clear areas. Larvae are torpedo-shaped and flattened, with skin (exoskeleton) appearing firm and tough. The head is small and narrower than the body and the body bears no legs or other features except hairs and spines. The back of the body is blunt and bears breathing pores (spiracles).

Other Stratiomyidae vary in color from black to metallic blue, green and purple or black and yellow patterns. They have characteristic "elbowed" antennae due to a long terminal segment. Larvae (**227**) are generally aquatic or semi-aquatic, feeding on algae, decomposing organic matter, or aquatic organisms. A few species are found in dung or in decaying fruit and vegetables or under the bark of rotting wood. Larvae of some species bear a rosette of hairs around the back end of their bodies used to float on the water surface and obtain air.

Life cycle: Larvae hatch from eggs and develop through several stages before pupating inside of the last larval skin.

Pest status: Adults superficially resemble wasps, but have no stinger and are harmless; larvae occasionally occur indoors when they breed in organic matter where faulty plumbing or another source of moist matter is present; larvae usually go unnoticed until they leave the larval habitat and crawl around the room in search of a drier pupation site.

Habitat and food source(s): Larvae have chewing mouthparts. Adult flies are commonly trapped indoors and are found around windows as they try to find an exit. Outdoors, they occasionally "buzz" by, but are otherwise rarely encountered. Larvae feed on decomposing organic matter, mold, and algae. The black soldier fly is commonly encountered indoors in bathrooms, kitchens, outdoor latrines, and earthworm beds. Larvae have also been extracted from carrion, and there are reports that larvae accidentally swallowed with contaminated food have caused myiasis (infestation within the body).

Literature: Drees 1990c.

228–230   ROBBER FLIES

Diptera: Asilidae   Many species

Description: Adult stages are medium to large (⅜ to 1⅛ inches) flies often observed on stems of plants, on the ground, or flying low. Species vary in appearance and some mimic wasps and bees. Most species are gray to black, hairy-bodied, have a long, narrow, tapering abdomen containing segments that may be banded, patterned, or contrasting in color. The heads of adults have a depression between the eyes when viewed from the front. They have long, strong legs for grabbing prey.

Some robber flies resemble bees (**229**) in appearance but can readily be separated because true flies have only one pair of wings. **Bee flies (230)** (Bombyliidae) include many species of stout-bodied, yellow-haired flies often seen hovering or resting on the ground or on flowers in open, sunny areas. Some bee fly species have wings marked with darker patterns and they hold their wings outstretched.

Life cycle: Adults lay eggs in the soil or in plants. Eggs hatch into slender, shiny, white, legless larvae that develop through several stages before pupating. The life cycle usually requires more than one year to complete.

Pest status: Adults prey on a variety of arthropods; they are considered to be beneficial insects, except for those that feed on bees and other beneficial insects; adults, handled improperly, are capable of inflicting a painful bite.

Habitat and food source(s): Adults have piercing-sucking mouthparts. They perch on stems of low plants or other objects and attack prey in the air, feeding on bees, beetles, dragonflies, other flies, grasshoppers, leafhoppers, wasps, and other insects. Larvae live in the soil, in wood and other habitats, feeding on organic matter, other arthropods such as white grubs, beetle pupae, and grasshopper egg masses.

Literature: Borror et al. 1989; Oldroyd 1964; Swan and Papp 1972.

231   LONGLEGGED FLIES

Diptera: Dolichopodidae   *Dolichopus* spp. and others

Description: This is a large family of flies, and species vary in their appearance and biology. In general, adult flies are medium to small, slender flies with green, blue or copper metallic-colored bodies and long legs. Their wings are clear or marked with darker areas toward the wing tips. Wing venation patterns are characteristic for identification to family.

Life cycle: Larvae develop through several stages (instars) in wet to dry soil and pupate in cocoons made up of soil particles cemented together. Adults mate after elaborate courtship behavior, involving the males displaying their legs to the female.

Pest status: Adult flies and larval stages are beneficial, being predaceous on other arthropods.

Habitat and food source(s): Mouthparts are for piercing (with a short proboscis). Longlegged flies are common in lightly shaded areas near swamps and streams, in meadows and woodlands. Adults and larvae are predaceous on small insects. Larvae are primarily aquatic and semi-aquatic, although immatures of some species tunnel in stems of grasses and other plants or live under bark of trees. Not much is known about larval feeding habits, although some species are known to be predaceous.

Literature: Borror et al. 1989; Swan and Papp 1972.

232, 233   SYRPHID FLIES OR FLOWER FLIES

Diptera: Syrphidae   Many species

Description: This is a large group of medium to large flies, ranging from ¼ to ¾ inch long. Most adult flower flies are black or brown with yellow banded abdomens and body markings, superficially resembling bees and wasps, except they have only two wings that are not held over the back of the body when at rest. Some species are hairy and have a long, thin abdomen. Antennae are short (not elbowed) and the last segment bears a strong hair (seta). Larvae (**233**) of most species are legless spindle-shaped maggots and vary in color from creamy-white to green or brown.

Flower flies, also called "hover flies," can be distinguished from other groups of similar flies by studying the wing venation: They have an isolated (spurious) vein in the wing between the third (radius) and the fourth (media) longitudinal veins.

Life cycle: Biology and developmental times vary between species and because of environmental conditions and availability of food. In general, females lay single white eggs on leaves near aphid infestations or near other suitable food sources for that species. Larvae or maggots hatch from eggs in about 3 days. Larvae develop through several stages (instars) over a period of 2 to 3 weeks before pupating, either on the host plant or in the soil. The skin of the last stage larva forms the tan-brown teardrop-shaped puparium. Adults emerge in 1−2 weeks unless the pupal stage remains through the winter. Up to 7 generations occur annually.

Pest status: Generally considered beneficial because the larval stages of many species are predaceous on insect pests such as aphids and adults pollinate flowers.

Habitat and food source(s): Larvae have chewing (teasing) mouthparts; adults have sponge-type mouthparts similar to house flies. Adult flies can be found hovering around flowers, feeding on nectar and pollen. They are often attracted to honeydew-covered leaves characteristic of infestations of sucking insects such as aphids. Legless larvae of these (Syrphinae) species are sluglike, adhering to leaf surfaces of infested plants while searching for aphids and other suitable prey (small caterpillars, thrips, etc.). Each larva can consume up to 400 aphids during development. Larvae of other species feed in the nests of ants, termites or bees, and others live in decaying vegetation and wood. Larvae of a few species feed on live plants. Those of *Eristalis* spp. are called "rattailed maggots" because of an unusually long breathing tube from the back of their bodies used to breath as they dwell in highly polluted water. Adults of this genus resemble bees and are known as "drone flies."

Literature: Borror et al. 1989; Mahr 1995; Swan and Papp 1972.

234, 235   LEAFMINER FLIES

Diptera: Agromyzidae   *Liriomyza* spp.

Description: Adult **serpentine leafminer** flies, *Liriomyza trifolii* Burgess, are small (¹⁄₁₆ inch), appear superficially like house flies but have bodies overall gray-black with yellow markings. Maggots grow to be about ¹⁄₁₆ inch long and whitish-yellow, while the pupae are yellow-brown, oval and seed-like. Mines appear snake-like or "serpentine," being narrow in width toward the end produced by younger maggots, and becoming progressively wider toward the end produced by larger mature maggots.

Common **leafminer** species include, *L. trifolii*, *L. brassicae* (Riley); and the **vegetable leafminer,** *L. sativae* Blanchard. One species attacks the base of Louisiana iris leaves. Several other insects have immature stages that produce serpentine- or blotch-shaped mines on leaves of host plants, including some species of beetles (Coleoptera: Chrysomelidae); sawflies (**325**)(Hymenoptera: Tenthredinidae), and moths such as the tomato pinworm (**248**) (Lepidoptera: several families).

Life cycle: Mated *L. trifolii* females produce punctures or "stipples" on leaves with their egg laying structure (ovipositor) and use some of these sites into which to insert an egg and others to feed upon. Maggots hatch from eggs in about 2 days, and develop through 3 stages (instars) while producing the mine over a period of 7 to 8 days. The last stage emerges from the leaf and drops to the ground, where it inflates its last skin to form the pupa or puparium. Adult flies emerge from the puparium in 7 to 11 days. Duration of the life cycle varies with temperature and time of the year. In the greenhouse, leafminers can breed throughout the year.

Pest status: Immature stages (maggots or larvae) tunnel through leaf tissue causing whitish winding tunnels or "mines" that can reduce yield and cause plants to look unsightly.

Habitat and food source(s): Larval mouth hooks are modified for rasping leaf tissue, while adults have lapping house fly type mouthparts. *L. trifolii* is primarily a pest of greenhouse plants including a wide variety of nursery crops (e.g., aster, chrysanthemum, dahlia, daisy, marigold, petunia, sunflower, zinnia) and vegetables (e.g., beans, cantaloupe, carrots, celery, cucumber, eggplants, lettuce, peas, tomatoes, and potatoes). Leaves are damaged as maggots tunnel through the inner leaf tissue (between the upper and lower leaf surface) producing whitish "mines" that reduce the energy-producing (photosynthetic) surface area. High levels of damage on vegetable crops cause stunted growth and reduced yield; leafy vegetable crops like lettuce, and ornamental plants become unsightly and occasionally unmarketable. High populations of adult flies can damage leaves by producing egg-laying and feeding scars called "stipples."

Literature: Carter et al. 1982b; Johnson and Lyon 1988.

235   SMALL FRUIT FLIES OR VINEGAR FLIES

Diptera: Drosophilidae   *Drosophila* spp.

Description: Adults are small, yellowish, tan to dark brown ⅛-inch-long flies, normally with red eyes. The antennae are characteristic in having a feathery bristle.

Life cycle: Adults lay cylindrical eggs near suitable larval habitat. Tiny maggots hatch from eggs and develop though several stages (instars) before leaving the food source in search of a drier location to pupate. Pupae are brown and seed-like with two horn-like stalks on the front end. Development from egg to adult can be completed in 8 to 10 days.

Pest status: Adult flies can be a nuisance in restaurants, wine cellars, near fruit and vegetable fields and food processing areas; anywhere where abundant breeding habitat is available. Fruit flies, particularly *Drosophila melanogaster* Meigen sometimes called the "banana fly," have been used extensively as laboratory animals for experiments in genetics, insect behavior, and physiology.

Habitat and food source(s): Mouthparts are for lapping in adults, while maggots have chewing or "teasing" mouthparts. Immature stages feed on overripe, fermenting, or rotting fruit and vegetables, fermenting liquids (vinegar, beer, wine, cider), and other rotting organic material in garbage and other unsanitary areas. Adults are attracted to fruit or fermenting liquid.

Literature: Ebeling 1978; Metcalf et al. 1962.

235   Darkwinged Fungus Gnats
(SEE PAGE 205)

236   Eye Gnats

Diptera: Chloropidae   *Hippelates* spp. and others

Description: Adults are small (¹⁄₁₆ to ⅛ inch), dark gray to black bodied flies with clear wings, somewhat similar to tiny houseflies.

Chloropid flies may be confused with fruit flies (*Drosophila*), but can be separated by characteristic antennal structures: The chloropid flies have a simple hair-like projection (arista) on the last antennal segment, whereas the arista on Drosophila are feathered.

Life cycle: Clusters of eggs are deposited on or in the soil by female flies. Larvae resemble tiny maggots and develop through several stages (instars) over 7 to 11 days in warm weather. Larvae pupate close to the soil surface and emerge as adults in about a week. Development from egg to adult can occur in about 21 days, but takes longer during colder winter months. They can occur year-round and may be locally abundant at certain times of the year, such as spring and fall, when conditions are favorable for their development.

Pest status: Adults are a true nuisance; although they do not bite, they are attracted to eyes and any wet areas on the body such as mucous, puss, and blood on and around wounds and exposed genitals of animals. They are capable of spreading some diseases of man and animals such as "pinkeye" (conjunctivitis).

Habitat and food source(s): Adults have lapping mouthparts capable of rasping (scarifying) because of spines covering the mouthpart (labella). Larvae develop in a variety of habitats such as decaying plant and animal matter and plant rootlets, particularly in freshly disturbed, well drained, and aerated sandy soils. Female flies attack animals while males are attracted to flowers.

Literature: James and Harwood 1969; Swan and Papp 1972.

Seedcorn Maggot

Diptera: Anthomyiidae   *Delia platura* (Meigen)

Description: The larval or maggot stages and puparia are most commonly encountered in association with rotting seeds and seedlings. Maggots are similar to house fly larvae, being cylindrical, whitish, and legless, but they are smaller (up to ¼ inch long). They are tapered toward the front end that bears the hook-like mouthparts, and the blunt back end supports a pair of breathing pores (spiracles). The puparium, made by inflating the last larval stage skin, is capsule-shaped about ³⁄₁₆ inch long and turns reddish-brown. Adults are small (³⁄₁₆ inch long) grayish-brown, black-legged flies resembling small house flies.

There are several other species of Anthomyiidae that feed on seeds and seedlings of various plants: the **onion maggot**, *Delia antiqua* (Meigen), on onions; and the **cabbage maggot**, *Delia radicum* (Linnaeus) on seedlings and transplants of broccoli, cabbage, cauliflower, brussels sprouts, radish, turnip, and some other vegetables. These species are similar to seedcorn maggots in appearance and biologies. Larvae can be identified by viewing differences in the structure of breathing pores (spiracles on the prothorax and last abdominal segments) and other characters using a dissecting microscope.

Life cycle: All life stages can occur year-round in Texas. Females lay eggs singly or in small clusters in suitable habitats. Maggots hatch in 1 to 9 days and develop through 3 stages (instars) over 1 to 3 weeks before pupating about 7 inches in the soil. Adult flies emerge in 7 to 26 days unless they overwinter. Development is influenced by temperature, with development beginning at 52°F and being most rapid in warmer conditions. Up to 5 generations can occur annually.

Pest status: Larvae infest soils high in organic matter and damage seeds and seedlings, particularly during cool, wet spring growing conditions.

Habitat and food source(s): Maggots have hook-like mandibles for teasing plant tissue. Seedcorn maggots feed mainly on decaying organic matter, but damage germinating seeds and seedlings of many vegetables and field crops, including alfalfa, beans, corn, cucurbits, onions, peas, peppers and soybeans. Maggots hollow seeds, leaving only seed coats, thereby reducing plant stands. Infested seedlings become wilted, yellowed (chlorotic), spindly and stunted, with stems and roots near the soil line showing characteristic damage produced by the maggots—tissues appear teased apart and rotting. Adults feed on nectar and honeydew produced by aphids and other sucking insects with lapping-type mouthparts that are similar to those of house flies.

Literature: Carter et al. 1982; Kogan and Kuhlman 1982; Metcalf et al. 1962; Peterson 1973.

237, 238   HOUSE FLY

Diptera: Muscidae   *Musca domestica* Linnaeus

Description: House flies are ³⁄₁₆ to ¼ inch long with robust bodies and two clear wings. The thorax is marked with four dark stripes. Larvae are called maggots and are creamy-white and cone-shaped, with the hind end blunt and bearing breathing holes (spiracles), tapering to the head, which bears black hook-like mouthparts.

Several flies resemble house flies. The **stable fly (238)**, *Stomoxys calcitrans* (Linnaeus), superficially resembles the house fly, but bears stiff, elongated mouthparts modified for biting animals and people and feeding on blood. They are very persistent and usually bite around the ankles. Their life cycle and food sources are similar to house flies, although development is slower (20 to 25 days from egg to adult).

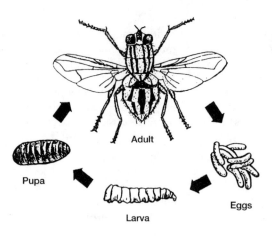

House fly life cycle

Life cycle: Female flies lay numbers of eggs in suitable larval food sources such as decomposing food in garbage, animal excrement, or other decomposing organic materials. Eggs hatch within a day into small maggots. Within a week, maggots grow and develop through 3 stages (instars) before they inflate their last larval skin into a puparium (pupa). After 4 to 6 days, adult flies emerge. Development from egg to adult can be completed in about 8 days under optimal conditions, and 12 generations can occur each summer. Adults normally live up to 25 days but may overwinter.

Pest status: Adults are a nuisance and a potential health threat. They can transfer disease organisms from an infested source, such as garbage and excrement, to a clean source, such as food, by crawling on surfaces between flights. They deposit "fly spots" on surfaces by regurgitating and defecating.

Habitat and food source(s): Adult flies have sponging-sucking mouthparts, with which they ingest mainly liquid food or food dissolved with regurgitated saliva. Larvae have mouthparts (mandibles) used to tease apart decomposing organic materials. Larvae feed with their narrow heads imbedded deep in the food source and the end of the bodies bearing the breathing pores on the surface. Just before completing larval development, they leave their food source in search of a dryer place to pupate. This is the time many larval infestations become noticeable. Large numbers of house flies can develop in poultry houses and around barns and feed lots where animal excrement accumulates. House flies developing there can fly to nearby homes and become a nuisance. Around the home, house flies can develop in garbage and piles of fermenting lawn clippings.

Literature: Ebeling 1978.

239 BLOW FLIES

Diptera: Calliphoridae *Calliphora* and *Phaenicia* spp.

Description: This group comprises several species including the **common blue bottle fly,** *Calliphora vomitoria* (Linnaeus) and the **green bottle fly,** *Phaenicia sericata* (Meigen). Adult flies are metallic blue, green, copper, or black flies that otherwise resemble house flies in appearance. The prominent hair on the terminal antennal segment (arista) is feathery (plumose).

Other Calliphoridae include the **black blow fly,** *Phormia regina* (Meigen), and the **cluster fly,** *Pollenia rudis* (Fabricius). Species of the family **Sarcophagidae** are also found in association with carrion and excrement, although some feed on decaying vegetation or are parasitic. One example of this family is the **flesh fly (244),** *Sarcophaga haemorrhoidalis* Fallen (Sarcophagidae). Adults are similar to blow flies, but are patterned a checkerboard of gray and black on the abdomen. The hair on the last antennal segment (arista) is bare or less feathery than those of Calliphoridae.

Life cycle: Female flies lay eggs on or near suitable habitats. Tiny maggots hatch from eggs in 6 to 48 hours. Maggots develop through 3 stages (instars) on carrion for 3 to 9 days before leaving the food source to pupate in soil. After 2 to 7 days in a prepupal stage, they form a puparium from their last larval stage skin. A fourth larval stage occurs within the puparium before pupation. Adult flies emerge 10 to 17 days after the formation of the puparium. Development from egg to adult occurs in 16 to 35 days, depending on temperature and environmental conditions.

Pest status: Blow flies are a nuisance similar to house flies when common indoors.

Habitat and food source(s): Maggots have hook-like mouthparts that tease apart tissues in which they live. Adults have sponge-like mouthparts similar to those of house flies. Larvae (maggots) primarily feed on dead animals and animal refuse. Some feed on vegetation and others are obligatory parasites.

Literature: Ebeling 1978; James and Harwood 1969.

240 HORN FLY

Diptera: Muscidae *Haematobia irritans* (Linnaeus)

Description: Adults are about half the size of house flies (about ³⁄₁₆ inch long) and are gray-black. Part of the mouthparts (proboscis or labium) are long and slender, projecting forward from the bottom of the head along with a pair of structures (palpi) which are almost as long. Immature stages are maggots similar to house fly maggots, distinguishable by the structure of the breathing pores (spiracles) on the back of the body.

The **stable fly (238)**, *Stomoxys calcitrans* (Linnaeus), is similar to, but larger than, the horn fly (see **house fly, 237, 238**).

Life cycle: Females lay eggs singly or in small clusters on the bottom edges of freshly passed cow manure. Maggots hatch in 2–3 days and develop for 8 to 10 days before crawling to a drier area to form a puparium. Adults emerge in 6 to 8 days. Rate of development is slowed in cooler temperatures. Overwintering occurs in a true diapause state in the pupal stage. Populations are most severe in spring and early fall.

Pest status: Flies build up in high numbers on cattle.

Habitat and food source(s): In the adults a mouthpart structure (the labella at the tip of the proboscis or labium) is modified for rasping. This part of the mouthpart is thrust into the host and blood is sucked up through other mouthparts that lie in a groove along the labium. Maggots are similar to house flies, having a single mouth hook. Horn flies are attracted to cattle where they rest during daylight hours. At night flies may leave the animal and rest in barns or on plants. When on the animal, they rest on the back, sides, and belly, usually with their heads pointed downward. Some animals can harbor thousands of flies at one time. Annoyance to cattle caused reduced food consumption, thereby reducing weight gain and milk production.

Literature: Hoelscher, et al. 1993; James and Harwood 1969.

Screwworm

Diptera: Calliphoridae   *Cochliomyia hominivorax*
                                       (Coquerel)

Description: Adult flies are similar in shape to house flies but are about twice as large. They have shiny blue-green bodies similar to blow flies and the back of the thorax is marked with three black stripes. Maggots are similar to house fly maggots in appearance, growing to about ⅔ inch long. Circles of elevated ridges around each segment of the body give them a screw-like appearance. The back end is blunt and supports two breathing pores (spiracles), while the front of the maggot tapers to a point supporting strong, black mouth hooks.

Blow fly maggots and the **secondary screwworm**, *Cochliomyia macellaria* (Fabricius), may also infest wounds.

Life cycle: Female flies mate only once in their lifetime. Thereafter, they are attracted to open wounds and lay eggs in shingle-like masses on dry skin along wound edges. Maggots hatch from eggs in 10 to 20 hours. After developing over 4 to 10 days through several stages, they drop to the ground and form puparia by inflating the last larval skin in which they pupate. Adult flies emerge 3 to 14 days later. Development from egg to adult can occur within 3 weeks, and up to ten generations can occur annually.

Pest status: This species no longer occurs in Texas. They still occur south of Mexico where the eradication program continues to be active. Formerly a common and widespread pest of Texas livestock; eradicated during the

1960s using the mass release of reared male flies that were sterilized by exposure to radiation. Occasionally, but less and less frequently, outbreaks continue to be reported, particularly if animals infested with screwworm maggots are brought north.

Habitat and food source(s): Maggots have mouth hooks that tear animal tissue. Adults have sponge-like mouthparts similar to house flies. Any wounded warm-blooded wild or domestic animal can serve as a host for screwworms, including cattle, dogs, goats, hogs, horses, humans, mules, and sheep. Maggots first feed in wounds but then begin to feed on healthy tissue, enlarging the wound and preventing it from healing by secreting a toxin. Infested animals may die if not found and treated.

Literature: Baumhover 1966; Knipling et al. 1959; Metcalf et al. 1962.

241 HORSE BOT FLY

Diptera: Oestridae

Gasterophilus intestinalis
(De Geer)

Description: Adult flies are brownish, hairy, robust, and about ⅔ inch long, superficially resembling bumble bees, except for having only one pair of wings. Wings of the horse bot fly have faint smokey spots on the wings. Fully-grown larvae (maggots) are ½ to ⅔ inch long and have yellow-white to pinkish thick, tough skin. They are blunt at one (the back) end, and taper to the other (front) end, which bears a pair of strong, hook-like mouthparts. Each body segment is ringed with strong spines.

Several other species of bot flies occur on horses: (**chin fly** or **throat bot fly,** *Gasterophilus nasalis* (Linnaeus); and, **lip** or **nose bot fly,** *G. haemorrhoidalis* (Linnaeus). They can be identified, in part, by the shape of the eggs.

Life cycle: Larvae develop in the digestive tracts of host animals during the winter. In the late winter and early spring months, full grown larvae are found in host's feces. From there, they burrow into the soil and form a puparium from their last stage (instar) larval skin. They transform into adult flies inside the puparium and emerge in 3 to 10 weeks. Adults are active from mid-summer through fall. Adult females glue eggs on the hairs of horses, particularly to hair on the front legs but also on the belly, shoulders, and hind legs. Eggs hatch in 10 to 140 days with the proper stimulus (moisture, heat, and friction) caused by the horse licking or biting egg-infested hair. Tiny first-stage (instar) larvae enter the mouth and burrow into the tongue for about 28 days before they molt and travel to the stomach where they remain for 9 to 10 months, developing into the third stage (instar) after about 5 weeks. There is one generation per year.

Pest status: Adults cannot bite or sting and are harmless to man and animals, although horses react evasively to egg-laying attempts by female flies; larval or maggot stages feed internally, damaging the digestive tracts of horses.

Habitat and food source(s): Maggots have mouth hooks that tear tissue apart in the digestive tracts; adults do not have functional mouthparts. Horses, mules, and donkeys are primary hosts. Adult female flies, attempting to lay eggs on host animals, cause horses to flee and resist fly "attacks" (hovering, buzzing, and striking), occasionally resulting in injury. Larvae live in the digestive tract, damaging the tongue, lips, stomach lining, and intestine. They apparently feed on the inflammatory products produced by the host in response to their presence. Infestations cause mechanical injuries and an infected ulcerous condition that progressively starves the host animal.

Literature: Metcalf et al. 1962.

242   COMMON CATTLE GRUB

Diptera: Oestridae   *Hypoderma lineatum*
                                      (de Villers)

Description: Adults are robust, black, ½-inch-long hairy flies that have white stripes and hair tufts on the thorax. Larvae (bots) are white and grow to 1 inch long, with a pair of breathing pores (spiracles) on the back end (posterior). They turn brown to black before leaving the host to pupate.

Life cycle: Winter is spent in the larval (bot or maggot) stage in the backs of host animals. Brown to black mature larvae, squeeze out of the hole on the animal's back and drop to the ground where they form pupae inside puparia made from the skin of the fifth and last larval stage (instar) from November through March. Adult flies emerge in about 5 weeks. Female flies lay rows of whitish eggs glued to hairs on the host animal. Larvae hatch from eggs in 3 to 7 days and burrow under the skin. Over about a 6-month period, larvae migrate through the body to the animal's back, developing through 3 instars. There, each bot cuts a hole in the skin and places its breathing pores (posterior spiracles) nearby. It remains there for another 2 months, developing through 2 more larval stages (instars). There is one generation per year.

Pest status: Also called the **ox bot, ox warble,** or **heel fly,** larvae (bots) develop inside cattle, causing health problems (inflammation and suffering) and reducing the value of hides; adults cannot bite or sting.

Habitat and food source(s): Maggots have hook-like mouthparts; adult flies do not feed. Cattle and bison are the primary hosts. Larvae hatching from eggs laid on the legs or flanks migrate beneath the skin and through the body to the gullet. They then migrate down to the diaphragm and up along the ribs to the back where they form bumpy cysts or "warbles" which cause inflammation and irritation. Larvae feed on secretions caused by the irritating presence of the maggot inside the inflamed cysts. Infestations reduce growth, milk production, and quality of meat and leather produced from infested animals. Adult flies attempting to lay eggs irritate host animals, causing cattle to run wildly and possibly injuring themselves.

Literature: Borror et al. 1989; Metcalf et al. 1962; Swan and Papp 1972.

Diptera: Tachinidae and others　　　　　　　Many species

Description: Adult tachinid flies can superficially resemble house flies, but vary by species in size, coloration, and shape. Many are gray or black or have bodies marked with stripes. Many have distinct long bristles on the ends of their abdomens. Other species are brightly colored (e.g., with a red abdomen and smokey-black wings), and they may have prominent fringes of hairs along their hind legs. Larval (maggot) stages are rarely seen, but may be observed when they emerge from host insects to pupate.

Some species of **flesh flies (244)** (Sarcophagidae) are also parasitic on some species of bees (Hymenoptera), beetles (Coleoptera) and caterpillars (Lepidoptera). Some species of **humpbacked flies** (Phoridae) parasitize species of ants and bees (Hymenoptera), beetles (Coleoptera) and scale insects (Homoptera). Some smaller groups of flies (Sciomyzidae, Pipunculidae, Pyrgotidae, Anthomyiidae) also contain parasitic species.

Life cycle: Life cycles vary by species. Eggs are sometimes laid on leaves and ingested by a host caterpillar during feeding. Female flies of other species may glue their eggs to the hosts' body after which the hatching larva tunnels inside. In other species, eggs are inserted directly into the hosts' body by the female. Once inside the body of the host, one or more larvae can develop through several stages (instars) for 4 to 14 days. They emerge from the host to pupate inside their last larval skin (puparium). Adults emerge 1 to 2 weeks later. Depending on species one or more generations occur per year.

Pest status: Larval stages develop inside developmental stages of other insects; beneficial insects.

Habitat and food source(s): Larvae (maggots) have hook-like mouthparts that tease apart tissues of their hosts. Adults have lapping mouthparts similar to those of house flies. Individual species are generally host-specific. As a group, most tachinid fly species parasitize caterpillars (Lepidoptera) or beetles (Coleoptera). However, some species develop in sawflies (Hymenoptera), true bugs (Hemiptera), grasshoppers (Orthoptera), or other insects. Adult flies can be found while they visit flowers.

Literature: Mahr and Ridgway 1993.

ORDER TRICHOPTERA
Caddisflies

DESCRIPTION

- Caddisflies are soft-bodied insects with 2 pairs of wings clothed with silky hairs, folded tent-like over their body. They resemble small moths.
- Adults have long antennae.
- Larvae are aquatic, resemble caterpillars and may have gill filaments on the abdomen. Many build cases made of silk and debris woven together and have hooks at the end of the abdomen to hold them in their case. Different groups of caddisflies can be recognized by the characteristics of their cases.
- Adults do not feed and have reduced, non-functional mouthparts. Larvae have chewing mouthparts and resemble caterpillars.
- Most caddisflies (adults and larvae) are under ½ of an inch in length.

LIFE CYCLE

- Metamorphosis is complete (egg, larva, pupa, adult).
- Larvae can spin silk webs which are used to build the cases and to capture food from the water.
- Larvae are scavengers, herbivores, or predators.

PEST STATUS

- Adults and larvae are important components of the food chain for fish and other aquatic organisms.

HABITAT

- Adults are common around streams and are attracted to lights at night.
- Larvae are found mostly in flowing water.

245 CADDISFLIES

Trichoptera: several families   Many species

Description: Adult caddisflies resemble small moths with wings held tent-like over their back when at rest. They have long hair-like antennae. Most species are small (usually ¼ inch or less) and are dull colored. However, some species are more brightly colored. Immature stages or larvae superficially resemble hairless caterpillars. They often have elongated fleshy gills on the underside of the abdomen. Most larvae have a pair of hooks on the (anal) prolegs on the last abdominal segment. Many of them fashion cases of plant material, sand, pebbles, or debris in which they live.

There are many species of caddisflies. Adults can be confused with small moths (Lepidoptera), but they never have coiled "siphoning" mouthparts as do moths, and they usually have long, hair-like antennae. The larvae may be confused with a few aquatic moth species (Lepidoptera), some beetle (Coleoptera) larvae or even dobsonfly larvae (Neuroptera: Corydalidae). The larvae of caddisflies can be distinguished by the claws on the thoracic legs and the anal prolegs.

Life cycle: Adult caddisflies are short lived and spend most of their time mating or laying eggs. Females lay eggs on the edge of the water or by dipping their abdomen into the surface of the water. Caddisfly larvae develop through 4 stages (instars) over several months or even a year. Pupation is almost always in water. There is usually one generation per year.

Pest status: Generally innocuous; adults are attracted to lights and occasionally abundant enough to be noticed; immature stages are aquatic, where they are an important part of the diet of fish.

Habitat and food source(s): Immatures are found in water, usually in flowing water. Larvae are scavengers, herbivores, or predaceous. They can spin silk and use it to form nets to strain material from the water to eat or to form cases in which to hide. The type of case or use of silk for a web depends on the species. Pupal cases are often attached to objects. Adults generally fly quickly from the water. Mating occurs on the ground or on vegetation. Adults are commonly found near lights at night or on foliage near water.

Literature: McCafferty 1981.

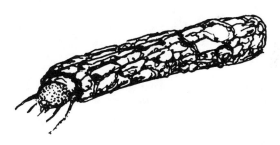

Caddisfly larva in case

ORDER LEPIDOPTERA
Moths, Butterflies, and Skippers

DESCRIPTION

- This is a large order of insects and one of the best known. How do you tell a butterfly from a skipper from a moth? A butterfly, which usually flies during the day, has "clubbed" antennae; a skipper, which looks much like a butterfly, has "hooked" antennae, instead of "clubbed"; and a moth, which generally flies at night, has antennae that are hair-like to feathery, not clubbed.
- Lepidoptera usually have 4 well-developed wings usually covered with overlapping scales as adults. A few adult Lepidoptera have their wings reduced or absent.
- Caterpillars are the feeding immature stages and those of some groups are known as cutworms, armyworms, hornworms, or by other common names.
- Caterpillars have chewing mouthparts, well developed head capsules, and very short antennae. Most caterpillars spin silk to form a cocoon in which they pupate.
- Some abdominal segments of caterpillars have protrusions, "false-legs", or "prolegs" used for locomotion. In most cases prolegs have small hooks (crochets) on the bottom of the prolegs even when the prolegs are reduced. Arrangement of the crochets is often used to identify certain groups of Lepidoptera.
- Mouthparts of adults are formed for siphoning, but some have reduced or non-functional mouthparts.
- Microlepidoptera are often under ¼ inch; the largest moths and butterflies in Texas have a wingspread over 5 inches.

LIFE CYCLE

- All Lepidoptera have complete metamorphosis (egg, caterpillar or larva, pupa sometimes in a cocoon or a naked chrysalis, adult).

PEST STATUS

- This order contains some of our most important pests: such as the bollworm, armyworms, cutworms, the codling moth, clothes moths, and the cabbageworm.
- Most species are rarely abundant or feed only on non-agronomic plant species.
- Many Lepidoptera are valuable food sources for birds, bats and other animals.

• Most caterpillars feed on leaves of plants, but some are leafminers; a few are borers in herbaceous and woody plants; and others feed on stored products including fabric.

• A few caterpillars are predators.

• Adults feed on nectar and some feed on pollen, contributing to pollination.

246 CLOTHES MOTHS

Lepidoptera: Tineidae

Tinea pellionella Linnaeus
and *Tineola bisselliella*
(Hummel)

Description: Adult moths have buff-colored, ¼ inch long wings fringed with hairs and held over their backs when at rest. The fore wings of the **case-making clothes moth**, *Tinea pellionella* Linnaeus, are brownish with three dark spots, while those of the **webbing clothes moth**, *Tinea bisselliella* Hummel, are uniformly golden. Caterpillars of the casemaking clothes moth feed from within a somewhat flattened silken case, which is dragged over the food source. Only their head and legs appear outside, but from either end of the case. The webbing clothes moth feeds inside of silken burrows spun over the fabric surface.

If moths are observed flying around the home, they are more likely to be stored product pests such as the **Indianmeal moth**, *Plodia interpunctella* (Hübner) (Pyralidae) or **Angoumois grain moth**, *Sitotroga cerealella* (Olivier) (Gelechiidae). If damage to fabric is observed, look for silk webbing and granular-looking excrement (frass or fecal pellets)—symptoms of caterpillar infestation. Larvae of **carpet beetles** (Coleoptera) do not produce silk.

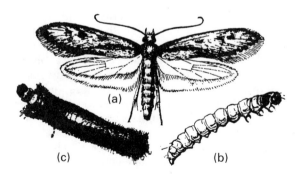

Casemaking clothes moth: (a) adult, (b) larva, and (c) larval case

Life cycle: Female moths lay eggs, singly or in small clusters, that hatch into tiny caterpillars within 4 to 10 days. Larvae develop through several stages (the casemaking clothes moth develops through 5 to 45 instars) until they reach almost ½ inch long. They pupate in silken cases in which fibers from the infested fabric and excrement are incorporated. The life cycle may be completed within 2 months but may take several years.

Pest status: Caterpillars feed mainly on stored fabric and materials of animal origin such as woolens and furs.

Habitat and food source(s): Larvae feed mainly on wool, feathers, fur, hair, upholstered furniture, leather, fish meals, milk powders, lint, dust, or paper. Sometimes they will damage fabrics of plant origin and synthetic materials soiled with oils or blended with animal fibers. The casemaking clothes moth will also feed on stored plant materials (e.g., spices, tobacco, hemp). These species avoid light in all stages and are located by examining stored animal product materials such as old clothing, woolens, yarn, furs, feather pillows and felt on piano strikers.

Literature: Cocke 1979; Ebeling 1978.

247 BAGWORMS

Lepidoptera: Psychidae

Thyridopteryx ephemeraeformis (Haworth) and others

Description: This insect is usually first detected by observing the bags produced by the larval (caterpillar) stages. Bags vary in size (up to 2 inches long and ½ inch wide) by growth stage (instar) of the larva and between species, and appearance varies with the bits and pieces of host plant leaves, twigs, and bark fragments woven into the silken bag in a shingle-like fashion.

Caterpillars of a few other species construct bags or sacks (i.e., casemaking clothes moths, cigar case makers), however, only bagworms incorporate plant debris into the sacs.

Life cycle: Bagworm species vary slightly in habits and life cycle. On evergreens the bagworm spends winter months in the egg stage within the sealed bag produced by females the previous fall. In the spring (late-May, early-June), tiny ⅛ inch long caterpillars hatch, lower themselves on silken strands to new foliage and construct a tiny conical bag that they carry upright as they move. As the caterpillar grows through 4 or more stages (instars), it enlarges its bag. Full-grown caterpillars within bags are up to 1 inch long before pupating in August or September. Seven to 10 days later, the pupae of male moths wriggle out of the bottom of the bag before the male emerges, leaving the empty pupal skin behind. Adult males with short ½ inch-long clear wings, hairy black bodies, and feathery antennae emerge. They fly and seek out a female to mate. Females do not develop into moths, but remain inside bags and resemble caterpillars, with no functional eyes, legs, mouthparts, or antennae. After mating, females produce a large clutch (500 to 1,000) of eggs inside their bodies and die. Other bagworm species spend winter months as partially-developed caterpillars that complete feeding and pupate in the spring. Adults emerge in the spring, although some emerge through October. Feeding larvae of all stages occur during the spring and summer.

Pest status: Caterpillar stages in bags feed on leaves and can defoliate shrubs and trees. Several species occur in the state and may occur on various trees and shrubs.

Habitat and food source(s): A wide range of boadleaf and evergreen trees and shrubs serve as hosts for bagworm species, including arborvitae and other ornamental conifers, boxelder, cedar, cypress, elm, fruit and nut trees, juniper, live oak, locust, maple, persimmon, pines, salt cedar, sumac, sycamore, wild cherry, willow, and many other ornamental plants. Leaves may be damaged by having the outer layer of cells (epidermis) removed by small caterpillars or all tissues but major leaf veins removed by larger caterpillars. Infested plants develop more bagworms each year because female stages do not fly. They may become abundant enough in some years to completely defoliate their host plant. Nearby host plants can remain unaffected. Completely defoliated evergreen species such as arborvitae and juniper, are killed. During leaf-feeding, the caterpillars emerge from the top of the bag and hang onto the host plant with their legs and sometimes with a silken thread. The bottom of the bag remains open to allow fecal material (frass) to pass out of the bag. During molts and pupation, caterpillars seal the bags. Dispersal of bagworms to new host plants occurs when young caterpillars hanging from silken threads are spread by wind or perhaps by birds.

Literature: Hamman 1981; Johnson and Lyons 1988.

Angoumois Grain Moth

Lepidoptera: Gelechiidae   *Sitotroga cerealella* (Olivier)

Description: Adult moths are small buff-colored, about ½ to ⅓ inch long. They are quite delicate and may show two small darker spots on the front wing. Larvae (caterpillars) are small, about ⅕ inch long, generally white with a darker head.

There are several other small moths that feed on grain and grain products; e.g., **Indianmeal moth (263),** *Plodia interpunctella* (Hübner), Pyralidae, and **flour moths,** *Ephestia* spp., Pyralidae.

Life cycle: Adults may be seen flying about infested grain storage areas. Female moths may lay several hundred eggs from which small caterpillars hatch. Larvae develop through several stages (instars) inside grain kernels. The larval stage normally lasts 20 to 24 days and the entire life cycle takes about 5 weeks. There may be 6 or more generations per year depending on the temperature and environmental conditions. Larvae pupate inside the kernels of the grain and later the adult emerges.

Pest status: Infests grain in stored grain in bins, groceries or ornamental wall hangings.

Habitat and food source(s): Angoumois grain moths feed on whole kernels of corn, wheat and other grains. Each larva usually feeds entirely inside one kernel. Adults are attracted to lights or can be seen flying about infested grain storage areas.

Literature: Metcalf et al. 1962.

248–250   TOMATO PINWORM

Lepidoptera: Gelechiidae   *Keiferia lycopersicella* (Walsingham)

Description: Caterpillars are small, ¼ inch long when fully grown, and yellowish-green to purplish-black with brown head capsules.

Other common members of Gelechiidae include: the **pink bollworm,** *Pectinophora gossypiella* (Saunders); and the **rednecked peanutworm,** *Stegasta bosqueella* (Chambers). Closely related families include Plutellidae, which contain the **diamondback moth,** *Plutella xylostella* (Linnaeus) (**249**), and the Yponomertidae, which contain the **ermine moth (250),** *Attera punctella* (Cramer).

Life cycle: The adult moth is small and brownish in color. Females lay eggs on the undersides of leaves in an erratic pattern on the upper half of the plant. Caterpillars hatch from the egg and grow incrementally through stages (instars) before pupating (into a chrysalis) in the soil. The life cycle is rather short, with 7 or more generations produced per year under greenhouse conditions within a 4-to-5-month period.

Pest status: Larval stages (caterpillars) damage leaves and fruit of field-and greenhouse-grown tomatoes.

Habitat and food source(s): Tomato pinworms are a major pest of greenhouse-grown tomatoes, but will also infest field-grown tomatoes, potatoes, and eggplant. Small caterpillars produce serpentine and/or blotch mines in leaves, and later cause leaves to fold or roll at the midrib using tight silk webbing. Larger larvae chew pin-holes into the base, near the stem (under the calyx) of developing buds and ripening fruit.

Literature: Little 1963; Metcalf et al. 1962; Westcott 1973.

251, 252   SQUASH VINE BORER

Lepidoptera: Sessidae   *Melittia cucurbitae* (Harris)

Description: The day-flying adults are very colorful and superficially resemble wasps (Hymenoptera). The fore wings are covered with metallic olive-brown scales. The hind wings are mostly clear with a brown edge. The abdomen is bright red and ringed with black bands. Adults have a wing spread of about 1–1½ inches. The larva (**252**) is white with a brown head. It does not appear to have prolegs and grows to be about 1 inch long.

There is at least one other species in Texas, the **southwestern squash vine borer,** *Melittia calabaza* Duckworth and Eichlin (**251**).

Life cycle: Adult females lay eggs on leaves and stems of squash. Larvae hatch from eggs and soon burrow into host plant stems. The caterpillars develop through several stages (instars). When full-grown the larvae climb from the stems and pupate a few inches deep in the soil. Adults feed on nectar and adults sit on the leaves of squash early in the morning. There are probably two generations in Texas.

Pest status: One of the most damaging and most common pests of squash, especially in home gardens.

Habitat and food source(s): They feed almost exclusively in squash and closely related wild plants. They may attack a few related plants like melons and cucumbers on occasion. Larvae are borers and tunnel inside the stems, causing considerable damage to squash. Excrement (frass) may extrude from the stems and stems may wilt and die.

Literature: Metcalf et al. 1962; Swan and Papp 1978.

PEACHTREE BORER

Lepidoptera: Sessidae   *Synanthedon exitiosa* (Say)

Description: The most commonly encountered stage of this insect is the caterpillar tunneling underneath the bark at the base of the trunk of its host plant. Fully-grown caterpillars are about 1¼ inches long, cream-colored with brown head capsules. Tiny hooks (crochets) on the underside of the abdominal prolegs are arranged in transverse rows. Adult moths are day-flying clearwing moths that superficially resemble wasps. They have a wingspan of 1 to 1½ inches. Females are bluish-black and have an orange band across the middle of the abdomen. The front wings are covered with black scales. Males are smaller and appear more wasp-like, with numerous small, yellow stripes and clear wings.

The **lesser peachtree borer,** *Synanthedon pictipes* (Grote and Robinson) is similar to the peachtree borer, but caterpillars feed under bark around wounds, usually in the upper trunk and large branches. Day-flying moths are metallic blue-black with yellow bands on the second and, to a lesser extent, on the fourth abdominal segments. The **American plum borer,** *Euzophera semifuneralis* (Walker) (Pyralidae), produces similar damage, but caterpillars

Peachtree borer, male (left) and female

are dingy-white to brownish-gray, have more hairy bodies and the pattern of tiny hooks (crochets) on the abdominal prolegs is circular.

Life cycle: Adult peachtree borers emerge primarily in August and September to disperse, mate, and seek new host plants. Female moths lay eggs around the base of host trees. Caterpillars hatch from eggs in about 10 days and tunnel into the bark. Caterpillars molt through several stages (instars) while they grow. Winter is spent as a partially-grown larva (caterpillar) in the tree trunk. After 10 to 11 months fully-grown caterpillars crawl out and pupate in the soil within bullet-shaped, brown silk cocoons. The life cycle is complete in about one year.

Pest status: Larvae tunnel into the trunks of peach trees and related trees, often killing young trees.

Habitat and food source(s): The peachtree borer attacks trees of the *Prunus* genus, including peach trees, apricot, cherry, and plum. Caterpillars feed on the inner bark (cambium layer) of the tree trunk, from 3 inches below to 10 inches above the soil line. Feeding in this area disrupts the tree's ability to transport water and nutrients, hampering tree growth. The site of infestation often oozes sap resembling a mass of amber-like gum and brown caterpillar excrement (frass). Extensive feeding can cause death of scaffolding limbs, and if the caterpillar tunnels around the circumference of the tree, "girdling" the trunk, the tree will die.

Literature: Holloway 1985; Johnson and Lyon 1988; Thomas et al. 1972; Westcott 1973.

253 GIANT LEOPARD MOTH

Lepidoptera: Arctiidae

Hypercompe scribonia (Stoll)

Description: The **giant leopard moth**, *Hypercompe scribonia* (Stoll), gets its name from the spots on the fore wings. The fore wings are about 3 inches across and nearly white with black spots that are solid black to nearly circular. The hind wings are nearly white with a few small black spots and streaks. The thorax is also white with black markings. The upper surface of the abdomen is primarily blue-black with orange spots. Caterpillars appear black and covered with stiff black hairs. The underlying skin is pink to red between the segments. The red color is easily seen when the larva curls into a ball when disturbed.

Adults of this species are sometimes confused with the **leopard moth**, *Zeuzera pyrina* (Linnaeus) (Lepidoptera: Cossidae), whose larvae are wood borers, but this species has not been recorded in Texas. The **carpenterworm**, *Prionoxystus robiniae* (Peck) (Lepidoptera: Cossidae), adults have a 3-inch wingspan with light gray wings mottled in black resembling bark. Hind wings of males are marked with orange. Caterpillars grow to 2 inches (leopard moth) or 3 inches (carpenterworm).

Also see sections on the clearwing moths (**251, 252**) (Lepidoptera: Sessiidae), metallic or flat-headed wood-boring beetles (**148—150**) (Coleoptera: Buprestidae) and long-horned or round-headed borer beetles (**171—178**) (Coleoptera: Cerambycidae). Some other insects, such as the **American plum borer**, *Euzophera semifuneralis* (Walker) (Lepidoptera: Pyralidae) also tunnel in poorly pruned branch stubs. Caterpillars, as opposed to beetle larvae, have false legs (prolegs) on the abdominal segments that bear rows of tiny hooks (crochets), a feature that can be used to distinguish between the two groups.

Life cycle: Caterpillars overwinter and are most abundant in the spring. The cocoon is covered in silk and the last larval skin with black hairs may be attached to the cocoon. Adults emerge in late spring and are most commonly seen at lights.

Pest status: The large black fuzzy caterpillars move rapidly during the day and therefore are conspicuous. They are not reported as causing skin irritation. Great leopard moths are commonly attracted to lights. Their relatively large size and bold markings make them conspicuous.

Habitat and food source(s): Caterpillars have chewing mouthparts. Caterpillars feed on leaves of many plants including plaintain, dandelion, honeysuckle, maple, willow, and banana. They probably feed on many other plants occasionally. They are most common in moist habitats on low growing plants.

Literature: Johnson and Lyon 1988, Mitchell and Zim 1987, Wright 1993.

CODLING MOTH

Lepidoptera: Tortricidae   *Cydia pomonella* (Linnaeus)

Description: Adult moths are grayish with wavy brown cross bands and coppery patches on the wing tips. The wingspan is ½ to ¾ inch, but wings are held over the back of the body when at rest. Caterpillars are pinkish-white with brown head capsules and grow to ¾ inch long. Also see **oriental fruit moth.**

Life cycle: Winter is spent as a fully-grown caterpillar in a silken cocoon under bark scales on host tree trunks or on nearby objects. They pupate in the spring and emerge as adult moths within 2 to 4 weeks. Mated females lay eggs singly on leaves, twigs and near fruit, 2 to 6 weeks after bloom. Tiny caterpillars hatch from eggs in 6 to 20 days and feed on leaves before tunneling into fruit where they develop through several stages (instars) over 3 to 5 weeks. They leave the fruit to seek a suitable pupation site. The life cycle can be completed in about 28 days, but is affected by temperature. Multiple generations occur annually.

Pest status: The typical "worm in the apple"; a major production pest of apples grown in the Texas Panhandle.

Habitat and food source(s): Codling moth caterpillars feed in fruit of apple, pear, English walnut and other fruits. Caterpillars enter fruit from the blossom end (calyx) and tunnel into the core where they feed on the seeds. Masses of excrement (frass) are associated with the tunneling and are expelled from the blossom end of the fruit. Damaged fruit may drop from the tree.

Literature: Metcalf et al. 1962.

ORIENTAL FRUIT MOTH

Lepidoptera: Tortricidae   *Grapholita molesta* (Busck)

Description: Moths are gray with brownish wing markings (bands) and are about ¼ inch long (½ inch wingspan). Caterpillars are pinkish-white with brown heads, growing to about ½ inch long. They possess a five-toothed comb-shaped plate on the last body segment.

In central Texas, similar damage to plums and peaches is produced by **peach twig borer,** *Anarsia lineatella* Zeller (Gelechiidae). These caterpillars grow to ⅜ inch long and are reddish-brown with yellow-white bands around the body. Apples can also be damaged by caterpillars of the **codling moth,** *Cydia pomonella* (Linnaeus) (Tortricidae). Peaches can also be infested with the creamy-white and legless larvae of the **plum curculio (199),** *Conotrachelus nenuphar* (Herbst) (Coleoptera: Curculionidae).

Life cycle: Fully-grown caterpillars (larvae) overwinter in a silken cocoon under bark, dried fruit or ground debris, and pupate in spring. Adults emerge in spring, mate, and females lay flat whitish eggs on leaves and twigs shortly after bloom. Caterpillars hatching from first generation eggs tunnel into twigs. Those of later generations tunnel into fruit. Up to 7 generations can occur per year.

Pest status: Caterpillars damage peaches, apples and other fruit trees in east Texas.

Habitat and food source(s): Caterpillars chew into twigs and fruit of peach and other fruit trees including apple, pear, apricot, and plum. In spring, caterpillars tunnel into succulent new growth of twigs, causing die back or terminals, a type of damage called "flagging." Heavily damaged trees appear bushy and stunted. Fruit injury may be severe in orchards where late-maturing peach varieties, apples, and pears are grown. Fruit of plum and early-maturing peach varieties are not attacked. Caterpillars enter fruit at the stem (so no external evidence of damage is visible) and into the sides where two neighboring fruit touch. Larvae feed around the seed and produce accumulations of fecal material (frass) where they feed. Infested fruit decompose rapidly in storage. Some ornamental shrubs, such as photinia, may be attacked in the fall.

Literature: Metcalf et al. 1962; Thomas et al. 1972.

HICKORY SHUCKWORM

Lepidoptera: Tortricidae   *Cydia caryana* (Fitch)

Description: Adult moths are about ⅜ inch long and the fore wings, which are held over the back when at rest, are gray-black. The caterpillar stage, commonly encountered while shucking pecans, is dirty white with a reddish-brown head capsule and grows to about ⅜ inch long. Caterpillars have

3 pairs of true legs on (thoracic) segments behind the head capsule and pairs of false legs (prolegs) on several of the abdominal segments.

Also see **pecan nut casebearer (Figure 26)**, **pecan weevil (200–201)** and **Indianmeal moth (263)**.

Life cycle: Winter is spent as a mature caterpillar within the pecan shucks. Caterpillars pupate in late winter or early spring. Adult moths begin emerging in early April. Early in the summer, mated females lay eggs on developing hickory nuts, leaves and the galls of pecan phylloxera (Homoptera: Phylloxeridae). Caterpillars hatching from eggs develop inside hickory nuts and phylloxera galls. For later generations from early July through harvest, eggs are laid on developing shucks of pecans. Larvae develop through several stages (instars) within developing pecans before pupating inside. Pupae wriggle out of the shuck through an exit hole cut by the larvae just before adult moths emerge, and thereafter leave the empty honey-colored pupal skin behind. Up to 5 generations can develop during the year. Adult emergence peaks occur in mid-May, late June, mid-August and early to mid-September.

Pest status: Caterpillar (larval) stages tunnel into the nutlets and shucks of pecans, which can result in loss of yield and quality.

Habitat and food source(s): This species attacks developing pecans and hickory nuts. Caterpillars feeding inside the developing nut before the pecan shell hardens (water stage, June through mid-August) cause nuts to drop from the tree. Later, after the pecan shell hardens, caterpillars tunneling through the shuck prevent proper development of kernels and cause a delay in nut maturity. Shucks sticking to pecans fail to open to release the nut, causing harvest difficulty. Scarring and black discoloration of pecan shell associated with larval tunneling also reduces quality.

Literature: Hall 1982; Holloway et al. 1984.

254, 255   NANTUCKET PINE TIP MOTH

Lepidoptera: Tortricidae   *Rhyacionia frustrana*
                                            (Comstock)

Description: The adult moth is slightly less than ¼ inch long with reddish-brown to copper and silver-gray marked wings, which are held over the back of the body when at rest. The larva (caterpillar) (**255**) grows to about ⅜ inch long with a black head, and as it develops the body color changes from cream to orangish-brown.

There may be a complex of tip moth species, particularly in west Texas. In addition, occasionally caterpillars of the **southern pine coneworm**, *Dioryctria amatella* (Hulst) (Pyralidae) also tunnel into shoots of southern pines. However, caterpillars are much larger and creamy white to dark gray-brown in body color, rather than orangish.

Life cycle: Winter is spent in the pupal stage within infested host plants. Adult moths emerge in early spring (February-March), mate and females lay whitish to orangish eggs on needles on developing tips or buds. Cream-colored, ¹⁄₁₆-inch-long larvae hatch from eggs within 5 to 31 days depending on temperature, and begin feeding on the surface of new growth before tunneling into needles. As they grow, they tunnel into shoot tips and produce protective webbing around their feeding sites. Fecal material and masses of resin accumulate on the outside of infested tips. Larval development occurs in 2 to 4 weeks. Thereafter, they form dark brown ¼-inch-long pupae in a silk cell within the tunnels. The pupae wriggle out prior to adult moth emergence, leaving the empty pupal skin protruding from the end of the tunnels. In central Texas, 4–5 generations may occur per year with overlapping generations occurring in the fall, while in north Texas there may be only 2.

Pest status: Caterpillars tunnel through the shoots and tips of pine host plants, destroying branch tips. It is a serious pest in seed orchards, Christmas tree plantings, and forest tree nurseries.

Habitat and food source(s): This species is the main pest of Texas-grown Virginia pines produced as Christmas trees. It also attacks other young southern pine trees, with shortleaf and loblolly pines less than 15 feet tall being most susceptible to attack. Damaged buds and shoots of pines turn brown and die. Afterward, tree growth can be stunted or deformed as new shoots grow around damaged shoots, producing branched growth referred to as "crow's footing." Trees so deformed have a lower value and can be unsightly.

Literature: Carter et al. 1980; Robinson 1984.

256 PUSS CATERPILLAR OR "ASP"

Lepidoptera: Megalopygidae   *Megalopyge opercularis*
                                  (J. E. Smith)

Description: Adults, known as **flannel moths**, are rarely encountered. The caterpillars grow to about 1 inch long and are furry in appearance, being completely covered by thick tan to grayish-white hairs that taper toward the back end. Among the long body hairs are shorter spines that discharge venom upon contact. The head and legs are not visible from above.

Other stinging caterpillars include larval stages of the **io moth (302, 303)**, *Automeris io* (Fabricius) (Saturniidae); the **hag moth,** *Phobetron pithecium* (J. E. Smith) (Limacodidae); the **saddleback caterpillar,** *Sibine stimulea* (Clemens) (Limacodidae); and the **buck moth,** *Hemileuca maia* (Drury) (Saturniidae). However, many hairy or spiny caterpillars may produce a similar skin irritation, and care should be taken to avoid skin contact with them. The io moth caterpillar is pale green with yellowish and maroon stripes edged with white along each side of the body. The body is adorned with clusters of stiff spines. They can grow to be about 2½ inches long. The buck moth caterpillar resembles the io moth caterpillar but is purple-black with a reddish head and lacks the body stripes. The saddleback caterpillar is an unusual looking caterpillar with a brown body marked with a bright green area resembling a saddle blanket with an oval purplish-brown spot in its center. Fleshy protuberances bearing spines occur along the sides of the body, with larger pairs near the front and rear. They grow to about 1 inch long before pupating. The even weirder hag moth caterpillar is about ⅝ inch long

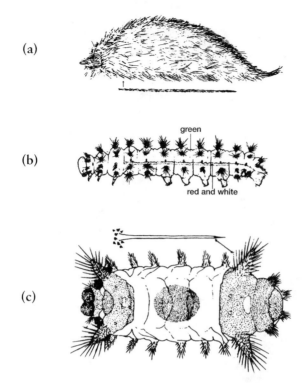

(a)

(b)

green

red and white

(c)

Stinging caterpillars: (a) puss caterpillar with enlarged featherlike hair; (b) io moth larva showing typical tubercles; (c) saddleback caterpillar and enlarged hollow spine

when fully grown and has 9 pairs of curved and twisted fleshy projections arising from the sides of the body bearing stinging hairs.

Life cycle: The puss caterpillar spends winter in the cocoon or pupal stage. Adult moths emerge in late spring or early summer and lay eggs on host plant leaves. Tiny whitish fuzzy larvae hatch from eggs and develop through several stages (instars) over a period of several weeks before they pupate.

Pest status: The caterpillar is called an "asp" by Texans, although there are other caterpillars that also produce a painful skin rash from contact with venomous spines. Hypersensitive individuals may experience a generalized systemic reaction requiring medical attention.

Habitat and food source(s): Caterpillars feed on leaves of many trees, shrubs and bushes, such as holly.

Literature: Hamman 1981.

PECAN NUT CASEBEARER

Lepidoptera: Pyralidae

Acrobasis nuxvorella Neunzig

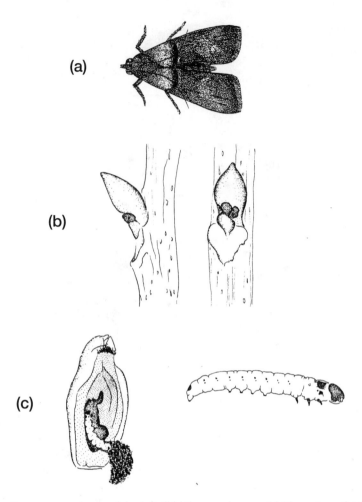

(a)

(b)

(c)

Pecan nut casebearer: (a) adult; (b) hibernaculum, and (c) larva in nutlet (left)

Description: Adult moths are ⅓ inch long, with wings held over the back of the body when at rest. Their silvery-gray fore wings are marked with a cross band composed of a ridge of dark scales followed by a line of lighter scales. Eggs are oval, flat and tiny (⅟₅₀ inch diameter). They are greenish-white when first laid, but become speckled with red and then turn pink just prior to hatching. Caterpillars (larvae) are first whitish and later olive-gray to jade green as they grow to be about ½ inch long before pupating.

The **hickory shuckworm**, *Cydia caryana* (Fitch) (Tortricidae), can be confused with this species, particularly when caterpillars of both species tunnel through pecan shucks after pecan shells harden in nut development (beginning in mid-August). However, shuckworm larvae can be distinguished by their dirty white to cream color and reddish-brown heads, and larvae tunneling in nutlets do not produce excrement (frass) visible on the outside of the nutlet.

Life cycle: Partially-grown larvae spend the winter in special silken cases (hibernacula) constructed on twigs and branches, usually next to the base of a dormant bud. Larvae emerge in the spring after bud break and complete development by feeding on buds and tunneling into developing shoots. They pupate in hollowed shoots and bark crevices. Adult moths appear in late April and May, depending on seasonal temperature levels and location within Texas. Eggs of this first generation are laid by mated females on the blackened tips of pollinated nutlets. In 4 to 5 days, tiny caterpillars hatch and crawl to buds and leaf stems (petioles) below the nuts to feed, leaving the empty egg shell behind. After a day or two, caterpillars begin tunneling into the base of nutlets and develop through several stages (instars) over a period of 4 to 5 weeks before pupating inside a hollowed out nutlet. Second generation moths emerge from the pupae in 9 to 14 days, generally from mid-June to mid-July. The duration of time from first to second generation egg stage is 42 to 45 days. From 2–4 generations occur annually. The larvae of the last generation feed on pecan shucks, buds, and leaf stems and form a hibernaculum by mid-November.

Pest status: Caterpillars tunnel into developing pecan nutlets and, when numerous, can cause a loss in yield; a major pest of pecan production.

Habitat and food source(s): Larvae feed on nutlets during late spring and early summer. Caterpillars of the first generation are the most damaging to the pecan crop because each larva can tunnel into the base of many pecan nutlets, often every nutlet in a cluster. Silk webbing and black granular excrement (frass), visible outside of the nutlet, are produced by caterpillars tunneling into the base of nutlets, and damaged nutlets often fall from the tree, reducing yield. Caterpillars of the later generations are less damaging because the nutlets are much larger at that time and fewer nuts are damaged by each larva.

Literature: Holloway et al. 1984; Knutson and Ree 1995.

257   SUGARCANE BORER

Lepidoptera: Pyralidae   *Diatraea saccharalis*
                                          (Fabricius)

Description: Adults are small brown moths with darker brown bands on each fore wing. Full-grown caterpillars are about 1 inch long, white to yellow with rich brown head capsules and first thoracic segment. Each body segment is marked with round brown to black spots.

Several other pyralid stalk borer species are agricultural pests in Texas. The **European corn borer,** *Ostrinia nubilalis* (Hübner), **southern cornstalk borer,** *Diatraea crambidoides* (Grote) and **southwestern corn borer,** *Diatraea grandiosella* Dyar, are primarily pests of corn in the Texas Panhandle. Caterpillars of European corn borers are brownish to pinkish with small dark spots on each body segment, whereas those of the southern cornstalk and

Sugarcane borer larva

southwestern corn borers are yellowish-white with round brown spots on each body segment similar to the sugarcane borer. In the southern part of the state, the **Mexican rice borer**, *Eoreuma loftini* (Dyar), has a similar biology and host range to the sugarcane borer. Caterpillars lack dark spots, but have two purple-red dash-like stripes on each body segment that do not connect to the stripes on adjacent segments. Along the Texas coast, **rice stalk borer**, *Chilo plejadellus* Zincken, caterpillars also lack dark spots, but have a pair of continuous light brown to purplish stripes all along the sides of their bodies.

Life cycle: Larvae overwinter in cells in crop stubble and pupate in the spring. Mated female moths lay elliptical to oval eggs in clusters that appear like fish scales on the midrib of the upper surface of leaves. Tiny caterpillars hatch in 3 to 7 days and develop through several stages (instars) over about 25 days before pupating. Adults emerge from pupae in about 10 days. Up to 5 generations can occur annually.

Pest status: Caterpillars (larvae) feed in stalks of crops, ornamental plants and weeds, occasionally reducing yield in heavily infested plantings. They occur in the eastern half of the state from south Texas through the coastal bend.

Habitat and food source(s): Host plants include sugarcane, corn, sorghum, rice, pampas grass, and other cultivated and wild tall grasses. Feeding by young larvae near the soil line on small plants causes the growing point to die, a symptom called "deadheart," which can reduce plant stands. On older plants, young larvae first tunnel into the leaf sheath and axil. Older larvae tunnel into the stalk (pith). On sorghum and some other plants, damaged areas develop a purple to reddish discoloration. Heavily damaged plants can be stunted, have reduced seed production, break over (lodge), and may die. In rice, seed head development is interrupted by larval tunneling causing a symptom called "white heads."

Literature: Browning et al. 1989; Little 1963; Teetes et al. 1983.

258   GREATER WAX MOTH

Lepidoptera: Pyralidae   *Galleria mellonella*
                                                (Linnaeus)

Description: Adult moths are grayish- to purplish-brown, have dark markings and lead-colored tips on the fore wings, pale brownish or yellowish hind wings, and a wingspan of about 1 to 1¼ inches. Wings are held over the back when at rest. Full-grown caterpillars vary in color but are generally dirty white, 1½ inches long.

Life cycle: Winter is spent mainly in the larval or pupal stages, although adult moths can emerge during warm periods. Mated females lay eggs at night. Tiny caterpillars hatching from eggs are initially white and turn yellow, brown to black on the upper side as they develop through 7−8 stages (instars). They pupate in tough silken cocoons in and around the bee hive in protected places. Up to 3 generations occur annually.

Pest status: Caterpillars (larvae) are destructive to bee hives because of their tunneling and feeding habits on honeycombs.

Habitat and food source(s): This is the only caterpillar pest known to infest bee hives. Caterpillars tunnel through wax of honeycombs during the night and construct silken tunnels and feed on wax, pollen, and cocoons. Older, dark honeycombs of weakened colonies are more frequently attacked and seriously damaged. Tunnels through infested honeycombs are littered with fragments, silk webs, and caterpillar excrement (frass). This insect is cultured for fish bait and scientific studies.

Literature: Little 1963; Swan and Papp 1972.

259−262   TROPICAL SOD WEBWORM

Lepidoptera: Pyralidae
Herpetogramma phaeopteralis Guenée

Description: Adult moths are dingy-brown moths with wingspans of about ¾ inch. Wings are held flat over the back when at rest, giving the insect a triangular appearance. Caterpillars (260) grow to almost ¾ inch long, appearing translucent green with small dark-colored spots or plates arranged on each body segment and a dark, yellowish-brown head capsule.

Several other species of **sod webworms** occur in Texas, mainly from the genus, *Crambus*. These sod webworms can be distinguished in the adult stage by the way the moths roll their wings around their bodies when at rest rather than holding them out. Larvae are distinguished by the different patterns of plates (panicula) on their thoracic segments. (See **fall armyworm (321).**) Other common plant-feeding pyralid moths include the **genista caterpillar (261)**, *Uresiphita reversalis* (Guenée), which occurs on Texas mountain laurel, and the **lesser canna leafroller (262)**, *Geshna cannalis* (Quaintance). (See **larger canna leafroller (264).**)

Life cycle: Females lay creamy white eggs in clusters of up to 15 eggs on grass blades, stems and turf debris. Tiny ½2-inch caterpillars hatch from eggs in 6 to 10 days and develop through 7 or 8 stages (instars) over 25 to 50 days, depending upon temperature. Full grown larvae form a ⅜-inch reddish-brown pupa in the thatch, sometimes within a shapeless bag spun by the caterpillar. Development from egg to adult occurs in about 6 weeks. Several generations occur during the year, but those occurring in the fall are larger, overlapping and potentially more damaging to turf grass. This species only survives in areas where mild winters allow all stages to continue to develop.

Pest status: Outbreaks occur in turf grass in Houston and elsewhere; numerous low-flying moths are usually associated with infestations.

Habitat and food source(s): Caterpillars feed during the night on turf grasses, including Bermuda grass, St. Augustine grass, centipede grass, Bahia grass, and zoysia grass. Damaged grass blades initially appear notched and ragged as tissues are removed from the edges until the entire leaf is consumed. Damaged turf is usually spotty within a lawn, but areas enlarge as caterpillars migrate in search of more food. Heavily damaged turf grass usually recovers, but may die. St. Augustine grass recovers much slower than Bermuda grass.

Literature: Kerr 1955.

263 INDIANMEAL MOTH

Lepidoptera: Pyralidae   *Plodia interpunctata*
                                          (Hübner)

Description: Moths are ⅜ to ½ inch long with wings folded over the back. Wings are two-toned, with the bases a pale gray and the ends reddish brown or copperish. Caterpillars are dirty white with brown heads. They grow to about ½ inch long and may become yellowish, pinkish, brownish or greenish.

Indianmeal moths are often mistaken for **clothes moths (246)** (Tineidae) or the **Angoumois grain moth,** *Sitotroga cerealella* (Olivier) (Gelechiidae). Other major stored-grain pests are **rice weevils (204),** *Sitophilus oryzae* (Linnaeus) and **granary weevils,** *S. granarius* (Linnaeus) (Coleoptera: Curculionidae).

Life cycle: Female moths lay eggs, singly or in clusters, on suitable larval food. Caterpillars hatch from eggs and produce silken tunnels for protection while feeding. Larval development varies in length with temperature and type of food material. Just before pupating, larvae leave the food source. Caterpillars can be found crawling on walls and ceilings searching for a place to spin a cocoon. Development from egg to adult takes from 27 to 305 days, and 7 or 8 generations can occur in a year.

Pest status: Moths are often found flying in kitchens and other rooms of the house, being a nuisance to occupants; appearance of moths is an indication of a breeding population of caterpillars in some type of stored food.

Habitat and food source(s): Caterpillars feed in flour (including whole wheat and cornmeal or Indian meal), shelled corn, and other broken stored grains, dried fruit, seeds, crackers, biscuits, nuts, powdered milk, chocolate, candy, red peppers, and dog food. Caterpillars produce a loose silken mat on the top surface of infested food material.

Literature: Ebeling 1978; Little 1963.

THE WATER LILY LEAFCUTTER

Lepidoptera: Pyralidae   *Synclita obliteralis* (Walker)

Description: Adult moths have a ⁷⁄₁₆ to ⅝-inch wingspan, with the wings of the smaller male dark brown mottled with brownish and white mottled markings and those of the larger female being grayish-brown with orange and dark brown mottled markings. The water lily leafcutter caterpillar's habits are truly unique. They live inside air-filled cases constructed from 2 disk-shaped pieces of leaves cut from a lily pad and held together with silk threads. They are sometimes called "sandwich man" moths. The caterpillars are creamy-white, although darker towards the yellow-brown head.

Life cycle: Adult moths lay eggs on water lily leaves. Caterpillars hatch from eggs and develop through several stages before pupating in the case constructed by the larva.

Pest status: Caterpillars feed on lily pads, causing water garden plants to look unsightly.

Habitat and food source(s): Caterpillars feed on a wide variety of water lily species, and this species is known to feed on nearly 60 species of plants. Caterpillars feed from the leaf margins, cutting disk-shaped pieces from leaves and leaving lily pads appearing ragged. Although water lily leaves can become severely tattered, damage is superficial and rarely threatens plant health. Although not truly aquatic insects (they do not have gills), air-filled cases in which caterpillars live allow them to remain underneath the water surface for extended periods.

Literature: Habeck 1991.

264   LARGER CANNA LEAFROLLER

Lepidoptera: Hesperiidae   *Calpodes ethlius* (Stoll)

Description: The adult stage is a large brown skipper butterfly with clear white spots on the front and hind wings. The wingspan is about 2 inches. Caterpillars hatching from eggs are initially clear white, but become semi-transparent pale green with dark orange heads marked with black as they grow. As with other skipper caterpillars, the "neck" behind the head capsule is somewhat constricted (strangulated).

The **lesser canna leafroller (262)**, *Geshna cannalis* (Quaintance) (Pyralidae), also feed on *Canna* species.

Life cycle: Adults lay hemispherical whitish eggs on host plant leaves. Caterpillars develop through several stages (instars) over a period of several weeks before pupating in rolled leaves in a pale green chrysalis with a projection (front tubercle) on the head. There are 3 or more generations annually.

Pest status: Also called the **Brazilian skipper,** caterpillars feed on leaves of canna lilies, causing these ornamental plants to look unsightly.

Habitat and food source(s): Caterpillars feed on *Canna* species. They use silk threads to "tie up" newly developed, unrolling leaves. They feed inside the rolled leaves through much of their development. Leaves become tattered and often malformed as terminal growth becomes tangled in rolled leaves. Adults are active, powerful flyers, and sip nectar from many types of flowers.

Literature: Arnett 1985; Holland 1913; Howe 1975; Klots 1960; Metcalf et al. 1962; Westcott 1973.

265   FIELD SKIPPER

Lepidoptera: Hesperiidae   *Atalopedes campestris*
                                       (Boisduval)

Description: The male butterfly is orange-brown with a single large black spot on each fore wing, whereas the female is dark brown with a few silver and orange spots on the fore wings. The wingspan is about 1 inch. Young caterpillars are greenish-white with oversized black heads. Mature larvae are smooth, olive-green, and tapered toward the back end. The body is constricted just behind the head, making larvae appear as if they had a neck. Two or three chalky-white spots occur on the underside between the back legs.

There are about 250 different skippers in North America, 11 of which feed on Bermuda grass. This is the only group of butterflies that feeds on the forage and turf grasses. The butterflies get their name from the rapid, direct and short flight behavior that make them appear to "skip" across the field.

Life cycle: Mated females lay ½₀ inch diameter eggs singly and glued to the grass blades. Tiny caterpillars hatch in 4 to 5 days and develop through several stages (instars), maturing in 3 to 4 weeks. They form a blackish-brown pupa in leaves and soil that may be wrapped with silk. The adult butterfly emerges in about 10 days. Caterpillar numbers are greatest in mid-July.

Pest status: Caterpillars (larvae) occasionally injure Bermuda grass hay fields in northeastern Texas, reducing yield.

Habitat and food source(s): Large numbers of larvae (50 or more per square yard) occasionally infest Bermuda grass hay fields, where they con-

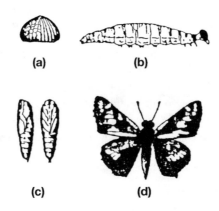

       (a)   **(b)**

       (c)   **(d)**

Life cycle of field skipper: (a) egg; (b) caterpillar; (c) pupa; (d) adult

sume leaves, leaving only stems and lower foliage and thereby reducing yield. They will also feed on St. Augustine grass. Heavy infestations are often very localized. When their food plants are consumed, large numbers of caterpillars migrate to adjacent areas, crawling up buildings and attacking lawns. Adults occur along roadsides and weedy areas where they visit flowers for nectar.

Literature: Knutson 1990.

266–269   BLACK SWALLOWTAIL AND PARSLEYWORM

Lepidoptera: Papilionidae   *Papilio polyxenes asterius* Stoll

Description: The black swallowtail is a black butterfly with yellow markings near the margins of the fore and hind wings and more limited blue and red markings on the hind wings. Its wingspan can reach 4½ inches. Full-grown parsleyworms or caterpillars can reach 2 inches in length and are smooth and green, marked with black bands and yellow spots.

The black swallowtail resembles the bad-tasting **pipevine swallowtail (269)**, *Battus philenor* (Linnaeus), which is all metallic black-blue on the upper surface of the wings, lacking the yellow and blue markings.

Life cycle: Winter is spent in the chrysalis stage (pupa). Adult black swallowtails emerge in the spring and seek host plants. Females lay round, yellow to cream-colored eggs on the leaves. Caterpillars (**267**) hatching from eggs are initially black with a white "saddle." After molting several times, each larva transforms into a pale green chrysalis (**268**) that is suspended from a plant stem by a thread.

Pest status: Caterpillars feed on dill and some other plants.

Habitat and food source(s): Host plants of the caterpillar include members of the parsley family (Umbelliferae) including carrot, parsley, dill, fennel, Queen Anne's lace, and some members of the Rutaceae (*Ruta graveolens* and *Thamnosma texana*). This caterpillar is bad tasting to birds and other predators because of toxins absorbed from the host plants. Like other larvae of swallowtail butterflies, parsleyworms have a defensive structure, called an osmetrium, right behind the head. This structure is usually concealed. However, when disturbed this "Y" or "V" shaped organ is everted. It emits a strong odor that is apparently distasteful to predators. This butterfly is easy to attract and raise by planting dill or fennel in your vegetable garden.

Literature: Howe 1975; Wright 1993.

270–273   GIANT SWALLOWTAIL OR ORANGE DOG

Lepidoptera: Papilionidae   *Heraclides (Papilio) cresphontes* Cramer

Description: Adult butterfly is one of the largest swallowtail species, with a wingspan of up to 6 inches. Wings are black with yellow markings near wing margins and spots forming a diagonal band across the fore wings. Caterpillars (**273**) are dark brown with creamy white mottled markings, making them appear much like bird droppings. When disturbed, caterpillars display a pair of horn-like, orange, glands (osmeteria), which emit a foul smell.

Other black and yellow swallowtail butterflies include the common **tiger swallowtail (273)**, *Pterourus (Papilio) glaucus* (Linnaeus), which has a 3½–4-inch wingspan and fore wings that are mostly yellow and marked with 4 black lines and wing margins. Females occur in 2 forms (they are dimorphic), one being similar to the male but with larger blue markings on the hind wings, and the other an all black form with similar blue markings on the hind wings. A remarkably similar species is the "**two-tailed swallowtail**," *Pterourus (Papilio) multicaudatus* (Kirby); although this species has reduced black stripe markings and each hind wing has 2 well-developed tails rather than one. It is more common in the canyon bottoms of west Texas. In the swampy woods of eastern Texas Gulf Coast counties, the **palamedes swallowtail (271)** *Pterourus (Papilio) palamedes* (Drury), is a common black-brown swallowtail with yellow markings forming a band near the middles of the wings (made of spots on the fore wings but being solid on the hind wing) and crescent-shaped spots closer to and along the wing margins. Like the black-and-blue **spicebush swallowtail (270)**, *Pterourus (Papilio) triolus* (Linnaeus), caterpillar stages feed on sassafras. However, caterpillars of the latter also feed on spicebush and are marked with 2 pairs of large black-ringed and yellow-orange eyespots (first pair black in center and second lacking center spot) and smaller black-ringed blue spots along the body. They roll up leaves to make nests in which they hide.

Life cycle: Adult females lay yellow-green eggs singly on host plants. Caterpillars hatch and develop through several stages (instars) before forming a chrysalis or pupa, which is attached to the host plant by the back end and held in an upright position by a silk thread around the middle.

Pest status: Caterpillar feeds on leaves of citrus.

Habitat and food source(s): Caterpillars feed on leaves of host plants including citrus, gas plant, *Dictamnus*, prickly ash, *Xanthoxylum* sp., rue, *Ruta graveolens*.

Literature: Howe 1975; Neck 1996; Wright 1993.

274   CLOUDLESS SULPHUR

Lepidoptera: Pieridae

Phoebis sennae eubule
(Linnaeus)

Description: One of the larger sulphur butterfly species, wingspans can be almost 3 inches. Males are brilliant yellow above with no markings. Females have some black marginal markings. Caterpillars, 1 inch long when fully grown, are pale yellowish-green with yellow stripes along their sides. Each body segment is also marked with rows of black dots.

Another subspecies, *Phoebis sennae marcellina* (Cramer), occurs in the Rio Grande Valley. Males are more patterned underneath with orange-brown and females have a warmer shade of yellow on the upper surface and a ground color of pinkish-orange on the underside. Thirty-six species of Pieridae, butterflies called "whites" or "sulphurs" occur in Texas.

Adults of the **alfalfa caterpillar (275)**, *Colias eurytheme* Boisduval, are commonly seen sulphur butterflies. Adults have a 2-inch wingspan and wings are yellow to orange-yellow with black markings along the wing margins (on males, markings are solid and on females, black markings are interrupted by spots). The caterpillar stages feed on leaves of alfalfa and soybeans, growing to 1½ inches long with green bodies marked on each side with a thin white stripe in which a finer red line occurs.

Life cycle: Adults overwinter in south Texas. Females lay eggs on host plants. Caterpillars hatching from eggs develop through several stages before forming a smooth chrysalis suspended from a plant stem by its base and a silk thread. Broods are continuous in the eastern half of Texas.

Pest status: This is a harmless, migrating species.

Habitat and food source(s): Larvae feed on wild senna, *Cassia,* species. In Louisiana, the primary host is the partridge pea, *Chamaecrista cinerea.* During the day, they hide in a "tent" made of cassia leaves webbed together with silk. Adults are strong migrators, particularly in late summer when their range expands northward. Adults can be common, as they visit flowers like thistle and morning glory.

Literature: Howe 1975; Neck 1996; Wright 1993.

276–278   COTTON SQUARE BORER OR GRAY HAIRSTREAK

Lepidoptera: Lycaenidae   *Strymon melinus* Hübner

Description: Adults are common on flowers; caterpillars can feed on developing fruit such as cotton squares, hops and beans. Adults have a 1–1¼-inch wingspan and are dark gray above and slate or bluish-gray below. They have a hair-like "tail" on each hind wing, along with a distinctive orange patch around a black spot on each surface. Caterpillar stages are reddish-brown or light green slug-like and are usually covered with short hairs (setae) making them appear velvety.

Most hairstreaks have fine, hairlike "tails" on their hind wings. When resting on plants, they move their wings back and forth, making the "tails" appear antennae-like, apparently to cause predators to attack this, less vital, part of their anatomy. One of the larger (1¾-inch wingspan), colorful species is the **great blue hairstreak (278)**, *Atlides halesus* Cramer, which has an iridescent blue patch of scales over a brown-black background on the upper surface of the wings, orange-red markings on the body and additional greenish iridescent markings around the tails. Caterpillars feed on mistletoe, *Phoradendron* sp. Caterpillars of some hairstreak species produce honeydew and are tended by ants. The Lycaenidae family is a large group of small butterflies, 65 occurring in Texas, and also include subfamily groups containing **blues (277), coppers, harvesters.** Blues are small butterflies, usually with upper wing surfaces colored blue to gray-brown and undersides marked with dark spots. One of the smallest butterflies is the **pygmy blue,** *Brephidium exilis* (Boisduval), with a wingspan of ½ to ¾ inch. Caterpillars feed on white pigweed, *Chenopodium album,* and some other plants. Another group, the **metalmarks** (Riodinidae), contain small brown butterflies with pink metallic markings.

Life cycle: Winter is spent in the chrysalis (pupal stage). Adult cotton square borers lay single, flattened eggs. On cotton, eggs are laid early in the spring. Eggs hatch in about 6 days. Caterpillars develop through several stages (instars) and feed over a period of about 20 days before forming a chrysalis. Adults emerge about 10 days later. There are 3 or more generations per year.

Pest status: Caterpillars may damage cotton squares or buds of hibiscus, but are not common.

Habitat and food source(s): Caterpillars generally feed on flowers and immature fruits, seeds and buds of host plants, that include 46 genera and 21 families of plants containing apple, blackberry, corn, cotton, lantana, legumes, and strawberry. In cotton, caterpillars hollow out squares, producing round entrance and exit holes and tunnels lacking excrement (frass) associated with other species of cotton boll feeders, such as bollworms and tobacco budworms (Noctuidae).

Literature: Bohmfalk et al. 1982; Howe 1975; Neck 1996.

279   SNOUT BUTTERFLIES

Lepidoptera: Libytheidae   *Libytheana bachmanii*
                                            (Kirtland)

Description: Snout butterflies have a prominent "snout" formed by elongated mouthparts (labial palpi). Wings (⅞-inch fore wing) are patterned on black-brown with white and orange markings. The fore wings have a distinctive squared-off, hook-like (falcate) tip. Caterpillars appear humpbacked, having a small head, swollen first and second abdominal segments, and a last abdominal segment that is tapered and rounded. They are dark green with yellow stripes along the top and sides of the body, and have two black tubercles on the top of the thorax. There are 2 subspecies that occur in the state; *L. b. bachmanii* (Kirtland) and *L. b. larvata* (Strecker). The latter is larger and darker and the tip (apex) of the fore wing and outer edge of the hind wing are straighter.

Libytheana carinenta mexicana Michener, the only other species in this family also occurs in southern Texas. It differs from *L. bachmanii* in that the orange coloration is paler and the tip (apex) of the fore wing and outer edge of the hind wing are straighter.

Life cycle: Winter is spent in the adult stage. Females lay eggs on host plants. Caterpillars hatching from eggs develop though several caterpillar stages (instars) and a pupa (chrysalis) to adult in 15 to 17 days. There may be up to 4 generations per year.

Pest status: Known for its mass migrations that occur at irregular intervals when populations explode in the south and southwest. They may become so numerous as to darken the sky. One of these migrations was reported south of San Antonio in mid-September 1996, where countless butterflies were observed flying across highways.

Habitat and food source(s): The primary food plant for caterpillars are hackberry (*Celtis*) trees. Caterpillars feed on tender foliage. Adults are frequently attracted to fermenting fruit and visit wild flowers. Males are encountered around host trees. When at rest, wings are held closed over the body and appear to mimic dead leaves.

Literature: Howe 1975; Opler and Rizek 1984.

280–282 BUCKEYE

Lepidoptera: Nymphalidae   *Junonia (Precis) coenia*
                                            (Hübner)

Description: This medium-sized brushfooted butterfly, with a 1½–2½-inch wingspan, is overall yellow-brown from above, but has 2 prominent intricately-colored eyespots on each of the fore and hind wings and additional white, red, and marginal markings. Caterpillars (**282**) are shiny black with 2 rows of orange spots on the back, and 2 rows of cream spots on the sides. The false legs (prolegs) on abdominal segments are orangish and the body is adorned with black branched spines with blue bases on the back and orange bases on the sides. The head is orange and bears a pair of spines.

In southern Texas, a darker subspecies, *Junonia (Precis) coenia nigrosuffusa* (Barnes and McDunnough), and another similar species, *Junonia (Precis) evarete* (Cramer), with smaller eyespots, occur. These species are sometimes migratory. The family Nymphalidae contains butterflies called "brushfooted" butterflies because their front pair of legs is reduced. This is the largest butterfly family, with 73 species found in Texas including fritillaries, checkerspots, crescents, and others. Other common and distinctive species of moderately-sized brushfooted butterflies are the **variegated fritillary (281)**, *Euptoieta claudia* (Cramer), a yellow-brown butterfly with upper wing surfaces marked with darker brown lines and spots along a double dark-lined wing margins (2¼-inch wingspan); the **American painted lady (281)**, *Vanessa virginiensis* (Drury), an orangish butterfly with white spots and markings at the tips of the fore wings in blackened areas and black-ringed blue spots and dark lines along the hind wing margins (2-inch wingspan); **red admiral (281, 282)**, *Vanessa atalanta* (Linnaeus), a brown-black butterfly marked with a brilliant red band that arches across the front wings and follows the margins of the hind wings, and with white markings on the tips of the fore wings (2-inch wingspan); the **red-spotted purple (281)**, *Basilarchia (Limenitis) arthemis* (Drury), a blue-black butterfly with iridescent blue to blue-green markings along the white-marked, scalloped wing margins (2¾-inch wingspan); and the **viceroy (281)**, *Bacilarchia (Limenitis) archippus*

(Cramer), a butterfly superficially similar to the **monarch butterfly,** *Danaus plexippus* (Linnaeus) (Danaidae), but easily distinguished by the presence of a black mid-wing cross-band on the upper surface of the hind wings on the viceroy (3-inch wingspan).

Life cycle: Larvae and adults overwinter. Female butterflies lay eggs on host plants and caterpillars develop through several stages (instars) before forming a chrysalis (pupa); 3–4 generations are produced annually.

Pest status: Caterpillars feed primarily on weeds.

Habitat and food source(s): Caterpillars eat leaves of broad-leaved weeds including gerardia, false loosestrife, monkey flower, plantain, snapdragon, stonecrop, toadflax, and Verbenaceae. Butterflies are found in open areas where they make short flights between stops where they rest on the ground, holding their wings out while basking in the sunlight. Adults frequent flowers and feed on nectar.

Literature: Howe 1975; Neck 1996; Wright 1993.

283   SILVERY CHECKERSPOT

Lepidoptera: Nymphalidae   *Charidryas nycteis*
                                            (Doubleday)

Description: The **silvery checkerspot,** *Charidryas nycteis* (Doubleday), is a medium-sized butterfly with a wingspan up to 1¾ inches. It is black-brown with a mottled wide orange band from the front edge to the hind edge of the wing. The hind wing is more orange and bordered with black-brown. There is a series of small dots near the outer edge and bands of black and orange. The underside of the fore wing is orange with dark brown mottling and a white spot near the tip. The underside of the hind wing is pale tan with brown lines and orange ringed black spots in a line near the outer margins. Full-grown caterpillars are velvety black with a dull orange stripe along each side and covered with barbed spines (tubercles with bristles). This species is found primarily in eastern and central Texas.

Several species closely resemble the silvery checkerspot and are often referred to as "crescent" butterflies. The **pearl crescent,** *Phyciodes tharos* (Drury), is a small- to medium-sized butterfly (1¼–1½-inch wingspan) is overall orange with black markings, but is highly variable in its markings geographically and even from season to season. The underside of the hind wings are relatively unmarked orange-brown to mottled gray-brown with a white crescent on the outer margin. The **bordered patch,** *Chlosyne lacinia* (Geyer), is one of eight closely related "patch" butterflies of the family, Nymphalidae, called the "brush-footed" butterflies. Also found in southern Texas, this species is highly variable but characteristically marked above with a wide curved yellow-orange band and small orange spots on a dark-brown background and with white dots along the wing margins. Larvae feed on a variety of Compositae including sunflowers and cocklebur.

Life cycle: Adults lay eggs in clusters on host plants. Caterpillars hatching from eggs develop through several stages (instars) before forming a mottled grayish-to-brownish, spine-covered chrysalis. They overwinter as partially grown larvae. There are two generations per year.

Pest status: Harmless.

Habitat and food source(s): Caterpillars have chewing mouthparts. Adults have siphoning mouths. Caterpillars feed on sunflowers, asters, and *Actinomeris* (Compositae). They occur in open meadows and along roadsides.

Literature: Howe 1975; Klots 1951, Neck 1996; Wright 1993.

284   HACKBERRY BUTTERFLY

Lepidoptera: Nymphalidae   *Asterocampa celtis*
                                       (Boisduval and LeConte)

Description: Adult is a medium-sized (1¾–2¼-inch wingspan) yellow-brown butterfly with white spots near the fore wing tips and a band of dark spots and two dark lines following along the wing margin. Caterpillars grow to 1¼ inches long, are green, tapered at both ends, and marked with a pair of yellow lines along the top of the body and V-shaped markings on the sides. The head bears a pair of branched knobs and the end of the body has two projections or "tails."

There are two subspecies in Texas; *A. c. celtis* (Boisduval and LeConte) has 1 distinct dark spot near the margin of the fore wing, while *A. c. antonia* (Edwards) has 2. **Empress leilia,** *Asterocampa leilia* (Edwards), in southwestern Texas, is similar to *A. celtis,* but can be distinguished by the 2 yellow-ringed black spots with white centers on the underside of the fore wings. The **tawny emperor,** *A. clyton* (Boisduval and LeConte) is similar to *A. celtis,* but is more dull orange to yellow-brown in color. It lacks the distinctive dark spot(s) and white markings on the fore wings. There are 3 Texas subspecies: *A. c. clyton* (Boisduval and LeConte), *A. c. louisa* (Stallings and Turner), and *A. c. texana* (Skinner). Caterpillars of these species also feed on hackberry, *Celtis* sp.

Life cycle: Caterpillars hatching from eggs develop through several stages (instars) before forming a green chrysalis. Three generations per year. Overwinters primarily in the egg stage.

Pest status: Very common butterfly on tree trunks and near hackberry trees; harmless.

Habitat and food source(s): Caterpillars feed on leaves and tender new growth of hackberry trees (*Celtis* sp.). Adults are found on foliage, flowers near host plants, resting on the ground and feeding at tree wounds.

Literature: Howe 1975; Neck 1996; Wright 1993.

285   GOATWEED BUTTERFLY

Lepidoptera: Nymphalidae   *Anaea andria* Scudder

Description: This is a red butterfly with tails. Adults have a 2–2½-inch wingspan; their fore wings have pointed tips (falcate) and hind wings each have one tail. Males are mostly reddish on top with darker wing margins; females have additional bands of dark and lighter markings that follow the wing margins. Caterpillars are green-gray and granular in appearance due to a covering of bumps (tubercles). The head bears orange "horns." They roll up leaves in which they hide.

There are several other species in Texas similar to, but less common or widely distributed than, *A. andria;* one example is the **tropical leaf wing,** *Anaea aidea* (Guérin-Méneville), which has hind wing margins toothed rather than smooth.

Life cycle: Females lay eggs singly on host plants. Several generations per year. Adults are commonly seen flying very late in the fall and early in the spring.

Pest status: Harmless.

Habitat and food source(s): Caterpillars feed on leaves of goatweed (*Croton* spp.).

Literature: Howe 1975; Neck 1996.

286–288   GULF FRITILLARY

Lepidoptera: Nymphalidae   *Agraulis vanillae incarnata* (Riley)

Description: This species is not a true fritillary and is sometimes separated into a separate family of "longwing" butterflies (Heliconiidae) rather than being included in the brush-footed butterflies (Nymphalidae). Adults, with a 3-inch wingspan, are brilliant orange with black markings on the elongated wings. The underside of the hind wing and tip of the fore wing have prominent silver spots and brown markings. Full-grown larvae (**287**) are about 1½ inches long, gray- to brown-black with three pairs of reddish-brown lengthwise stripes. The head and body segments have black, branched spines.

Another subspecies, *Agraulis vanillae nigrior* Michener, occurs in the southeast, with darker black markings. Seven species of longwing butterflies occur in Texas. The **Mexican silverspot,** *Dione moneta poeyi* Butler, is similar to the gulf fritillary, but the upper wing surfaces are yellow-brown and not marked with white spots. Underneath, the silver spots are not rimmed with black. Its range is restricted to the Rio Grande Valley and occasionally far west Texas. Other distinctive members of this family include the **zebra longwing (288),** *Heliconius charitonius vazquezae* Comstock and Brown, a jet black butterfly with brilliant narrow yellow stripes on wings that span 3–3½ inches. The **Julia longwing,** *Dryas julia moderata* Stichel, is predominantly brownish- to yellowish-orange with only darker hazy markings on the upper surface of the fore wing and wing margins.

Life cycle: Adult females lay elongated, ribbed, buff-yellow eggs on host plants. Larvae develop through several stages (instars) before forming a brown chrysalis.

Pest status: Harmless.

Habitat and food source(s): Caterpillars feed on leaves of passion flower, *Passiflora* spp. Adults visit numerous flowers and migrate northward and feed on nectar.

Literature: Howe 1975; Neck 1996; Wright 1993.

289   HERMES SATYR

Lepidoptera: Satyridae

Hermeuptychia hermes
(Fabricius)

Description: This butterfly, with a 1¼-inch wingspan, is brown with faint lines on top. The underside is brown with a grainy white haze, several wavy narrow dark brown lines and yellow circling and black eyespot markings along the margins of the front (5 eyespots) and hind (6 eyespots) wings. Caterpillars are light green with darker stripes along their sides and their bodies are covered with yellow, hairy tubercles.

This is one species in the family of butterflies (Satyridae) known as "satyrs" and "wood nymphs." Eight other species occur in the state, mainly in semi-wooded areas. These include the **gemmed satyr**, *Cyllopsis gemma* (Hübner), which has a reflective patch (black oblong spots in small silver outer margin) on the underside of the hind wing; the **little wood satyr,** *Megisto cymela cymela* (Cramer), with 2 eyespots along the margin of each wing on the upper surface (both in eastern half of Texas); the **red satyr,** *M. rubricata* Edwards, upper wing surfaces orange-brown with single yellow-ringed black eyespots on front and hind wings (western half of Texas); and, the **common wood nymph,** *Ceryonis pegala* (Fabricius), a larger (2½-inch wingspan) butterfly with upper surfaces of fore wings marked with yellow to orange patches containing 1 or 2 eyespots (central and north central to east Texas).

Life cycle: Two or three generations annually.

Pest status: Harmless.

Habitat and food source(s): Common in the eastern half of the state in moist wooded areas. Caterpillars feed on grasses, *Axonopus compressus* and *Cynodon dactylon*.

Literature: Howe 1975; Neck 1996; Wright 1993.

290–292   MONARCH BUTTERFLY

Lepidoptera: Danaidae

Danaus plexippus
(Linnaeus)

Description: Adult butterflies are orange with black wing veins and bodies. Caterpillars (**291**) are 2¾ inches long fully grown, with a pair of black antennae-like appendages (filaments) at either end of the body (2nd thoracic segment, 8th abdominal segment). The body is ringed with black, yellow and white stripes. The chrysalis (**292**) is smooth and light green or blue with gold markings.

The **viceroy butterfly (281)**, *Basilarchia archippus* (Cramer) (Nymphalidae), although not closely related to the monarch butterfly, appears strikingly similar in color and pattern. It can be distinguished by the dark band arching across the center of the hind wing. This species mimics the monarch's appearance to avoid heavy predation by birds who mistake this tasty mimic for the distasteful monarch. Caterpillars feed on willow leaves and mimic bird droppings in appearance. The **queen**, *Danaus gilippus* (Cramer), is closely related to the monarch, but differs in color patterns. Butterflies lack dark-colored wing veins and the white spots on the wings are more diffuse. Larvae also feed on milkweeds, but bear an extra pair of filaments in the middle of the body (2nd abdominal segment) and each body segment bears a pair of yellow dots.

Life cycle: Development progresses from an egg, which hatches in 7 to 9 days, through 5 caterpillar stages (instars) in roughly 5 weeks, and a chrysalis (pupa) for about 9 days before the adult butterfly emerges. Monarch butterflies migrate south through Texas from Canada and the eastern half of North America every fall to the 10,000-ft tall hills near Angangueo, Mexico where they spend the winter. (This site was discovered in 1976!) In the spring, surviving adult butterflies begin migrating north, breeding and developing through 2 to 4 or more generations as they spread north. About 100 million members of the last generation produced each season migrate in the fall to Mexico and live for about 9 months.

Pest status: Harmless.

Habitat and food source(s): Caterpillars feed exclusively on milkweed. Adults feed on nectar from numerous wild flowers. The monarch butterflies are distasteful to birds because of chemicals obtained from caterpillar feeding on milkweed leaves.

Literature: Howe 1975; Neck 1996; Wright 1993.

293   SPRING AND FALL CANKERWORM

Lepidoptera: Geometridae   *Paleacrita vernata* (Peck)
                                       and *Alsophila pometaria*
                                       (Harris)

Description: Adult moths are drab gray, delicate with green markings. Males have a wingspread of about 1 inch while the females are wingless. Cankerworms, like other members of this family, often are called "inchworms" because of the way they crawl. They arch their back into a loop, anchor the hind legs and extend the front to move ahead. The **spring cankerworm**, *Paleacrita vernata* (Peck), has 2 pairs of prolegs, while the **fall cankerworm**, *Alsophila pometaria* (Harris), has 3 pairs of prolegs. Larvae grow to 1

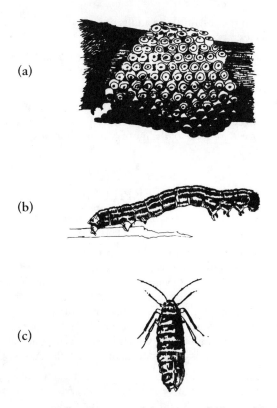

(a)

(b)

(c)

Fall cankerworm: (a) egg mass; (b) larva; (c) adult

inch, are variable in color, and marked predominantly with green, brown, and pale yellow longitudinal stripes.

There are many other species of inchworms, many of which are cryptically colored. Inchworms may sometimes be confused with loopers, which are in the family Noctuidae. Most adult Geometridae have winged females. Wings may be rounded or highly irregular in shape, and dull to brightly colored. Moths in this family often hold their wings together over the back like a butterfly at rest.

Life cycle: Wingless females can only migrate by walking. They crawl up the tree trunks and onto branches to lay eggs in clusters of about 100 in bark crevices or on the limbs. Spring cankerworms lay eggs in the spring, which hatch in a few weeks, while fall cankerworms lay eggs in the fall, which remain on the tree from November until March or April. Both species hatch from eggs in the spring when trees are just reaching budbreak and new foliage is expanding. Larvae feed on leaves for about 3 to 4 weeks before they drop to the ground on a silken thread and pupate in the soil. Caterpillars may be blown in the wind to new locations when suspended on silken threads. Pupae remain in the soil until the adults emerge in the spring or fall depending on the species.

Pest status: Cankerworms can be major defoliators of broad leaf trees in east and central Texas with widespread outbreaks occurring in some years; defoliated trees typically survive and leaf out again; caterpillars can be a nuisance when abundant.

Habitat and food source(s): Nearly any broad-leaved tree or shrub could be attacked. Oak and elm trees are some of the more commonly attacked trees.

Literature: Jackman 1981.

294 EASTERN TENT CATERPILLAR

Lepidoptera: Lasciocampidae   *Malacosoma americanum*
                                          (Fabricius)

Description: Adult moths have a 1-inch wingspread and are brown and yellowish with two diagonal markings on the fore wings. Caterpillars (larvae) grow to over 1½ inches long. They are brightly colored with long hairs on their bodies, mostly along the sides and marked with a solid white line down the center of the back. Other colors may vary but solid or broken lines of blue, yellow, and black are also present. Larvae form a dense silken web usually in the crotch of small limbs, which is used as a refuge at night and during rainy spells. The tent is expanded as the caterpillars grow.

Other tent caterpillar species include the **forest tent caterpillar (295)**, *M. disstria* Hübner; the **western tent caterpillar**, *M. californicum* (Packard), which builds large tents and is found on a variety of trees and shrubs, including oaks and wild plums (caterpillars have a series of white dashes on the back); and the **Sonoran tent caterpillar**, *M. tigris* (Dyar), found on oaks and builds a small tent (caterpillars have one black segment and lack white markings on the back). Tent caterpillars are sometimes confused with **fall webworms (315)**, *Hyphantria cunea* (Drury) (Arctiidae), which form loose silken webs around foliage upon which they are feeding rather than dense webs in crotches of branches, which they leave to feed.

Life cycle: The winter is spent as a hard mass of eggs that encircle a twig. Larvae hatch in early spring just as the plants leaf out (mid-February to mid-March). Caterpillars develop through several stages (instars) over several weeks before leaving the host plant to pupate in a cocoon. There is only one generation per year and activity is usually completed by May.

Pest status: Caterpillars feed on leaves of host plants and produce silken tents that are persistent, unsightly, and must be physically removed in ornamental plantings.

Habitat and food source(s): Eastern tent caterpillars prefer cherry, plum, peach, apple, hawthorne, and related plants. If the food plant is defoliated, they may move to less preferred hosts. Caterpillars leave their tents to feed on leaves and can quickly defoliate sections of a tree. Caterpillars may migrate and wander before they form a cocoon, which may bring them into contact with homeowners.

Literature: Jackman 1988; Metcalf et al. 1962.

295   FOREST TENT CATERPILLAR

Lepidoptera: Lasciocampidae   *Malacosoma disstria* Hübner

Description: Adult moths have a wingspan of about 1 inch and are brown and yellowish with 2 diagonal markings on the front wings. Larvae (caterpillars) are brightly colored with long hairs on their bodies, mostly along the sides and with distinctive white keyhole-shaped markings on each segment down the center of its back. Other colored markings vary, but solid or broken lines of blue, yellow and black are also usually present. Larvae can reach over 1½ inches in length.

Also see **eastern tent caterpillar (294),** *M. americanum* (Fabricius). Tent caterpillars are sometimes confused with **fall webworms (315)** and **bagworms,** which are quite different in appearance and biology. In central Texas, forest tent caterpillars often occur with **Sonoran tent caterpillars,** *M. tigris* (Dyar), and **buck moth** larvae, *Hemileuca maia* (Drury) (Saturnidae).

Life cycle: Winter is spent as a hard, darkened mass of eggs that encircle a twig. Larvae hatch in early spring (mid-February through mid-March) just as the plants leaf out. Larvae form a mat of silk on bark of the trunk or major branches at molting time but otherwise do not form a tent. Larvae feed in groups and concentrate their defoliation. Larvae develop through several stages (instars) before leaving the host plant to pupate inside a cocoon. Adults emerge, mate, and females lay eggs. There is only one generation per year, and activity is usually completed by May or June.

Pest status: Caterpillar feeds on leaves of some deciduous trees; in spite of the name, caterpillars do not form tents; large numbers of caterpillars leaving host plants become a nuisance.

Habitat and food source(s): In Texas, forest tent caterpillars prefer oaks, but also feed on tupelo gum, black gum, sweet gum, and other deciduous trees. They can defoliate whole or sections of a tree. If the food plant is defoliated, they may move to less preferred hosts. They seem to avoid red maple, pear, buffaloberry, and silverberry. Caterpillars may migrate and wander after leaving the host plant, which may bring them into contact with homeowners.

Literature: Jackman 1988; Metcalf et al. 1962.

296–304   LUNA MOTH

Lepidoptera: Saturnidae   *Actias luna* (Linnaeus)

Description: These moths are large, with a 4–5-inch wingspan. Wings are light green, marked with transparent spots and a pink-purple or yellow fore wing margins, and hind wings bearing long twisted tails. Antennae are feathery, with antennae of males being more feathery than those of females. Caterpillars (**297**) are translucent light green with a pale yellow horizontal line along each side and reddish-orange fleshy knobs (tubercles) on each body segment. They grow to be 2¾ inches long.

There are several other common silk moths (Saturnidae). Luna moth caterpillars superficially resemble those of the **polyphemus moth (304)**, *Antheraea polyphemus* (Cramer), but differ because they have vertical yellow lines on each segment rather than single horizontal lines along each side of the body. Other common silkworm (Saturnidae) species include: **cecropia moth (300, 301)**, *Hyalophora cecropia* (Linnaeus), has mature (4 inches long) green larvae adorned with blue and yellow spined knob-like structures (tubercles) on each body segment, with red tubercles on the first two segments behind the head; adults are large (4–6-inch wingspan), with a background of shades of brown and marked with reddish and white and darker markings; **polyphemus moth** caterpillars grow to 3 inches long, are smooth, light green with red, orange or yellow tubercles adorned by short hairs; adults (up to 6-inch wingspan) are overall light brown with small clear spots on the fore wings and large eye-spots on the hind wings; **hickory horned devil**, *Citheronia regalis* (Fabricius), caterpillars grow to 6 inches and have long orange and black filaments or "horns" arising from the body segments directly behind the head; adults (5½-inch wingspan) have orange stripes along wing veins and yellow spots on the fore wings; **imperial moth,** *Eacles imperialis* (Drury) **(298, 299)**, larvae grow to 4 inches long, are smooth green or light brown with yellow-orange tubercles adorning fine hairs; adult moths (5½-inch wingspan) are overall yellow with brownish markings; full-grown (2 inches long) caterpillars of the **io moth (302, 303)**, *Automeris io* (Fabricius), are green and marked with a 2-color (pink and white) stripe along the sides, and covered with clusters of branched spines capable of "stinging" like an "asp" (see **puss caterpillar (256)**) if handled; adults (2⅓-inch wingspan) have yellow to brownish fore wings and hind wings marked with prominent eyespots.

Life cycle: Adults begin to emerge in the spring (March) to mate and lay oval eggs. Caterpillars develop through several molts before spinning a papery cocoon among dead leaves that usually falls to the ground. There are 2 generations per year.

Pest status: Luna or "moon" moths are active at night and are harmless; caterpillars feed on tree leaves but are rarely found in large numbers.

Habitat and food source(s): Caterpillars feed on leaves of walnut, hickory, sweetgum, maple, oak, persimmon, willow, and other trees.

Literature: Holland 1968; Wright 1993.

BUCK MOTH

Lepidoptera: Saturnidae   *Hemileuca maia* (Drury)

Description: Adult buck moths have semi-transparent white wings, almost devoid of scales with reddish-brown bases, outer wing margin and a center spot. The wingspan is 2 to 3 inches. The abdomen is black or brown with a red tuft at the tip. Full-grown caterpillars are 2½ inches long, have dark black-brown bodies with yellowish dots and are covered with branched stinging spines or bristles arising from bumps (tubercles).

Similar in size and biology to the buck moth, the **range caterpillar,** *Hemileuca oliviae* Cockerell, occurs in the northwest corner of the Texas Panhandle and occasionally causes serious losses of range grasses. Its wings are white with a light to dark dusting of brownish-gray. Four other species in this genus have been reported from Texas.

Life cycle: The buck moth spends the winter in the egg stage, which occur in clusters around twigs. In the spring (March to April), caterpillars hatch from egg masses and feed together (gregariously). They develop through 5 molts and pupate in the ground. Adult moths appear mainly in the fall.

Pest status: Caterpillars (larvae) feed on leaves of trees.

Habitat and food source(s): Buck moth caterpillars, common in the hill country of central Texas in the spring, feed primarily on leaves of oaks, but will also feed on leaves of willow and cherry trees. Buck moths fly during the daytime and evening hours.

Literature: Arnett 1985; Holland 1968; Swan and Papp 1972; Werner and Olson 1994.

305–307   CATALPA SPHINX

Lepidoptera: Sphingidae   *Ceratomia catalpae*
                                             (Boisduval)

Description: The caterpillar is one of the "hornworm" species, having a prominent black spine on the back end of the body. The caterpillar has a shiny black head and may grow up to 3 inches long. Although body coloration and markings change as caterpillars grow, lengthwise yellow or green and black stripes become more apparent in larger caterpillars. This night-flying adult hawk moth has long, narrow mottled gray or brown wings, which have a wingspan of about 3 inches, and robust, spindle-shaped bodies.

Hornworm caterpillars of the **whitelined sphinx (306),** *Hyles lineata* (Fabricius), feed on leaves of apple, azalea, chickweed, elm, evening primrose, portulaca, purslane, Virginia creeper, and many other plants. Caterpillars grow up to 3⅛ inches long, have yellowish-orange heads, and their bodies are generally green with 2 black stripes along their sides. A black form with yellow-green stripes also occurs. Adult moths have a wingspread of about 3 inches, with long narrow brown and black fore wings marked with white veins, borders, and a broad white stripe running across the middle. Hind wings are dark brown with a rosy-white band across the middle, and the moth's body is brown with white stripes on the head and thorax, and bands of black and white spots on the abdomen. These moths fly in daylight and evening hours, with hovering flight resembling that of hummingbirds as they sip nectar from flowers. This is one of the most commonly observed sphinx or hawk moth species. Another species occassionally found at lights is the **walnut sphinx,** *Laothe juglandis* (J. E. Smith) (**307**).

Life cycle: Winter is spent in the pupal stage, which appears naked, brown and spindle-shaped, 2 to 3 inches deep in the soil. Adult catalpa sphinx moths emerge in the spring and mate. Females lay clusters of up to 1,000 white eggs on catalpa tree leaves, usually in April or early May. Tiny caterpillars hatch from these eggs in about 10 to 14 days and feed together. Caterpillars molt several times during development before they crawl down the tree trunk and pupate in the soil. Adults emerge several days later. There may be 4 to 5 generations per year in Texas.

Pest status: Catalpa trees are occasionally planted intentionally to produce caterpillars, sometimes called "catawba worms" for fish bait. High numbers of hornworms can defoliate ornamental catalpa trees, making them appear unsightly.

Habitat and food source(s): Caterpillars feed on leaves only of catalpa trees. Adults are attracted to lights.

Literature: Metcalf et al. 1962; Swan and Papp 1972; Thomas 1968.

308, 309 TOMATO HORNWORM

Lepidoptera: Sphingidae   *Manduca quinquemaculata*
                                           (Haworth)

Description: Adults are large-bodied moths with a 4–5-inch wingspan that resemble hummingbirds in flight as they hover around flowers from which they obtain nectar at dusk. The moth's abdomen is marked with five pairs of orange-yellow spots. Caterpillars (**309**) can reach 3 to 4 inches in length, are green with prominent diagonal white stripes (appearing as "/" marks with the head to the left) along the sides of the body and a black-colored "horn" on the back end.

There are several common hawk moths or sphinx moths in Texas. The **tobacco hornworm,** *Manduca sexta* (Linnaeus), is very similar to the tomato hornworm in biology and the 2 species may be found together. The tobacco hornworm larva differs in that the white diagonal stripes on the sides of the body appear as "/" marks. They also have a red-colored horn. Adults of the tobacco hornworm have differently patterned hind wings and 6 pairs of orange-yellow spots along the abdomen.

Life cycle: The winter is spent as a pupa in the soil. The pupa is about 2 inches long, dark brown in color and spindle-shaped, with the encased mouthparts prominent and separated from the body—appearing like a handle. Adult moths emerge in the spring. Female moths deposit greenish-yellow eggs singly on the undersides of host plant leaves. Caterpillars hatch from the eggs in about 7 days and caterpillars develop through 5 stages (instars) for 3 to 4 weeks until they pupate 3 to 4 inches deep in the soil. Unless the pupa overwinters, adults can emerge in about 3 weeks, producing 2 generations per year.

Pest status: Caterpillars feed on certain plants.

Habitat and food source(s): Caterpillars feed on leaves of tomato, eggplant, pepper, potato, and some weeds. Adults are attracted to lights.

Literature: Metcalf et al. 1962; Selman 1975.

310–312   WALNUT CATERPILLAR

Lepidoptera: Notodontidae   *Datana integerrima* Grote
                                             and Robinson

Description: The adult moth has a 2-inch wingspan, is brown and tan with a dark region on the body behind the head, and has wavy, dark lines across the front wings. Caterpillars are reddish-brown to black with white markings and long white hairs. Large larvae are conspicuously fuzzy and may grow up to 2 inches long. Larvae characteristically arch their heads and tails in a defensive posture when disturbed.

Another common species of Notodontidae is the **yellownecked caterpillar (311)**, *Datana ministra* (Drury). Caterpillars grow to 2 inches long, have yellow stripes along their orange to black body, and have a yellow "neck" just behind their black head capsule. They feed in groups (aggregates) on leaves of cherry, crabapple, elm, maple, peaches, oak, and walnut and display a defensive posture, raising the head and tip of the abdomen when disturbed. The **unicorn caterpillar (312)**, *Schizura unicornis* (J. E. Smith), occurs on apple, cherry, rose and other woody ornamental plants. Caterpillars grow to 1⅓ inches long and are variegated brown. They have a prominent projection on the first abdominal segment and feed together.

Life cycle: Adults emerge from pupae that overwinter in the soil at the base of a host tree. The female moth deposits about 300 eggs on the underside of a leaf. Caterpillars (larvae) hatch from the eggs in about 9 days, living together in a group. The caterpillars often move to the tree trunk to molt from one stage (instar) to the next, leaving a patch of fur-like hair and cast skins. When they finish feeding, they drop to the ground and pupate in the soil. They do not spin a cocoon but form a naked pupal case. Populations of this species vary from year to year and there may be several years between outbreak levels. In Texas, at least 2 generations of the insect develop each year. The second generation is usually larger in number and causes more damage.

Pest status: A serious but occasional threat to certain trees and shrubs; can cause defoliation.

Habitat and food source(s): Host plants include hickory, walnut, oak, willow, honey locust, and certain woody shrubs. Young larvae feed only on soft tissue, leaving a skeletonized leaf behind, while older larvae feed on the entire leaf, including the petiole. The last few stages, or instars, do most of the feeding. Damage may be localized to just a branch to two because they feed together. Isolated trees are more subject to attack than forest or orchard trees. They can rapidly defoliate ornamental and orchard trees if not controlled. In some past years, almost all of the native pecan trees in certain areas of the state have been defoliated by walnut caterpillars.

Literature: Jackman 1981c.

313   WHITEMARKED TUSSOCK MOTH

Lepidoptera: Lymantriidae   *Orgyia leucostigma*
                                             (J. E. Smith)

Description: The male moth, with a wingspan of about 1¼ inches, is ash gray and the fore wing is marked with darker wavy bands. Females are white to gray and do not have fully-developed wings. Caterpillars grow to 1¼ inches long and are unique in that there are 4 brush-like tufts or bunches of light tan hairs on the back (top of the first 4 abdominal segments) and red dots (abdominal segments 6 and 7). In addition, there is a pair of longer tufts of black hairs (pencil-lead-sized tufts called pencil hairs) arising from the front (the prothorax) and a light-haired one from the back (abdominal segment 8) of the body. The body is overall cream-colored, has a broad black stripe on the back, a broader gray stripe along each side, and a red-orange head.

The **pale tussock moth**, *Halysidota tessellaris* (J. E. Smith), (Arctiidae), lacks the upright tufts of short, light hairs on the first 4 abdominal segments. Its body is covered with whitish hairs, may have a line of darker hairs along the back, and has pairs of longer hair tufts (pencil hairs) arising from both ends of the body. The **sycamore tussock moth**, *Halysidota harrisii* Walsh, (Arctiidae), which feeds on American sycamore and London plane tree throughout the range of these plants, has white body hair and hair tufts (pencils) on the ends of the body. Several other species of tussock moths occur and, when in high numbers, may damage ornamental host plants. Another notable species in the family Lymantriidae is the **gypsy moth**, *Lymantria dispar* (Linnaeus), which was introduced in northeastern America and has been spreading south and westward. Although adult specimens have been collected in Texas using sex attractant (pheromone) traps along routes of transportation, larval infestations have not occurred in the state.

Life cycle: Winter is spent in the egg stage. Caterpillars hatch from eggs from April to June and develop through several stages (instars) over a period of 30 to 40 days. Caterpillars pupate within grayish cocoons made of silk and larval hairs on the trunk, on branches of the host plant or on nearby objects. Adults emerge in about 2 weeks and mate. Females lay masses of eggs on the surface of old cocoons. There are 3 generations per year.

Pest status: A serious but occasional threat to certain trees and shrubs.

Habitat and food source(s): Caterpillar host plants include apple, basswood, elm, maple (Norway and silver), pear, plums, poplars, rose, sycamore, willow, wisteria, and others. The subspecies in the south feeds on live oak, redbud, pyracantha, and mimosa. Young larvae skeletonize leaves while older larvae eat all of the leaf surface except for the larger veins.

Literature: Johnson and Lyon 1988; Metcalf et al. 1962; Peairs and Davidson 1956.

314, 315   FALL WEBWORM

Lepidoptera: Arctiidae   *Hyphantria cunea* (Drury)

Description: Adult moths are mostly white with dark spots on the wings. Webs can cover leaves, clusters of leaves or leaves on whole branches, becoming several feet in diameter. They contain many hairy caterpillars that hatched from one egg mass. Some trees can have many webs. Caterpillars grow to about 1 inch long, with black or reddish heads, pale yellow or greenish bodies marked with a broad mottled stripe containing two rows of black bumps (tubercles) down the back (one pair on each body segment), and yellowish patterns on the sides. They are covered with tufts of long whitish hairs.

Webs of fall webworms are often confused with webs produced by **eastern tent caterpillars (294)**, *Malacosoma americanum* (Fabricius) (Lasciocampidae). Another web-producing caterpillar is the **genista caterpillar (261)**, *Uresiphita reversalis* (Guenée) (Pyralidae), commonly found on Texas mountain laurel. Caterpillars are less hairy and lack the double row of black dots on the top of each body segment. Fall webworms are also sometimes called "bagworms," but this term is more accurately used for the true **bagworms (247)** (Psychidae).

Life cycle: Winter is spent in the pupal stage in a silken cocoon in leaf litter or in cracks on rough bark. Adults emerge in spring after host plants have developed leaves, and mate. On the underside of leaves female moths deposit eggs in masses that appear covered with hair. Caterpillars hatch and begin feeding on leaves, spinning loose silken webs enveloping their feeding sites. Caterpillars molt up to 11 times between growth stages (instars) before leaving the host plant to pupate. Two to four generations occur per year, depending on locality within Texas.

Pest status: Caterpillars produce unsightly "nests" of loose webbing around leaves and branches in which they feed on leaves; they cause loss of leaves and some plant stress; hairs on larvae may cause skin irritation.

Habitat and food source(s): Caterpillars will feed on leaves of many trees including hickory, mulberry, oak, pecan, poplar, redbud, sweetgum, willow and many other woody plants. Preferences for different host plant species appear to be regional and seasonal. They feed on tender parts of leaves, leaving the larger veins and midrib. Webworms can appear as early as April in south Texas and high numbers of webs can occur during any of the generations that occur through the summer. However, the last generation is generally the most damaging. Adults are attracted to lights.

Literature: Johnson and Lyon 1988; Robinson and Hamman 1980.

SALTMARSH CATERPILLAR AND WOOLLYBEAR

Lepidoptera: Arctiidae

Estigmene acrea (Drury)
Pyrrharctia isabella
(J. E. Smith)

Description: The **saltmarsh caterpillar,** *Estigmene acrea*, grows to 2 inches, has bunches of short bristles and longer, whitish hairs covering its yellow to dark brown body. It curls up when disturbed. Adult moths (2-inch wingspan) are overall white, with the fore wings having some small black spots and the abdomen yellow with black spots. The **banded woollybear,** *Pyrrharctia isabella*, grows to 2¼ inches, and is red-brown with black at both ends of the spine-covered body. The adult stage, called the **Isabella tiger moth,** has a 2-inch wingspan, and is overall yellow-brown with the abdomen marked with black spots.

There are several other common moths in the family Arctiidae that occur at lights. Two of the more colorful are the **tiger moths (316),** such as *Grammia parthenice intermedia* (Stretch), with a 3-inch wingspan, cream-colored fore wings with black patterns and hind wings that are orange with black patches; and the **giant leopard moth (253),** *Hypercompe scribonia* (Stoll), with a 3-inch wingspan, is white with black open-circular spots on the fore wings and a metallic blue abdomen with orange markings. Caterpillars of this species grow to 3 inches long, are black with red bands between the body segments and clusters of short stiff spines.

Life cycle: Both species overwinter as larvae. Woollybear caterpillars in the fall are thought to indicate the severity of the oncoming winter by the proportion of red-brown to black on the body, although this is interesting folklore, there is no scientific evidence supporting this idea. Adults occur in the spring.

Pest status: Caterpillars may cause a problem when occurring in high numbers on landscape plants or crops. Contact with their hairy bodies can cause irritation to the skin.

Habitat and food source(s): Caterpillars are general feeders, eating leaves of weeds and grasses. Partially-grown caterpillars often migrate into row crops such as soybean fields, gardens, and landscapes.

Literature: Wright 1993.

YELLOWCOLLARED SCAPE MOTH

Lepidoptera: Arctiidae

Cisseps fulvicollis (Hübner)

Description: Adult is small (⅝ inch long) has black fore wings and paler, black-margined hind wings. The part of the thorax behind the head (prothorax) is yellow.

This is one of several species of day-flying moths called "wasp moths." Other species of day-flying moths are often colorful. Another species, the ermine moth (250), *Atteva punctella* (Cramer) (Yponomeutidae), is also a small (½ inch long) moth with narrow fore wings (held over the back when at rest) that are bright yellow with 4 bands of yellow spots edged in lead blue. Caterpillars feed on leaves of ailanthus and produce silken webs. The **eightspotted forester**, *Alypia octomaculata* (Fabricius) (Noctuidae), is black with 2 whitish or yellowish spots on each wing, with a ¾-inch wingspan. Caterpillars feed on Virginia creeper and grape leaves. Because antennae are slightly clubbed, it can be confused with a **skipper butterfly (265)** (Hesperiidae).

Life cycle: Development progresses through egg, larval stages (instars), and pupa. Adults are common in the fall.

Pest status: Harmless.

Habitat and food source(s): Caterpillars feed on grasses. Adults commonly visit goldenrod flowers during daytime in late summer.

Literature: Borror et al. 1989; Holland 1968.

318   GRANULATE CUTWORM

Lepidoptera: Noctuidae   *Agrotis subterranea*
                                        (Fabricius)

Description: Adults are dingy, grayish-brown moths marked with light or dark spots on the wings. They have a wing spread of 1 to 2 inches. Caterpillars are dingy, grayish-black, smooth-skinned, and may reach 1½ inches in length. When disturbed, the caterpillars curl up tightly into a C-shape.

There are 4 major groups of cutworms based on habitat and feeding behavior: (1) **subterranean cutworms,** such as the **pale western cutworm,** *Agrotis orthogonia* Morrison, that feed almost entirely below the soil surface on roots and underground stems; (2) **tunnel dwellers** such as the **black cutworm,** *Agrotis ipsilon* (Hufnagel), which cuts a tender plant at the soil surface, pulls it into the tunnel and devours the plant; (3) **surface feeders** such as the granulate cutworm and the **army cutworm,** *Euxoa auxiliaris* (Grote); and (4) **climbing cutworms** such as the **variegated cutworm,** *Peridroma saucia* (Hübner), which can devour the spring buds of grapes. The army cutworm overwinters in the mountains of west Texas as adults. It can be very numerous and a nuisance in buildings. Adult moths that are about 1–2 inches long are often referred to as "millers" or miller moths. This is a general term for moths which are often in the family Noctuidae, which includes cutworms, armyworms, bollworms, and many other species.

Life cycle: Winter is spent in the larval stage. After emerging from the pupa (cocoon), mated female moths deposit eggs that hatch into larvae (caterpillars), which then develop through several larval stages (instars) before pupating in the soil. There may be 3–5 generations per year in central and south Texas, depending on weather conditions and temperature.

Pest status: Caterpillars chew on stems and leaves of plants.

Habitat and food source(s): The granulate cutworm is a surface-feeding cutworm. Like other cutworm species, it spends the winter months as a partially-grown larva in the soil, feeding on weeds and grasses at night. In the spring when gardens and fields are plowed and planted, caterpillars that were feeding on weeds and other host plants move to young plants and transplants. Caterpillars cut off small plants at or near the soil surface and feed on them during the night. In field crops, damage usually appears as skips or sections of rows where all plants are missing. Caterpillars can do tremendous damage in a short period of time. Many turf, forage, ornamental, and vegetable plants are attacked, particularly cabbage and tomato transplants and corn seedlings. Caterpillars dwell in soil around damaged plants or under debris on the ground during the day. Adult moths are attracted to lights at night.

Literature: Stewart 1985.

319 CORN EARWORM, BOLLWORM, TOMATO FRUITWORM, (SORGHUM) HEADWORM, (SOYBEAN) PODWORM

Lepidoptera: Noctuidae   *Helicoverpa zea* (Boddie)

Description: Adult moths are brown with darker brown patterned wings. Caterpillars can grow up to about 1⅝ inches in length and vary in body color from yellowish, greenish, reddish or brownish with more or less prominently colored longitudinal lines. The body is covered by regularly occurring body-colored to black bumps sporting stiff black hairs or setae. The head capsules are tan to dark brown.

There are many species within the noctuid family. In agriculture, however, the **tobacco budworm,** *Heliothis virescens* (Fabricius), is similar to the corn earworm and presents control problems because of insecticide resistance. Tobacco budworm caterpillars can be separated from the corn earworms by the shape of the "jaw" or mandible (basal molar or mandibular retinaculum is absent on corn earworm) and by the presence of microspines on the bumps along the body sporting black hairs. Caterpillars of the **fall armyworm,** *Spodoptera frugiperda* (J. E. Smith), and in the Texas Panhandle, the **European corn borer,** *Ostrinia nubilalis* (Hübner) (Pyralidae), and the **western bean cutworm,** *Loxagrotis albicosta* (Smith), also enter the ears of corn and feed on kernels. Full-grown western bean cutworm caterpillars are light brown to pale gray with light brown heads. Behind the head is a wide, dark brown collar (prothoracic shield) marked with three narrow, pale stripes.

Another "headworm" affecting sorghum production is the **sorghum webworm,** *Nola sorghiella* Riley. Adult moths have a ⅝-inch wingspan, with whitish, poorly-patterned fore wings. Caterpillars grow to about ½ inch long and their bodies are covered with spines or hairs, green to tan in color, and marked with 4 reddish-brown lengthwise stripes. Caterpillars feed on ripening grain, consuming the contents and leaving the hull intact.

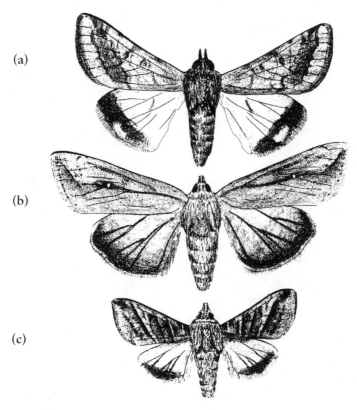

(a) Corn earworm; (b) armyworm; (c) tobacco budworm

Life cycle: Corn earworm eggs are pin-head sized and have characteristic ridges. They are laid singly by female moths and turn from white to dark brown before hatching in 3 to 10 days. Larvae pass through 6 stages (instars) with the first being about 1/16 inch long. Larval development takes about 18 days before they pupate in the soil and remain for about 8–14 days. Development from egg to adult takes 3 to 4 weeks during the summer. There are several generations each year.

Pest status: Caterpillar stages are pests of many agricultural crops.

Habitat and food source(s): The newly hatched caterpillar will eat its egg shell and then feed on tender leaves. Older caterpillars feed on older leaves and tunnel into fruit. A wide variety of wild plants and crops including beans, corn, cotton, peanuts, sorghum, tomato, and ornamental (bedding and flowering) plants are suitable hosts. Caterpillars have silk glands and produce silk threads around feeding sites. Adults are attracted to lights.

Literature: Mock et al. 1981; Neunzig 1964; Stinner et al. 1980.

Lepidoptera: Noctuidae   *Spodoptera exigua* (Hübner)

Description: Adult moths have a wingspan of 1 to 1¼ inches. However, wings are held over the back when at rest. The fore wings are grayish-brown with two pale spots near the center. The caterpillars (larvae) are overall green or marked in shades of green with stripes, grow up to about 1¼ inches long, and can best be identified by a characteristic small black spot on each side of the second body (thoracic) segment behind the head.

See **fall armyworm (321).**

Life cycle: Winter is usually spent in the pupal stage. In spring, mated female moths lay clusters of about 80 spherical, ribbed eggs covered with hairs and scales from her body. Tiny caterpillars hatch from the egg mass in 2 to 5 days and develop through 5 stages (instars) over a period of about 3 weeks. Thereafter, caterpillars pupate in the ground within a cell constructed ¼ inch deep and made of soil and trash particles glued together with a sticky secretion. Moths emerge within 5 to 8 days. The life cycle requires 30 to 40 days, depending on temperature, and several generations can occur annually. Beet armyworm moths are known to migrate northward each year.

Pest status: Caterpillars feed on foliage on a wide variety of agronomic and horticultural crops and cause severe crop losses when they occur in large numbers.

Habitat and food source(s): Young larval stages feed close together, often grazing on the outer (epidermal) layer of cells on the underside of leaves. They may spin a light web over the foliage. Older, larger caterpillars feed alone and consume leaf tissue that can result in complete defoliation of host plants. In cotton fields, they also feed on developing squares and bolls. Alfalfa, citrus, corn, grasses, legumes, onion, ornamental plants, pea, pepper, potato, soybeans, sugar beets, sunflower, tomato, vegetables and weeds such as plantain and pigweed also serve as hosts for this species.

Literature: Bohmfalk et al. 1982; Cameron et al. 1982.

321, 322   FALL ARMYWORM

Lepidoptera: Noctuidae   *Spodoptera frugiperda*
                                          (J. E. Smith)

Description: Adult moths have dark gray mottled fore wings marked with light and dark areas. Wings are held over the back of the body when at rest. Outstretched wings measure about 1½ inches from tip to tip. The hind wings are whitish. Caterpillars grow to about 2 inches long and are marked with green, brown, or black colors arranged in stripes, with darker stripes along the sides. The top of each abdominal segment is marked with two pairs of black dots from which stiff hairs arise. The front of the dark head capsule is marked with a pale-colored upside-down "Y."

The "true" **armyworm,** *Pseudaletia unipuncta* (Haworth), is difficult to distinguish from the fall armyworm in the larval stage. Caterpillars are pale-green to yellowish or brownish-green with bodies that are somewhat wider in the middle. Adult moths have predominantly pale brown to grayish-brown wings. The center of each fore wing is marked with a single small white spot.

Adult moths of several groups can sometimes be abundant at lights at night, which may be confused with other "armyworms." One such genus is *Melipotis* (322) which has larvae that feed on mesquite and other wild plants.

Life cycle: Winter is spent primarily as pupae, although all stages may be encountered during mild winters. Adults emerging in early spring mate, disperse, and lay eggs on host plants. Females lay clusters of a hundred or more eggs that are covered with fuzzy, gray scales from the female's body. Caterpillars hatch from eggs in about 10 days and begin feeding together, first on the remains of the egg mass and then on the host plant. Larvae grow and molt between several stages (instars) over a period of 2 to 3 weeks, before digging a burrow up to 8-inch deep in the ground in which to pupate. The pupa is about ½ inch long, reddish brown to black, smooth and hardened. Adults emerge in about 2 weeks. Several generations can occur annually. It is most common in late summer or fall.

Pest status: Caterpillars are commonly encountered in agricultural fields, landscape plants and turf.

Habitat and food source(s): Fall armyworms feed on a wide range of plants, including Bermuda grass, corn, fescue, Johnson grass, rice, rye grass, small grain crops, sorghum, Sudan grass, and timothy. In corn, caterpillars can damage foliage as well as the ears. Caterpillars often occur locally in large numbers and migrate together like an army as they devour host plants, eating all above ground plant parts. They feed at all times of the day or night. Adult moths are attracted to lights.

Literature: Brook et al. 1982.

323 YELLOWSTRIPED ARMYWORM

Lepidoptera: Noctuidae　　　　　　　　*Spodoptera ornithogalli*
　　　　　　　　　　　　　　　　　　　(Guenée)

Description: Adult moths have a wingspan of 1½ to 1¾ inches. Caterpillars are up to 2 inches long and vary in color from green when small to almost black when large. They have two cream yellow to orangish stripes along the back, and a prominent dark spot on the sides of the fourth body segment behind the head (the first legless abdominal segment). Partially-grown larvae appear to have pairs of triangular dark markings along the back of each body segment inside of the light-colored stripes.

Yellowstriped armyworm caterpillars can be identified by examining the front of the head capsule. They have light-colored markings along the seams (sutures) of the "face" that appear as an upside-down "Y." Also see **beet armyworm** (320) and **fall armyworm** (321, 322).

Life cycle: Adult moths lay clusters of eggs on host plants and then cover them with scales from their bodies. Small (⅛ inch) caterpillars hatch from eggs in about 6 days. Caterpillars develop through several molts to increasingly larger stages (instars) over a period of about 20 days until they pupate in the soil for 14 days or overwinter. Adult moths emerge from the pupae. Several generations can be produced each year, each being completed in 35 to 45 days to several months depending on temperature, food, and environmental factors.

Pest status: Caterpillars feed on many plants.

Habitat and food source(s): This is one of the most common caterpillars encountered in the vegetable garden, feeding on leaves during the day. Caterpillars strip foliage from one plant and then move on to the next available food plant. Although certain plants are preferred hosts, such as cotton, tomatoes, chrysanthemums, forages, and turf grasses, larvae will feed on many plants. In cotton, larvae also tunnel into developing cotton bolls.

Literature: Bohmfalk et al. 1982; Jackman 1981a; Metcalf et al. 1962; Rings and Musik 1976.

324 CABBAGE LOOPER

Lepidoptera: Noctuidae   *Trichoplusia ni* (Hübner)

Description: Adult moths are mottled grayish-brown with a 1½-inch wingspan. Each fore wing is marked near its center with a pair of characteristic silver markings: a spot and a mark resembling a "V" or an "8" with an open end. The caterpillar (larva) grows to be about 2 inches long, is light green and has 3 pairs of "true" legs behind the head plus pairs of fleshy "false legs" (prolegs) on the 3rd, 4th and last, or 6th, segments behind the segment with the last pair of true legs (the abdominal segments). This arrangement of legs causes the caterpillar to crawl with a "looping" motion, similar to that of inchworms. Some specimens are marked with light stripes along the body.

Other looper species include the **celery looper,** *Anagrapha falcifera* (Kirby), and the **soybean looper,** *Pseudoplusia includens* (Walker). "Loopers" (Noctuidae) usually can be separated from **"inchworms" (293)** (Geometridae) by the configuration of the "false legs" or prolegs. Inchworms generally have 2 pairs of prolegs, while loopers generally have 3 pairs.

Other caterpillars found on cabbage include white butterflies (Piercidae) such as the imported cabbageworm, *Pieris rapae* (Linnaeus).

Life cycle: Winter is spent in the pupal stage inside of a cocoon attached by one side to the host plant material. Adults emerge in the spring, mate, and fly to a suitable host plant. Eggs are smooth, light green, and slightly flat. Within about 3 days, small caterpillars hatch from the eggs. During a period of about 4 weeks, caterpillars feed and develop through several stages (instars) before spinning a silk cocoon in which they form a greenish to brownish ¾-inch pupa. Adults emerge in about 13 days unless they overwinter. Development from egg to adult can be completed in about 35 days. Four generations or more can be produced each year.

Pest status: One of the most common caterpillars found in garden and bedding plants.

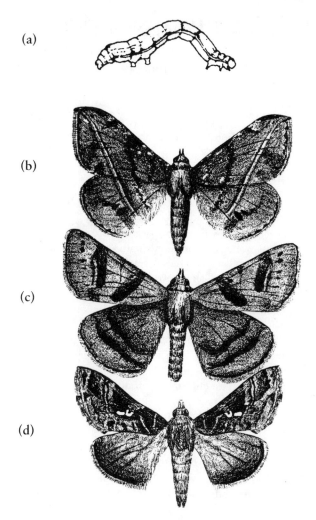

(a)

(b)

(c)

(d)

(a) Cabbage looper; (b) velvetbean caterpillar moth; (c) green cloverworm moth; (d) soybean looper moth

Habitat and food source(s): Cabbage loopers feed on leaves of a wide variety of plants, including beets, cabbage, carnation, cotton, kale, lettuce, nasturtium, parsley, peas, potato, soybeans, spinach, and tomato. Injured leaves appear tattered, with irregular-shaped holes removed between major leaf veins. Adults are attracted to lights at night.

Literature: Bohmfalk et al. 1982; Metcalf et al. 1962.

ORDER HYMENOPTERA
Sawflies, Ichneumonids, Gall-Forming Chalcids, Ants, Wasps, and Bees

DESCRIPTION

- Adult Hymenoptera are winged or wingless; winged members have 2 pairs of membranous wings with relatively few veins.
- Most Hymenoptera like bees, ants, and wasps have the body constricted greatly between the abdomen and thorax, although sawflies and horntails have wide waists.
- The abdomen in the females ends in an egg-laying structure (ovipositor), which may be modified into a stinger or a saw-like organ.
- Immature stages have chewing mouthparts and are maggot-like for ants, bees and wasps. Legs are present in some forms like sawflies, which resemble caterpillars, and these even have prolegs but without crochets (see Lepidoptera). They have a more or less well developed head capsule.
- Habits of these insects are varied: some are predaceous; some are parasitic; some cause plant galls; and some feed on plant foliage. Sawfly larvae feed on foliage. Horntail larvae feed in wood like borers. Others, such as bumble bees and honey bees feed on plant pollen and nectar.
- Mouthparts are formed for chewing or modified like in honey bees for both chewing and sucking.
- Hymenoptera are microscopic to about 3 inches in length.

LIFE CYCLE

- Metamorphosis is complete (egg, larva, pupa, adults).
- Some species (Cynipidae) have complex life cycles that produce more than one form of adult.

PEST STATUS

- Many Hymenoptera have a painful sting and should be avoided if possible.
- Some groups contain many species that parasitize other insects and are considered to be important biological control agents. Many others are predaceous on other insects as adults and are considered beneficial even though they sting.

HABITAT

- Hymenoptera can be found in a wide variety of habitats.
- Many Hymenoptera are social insects that live in colonies and feeding is communal.
- Bees are important pollinators of plants.

Hymenoptera: Cimbicidae,   Many species
Diprionidae and Tenthredinidae

Description: These primitive wasps are not flies (Diptera), which have only 2 pairs of wings. Common sawflies (Tenthredinidae) are wasp-like, often brightly colored and up to ¾ inch long. The adult **elm sawfly,** *Cimbex americana* Leach (Cimbicidae), is ¾ to 1 inch long, dark blue, parallel-sided, and females have 4 small yellow spots on each side of the abdomen. The full-grown elm sawfly larva is 1½ inches long, greenish-yellow with a black stripe down the center of the back. **Conifer sawflies** (Diprionidae) have somewhat more compact bodies and the antennae of females are feathery (pectinate or bipectinate). They are called sawflies because females of most species have a saw-like structure on the tip of their abdomens used to deposit eggs into plant tissue. Larval stages are caterpillar-like, with a well-developed head capsule and 3 pairs of true legs behind the head and a hairless body. Unlike caterpillars (Lepidoptera larvae), fleshy "false legs" (prolegs) occur on at least the 2nd–6th abdominal segments, and the bottoms of these prolegs lack rows of tiny hooks (crochets) found only on caterpillars. Some sawfly larvae are slug-like, appearing slimy, unsegmented and translucent, greenish to black, while others appear wax-covered in some of their developmental stages. Larvae can change in appearance and coloration through developmental stages.

Life cycle: Life cycles vary by species, but generally they overwinter as a pre-pupa in a cocoon in the ground or other protected place, pupating in the spring. In early summer, adults lay eggs in or on plant tissue. Larvae develop through several stages (up to 6 instars) before pupating, producing up to several generations per year.

Pest status: Adults are rarely seen and do not sting. Larvae feed on the leaves of plants and can occasionally become numerous enough to cause damage to some trees.

Habitat and food source(s): Most sawflies are somewhat host-specific. The elm sawfly feeds on elm and willow. Some sawflies, e.g., the **loblolly pine sawfly,** *Neodiprion taedae linearis* Ross (Tenthredinidae), can occasionally cause serious damge to pines and other evergreens by feeding on foliage, tunneling into buds or boring into shoots. Larvae of the **blackheaded ash sawfly,** *Tethida barda* (Say) (Tenthredinidae), and **brownheaded ash sawfly,** *Tomostethus multicinctus* (Rohwer) (Tenthredinidae), feed on red and white ash. Common sawfly larvae feed together (gregariously) and may hold their abdomens coiled over the edge of the leaf. On broad-leaved tree leaves, larvae usually feed on the underside of the leaf. Larvae of *Caliroa* spp. (Tenthredinidae) skeletonize leaves, while pecan sawfly larvae produce round holes of various sizes in leaves. Some species are leaf rollers, web formers, leaf skeletonizers, leafminers or cause plant galls. Adults can be found on flowers.

Literature: Borror et al. 1989; Johnson and Lyon 1988.

326   PIGEON TREMEX

Hymenoptera: Siricidae   *Tremex columba* Linnaeus

Description: The adult wasp is 1 to 1½ inches long, with a straight-sided cylindrical reddish-brown body marked with a yellow banded and black pattern on the abdomen. Wings are tinted dark brown to black. Both sexes possess projections on the end of the abdomen ("horntails"). In addition, females have a longer projection that arises from the undersurface of the abdomen called an ovipositor, used to deposit eggs in tree trunks.

Siricidae are also called "wood wasps." Adults may be confused with sawflies.

Life cycle: Females deposit eggs singly, into the wood of host trees. Larvae are grub-like, whitish, deeply segmented and have poorly-developed legs. They develop through several stages (instars) reaching a size of about 2 inches before pupating. Development is normally completed in 2 years.

Pest status: Although larval stages develop in trunks of trees, host trees are usually stressed, dying or dead from other causes; damage caused by larvae seldom threatens tree health, although female wasps can infect the host tree with a tree-rotting fungus, *Cerrina unicolor*; adults do not sting.

Habitat and food source(s): Larvae develop in the trunks of dead and dying trees, including beech, elm, maple, oak and others. Larvae produce a round tunnel in the sapwood and heartwood.

Literature: Borror et al. 1989; Johnson and Lyon 1988; Swan and Papp 1972.

327, 328   ICHNEUMONS

Hymenoptera: Ichneumonidae   *Megarhyssa macrurus*
                                          (Linnaeus) and others

Description: Adults of *Megarhyssa macrurus* (**327**) have brown bodies, up to 1½ inch long, marked with black and yellow markings and transparent wings. Females have a very long (up to 3 inches long) thread-like egg-laying structure (ovipositor) on the end of their abdomens.

Rhyssella species are black with white markings, not as large as *Megarhyssa,* and parasitize wood-boring wood wasp larvae (Xiphydriidae) in conifers. Possibly a more common ichneumon is *Ophion nigrovarius* Provancher, which is reddish or dark yellow-brown, 1-inch long, with brown-tinted wings. Larvae feed on immature stages of white grubs (Coleoptera: Scarabaeidae). Adults can sting and are frequently encountered around lights in and around the home (**328**).

Life cycle: The larva of *M. macrurus* hatch from eggs inserted into the tunnels of the **pigeon tremex (326)**. Larvae are grub-like and develop through several stages (instars) before pupating inside a cocoon in host insect tunnels. Adults emerge in the spring. Most species overwinter in the cocoon as a mature larva, although some spend the winter as adult females. There may be 1–10 generations produced annually depending on the species.

Pest status: The family, Ichneumonidae, contains many species considered to be beneficial insects because their larvae develop on other insect pests; although generally considered to be harmless some species are capable of stinging when improperly handled.

Habitat and food source(s): Females of *M.* macrurus insert their ovipositor through the bark of dead deciduous trees and lay eggs in the tunnels of the pigeon tremex. Larvae crawl along the tunnel until encountering a host larvae on which they feed. Adult wasps can occasionally be found in the spring (March), attached to the trunk on a dead tree with their long ovipositor.

Most ichneumons are smaller parasitic wasps. Adults often feed on body juices of hosts and larvae feed on immature stages, such as larvae and pupae of butterflies and moths (Lepidoptera), beetles (Coleoptera), flies (Diptera), sawflies, and wasps (Hymenoptera). Some species attack spiders or are hyperparasites (parasites that feed on other parasites) and, thus, might not be considered to be beneficial insects.

Literature: Arnett 1985; Borror et al. 1989; Metcalf et al. 1962; Swan and Papp 1972.

329   PARASITIC WASPS

Hymenoptera: Braconidae,   Many species
Ichneumonidae, and others

Description: Adults of many species are very small (ranging from $\frac{1}{100}$ to $\frac{3}{4}$ inch long) and often go unnoticed. They vary in shape and coloration, but usually have long, thread-like (filiform) antennae that may appear elbowed. They have clear or colored wings with characteristic venation, and a narrow "waist" between the thorax and abdomen. Females of many species have a spine-like egg-laying structure (ovipositor) at the tip of the abdomen. Larval stages are usually not observed unless they are dissected from hosts (internal parasites) or detected on the host (external parasites). They are usually cream colored, legless, and tapered at both ends. Occasionally, caterpillars are observed with white silken cocoons of parasites (Braconidae) attached to their bodies (**329**). Stages of immature whiteflies parasitized with *Encarsia formosa* (Gahan) (Encyrtidae) are darker or black when late in the parasite development compared to yellowish to creamy healthy ones (see figure 100). Aphids are hosts for species in the subfamily Aphidiinae (Braconidae) such as *Aphidius* spp. and others in the family Aphelinidae. Parasitized aphids, called "aphid mummies," appear puffed up, brown, and hardened. The adult parasitic wasps chew a round hole in the abdomen to emerge.

Life cycle: Biology and details of development vary with species. Adult wasps emerge from pupae and females seek suitable host insects into or on which to lay eggs singly or in clusters. Usually, a larva hatches from an egg and develops through several stages (instars) before forming a pupa. However, some parasitic wasps, such as *Copidosoma* spp. (Encyrtidae), undergo a process called polyembryony, whereby an egg inserted into a host divides and gives rise to hundreds of larvae. Most parasitic species have high reproductive capacity and develop rapidly. Several generations can sometimes develop during a single generation of the host, although some species have only a single generation per year.

Pest status: Numerous tiny wasps parasitize various stages of other insects; many are beneficial parasites that kill other insect pests, while some are considered harmful because they parasitize parasites (a process called hyperparasitism) or other beneficial insects; some may sting if mishandled.

Habitat and food source(s): Larval stages of parasitic wasps develop inside or outside of a single host during one or more of the host's developmental stages (egg, larvae, pupae or adult). Most insect groups (including aphids, beetles, caterpillars, flies, sawflies, scale insects, and true bugs) are attacked by parasitic wasps. Many species are host specific, developing in one or a limited number of related host species. For example, the species of *Trichogramma* (Trichogrammatidae) primarily parasitize the eggs of caterpillars. Adults of some parasitic wasps feed on other insects to obtain energy to seek other suitable hosts into or on which to lay eggs. This behavior is called host feeding.

Literature: Arnett 1985; Mahr and Ridgway 1993.

330 MEALY OAK GALL WASP

Hymenoptera: Cynipidae   *Disholcaspis cinerosa* (Bassett)

Description: This wasp produces 2 kinds of galls. The most notable are produced by the asexual generation that are spherical, corky, ⅛ to 1 inch in diameter and appear on twigs and branches of live oak in late summer and early fall. When first formed, they are pink to pinkish brown and the yellow-green tissue inside is moist and soft. The other type of gall is produced in the spring, but is small, beige-colored, and resembles a kernel of wheat.

A number of cynipid wasps cause unique galls on oak trees: the **gouty oak** and **horned oak gall (woody twig galls)**, *Callirhytis* spp.; **hedgehog gall**, *Acraspis erinacei* Beutenmuller (leaf galls with orangish "hair"); **wool sower gall**, *Callirhytis seminator* Harris (stick, spongy galls on twigs with seed-like structures inside); **woolly leaf gall**, *Andricus laniger* Ashmead (leaf galls on post oak); and, **oak apple**, *Amphibolips* spp. (spherical, spongy-filled galls on red oak). Galls on trees are also caused by other insects such as some species of aphids, flies, *Phylloxera*, psyllids, thrips, and mites.

Life cycle: Adults emerge from galls of the "asexual generation" during December. All adults are female and do not mate before laying eggs on swollen leaf buds. Eggs hatch in early spring as leaf buds begin to open. Larvae develop quickly in leaf tissue and stimulate the development of the small type of gall. Adults of both sexes emerge from these galls or the "sexual generation" after a few weeks. After mating, females lay eggs in post oak twigs and branches. These eggs remain dormant for 3 to 5 months. Then they hatch and stimulate the formation of the larger type galls of the asexual generation.

Pest status: Although adult wasps are rarely seen, the galls produced on live oak trees around developing stages are noticeable when numerous and can disfigure trees.

Habitat and food source(s): This cynipid wasp species only affects post oak trees.

Literature: Drees 1994; Frankie et al. 1978; Johnson and Lyon 1989.

331–333 CICADA KILLER

Hymenoptera: Sphecidae   *Sphecius speciosus* (Drury)

Description: These wasps reach up to 1½ inch in length. Except for a rusty red head and thorax, they are overall black or rusty in color, with yellow band markings on the abdominal segments. They have russet colored wings. Other sphecid wasps include **digger wasps, sand wasps (332),** *Bembix* sp., and **mud daubers (334, 336).**

The **tarantula hawk (333),** *Pepsis* sp., (Pompilidae) is about 1½ inches long, black with long legs and yellow-orange wings edged in black. Spider wasps (Pompilidae) provision their nests with spiders, including tarantulas, as food for their immatures. Pepsis sting the tarantulas and drag them into burrows in the ground.

Life cycle: Cicada killers spend winters in the larval or pupal stage. Adults emerge in the summer, feed, mate, and produce new nesting burrows. The female provisions each cell in the burrow with one or more paralyzed cicadas on which an egg is deposited, and then seals it. The wasp larva hatches from the egg and develops through several molts (instars) before pupating inside a woven, spindle-shaped brown case measuring up to 1¼ inches long. One generation occurs per year.

Pest status: One of the largest wasps encountered; although females are capable of stinging, they are rarely aggressive towards man or animals; males are incapable of stinging, but can be more aggressive; large numbers of females nesting in localized areas such as sandy embankments can be a nuisance and cause concern because of their large size, low flight and nesting activities; nest entrances are often accompanied by a pile of soil excavated from the burrow that may disturb turf grass.

Habitat and food source(s): Cicada killers nest in sandy areas, digging burrows about 6 inches deep before turning and extending another 6 or more inches. Tunnels may be branched and end in one or more globular cells. Females are solitary, each provisioning their own nests even though they appear to be nesting in a common area. Cicada killers are active during July and August, coinciding with the appearance of cicadas which they attack, sting, and paralyze. They then fly, glide, or drag the cicadas back to their nests, provisioning the cells in their burrows. Larvae feed only on cicadas; the adult will feed on flower nectar.

Literature: Borror et al. 1989; Brook et al.1982; Swan and Papp 1972.

Hymenoptera: Sphecidae   Many species
and Vespidae

Description: Adult **mud daubers** (Sphecidae) are ¾–1 inch wasps, varying in color by species from dull black to black with bright yellow markings to iridescent blue-black. The best identifying feature is the longer, narrow "waist" or petiole–the section between the thorax and abdomen. **Potter wasp (336),** (*Eumenes fraternus* Say (Vespidae), wings are folded in half, lengthwise, when at rest. Their bodies are smaller (⅜ to ¾ inch long), black with yellow markings on the abdomen and thorax, and also with a narrow "waist."

Life cycle: These are solitary wasp species, with nests constructed and provisioned by individual mated females. Eggs of mud daubers are laid singly on hosts in cells in mud nests provisioned with food, sealed, and abandoned. Larvae grow up to 1 inch long and are cream-colored, legless, and maggot-like. They pupate in cocoons within the cells and overwinter in nests. There can be several generations annually. Eggs of potter wasps are attached to the top inner surface of cells before the nest is provisioned with food and sealed.

Pest status: Although capable of stinging, they are rarely aggressive. Mud dauber nests can be a nuisance in garages, under eaves and in other buildings, while potter wasps construct tiny clay vase-like nests usually attached to twigs but sometimes to structures.

Habitat and food source(s): Mud daubers build small nests of mud under overhangs like eaves of buildings. The **pipe organ mud dauber,** *Trypoxylon politum (*Say), builds mud nests of long parallel tubes and provision their nests with spiders. The **black and yellow mud dauber,** *Sceliphron caementarium* (Drury), constructs a globular nest containing one cell to several cells, also provisioned with paralyzed spiders. Adults are commonly seen in wet spots, making balls of mud for building their nests. The iridescent **blue mud dauber,** *Chalybion californicum* (Saussure), takes over nests of the black and yellow mud dauber and provisions it mostly with black widow spiders. The **potter wasp (336),** constructs a nest of clay that appears like a tiny vase attached to a twig or other object, provisioned with insect larvae (stung, paralyzed caterpillars and beetle larvae). Some potter wasp species use hollowed twigs, deserted mud wasp nests, or holes in brick walls for nesting sites. Adults are commonly seen foraging on flowers. The cuckoo wasp (**337**) (Chrysididae) is often found with mud dauber nests and ground-nesting bees.

Literature: McIlveen 1991; Metcalf et al. 1962; Swan and Papp 1972.

338   LEAFCUTTING BEES

Hymenoptera: Megachilidae   *Megachile* species and others

Description: Adults resemble honey bees. They are mostly black with light bands across the abdomen and a covering of pale hairs on the underside. Females carry pollen on stiff yellow hairs on the underside of the abdomen rather than on the sides of the hind legs like honey bees. Leafcutting bees can be distinguished from other bees by their wing venation.

Not all species of Megachilidae construct nest cells with pieces of leaves. **Carpenter bees** (339), *Xylocopa sp.* (Anthophoridae) also construct cells in holes they dig in structural beams or branches. However, carpenter bees do not construct their cells from pieces of leaves.

Life cycle: They are solitary nesters. Females stack cylindrical, blunt-ended leaf-lined cells in deep nesting holes. One egg is laid in each cell. A white, legless, grub-like larvae hatches from the egg and develops through several stages (instars) before pupating within the cell. Cells are stacked end-to-end. Some species of leafcutting bees are parasitic.

Pest status: These bees cut nearly circular pieces of leaves causing minor plant damage. Nests made in walls of buildings can be a nuisance and cause minor structural damage. They are important pollinators of plants. Another member of the family Megachilidae, the **alfalfa leafcutting bee,** *Megachile rotundata* (Fabricius), is an important pollinator of alfalfa, and can be encouraged to nest in man-made structures. Females are capable of stinging.

Habitat and food source(s): Adult females cut circular or elongate pieces from leaves, particularly from rose, but also from azalea, ash, bougainvillea, redbud, and other cultivated and wild plants. They use leaf pieces to construct walls and partitions of nesting cells in which young develop. Nests are located in hollow twigs, other natural cavities, holes in buildings, and occasionally in the ground. Cells are provisioned by adults with nectar and pollen collected from flowers.

Literature: Borror et al. 1989; Johnson and Lyon 1988; Werner and Olson 1994.

339   CARPENTER BEES

Hymenoptera: Anthophoridae   *Xylocopa* spp.

Description: Adult carpenter bees are large (¾ to 1 inch long) and resemble bumble bees, *Bombus* sp., except that the abdomen is hairless and shiny black rather than being covered by patches of orange to yellow hair found on bumble bees. The carpenter bees in the genus, *Ceratina,* are much smaller (¼ inch) and are dark bluish-green, and make nests in plant stems.

Life cycle: Adults spend the winter in nests constructed the previous year, and become active in April or May. After mating, females construct new nesting tunnels or use pre-existing tunnels. Nesting tunnels are about ½ inch wide and start on the end of wooden beams or at right angles to a surface for ½ to 1 inch before turning and following the wood grain. Tunnels are clean cut and may extend 6 to 8 inches. Females collect pollen and nectar to produce a dough-like mass called "bee bread." Eggs hatch into larvae that feed on the bee bread in their cells. Development varies with species and temperature, but can progress from egg to adult in a little over a month. There may be 2–3 generations per year. Continuous generations may occur in south Texas. Adults emerging in late summer or fall do not mate until spring but may gather and store pollen in their tunnels.

Pest status: Adult female carpenter bees can sting but usually only if aggravated; most carpenter bees "attacking" people passing by nesting sites are territorial males incapable of stinging; structural damage produced by nest-making activities can be somewhat damaging to homes, garages, fences, and other buildings, although damage is largely cosmetic unless nesting sites are used repeatedly over years.

Habitat and food source(s): They prefer unfinished softwoods such as redwood, cypress, cedar, and pine in structures for constructing nests. Carpenter bees do not consume wood like termites, but use wood merely to construct nests. While gathering nectar and pollen carpenter bees pollinate flowers.

Literature: Borror et al. 1989; Hamman and Owens 1981b.

340   BUMBLE BEES

Hymenoptera: Apidae   *Bombus* spp.

Description: Bumble bees are easily recognized, being large (¾ inch long) with black and yellow or orangish hair patterns on their abdomens. Queens and workers have pollen baskets on their hind legs. Bumble bees can be distinguished from carpenter bees because of the presence of orangish or yellow hair patterns on the upper surface of the abdomen of the bumble bee. Some bumble bees in the genus *Psithyrus* are parasites of bumble bees, feeding on larvae.

Life cycle: Fertilized queens survive the winter, select an underground nesting site in the spring and construct a nest in which worker bees are raised. Queens lay eggs that hatch into larvae and develop through several stages (instars) before turning into a pupa. Male and female bees are produced later in the summer. In the fall, all members of the colony die except the fertilized queens.

Pest status: Bumble bees are important pollinators; females are capable of stinging. They can be aggressive around nesting sites but they are rarely aggressive during foraging activities; occasionally, they become a problem when their nest is located next to a building or walkway.

Habitat and food source(s): Nesting sites include clumps of dry grass, old bird nests, abandoned rodent burrows, old mattresses, car cushions or even in or under old abandoned buildings. Most colonies contain a few hundred bees although thriving colonies can contain up to 2,000 bees. Nests may be up to 12 inches in diameter and may have several entrances. Foraging worker bees use long tongues to pollinate clovers and other flowers, collecting pollen and nectar that they bring back to the hive to feed to the colony. Honey is stored in "pots" rather than combs in the nest. Foraging activities occur only during the daylight hours.

Literature: Borror et al. 1989; Hamman 1980.

Hymenoptera: Apidae   *Apis mellifera* Linnaeus

Description: Honey bees are somewhat variable in color but are some shade of black, brown or brown intermixed with yellow. They have dense hairs on the pronotum and sparser hair on the abdomen. Microscopically, at least some of the body hairs of bees (Apoidea) are branched (plumose). The abdomen often appears banded. Larvae are legless grubs, white in color.

Honey bees are the only bee in the genus *Apis* in Texas. They have several varieties or races and have been bred for honey production, temperament, and resistance to disease. These varieties may be recognized to some extent by color and size. However, cross breeding may occur in the wild, so queens from commercial breeders should always be purchased to re-queen colonies. **Africanized honey bees** or "killer bees" cannot easily be differentiated from commercial varieties and requires measuring several bees from a colony and comparing measurements. There are several other bees including **bumblebees** and **leafcutting bees** that also collect pollen and nectar.

Life cycle: Honey bees are social insects. There are three castes of bees: queens, which produce eggs; drones or males, which mate with the queen; and, workers, which are all non-reproducing females. The queen lays eggs singly in hexagonal cells of the comb. Larvae hatch from eggs in 3–4 days, are fed by worker bees, and develop through several stages (instars) in the cells. Cells are capped by worker bees when the larvae pupates. Queen and drones (which develop from unfertilized eggs) are larger than workers and require enlarged cells to develop. Queens complete development in 15½ days, drones in 24 days, and workers in 21 days for larvae and pupae stages. Only one queen is usually present in a hive. New queens develop in enlarged cells and by differential feeding by workers when the existing queen ages, dies, or the colony becomes very large. Virgin queens fly on a nuptial flight and are mated by drones from their own colony or other colonies. Queens mate with several drones during the nuptial flight. New colonies are formed when newly mated queens leave the colony with worker bees, a process called "swarming." Swarms of bees are often noticed and sometimes cause concern until they find a suitable nesting location. A queen may live 3–5 years; drones usually die before winter; and, workers may live for a few months. A colony may consist of 20,000 to 90,000 individuals.

Pest status: Mostly considered beneficial because they pollinate many fruits, vegetables, and ornamental flowers; they produce honey, beeswax, and royal jelly; adult bees can sting, making them a nuisance to man and animals. They are a hazard only to sensitive individuals. Recently, the **Africanized honey bee** (sometimes called the "killer bee"), a race (some consider it a subspecies) of honey bees has entered Texas. Their stings are no more potent than stings of "domesticated" commercially-produced and kept **European honey bees**, which were originally introduced into North America by early European settlers, but the Africanized honey bees tend to be more aggressive in defending their hives and thus are more inclined to sting en masse. Historically in Texas, an average of one human per year dies from insect stings.

When worker honey bees sting, they leave the barbed stinger in the skin with the poison sac still attached. This is fatal for the bee, so each bee can only sting once. Stings should be removed promptly to prevent injection of additional venom. Scrape the sting and poison sac away with a knife or fingernail in such a way as to avoid slapping or pinching the poison sac because this will inject more poison into the skin.

Habitat and food source(s): Complex mouthparts of adults can be used for chewing and sucking. Larvae ingest liquids and have mouthparts reduced. Honey bee workers visit flowers to collect pollen and nectar. During transport to the hive, pollen is held in a structure on each hind leg called the "pollen basket," and nectar is carried in a structure in the front part of the digestive system, called the "honey sac." They return to the hive, which may be provided by man or located in a hollow tree, wall void, or some other sheltered habitat. Pollen is stored in the cells of the comb within the hive. In other cells ("honeycombs"), nectar is converted into honey when the bee regurgitates the nectar, adding an enzyme (invertase) that facilitates the conversion. Nectar must also be concentrated by evaporation. Worker bees feed the larvae, drones, and queen. Wax is produced between the segments of the worker bees' body wall in small flakes. It is chewed and reshaped to form honey comb. Worker bees communicate with other worker bees, conveying information about the type of nearby nectar source, distance, and direction from the hive using "dances." They also regulate the temperature (thermoregulate) in the colony and collect water to use as an evaporative coolant during hot times of the year. Worker bees are generally not aggressive (defensive) during foraging or swarming activities. However, when the hive contains developing larvae and pupae, they (particularly Africanized honey bees) will aggressively attack intruders to defend their colony. They also communicate with sound, queen pheromone, and alarm pheromone.

Literature: Dadant 1979; Metcalf et al. 1962; Swan and Papp 1972.

344, 345   RED VELVET-ANT OR "COW KILLER"

Hymenoptera: Mutillidae

Dasymutilla occidentalis (Linnaeus)

Description: These insects are wasps, not ants. Females are wingless and covered with dense hair, superficially resembling ants. The red velvet-ant is the largest velvet-ant species, reaching about ¾ inch in length. They are black overall with patches of dense orange-red hair on the thorax and abdomen. Males are marked differently, have wings, and cannot sting.

Several other species of velvet ants are common in Texas, including the **gray velvet-ant** or **thistle down mutillid**, *Dasymutilla gloriosa* (Saussure), and another species *D. vestita* (Lepeletier). Most are solitary parasites of immature wasps (Vespidae and Sphecidae), solitary bees, and some other insects such as beetles (Coleoptera) and flies (Diptera). Winged males can be confused with other Hymenoptera. Adults of the **tiphiid wasp (345),** *Myzinum* sp. (Tiphiidae) are black and yellow, ¾ inch long . They can occur in large numbers, sometimes on flowers of landscape plants. Larvae are parasites of white grubs (Coleoptera: Scarabeidae).

Life cycle: Females seek the immature stages of ground-nesting bees, digging to the nesting chambers and eating a hole through the cocoon. She deposits an egg on the host larva, which soon hatches into a white legless grub. The immature velvet-ant eats the host larva, developing through several larval stages before forming a pupa.

Pest status: The common name, "cow killer," is thought to describe the painful sting these insects can inflict to man and animals, although it is doubtful that many cows are actually stung.

Habitat and food source(s): Lone females can be found crawling on the ground, particularly in open sandy areas. Adults are most common during the warm summer months. Larvae are solitary, external parasites of developing bumble bees.

Literature: Borror et al. 1989; Brook et al. 1982; James and Harwood 1969; Swan and Papp 1972.

346, 347   BALDFACED HORNET

Hymenoptera: Vespidae   *Dolichovespula maculata*
                                                      (Linnaeus)

Description: Baldfaced hornets are large (¾ inch long) and black with white markings, particularly on the front of the head and the tip of the abdomen. Front wings of hornets and other Vespidae are folded lengthwise when at rest. They construct an inverted, pear-shaped, enclosed papery nest which can be up to 3 feet long. The grayish brown nest has 2–4 horizontally arranged combs and an entrance hole at the bottom. Also see other Vespidae, e.g., **paper wasps, southern yellowjackets (348–352).**

Life cycle: Baldfaced hornets are social insects. The mature colony consists of a queen, 200 to 400 winged infertile female workers, brood (eggs, larvae and pupae) and, in late summer, males and reproductive females. Eggs are laid in cells of the nest by the queen. Larvae hatching from eggs are fed by workers. Larvae are legless and maggot-like, and develop through several stages (instars) before pupating. Cells are left open during larval development, but are capped by workers when larvae pupate. Mated female wasps or queens overwinter in protected habitats such as cracks and crevices, and begin a new colony the following spring.

Pest status: The only "hornet" reported in Texas, it actually belongs to the yellowjacket family (Vespidae); their sting can be intensely painful.

Habitat and food source(s): Nests usually hang in trees, but may be attached to the sides of buildings. Larvae are fed sugary solutions (nectar, honeydew, juices of over-ripe fruits) and insects (flies and caterpillars) collected and brought to the colony by adult foraging worker wasps. Larvae also feed the adults a sweetish secretion from their mouths. Nests are made of "paper," which workers make from chewed weathered wood from old boards, fences, or siding.

Literature: McIlveen 1991; Metcalf et al.1962; Swan and Papp 1972.

348–350   PAPER WASPS

Hymenoptera: Vespidae   *Polistes* spp.

Description: Paper wasps are ¾ to 1 inch long slender, narrow-waisted wasps with smokey black wings that are folded, lengthwise when at rest. Body coloration varies with species: *Polistes exclamans* Viereck (**348**) is brown with yellow markings on the head, thorax and bands on the abdomen; *Polistes carolina* (Linnaeus) (**349**) is overall reddish-brown.

Unlike nests of **southern yellowjackets,** *Vespula squamosa* Drury, and baldfaced hornets, *Dolichovespula maculata* (Linnaeus), paper wasp nests are open and combs are not encased in a papery outer covering.

Life cycle: Paper wasps are semi-social insects and colonies contain three castes: workers, queens, and males. Fertilized queens, which appear similar to workers, overwinter in protected habitats such as cracks and crevices in structures or under tree bark. In the spring they select a nesting site and begin to build a nest. Eggs are laid singly in cells and hatch into legless grub-like larvae that develop through several stages (instars) before pupating. Cells remain open until developing larvae pupate. Sterile worker wasps assist in building the nest, foraging for food, feeding young and defending the nest. A mature paper wasp nest may have 20 to 30 adults. In late summer, queens stop laying eggs and the colony soon begins to decline. In the fall, mated female offspring of the queen seek overwintering sites. The remainder of the colony does not survive the winter.

Pest status: Nests commonly occur around the home underneath eaves, in or on structures and plants; wasps attack when the nest is disturbed and each one can sting repeatedly; stings typically cause localized pain and swelling, but in sensitive individuals or when many stings occur (as with most arthropod stings) whole body (systemic) effects can occur including allergic reactions that may result in death; males are incapable of stinging because the stinger on the females is a modified egg-laying structure (ovipositor) and it is not present in males; wasps feed on insects, including caterpillar pests, and thus are considered to be beneficial insects by many gardeners.

Habitat and food source(s): Nests are built from wood fiber collected from posts and occasionally from live plant stems, causing some plant damage. This fiber is chewed and formed into a single paper-like comb of hexag-

onal cells. Nests are oriented downward and are suspended by a single fila-
ment. Mature nests contain up to 200 cells. Paper wasps prey on insects such
as caterpillars, flies, and beetle larvae, which they feed to larvae. They actively
forage during the day and all colony members rest on the nest at night.
Wasps can be found on flowers, particularly on goldenrod in late fall.

Literature: McIlveen and Hamman 1991.

351, 352   SOUTHERN YELLOWJACKET

Hymenoptera: Vespidae   *Vespula squamosa* (Drury)

Description: Workers are about ½ inch long, with clear wings. The body is
black with yellow characteristic markings on the head, thorax and
abdomen. The body is not hairy.

   Another "yellowjacket," the **eastern yellowjacket,** *Vespula maculifrons*
(Buysson) is found in eastern Texas.

Life cycle: The colony is initiated by a single queen that survived the winter.
The queen is very large and predominately orange, differing from the worker
and male wasps in a colony. After feeding on nectar and arthropods in early
spring, the queen's ovaries develop and she seeks a nesting site. There she
constructs a nest of 20 to 45 cells and produces eggs that hatch into larvae.
The queen feeds nectar and arthropod prey to these larvae and in about 30
days the first worker wasps emerge from the pupal stage. After the number of
worker wasps increases, the queen no longer leaves the nest. Colonies can
contain up to 4,000 workers. Late in the summer, workers construct larger
reproductive cells in which male and female wasps are produced. After they
emerge, they leave the nest and mate. Thereafter, queens seek hibernation
sites while males swarm in high numbers over hilltops and vegetation.

Pest status: This is a venomous, stinging, social insect, that is abundant in
urban areas. When nests are disturbed, defending worker wasps can inflict
multiple stings; foraging worker wasps may be a nuisance at picnics and
other outdoor events.

Habitat and food source(s): Colonies, constructed out of chewed vegetable fiber that forms paper carton, occur in disturbed habitats such as yards
and roadsides. Nests are most often underground, but occasionally are
found in wall voids and indoors. In Texas, some colonies can survive for several years and continue to grow. Colonies in Texas and other southern states
have been reported that are 6 ft across. In exposed and underground sites,
nests are spherical and consists of a number of roundish combs, attached
one below another, and surrounded by a many-layered outer cover. Worker
wasps leave the nest and seek protein sources such as live insects and animal
carcasses, foraging around picnic tables, garbage cans and other locations.
They do not make or store honey.

Literature: Akre et al. 1981; McIlveen 1991.

TEXAS LEAFCUTTING ANT

Hymenoptera: Formicidae   *Atta texana* (Buckley)

Description: Also known as town ant, cut ant, parasol ant, fungus ant, and night ant, sterile female worker ants are rust brown, ⅟₁₆ to ½ inch long and have 3 prominent pairs of spines on the thorax. The queen is much larger with the body being about ¾ inch long.

Damage to plants produced by Texas leafcutting ants can resemble damage produced by some other chewing insects such as **leafcutting bees (338)**. However, ants and characteristic ant mounds around damaged plants should help determine the cause. Several other Texas ants produce mounds, including the **red imported fire ant (362, 363)**, *Solenopsis invicta* Buren. The other large ants that produce colony entrances with a central opening surrounded by coarse soil are harvester ants such as the **red harvester ant (361)**, *Pogonomyrmex barbatus* (F. Smith). However, the red harvester ants do not have spines on the thorax and usually only gather seeds.

Life cycle: Texas leafcutting ants are social insects. Queen ants deposit eggs that hatch into cream colored larvae that develop through several stages (instars). Fully-developed ¼–½- inch long larvae form pupae. In the spring, some larvae develop into larger (¾ inch) winged male and female ants, called reproductives. Males have much smaller heads than do females and both have long smokey black wings. Sometime between April and June, on clear moonless nights, and usually after heavy rains, these winged ants leave the colony on mating flights. These ants are attracted to porch lights and are some of the largest encountered in Texas. Virgin queens carry a small piece of the fungus from their parent colony in a small cavity inside their mouths. After mating, the males die. The queen looses her wings and digs a small tunnel or gallery in which she begins laying eggs and culturing her fungus garden on her feces. The queen feeds largely on her own eggs until small worker ants develop from the surviving eggs and begin to collect foliage on which to culture the fungus. Colonies can survive for many years and colonies may contain over 2 million ants. The nest interior may be 15 to 20 ft deep and contain numerous chambers interconnected by tunnels.

Pest status: Worker ants bite. This species is primarily a pest of plants because they remove leaves for growing fungi. Large underground colonies are marked on the surface by the presence of many 5–14-inch tall, 1–1½-ft-diameter mounds made of coarse particles of sandy soils and with single central openings. Around colonies, foliage can be stripped from plants in an area over an acre. Colonies are more commonly encountered in deep, well drained sandy or loamy soils; large colonies can excavate soil from underneath roadways, causing a structural threat.

Habitat and food source(s): Worker ants remove leaves and buds from weeds, small grains, forage and turf grasses, fruit and nut trees, including plum and peach trees, blackberry bushes, and many ornamental plants. Pine trees and pine seedlings may also be damaged when other plant material is scarce. Defoliation is particularly noticeable during winter months. Worker ants forage when temperatures range from 45 to 80°F during the year, and mainly at night during the summer. Worker ants travel up to 600 ft or more along foraging trails and dismantle foliage into leaf pieces that they carry back to the colony over their bodies. In the colony the pieces of leaves are used to raise a fungus. Members of the colony feed almost exclusively on the fungus.

Literature: Stewart 1982.

356, 357   CARPENTER ANTS

Hymenoptera: Formicidae   *Camponotus* spp.

Description: Fourteen species of carpenter ants occur in Texas. The largest species is the **black carpenter ant**, *Camponotus pennsylvanicus* (De Geer) and is found primarily in wooded areas outdoors. Common indoor species, *Camponotus rasilis* Wheeler and *C. sayi* Emery, have workers that are dull red bodied with black abdomens. Worker ants range in size from ¼ to ½ inch. They can be distinguished from most other large ant species because the top of the thorax is evenly convex and bears no spines. Also the attachment between the thorax and abdomen (pedicel) has but a single flattened segment.

Winged reproductive carpenter ants should not be confused with winged **termites** (Isoptera). Ants have elbowed antennae, distinctly veined wings of different sizes (large fore wings and small hind wings) and a narrow portion of the body (waist) between the thorax and abdomen. The **acrobat ants,** *Crematogaster* spp., also occasionally nest in wood. These ants are much smaller and have a heart-shaped abdomen that is often held up over their bodies. They feed primarily on honeydew produced by aphids (Homoptera).

Life cycle: Carpenter ants develop through several stages: egg, larva, pupa, and adult. Larvae are legless and grub-like and pupae are cream-colored to tan cocoons, which are often mistakenly called "ant eggs." Development from egg to worker ant occurs in about 2 months. Carpenter ants are social insects and live in colonies made of different forms of ants or "castes." Mature colonies contain winged male and female forms (reproductives), sterile female workers of various sizes, and a wingless ⁹⁄₁₆-inch queen. Winged forms swarm during May through late July.

Pest status: Although these ants can bite, they do not sting. Galleries excavated in wood by carpenter ants to produce nesting sites can weaken structures. Foraging worker ants in the home can be a nuisance.

Habitat and food source(s): These ants usually nest in dead wood, either outdoors in old stumps and dead parts of trees and around homes (in fences, fire wood, etc.) or indoors (between wood shingles, in siding, beams, joists, fascia boards, etc.). Although indoors, colonies are often located in cracks and crevices, the ants can also tunnel into structural wood to form nesting galleries. They often appear to prefer moist, decaying wood, wood with dry rot or old termite galleries. However, structural damage is often limited because these ants tunnel into wood only to form nests and do not eat wood. Galleries (nesting tunnels) produced by carpenter ants usually follow the grain of the wood and around the annual rings. Tunnel walls are clean and smooth. Nests can be located by searching for piles of sawdust-like wood scrapings (frass) underneath exit holes. These piles accumulate as the nests are excavated and usually also contain parts of dead colony members. Occasionally, carpenter ants, particularly *Camponotus rasilis* Wheeler, nest under stones or in other non-wood cracks and crevices. Foraging worker ants leave the nest and seek sources of sweets and other foods such as decaying fruit, insects and sweet exudates from aphids or other sucking insects.

Literature: Ebeling 1978; Hamman and Owens 1981a; Owens 1983.

358–360   PHARAOH ANTS

Hymenoptera: Formicidae   *Monomorium pharaonis*
                                                                                    (Linnaeus)

Description: Also called the sugar ant or piss ant, these are some of the smallest ants, about $1/12$–$1/16$ inch long, with a light tan to reddish body. Over 200 species of ants are known to occur in Texas, and many are occasionally encountered in and around the home. Workers of the **crazy ant (359)**, *Paratrechina longicornis* (Latreille), are fast-running grayish-black ants with long legs and antennae. The **pyramid ant,** *Dorymyrmex insana* (Buckley) **(360)**, is another small ant that usually occurs outdoors and builds small mounds with central openings.

Life cycle: Development of worker ants progresses from eggs (5–6 days), to several larval stages (22-24 days), prepupal stage (2 to 3 days), pupae (9–12 days) and adult ants, thus taking from 38 to 45 days from egg to adult (4 days longer for sexual forms). Colonies consist of one to several hundred queen ants, sterile female worker ants, periodically produced winged male and female reproductive ants (sexuals) and brood (developmental stages). These ants do not swarm. Colonies multiply by "budding," whereby a part of an existing colony migrates carrying brood to a new nesting site.

Pest status: This is the most commonly occurring indoor ant in Texas. In hospitals, it can be a carrier of more than a dozen pathogenic bacteria including *Staphylococcus, Salmonella, Pseudomonas,* and *Clostridium.* These ants do not sting and usually do not bite.

Habitat and food source(s): Pharaoh ants are omnivorous, feeding on sweets (jelly, particularly mint apple jelly, sugar, honey, etc.), cakes and breads, and greasy or fatty foods (pies, butter, liver and bacon). Nests can be found outdoors and almost anywhere indoors (light sockets, potted plants, wall voids, attics, in any cracks and crevices) particularly close to sources of warmth and water.

Literature: Ebeling 1978; McIlveen 1986.

361   RED HARVESTER ANT

Hymenoptera: Formicidae   *Pogonomyrmex barbatus*
                                           Smith

Description: Worker ants are ¼ to ½ inch long and red to dark brown. They have square heads and no spines on the body.

There are 22 species of harvester ants in the United States with most occurring in the West. Worker harvester ants are often sold as inhabitants for ant farms.

Life cycle: Winged males and females swarm, pair and mate. Males soon die and females seek a suitable nesting site. After dropping her wings, the queen ant digs a burrow and produces a few eggs. Larvae hatch from eggs and developed through several stages (instars). Larvae are white and legless, shaped like a crookneck squash with a small distinct head. Pupation occurs within a cocoon. Worker ants produced by the queen ant begin caring for other developing ants, enlarge the nest, and forage for food.

Pest status: Worker ants can bite and produce a painful sting but are generally reluctant to sting. Effects of the stings can spread along lymph channels and may be medically serious; worker ants remove vegetation in circular areas or craters around nests. They are the primary food source of the horned lizard.

Habitat and food source(s): Red harvester ant foragers collect seeds and store them in their nests. In addition to seeds, dead insects are also collected for food. Nests occur in open areas. Often there is no vegetation within a 3–6 ft circle around the central opening of their colony and along foraging trails radiating from the colony. Heavy infestations in agriculture may reduce yield but colonies are usually widely separated. They do not invade homes or structures.

Literature: Brook et al. 1982; Cole 1982; Ebeling 1978; Wheeler and Wheeler 1985.

362, 363   RED IMPORTED FIRE ANT

Hymenoptera: Formicidae   *Solenopsis invicta* Buren

Description: Red imported fire ants produce hills or mounds in open areas where the colonies reside, although colonies occasionally occur indoors and in structures such as utility housings and tree trunks. Disturbance of mounds results in a rapid defensive response by worker ants, which quickly run up vertical surfaces. Worker ants range from ¹⁄₁₆ to ³⁄₁₆ inch in length and are reddish brown. Queen ants are larger (⅜ inch) and remove their wings after mating.

There are 3 other species of fire ants that are native in Texas: the **tropical fire ant,** *Solenopsis geminata* (Fabricius); the **southern fire ant,** *S. xyloni* McCook; and the **desert fire ant,** *S. aurea* Wheeler.

Life cycle: Eggs hatch in 8 to 10 days and larvae develop through 4 instars before pupating. Development requires 22 to 37 days, depending on temperature. Fire ants are social insects, and each colony contains one or more queen ants. Queen ants can produce about 800 eggs per day. A "mature" colony can contain over 200,000 ants along with the developmental and adult stages of winged black-colored male and reddish-brown female ants called "reproductives." These ants stay in the colony until conditions exist for their nuptial flight.

Pest status: Sterile female fire ant workers can sting repeatedly; they first bite, and while holding on to the skin with their jaws, inject venom with stingers at the end of their abdomens. Their unique venom produces a fire-like burning sensation and most people react by developing a whitish pustule or fluid-filled blister at the site of the sting after a day or two; some people are hypersensitive to stings and should be prepared for a medical emergency if stung; most people can tolerate multiple stings but may have problems with secondary infections at the sites of the stings. Fire ants are considered to be medically important pests of people, pets, livestock, and wildlife; they can also damage crops such as corn, sorghum, okra, potatoes, sunflowers, and others by feeding on seeds, seedlings, and developing fruit.

Habitat and food source(s): Only the last larval stage can ingest solid food particles. Sieve plates in the mouths of worker ants prevent ingestion of food particles and thus, they consume mainly liquids. Fire ants infest the eastern two-thirds of Texas. They are omnivorous, but their primary diet consists of insects and other invertebrates. Predatory activities of fire ants suppress populations of ticks, chiggers, caterpillars, and other insects. Predatory activity attributes to wildlife reductions in some areas.

Literature: Brandenburg and Villani 1995; Drees et al. 1996.

Non-Insect Arthropods

Description

- Body with 1, 2, or multiple regions, but never 3.
- All have exoskeletons.
- Body of adults may have 8, 10, or more legs, but never 3 pairs. Legs of all arthropods are jointed.
- No wings are present. Simple eyes, but no compound eyes, may be present.

Life Cycle

- All arthropods molt their exoskeletons periodically during development.
- Development is simple (egg, immature stage, adult).
- Immature stages resemble adults although some may change form to some extent.

Pest Status

- Most terrestrial arthropods are not pests although they can become locally abundant. Some (e.g., spiders, centipedes, scorpions) can bite or sting and are medically important. Others (e.g., pillbugs and sowbugs) can feed on and damage plants.
- Several groups are important predators (e.g., spiders, windscorpions) of insects and other organisms and are therefore considered beneficial.

Habitat

- Many terrestrial arthropods are active at night and hide during the day, while others are day active.
- Some are specific in habitat while others may be widespread.

ORDER SCORPIONIDA
Scorpions

DESCRIPTION

- Scorpions are easily recognized by the pincers on the first set of appendages, the long tail with a stinger at the end and the flattened appearance of the body.
- They have 4 pairs of walking legs.
- Scorpions have 2 eyes on the top of the head region and usually 2–5 along the side of the head.
- There are about 18 species of scorpions in Texas. Many of these are uncommon or are known only locally.
- Size ranges from 1–3 inches.

LIFE CYCLE

- Development is simple (egg, immature stages, adult).
- Females care for the young by carrying them around on their bodies for a short time after hatching.

PEST STATUS

- All scorpions can sting, but no Texas species are considered deadly poisonous.

HABITAT

- They are often found under loose bark of logs and under rocks or ground trash.
- They are usually active at night when they search for prey.

---

364 STRIPED CENTRUROIDES

Scorpionida: Buthidae   *Centruroides vittatus* (Say)

Description: Adults average about 2⅜ inches in length, with the tail being longer in the males than in the females. Body color of adults varies from yellowish to tan, marked with two broad, blackish stripes on the upper surface of the abdomen. Populations in the Big Bend area may be only faintly marked or completely pale. There is a dark triangular mark on the front (anterior) portion of the head region (carapace) in the area over the (median and lateral) eyes. Younger specimens may be overall lighter in color, and bases of the pedipalps and the last segment of the body (postabdomen) is dark brown to black. The key recognition characters for this species are the slender pedipalps and the long slender tail.

Life cycle: Scorpions are capable of reducing their metabolic rates to very low levels. Mating apparently occurs in the fall, spring, and early summer. All scorpions are born live (viviparous), and embryos are nourished in the female's body (in utero or via a "placental" connection). Development (gestation) is estimated to take about 8 months, but varies depending on the species. Young are born in litter sizes from 13 to 47, averaging about 31. The young climb to the mother's back after birth and soon molt. After the first molt they disperse to lead independent lives. Immature scorpions molt an average of 6 times before maturity. Some species may live for 20 to 25 years but the typical scorpion probably lives 3–8 years. Individual adults may produce several broods.

Pest status: The striped centruroides is the most common and widespread scorpion in Texas; stings are painful and produce local swelling and itching that may persist for several days. Reaction to the bite may vary based on sensitivity of the individual. Non-lethal stings may be mild to strong and produce swelling (edema), discoloration, numbness, and pain that may last for several minutes to several days. Deaths attributed to this species are not well substantiated.

Habitat and food source(s): Scorpions use the pincers to capture and hold prey. This species occurs under rocks, under boards, and in debris. It can be found indoors or outdoors in a wide variety of habitats (pine forests in east Texas, rocky slopes, grasslands, juniper breaks in other parts of the state). *Centruroides* are active foragers and do not burrow. They are considered "bark scorpions" with a distinct association with dead vegetation, fallen logs, and human dwellings. It is common for them to climb and many reports in homes are associated with attics. Scorpions remain sheltered in the daytime and become active at night. This behavior helps with regulating temperature (thermoregulation) and water balance. Their bodies are covered with a waxy cuticle that also helps reduce water loss. For reasons yet unknown, the scorpion cuticle fluoresces under ultraviolet light.

Literature: Polis 1990; Shelley and Sissom 1995.

ORDER UROPYGI

365 "VINEGAROONS"

Uropygi: Thelyphonidae

Mastigoproctus giganteus
(Lucas)

Description: Vinegaroons have heavy mouthparts (pedipalps) that are formed into pincers. The first pair of legs is long and thin and is used like antenna to feel their way around. The next 3 pairs of legs are used for walking. The abdomen is attached widely to the head-thorax region (cephalothorax). The tail is long and thin suggesting a whip, which is where the common name "whipscorpion" originates for the order Uropygi. The only species that occurs in Texas is *Mastigoproctus giganteus* (Lucas). Our Texas species is nearly black in color. Bodies of adults are 1½–3 inches long. It is found primarily in west Texas especially in the Trans-Pecos region but has been reported as far north as the Panhandle and in south Texas.

Life cycle: Eggs are carried in a sac by the female. After hatching, they ride on the female's back similar to scorpions.

Pest status: Considered non-poisonous but they can pinch; capable of spraying a mist from scent glands at the base of the tail when disturbed. The mist produced by our species contains 85% concentrated acetic acid, or vinegar, hence the name.

Habitat and food source(s): Vinegaroons are nocturnal with poor vision, relying on sensing vibrations to locate prey. They are more commonly found in desert areas, but they have also been reported in grassland, scrub, pine forests, and mountains.

Literature: Borror et al. 1989; Levi et al. 1990; Rowland and Cooke 1973.

ORDER ARANEAE

Spiders

DESCRIPTION

- Spiders have 2 body regions (cephalothorax and abdomen) and are highly variable in size and shape.
- They also have a pair of palpi by the mouth that act as sense organs and in males are used during mating.
- They are wingless and lack antennae. Most have 6 or 8 eyes.
- Most spin webs of various sorts to capture prey or to serve as a refuge.
- Mouthparts are a pair of chelicerae, each with a piercing tooth or "fang," which are used to manipulate captured prey but all food intake is liquid.
- Size ranges from ⅛ of an inch to over 4 inches.

LIFE CYCLE

- The stages are egg, immature (often called spiderlings) and adult.

PEST STATUS

- All spiders are predators.
- A few (such as the widow spiders and the recluse spiders) are considered poisonous and medically important.

HABITAT

- There are about 900 species of spiders in Texas that can be found in almost any habitat. (For more detailed information see *Texas Monthly Field Guide to Spiders and Scorpions of Texas* by J. Jackman, Gulf Publishing Co., Houston, Texas.)

366 TARANTULAS

Araneae: Theraphosidae *Aphonopelma* spp.

Description: Tarantulas are our heaviest spiders by weight and have a body length of about 1½ inches. They are relatively common throughout Texas and their large size makes them quite recognizable. Typically, the head-thorax region (cephalothorax) and legs are dark brown, the abdomen brownish black. Color may vary between individuals and certainly changes after a molt. There are 14 species of tarantulas in the genus *Aphonopelma* listed from Texas in a recent work. Identification of species is difficult and requires mature males, a microscope, proper literature, and experience.

Life cycle: Females lay 100 to 1,000 eggs in a web that is constructed like a hammock. The egg sac is retained in the burrow, guarded, and usually held by the female. Eggs hatch in 45 to 60 days. Spiderlings hatch in July or later in the year within the egg sac. Once they leave the egg sac, the spiderlings may stay with the females for 3 to 6 days or longer before dispersing. Many of the young fall prey to other spiders or predators as they disperse to begin their own burrows. Females have lived in captivity for over 25 years. Males in Texas rarely live over two or three months after maturity.

Pest status: The large size and hairiness of tarantulas attract attention and concern. Bites of Texas species are generally not serious to humans. When disturbed, tarantulas maneuver to face the threat and will raise up on their hind legs and stretch out their front legs in a threatening posture. When disturbed, they also may rapidly brush the top of their abdomen with their hind legs, which dislodges urticating hairs from the spider abdomen that can irritate the eyes or skin of an attacker.

Habitat and food source(s): Like other spiders, tarantulas have "fangs" on the end of the chelicerae, which inject poison when they bite prey. Spiders only injest liquid food, but they will chew the food somewhat while they feed. Tarantulas occur throughout Texas and are common in grasslands and semi-open areas. They use burrows, natural cavities under logs or stones, spaces under loose bark of tree trunks, and even old rodent burrows as shelters. They also dig their own burrows. Webbing is sometimes used to line the shelter and a few lines of silk are placed on the ground in front of the shelter to detect passing prey. These spiders usually are restricted to the ground but can climb. They usually remain in the burrow waiting for prey to come by but may move a few meters out to forage when necessary. They typically feed on crickets, June beetles, ground beetles, grasshoppers, cicadas, and caterpillars. One of the most spectacular spider events in Texas occurs for a few weeks each summer when male tarantulas actively wander, apparently seeking females. This phenomenon is not well understood and may be related to migration more than mating.

Literature: Janowski-Bell and Horner 1995; Kaston 1978; Levi et al. 1990; Smith 1994.

367   BROWN RECLUSE

Araneae: Sicariidae   *Loxosceles reclusa* Gertsch
                                                       and Mulaik

Description: The shape of the head-thorax (cephalothorax) region and darkened violin markings on the carapace (top of the cephalothorax) are useful identification marks for most of our recluse spiders. Recluse spiders have 6 eyes in 3 pairs, or diads, and a carapace that is quite flat when viewed from the side and highest near the head. The mouthparts (chelicerae) are fused at the base. The color is generally yellowish brown but it can vary. The most distinctive mark is the darker violin shape on top of the carapace. The base of the violin mark is at the front of the carapace and the "neck" of the violin extends backward toward the abdomen. Body length of the female is ⅜ inch; length of the male ⁵⁄₁₆ inch.

Recluse spiders are also known as violin spiders, or brown spiders. There are 13 species of *Loxosceles* in North America; 4 other species in the genus recorded from Texas are the **Big Bend recluse,** *L. blanda* (Gertsch and

Ennik), from west Texas; the **Texas recluse,** *L. devia* (Gertsch and Mulaik), from central and south Texas; *L. apachea* (Gertsch and Ennik); and *L. rufescens* (Dufour) from scattered locations across the state. The Texas recluse may be the most common species in Texas and is often mistaken for *L. reclusa*. Other species in the genus should also be considered poisonous. These other species are very similar but the "violin" markings vary somewhat. Species determinations should be completed using genitalia.

Life cycle: Mating season is from April to July. Females produce up to 5 egg sacs containing about 50 eggs in each. Development to adult may take nearly one year. Laboratory records indicate that they may live for several years as adults. The spiders form a loose irregular sheet web that is used to capture prey and as a retreat. They also form loosely constructed egg sacs that are attached to a surface.

Pest status: This spider is most frequently associated with bites of medical significance; venom is potentially harmful to humans. Recluse bites usually produce a red circular area on the skin, which sloughs off leaving an open wound that is difficult to heal and may require several months before it is completely healed. Reactions vary in severity, depending on the sensitivity of the individual. This spider is quite non-aggressive and bites occur most frequently when it is injured or killed. This may happen when trapped in clothing or bedding. Bites often occur on the buttocks or legs. They typically produce local pain and itching, which may take days or over a week to occur. The bite site may develop a discolored pustulate area that progresses to a necrotic area with an open wound the size of a quarter or larger. Systemic reactions usually are evident within 72 hours and may include rashes, fever, generalized itching, vomiting, diarrhea, shock, or death.

Habitat and food source(s): The brown recluse occurs nearly throughout Texas (although there are no records yet from the Lower Rio Grande Valley). They usually occur found under logs, stones, or other sheltered areas, preferring undisturbed habitats. They can be found indoors where they hide in dark corners, in trunks, under stored clothing, and around almost any undisturbed structure. They are commonly seen moving around at night, undoubtedly hunting.

Literature: Demmler et al. 1989; Gertsch and Ennik 1983; Kaston 1978; Levi et al. 1990.

368 SOUTHERN BLACK WIDOW

Araneae: Theridiidae

Latrodectus mactans (Fabricius)

Description: The body of the female, consisting of 2 regions (cephalothorax and abdomen), is typically shiny black with red markings. The red is usually an hourglass-shaped mark on the underside (venter) of the abdomen, but this may be reduced to remnants. Usually there is a single red spot just behind the spinnerets and sometimes a row along the back. There is much variation in body color with southern and western specimens being more strikingly marked than northern and eastern ones. The male and immature stages have the abdomen narrower, with white lines along the sides. Young spiderlings are orange and white, and acquire more black in later developmental stages (instars) until some have little or no red except for the hourglass markings. Immatures have the abdomen gray with white curved stripes. The body length of the female is about ⅜ inch and that of the male is about 3⁄16 inch, but sizes within different geographical populations can vary widely.

There are more than 25 *Latrodectus* species worldwide. Contrary to common belief, the female does not typically consume the male; this only happens when both are held together in cages and the male cannot escape. Examination of the genitalia is the proper way to identify species in this group. The species in Texas can be separated to some degree by the shape of the red markings on the abdomen and the geographic location.

The **western black widow**, *Latrodectus hesperus* Chamberlin and Ivie, usually has the hourglass marking connected or complete with the anterior triangle larger and wider than the posterior triangle. This species largely displaces the southern black widow in the western half of the state. In southwestern Texas through the Lower Rio Grande Valley and adjoining parts of Mexico, specimens of *L. hesperus* have been found in which the adults retain their brilliant immature colors. Further west, the coloration of the species appears to grade back to black.

The **northern black widow**, *Latrodectus variolus* Walckenaer, usually has the hourglass divided, typically with red spots on the dorsum and white lines on the sides. This species occurs throughout much of the eastern half of the U.S.

The **brown widow**, *L. geometricus* C. L. Koch, is dark to light brown with a pattern and an orange hourglass. They are sometimes called "gas station spiders" because of their habit of building webs in service stations. They are extending their range from the east but their presence in Texas is uncertain.

Life cycle: Adults of both sexes have been found throughout the year in buildings. They can be very common at some locations and times. During the course of a summer a female may lay several egg sacs. The egg sacs are white to tan or gray, pear-shaped to almost globular, of tough papery texture, and about ¼ to ½ inch in diameter. Each egg sac contains from 25 to 400 or more eggs. Egg sacs are suspended in the web and the female stands guard nearby. The second stage (instar) spiderlings typically emerge about 4 weeks after egg sac production. Newly emerged spiderlings are not cannibalistic until 10 to 14 days after emergence, whereupon they may suddenly become highly cannibalistic. Males generally require fewer molts to mature than females.

Pest status: Most notorious of all spiders in the United States; venom is highly virulent, but the spider is quite timid. Even when disturbed in its web it attempts to escape rather than to attack.

Habitat and food source(s): Widow spiders feed on a wide variety of arthropods. Red imported fire ants have been reported as their main food in cotton fields of east Texas. Boll weevils, grasshoppers, June beetles, and scorpions are also known prey. They are found in houses, outhouses, cotton fields, trash and dumps. Webs are commonly found in spaces under stones or logs, or holes in dirt embankments, and in barns, and other outbuildings. The web is an irregular mesh usually built in a dark spot sheltered from the weather. The webs may also have a retreat, typically a $\frac{1}{16}$ to $\frac{5}{16}$ inch circular or semicircular silken tent. The spider spends most of the time in the retreat, venturing out onto the web for web maintenance or when attracted by prey vibrations. Webs are usually placed low to the ground.

Literature: Breene et al. 1993b; Kaston 1978; Levi et al. 1990; Platnick 1993.

ORDER OPILIONES

369   HARVESTMEN

Description: Harvestmen have a globular body. They can be separated from spiders, which have two distinct body segments, because harvestmen have the entire body as one unit. The abdomen is distinctly segmented and the 2 eyes are mounted on a large dorsal tubercle on the top surface of the body (carapace). While most species have extremely long spindly legs, there are species with shorter legs.

Worldwide, there are 37 families of harvestmen; 18 species in Texas. Members of only one family, Phalangiidae, are properly referred to as **daddylonglegs.**

Life cycle: Immature stages resemble adult stages, but are smaller.

Pest status: Harvestmen are not spiders; they are harmless.

Habitat and food source(s): Some species occur nearly everywhere. They are especially common in wooded areas, under rocks or logs, caves, and similar sheltered areas. Harvestmen are primarily predaceous on insects and other arthropods, but sometimes feed on dead insects and plant juices. They have scent glands with ducts to the outside above the bases of the legs (first or second coxae). These glands produce a smelly fluid, which may be the reason for the common belief that they are poisonous. No scientific literature verifies that claim.

Literature: Cokendolpher and Lee 1993; Levi et al. (1990); Rowland and Reddell 1976.

ORDER ACARI
Ticks and mites

DESCRIPTION

- Adults and immatures appear to have a single body "region." They have 8 legs, although some immature stages have only 6 legs. Ticks and mites are wingless, lack antennae, and usually are flat- or round-bodied.
- All members have piercing-sucking mouthparts.
- Many mites are microscopic, but engorged ticks can be over ½ of an inch long.

LIFE CYCLE

- There are usually 4 stages; egg, larva, nymph, and adult. (The terms larva and nymph are not used the same here as in the true insects.)

PEST STATUS

- Ticks only feed on blood of animals.
- Ticks are responsible for spreading disease organisms such as the organism that causes Rocky Mountain spotted fever in man and cattle fever in cattle.
- Some groups of mites feed on plants and may injure crops and ornamental plants. Others are of veterinary or medical importance.

HABITAT

- Ticks may be found almost anywhere but are most common around animals or birds.
- Mites vary greatly between groups. There are: plant feeders found on plants; external parasites of animals; stored products pests; predators on other arthropods; and decomposers that feed on organic matter.

370 LONE STAR TICK

Acari: Ixodida

Amblyomma americanum
(Linnaeus)

Description: Adult ticks have 8 legs and the body is fused into a single region. Lone star tick adults are brown to tan, ⅓ inch long before feeding and up to ½ ich long engorged. Females have a single silvery-white spot on their back while males have scattered spots or streaks around the margins of the body.

Other "wood ticks" include several other *Amblyomma* species; the **American dog tick**, *Dermacentor variabilis* (Say), and the **brown dog tick,**

Rhipicephalus sanguineus (Latreille). Ticks can belong to either of two family groups: "hard ticks" (Ixodidae) and "soft ticks" (Argasidae).

Life cycle: Ticks develop through 4 stages: egg, 6-legged larva or "seed ticks," an 8-legged nymph, and adult. Tick species like the lone star tick are referred to as 3-host ticks because they use different hosts for each feeding stage. Females occur in late spring and early summer. After feeding, they drop from the host and lay clusters of thousands of eggs in ground litter. Males die soon after mating with one or more females and females die soon after laying eggs. There may be overlapping generations, with peak adult and nymphal activity occurring from March through May and again from July through August. Larvae occur in mid-June or July. Its life cycle may take years to complete.

Pest status: This is one of several tick species in Texas. All ticks feed on warm-blooded animals by attaching themselves to the skin using their mouthparts. Tick "bites" can be painful and cause localized inflammation, swelling, loss of blood (anemia), wounds that can get secondary infections, and possibly transmit disease agents such as those causing Rocky Mountain spotted fever, Lyme disease, and tularemia. The bite of a tick is not initially felt. If the tick attaches near the back of the neck and feeds there a while, injecting salivary secretions, the vertebrate victim may suffer from "tick paralysis," which can result in total paralysis and death unless the tick is removed.

Habitat and food source(s): Ticks feed by making a small incision in the skin with their barbed, piercing mouthparts (chelicerae). After inserting their mouthparts they set the barbed teeth on the anchoring device (hypostome) and secrete a fluid that cements their mouthparts into the skin. Lone star ticks live in wooded areas with underbrush, along creeks and rivers near animal resting places. This 3-host tick tends to have a serial host preference: e.g., larval and nymphal stages feed on the blood of separate small wild animals, birds or rodents, while adults feed on larger animals, including livestock and deer. All 3 stages will feed on humans.

Literature: Ebeling 1978; Hair and Bowman 1986; Hamman 1983; McDaniel 1979; Teel 1985.

371 TWOSPOTTED SPIDER MITE

Acari: Tetranychidae   *Tetranychus urticae* Koch

Description: Adult mites are small, ½ inch or less. Body is globular, yellowish to greenish and is often marked with darker spots on the back. The body has 8 legs. The mites spin protective webs of silk over infested plant surfaces.

There are many other spider mites common in Texas, the **southern red mite**, *Oligonychus ilicus* (McGregor) is similar to the twospotted spider mite.

Life cycle: Outdoors, twospotted spider mites may overwinter as adults or continue to breed on host plants in mild winters. Adults lay clear to yellowish spherical eggs, often suspended in a fine web of silk on the underside of host plant leaves. Spotless, clear greenish to brownish, 6-legged nymphal stages hatch from eggs and develop into 8-legged nymphs as they molt 2 more times. Adult male and female mites mate soon after emerging from the last nymphal stage. Generation from egg to adult occurs in 5 to 20 days, depending upon temperature. Many generations can occur per year. When heavily infested host plants decline, the mites spin silk threads and use these strands to passively "fly" or "balloon" in wind to disperse.

Pest status: Plant feeder, causing stippling or bronzing of leaves.

Habitat and food source(s): Mouthparts (chelicerae) appear as tiny microscopic toothpick-like structures with which they can pierce plant cells. Mites pierce clusters of surface (epidermal) cells and use their other mouthparts (palpi) to suck out the contents (mesophyll). Damaged clusters of cells appear as yellow (chlorotic) and later, bronzish (necrotic) stipples on the leaves. On light to moderately infested leaves, stipples are concentrated around the leave's midrib and larger veins. Leaves on more heavily damaged plants can become yellowed, bronze, and fall off.

Pests of many (over 180) agronomic and horticultural crops including soybeans, cotton, small grains, vegetables, and ornamental plants, they also thrive on some weed species (chickweed, pokeweed, wild mustard) and blackberries. All stages occur primarily on the undersides of leaves.

Literature: Carter et al. 1982b; Drees 1994.

TOMATO RUSSET MITE

Acari: Eriophyidae

Aculops lycopersici
(Massee)

Description: Microscopic, about ¹⁄₂₅ inch long, mites with cigar-shaped bodies and 2 pairs of legs.

There are several common mites in the family Eriophyidae in Texas. **Bermuda grass mites,** *Eriophyes cynodoniensis* Sayed, which infest Bermuda grass in low humidity areas of Texas, cause a thickening of the shoots and shortening of internodes. Damaged grass appears pale and stunted. The **citrus rust mite,** *Phyllocoptruta oleivora* (Ashmead), is an occasional pest of Texas citrus that causes bronzing of leaves and green twigs.

Life cycle: Development from egg to adult can occur in 6 to 7 days.

Pest status: Tomato russet mites damage stems, leaves, and fruit of tomatoes and related plants.

Habitat and food source(s): Mites insert their mouthparts into plants and suck out the plant juices. Infested plants are often reddish in color due to the presence of large numbers of mites on the stems and petioles. Mites damage plants and cause bronzing or russeting of the surface of stems, leaves, and fruits. Plant damage starts at the base of the plant and spreads from the stems to the leaves and fruit. On tomatoes, damaged leaves turn brown and paper-like, and may fall off infested plants. Damaged fruit turns bronze and can crack longitudinally. In addition to tomatoes, the tomato russet mite also infests eggplant, pepper, potato, petunia, groundcherry, datura, and various solenaceous plant species.

Literature: Hamman and McIlveen 1983.

CHIGGERS

Acari: Trombiculidae

Trombicula alfreddugesi (Oudemans) and T. *splendens* Ewing

Description: Chiggers are mites that are also called "jiggers" and "redbugs." The parasitic larval stages are very small, requiring a hand lens or microscope to see. The larval stage is less than ⅟₁₅₀ inch long, having a hairy yellow, orange to light red body, and 6 legs. The nymphal stage resembles the adult, having 8 legs, and brilliant red, ⅟₂₀ inch long, figure-8-shaped bodies.

There are many chigger species in Texas, but only a few are annoying to humans. Other species live in moist habitats, swamps, bogs, rotten logs, and stumps.

Life cycle: Adult chigger spend the winter in protected sites such as cracks in the soil and leaf litter on the ground. In the spring, they lay eggs that hatch into the parasitic larval or "chigger" stage. This is the stage that attaches to humans or animals. After feeding for several days, the larva dislodges, drops to the ground and changes into a non-feeding pupal-like second larval stage (the nympho-chrysalis), where it develops into a free-living nymphal stage. After passing through two nymphal stages (one feeding, one non-feeding), the mite becomes an adult. Development can be completed in 40 to 70 days, with up to 4 generations being produced per year.

Pest status: Chiggers cause intense itching and reddish, swollen welts on people and animals due to their parasitic feeding activities. Adult and nymphal stages are free-living and predaceous, feeding on other small arthropods.

Habitat and food source(s): The parasitic larval stage attaches to tender skin with their mouthparts to feed for several days, much like ticks. They prefer to attach in areas where clothing fits tightly such as underneath belt lines and sock bands, and where skin is wrinkled such as behind the knees. The larva injects a digestive fluid that disintegrates the skin cells and forms a feeding tube (stylastome) into the skin. The skin swells around the chigger, making the chigger appear to be burrowing into the skin. The itching, caused by the injection of digestive enzymes, may persist for several days after the chigger dislodges.

In addition to humans, the parasitic larval stage of chiggers feed on domestic and wild animals, including birds, reptiles, and some amphibians. Chigger populations develop in fields and weedy areas, particularly in areas with tall grasses and wild berry patches. Although active from spring through fall, they are more of a problem in early summer, when lush vegetation is prevalent. The larval stages congregate on the tips of plants and other objects from where they crawl onto hosts detected by movement, carbon dioxide, odor and other stimuli. The free-living nymphal and adult stages are predaceous, feeding on insect eggs, small insects, and other organisms such as Collembola in ground litter where they occur.

Literature: Hamman 1983.

STRAW ITCH MITE

Acari: Pyemotidae

Pyemotes tritici (LaGrèze-Fossat and Montané)

Description: These soft-bodied mites are almost microscopic ($\frac{1}{125}$ to $\frac{1}{16}$ inch). They have 4 pairs of legs, with the first 2 spaced far apart from the last 2.

Also see **chiggers.**

Life cycle: Mated females attached to man or insect hosts enlarge to $\frac{1}{16}$ inch, with greatly-distended abdomens containing eggs and developing young. Up to 300 adult mites develop inside the mother and mate soon after leaving the female. These adults seek a host, and produce another generation within a week.

Pest status: Although occasionally sold as a biological control agent for the red imported fire ant, *Solenopsis invicta* Buren (Hymenoptera: Formicidae), it is historically known for medical importance because it is capable of causing rashes to humans; also known as "hay" or "grain itch mites."

Habitat and food source(s): Mouthparts are irritating with reduced stylet-like chelicerae and injection of salivary fluids. Straw itch mites parasitize a wide variety of insects, including stored-grain pests, e.g., Angoumois grain moth, and others. Therefore, they are considered to be natural enemies of arthropod pests. Humans, particularly in grain-growing areas, handling infested straw, crops (beans, cotton, small grains) or crop residues, can be severely affected. Symptoms are similar to those caused by chiggers and develop into a hive-like rash over much of the body. Intense itching may last a week or so, and may be accompanied by fever, headaches, mild diarrhea, vomiting, and joint pain may occur in severe cases. These mites are cultured on caterpillar-infested wheat seeds and sold commercially for application to fire ant mounds.

Literature: James and Harwood 1979; Metcalf et al. 1962.

BROAD MITES

Acari: Tarsonemidae

Polyphagotarsonemus latus (Banks)

Description: Adult mites are microscopic (100 to 300 microns). Eggs are clear, oval, and marked with characteristic rows of white tubercles that appear gem-like under proper lighting. Immatures resemble adults, although smaller in size. Adult males and females have 4 pairs of legs, with 2 pairs toward the front of the body and 2 near the rear. The middle of the body may be constricted to look waist-like. Males are shorter, broad, and have longer hind legs. These mites are very similar to **cyclamen mites,** *Phytonemus pallidus* (Banks), but can be separated by the lack of tubercles on cyclamen mite eggs and by the structure of the hind legs of the males.

Life cycle: The life cycle takes from 4 to 10 days depending on temperature.

Pest status: Feeding causes deformed buds and newly-expanded leaves on host plants.

Habitat and food source(s): Mouthparts are piercing and sucking, similar to spider mites. Broad mites infest a wide range of host plants, including peppers, cotton, citrus, tomatoes, potatoes, beans, gerber daisy, dahlias, zinnias, and chrysanthemums. They are a particular problem on greenhouse grown nursery crops during the winter months. The mites are found on the underside of leaves and in cupped young foliage and flower buds. Affected leaves turn bronzish in color, may thicken, become brittle and appear cupped or otherwise deformed as they emerge. Occasionally, the growing point of the plant is killed.

Literature: Riley 1992.

372   HOUSE DUST MITE

Acari: Epidermoptidae   *Dermatophagoides* spp.

Description: The **American house dust mite,** *Dermatophagoides farinae* Hughes, and the **European house dust mites,** *D. pteronyssinus* (Trouessart), are microscopic ($\frac{1}{80}$ inch long) and rarely seen without the aid of a microscope.

Life cycle: Female mites lay up to 50 eggs each. Eggs hatch into tiny mites that develop through several stages to adults within about 3 weeks.

Pest status: House dust mite infestations cause allergic reactions in some people, including bronchial asthma, nasal allergies, skin allergies, and other symptoms. They are common in almost every home. House dust mites do not bite.

Habitat and food source(s): House dust mites live in warm, humid environments in carpets, upholstery, feather pillows, and under furniture and bedroom mattresses. They feed on shed scales from human skin such as dandruff. Waste product particles (droppings) produced by the mites are the main substance in house dust to which allergic people react. Each mite can produce about 20 waste particles per day, and these particles can cause reactions even after the mites have been removed.

Literature: Ebeling 1978.

373   HONEY BEE MITE

Acari: Tarsonemidae   *Acarapsis woodi* (Rennie)

Description: These mites, which must be dissected from the bee, are very small and a microscope is required to detect them. They are whitish in color with oval bodies, and have a shiny cuticle with a few long fine hairs on the body and legs. They are sometimes referred to as "tracheal bee mites" or "honey bee tracheal mites."

Life cycle: This small mite is an internal parasite of honey bees. It infests and lives entirely within the tracheal (respiratory) system of honey bees primarily in the prothoracic section, except for short migratory episodes. The queens, drones, and workers are all attacked.

Pest status: Honey bees infested by this parasite may become unable to fly. Heavily infested bees may crawl on the floor of the hive or cluster in the hive. Life spans of bees are shortened by heavy mite infestations, which cause a condition called acarine disease or acariosis.

Habitat and food source(s): Tracheal bee mites feed by puncturing the breathing tubes of the host with their mouthparts. They feed on blood from the host.

Literature: Merchant 1995; Pettis and Wilson 1990.

374   VARROA MITE

Parasitiformes: Varroidae   *Varroa jacobsoni*
                                             (Oudemans)

Description: This mite is large enough to see with the naked eye. It appears somewhat like a brown tortoise on the back of adult bees or on developing bees.

Life cycle: Honey bee colonies infested with this parasite may take 2–3 years before they develop signs of infestation.

Pest status: Varroa mites can be a severe problem. An infested bee colony becomes weakened or may even be destroyed by this pest.

Habitat and food source(s): This mite feeds on hemolymph (body fluids) of bees while living on the exterior of adult and immature stages of honey bees.

Literature: Merchant 1995; Pettis and Wilson 1990.

ORDER PSEUDOSCORPIONES

375 PSEUDOSCORPIONS

Description: The body of pseudoscorpions is divided into 2 general regions; the head-thorax (cephalothorax) and the abdomen. The body and appendages have many hairs. The cephalothorax is covered by a shield or carapace that is not segmented. There is usually one or more pairs of eyes on the edge of the cephalothorax. There are 6 conspicuous appendages on the cephalothorax: the chelicerae, the palps, and 4 pairs of walking legs. Chelicerae are short and have a clasping mechanism with a fixed and a movable finger. The pedipalps are longer and have a claw that resembles that of a scorpion. The abdomen has 12 segments but the last 2 are reduced and inconspicuous. They do not have a long tail like scorpions, and they do not sting. Pseudoscorpions are quite small with a body length generally under ⅛ inch.

Life cycle: Pseudoscorpions have spinnerets and produce silk that is used to construct nests and temporary sheets for sperm transfer. Females usually produce only 3 or 4 clutches of eggs but some produce up to 30 eggs per clutch. Immatures hatch from eggs carried by the female. There are 3 additional immature stages which are free living, followed by the adult stage. Although data are sparse, adults are apparently long lived, probably surviving for 6 months to 2 years.

Pest status: Rarely observed; harmless.

Habitat and food source(s): Pseudoscorpions are predators that feed on a variety of small insects and other arthropods. They can be found in a wide variety of habitats, and habitat preference by species is well documented. They can be found in ground cover, leaf litter, in rotten logs, under bark, in bogs, swamps, in rock outcrops, caves, and homes. None are known to be external parasites (ectoparasites), but they can be found in bird and rodent nests where they feed on arthropods in the nests. They are sometimes found on beetles or large insects where they apparently feed on mites.

Literature: Hoff 1949; Weygoldt 1969.

ORDER SOLIFUGAE

WINDSCORPIONS

Solifugae: Eremobatidae and   *Eremobates* and other genera
Ammotrechidae

Description: Also known as sunspiders, windspiders, and sunscorpions, windscorpions are from ⅜ to 2 inches long. Most are yellowish to brown in color, and have 4 pairs of legs. The pedipalps are thin and used like feelers. The first pair of legs are more slender than the others and act as sense organs. The mouthparts (chelicerae) of windscorpions are formed into large jaws that work vertically and project forward from the mouth. The shape of the head with its enormous jaws is quite distinctive. The males often have a more slender body, which is often longer in the males than in the females, and with their longer legs males look bigger.

There are 26 species reported in Texas and most belong to the family Eremobatidae and the largest genus is *Eremobates*. In this family, the front of the head is straight across and the first pair of legs have 1 or 2 claws. The species are difficult to identify. Many are localized or have records from only a few locations.

Life cycle: Females bury their eggs and some guard them. Windscorpions are short lived, probably surviving only 1 year.

Pest status: They do not have venom glands but are capable of biting.

Habitat and food source(s): Present throughout the western and southern parts of the state, they are unknown or at least uncommon in east Texas. They are primarily found in deserts and dry areas. They feed by using their powerful curved jaws that project out the front. Windscorpions are rapidly-moving predators that readily attack prey. They feed on almost any invertebrate and have been known to feed on lizards and other small vertebrates. They can move very fast and run "like the wind," hence the name. They may burrow into the sand or hide under stones and are mostly active at night (nocturnal).

Literature: Levi et al. 1990; Muma 1951, 1962; Rowland and Reddell 1976.

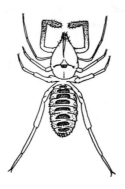

Windscorpion

ORDER ISOPODA

377, 378   SOWBUGS AND PILLBUGS

Description: Adults grow to about ⅜ inch long, have several rounded body segments and 7 pairs of legs. Sowbugs possess a pair of tail-like structures on the back end of the body. Pillbugs do not have these structures and are capable of rolling into a tight ball when disturbed, a behavior that resulted in their common name, "roly-polies."

Isopoda (sowbugs and pillbugs) are terrestrial crustaceans, and are more closely related to lobsters, shrimp, and crayfish. They even have gills. **Saltwater isopods,** *Ligia* sp. occur along the Texas seashore among jetty rocks and pilings. They are active in the evening and run rapidly, superficially resembling cockroaches in form and behavior. They are called "sea roaches" and occasionally enter structures near the waterline. Another group of crustaceans, Order **Amphipoda,** occurs in salt and freshwater habitats. Freshwater amphipods, *Hyalella* sp., build up in large numbers in temporary ponds and puddles. When their aquatic habitats dry up, they leave in search of other bodies of water and occasionally invade homes and structures, hopping about. Members of this group are commonly called "**scud**" (**378**). They are about ¼ inch long, grayish to pinkish and shrimp like in form. **Crayfish** (also called "crawdads"), shrimp, crabs and lobsters belong to the Order **Decopoda.** They have a shield (carapace) that covers the throax and have 5 pairs of legs, the first of which have a large claw. Texas crayfish are poorly known, with 5 species occurring in Brazos County (per. comm. M. Wicksten).

Life cycle: Females lay eggs that they carry in a pouch underneath the body. Eggs hatch into young sowbugs and pillbugs that resemble adults but are smaller. They remain in the pouch up to 2 months after hatching. Development to adults occurs in about a year and they breed mainly in the spring. They may live up to 3 years. Up to 3 broods may be produced annually.

Pest status: Mainly a nuisance, particularly when they venture indoors, they are capable of feeding on tender plant tissue and occasionally cause considerable damage to garden transplants and seedlings; medically harmless.

Habitat and food source(s): Sowbugs and pillbugs spend bright daylight hours in damp dark habitats such as underneath stones, logs, leaf litter and other debris. At night they venture out and feed on decomposing organic material, including mulch and grass clippings. They will feed on the tender foliage, stems, and roots of young garden vegetable transplants, seedlings, and bedding plants. They also rasp the outer skin of cucumbers laying on the ground in gardens, causing fruit to be deformed and blemished.

Literature: Brook et al. 1982; Drees and Wicksten 1990.

CLASS CHILOPODA AND DIPLOPODA

379–381   CENTIPEDES AND MILLIPEDES

Description: Centipedes (Chilopoda) can easily be distinguished from millipedes (Diplopoda) by counting the number of pairs of legs arising from body segments: millipedes have 2 pairs, while centipedes bear 1 pair per segment, with the first pair of legs being modified into fangs. Centipedes are generally flattened and have a pair of well developed antennae on the head. Some centipedes, such as the **house centipede**, *Scutigera coleoptrata* Linnaeus, have long legs and are capable of running rapidly. The largest centipedes, *Scolopendra* spp. (Scolopendridae) may grow to be about 6 inches long. Millipede bodies are rounded or somewhat flattened. Legs are short and movement is slow, with movement of legs appearing wave-like. Most species are less than 1½ inch long, although one species, *Narceus americanus* (Beauvois) (Order Spirobolida), in west Texas grows up to 4 inches long.

Life cycle: Centipedes and millipedes spend the winter as adults in protected habitats and become active in the spring. During the warmer months, females lay eggs in soil and cover them with a sticky substance, although some species give birth to living young. Immature stages (larvae) hatching from eggs several days later are similar to adults but smaller, having fewer leg-bearing body segments. Additional leg-bearing segments are produced with each molt. Millipedes develop through about 7 stages (instars) in 21 to 25 weeks. Some centipedes are known to have lived up to 6 years.

Pest status: Mainly nuisance pests, centipedes have poison glands connected to a pair of jaws and will bite if provoked. The bite is usually not medically threatening except to small children and individuals allergic to venoms. The larger species have more painful bites. Millipedes do not bite; but when disturbed, they can produce an irritating fluid (using repugnatorial glands opening at the base of the legs). This fluid can irritate eyes, blister the skin, produce an unpleasant odor and cause allergic reactions in venom sensitive people. Some species can squirt their fluids several inches. Millipedes, such as the **garden millipede**, *Oxidus gracilis* (Koch) (Polydesmida: Paradoxosomatidae), can become numerous in the greenhouse and damage crops; they may invade homes during cooler weather.

Habitat and food source(s): Mouthparts are for chewing. Centipedes and millipedes prefer to live in moist habitats and during the day stay underneath rocks, logs, and other objects in contact with the ground. They are active at night. Centipedes feed on insects and spiders they kill by grasping them with their powerful fangs and injecting venom. The fangs are located on the body segment just behind the head. Millipedes feed on decomposing organic matter, but will occasionally damage seedling plants by feeding on leaves, stems, and roots. They curl up tightly when disturbed resulting frequently in the release of their repugnatorial fluids.

Literature: Borror et al. 1989; Brook et. al. 1982; Stewart 1979.

Appendix A
Collecting and Preserving Insects

Making an insect collection is one of the best methods of learning about insects. In the process of locating, handling, and preserving insects many observations about the life cycle, habitat, behavior, and appearance of insects are naturally made. These observations contribute greatly to understanding insects and their relationships and roles in the environment.

Insect collections are necessary for the proper identification of insects, a necessary step to properly communicate any information about insects. An insect collection can also be an item of beauty. A well preserved and neatly presented collection can make an attractive display in a home or office. Displays of insects usually become a conversation piece anywhere they are on display.

Collecting Insects

Insects can be found in nearly any habitat. Sometimes they are very obvious, but other times it is necessary to do some hard work or careful observation to discover them. It is important to visit a variety of habitats to collect a wide variety of insects. Be sure to look around lights, under logs or boards, in grassy fields, near ponds or streams, and on flowers, which are all productive locations for insect collecting. Most insects are active in the spring, so concentrate your effort at that time of year. However, grasshoppers, stinkbugs, and other insects may not mature until later in the fall of the year. Therefore, it is necessary to collect in the fall to acquire adult specimens of some of these insects. Be aware of and abide by legal restrictions that apply to collecting insects. National, state, or local laws may apply to species or areas.

Capturing insects for observation or to preserve them in a collection is sometimes quite easy but may be a challenge for some types of insects. Collecting a specific insect or group of insects requires special skills and patience. The most important piece of collecting equipment is the *jar*. Many insects can simply be knocked into an open jar and the lid closed quickly. Forceps are also useful to pick up small or hazardous insects. A soft forceps is preferred for most field use because it is less likely to damage soft specimens.

Perhaps insect nets are the most recognized piece of insect collecting equipment. The typical net is an *aerial* or *butterfly net*. However, aerial nets are best used by dropping them over a resting insect or by scooping an insect from a resting site on a plant. Running across a field with a net overhead and swinging wildly to catch a flying insect is very inefficient and typically results in a broken specimen, although sometimes it is the only way to get one! A *sweep net* has a heavy frame and a heavy cloth bag. It is used by brushing the net bag back and forth (somewhat like a broom) with the net bag in foliage like grass and flowers. The sweep net motion should flip the bottom of the bag around at the end of each stroke into position to make the next stroke through the foliage. The number of "sweeps" can be just a few to 100 or more to amass a large number of specimens in a short time. It is not a very good method to collect delicate specimens because many will be broken in the thrashing of the net.

Aquatic nets are extra heavy and often have a flat side giving the net bag a D shape or triangle shape. These nets are used by placing the net bag on the bottom of a flowing stream. Insects are dislodged upstream by rubbing rocks on the bottom or kicking up the bottom of the stream. Dislodged insects then accumulate in the net.

Another useful tool is the *beating sheet.* This is simply a piece of heavy cloth held flat by sticks (usually in an X fashion attached to the sheet corners). The beating sheet is held or laid under trees or shrubs and the foliage above is beaten with a heavy stick or simply shaken. This action dislodges many insects that fall onto the sheet. Once on the sheet the insects can be viewed, sorted or collected in a jar.

Insects traps can be purchased or made, often fashioned with common household items such as plastic milk jugs or soda bottles. Traps can be passive or include an attraction to insects like bait or light. Lights are very effective at attracting insects of many types. *Black lights* and mercury vapor lights are used and sometimes in combination. A simple white sheet with a black light shining on it can be very effectively used to attract insects. Passive traps are designed to intercept insects as they pass by. *Window pane traps* consist of a pane of glass with a trough below that is filled with liquid to collect the insects that fly into the window and fall. Liquids in these traps can be salt water, soapy water, or ethylene glycol. Ethylene glycol should not be used if wildlife or pets may have access to the liquid. *Pit fall traps* are placed in the ground flush with the surface. Insects walking by simply fall into the traps. Pit fall traps collect crawling insects that are active on the ground at night.

Baits should be selected or made to attract the specific insects of interest. Sugar baits consist of a mixture of brown sugar, water, yeast, and, overripe fruit such as bananas or peaches. Sugar baits are allowed to ferment for a few days and then they are used in a trap or simply painted on the side of a tree. Many moths, beetles, and other insects are attracted to the sugar baits where they can be collected easily. Other insects are attracted to dung or decaying meat. *Pheromones* are chemicals that are given off by an insect to affect the behavior of other members of the same species. There are pheromones for alarm and aggregation. However, the most effective pheromones for traps are sex lures. Sex pheromones for traps are chemicals given off by an insect to attract mates (usually emitted by females to attract males). There are several hundred sex pheromones that are available commercially.

A *Berlese funnel* is a good tool to collect small insects from leaf litter, plant debris, or old logs. The funnel has a coarse screen on the inside on which material is placed and a dish of alcohol below to catch the insects as they move out of the drying debris. The plant material can be allowed to dry or force dried using a light bulb or other heat source to drive the insects out. These funnels can be home-made using plastic soda bottles by cutting off the bottom and inserting a piece of screen.

Killing Insects

Insects should not be killed needlessly. However, when insects are collected for study, killing them usually becomes a necessary step to acquiring a complete, quality specimen. Perhaps the easiest method to kill an insect is simply to put it in a *freezer*. Most specimens will die over night but some cold resistant insects may require a week or more. Usually in field work, insects are collected into a killing jar. Killing jars may be in any size but seldom need to be larger than a pint. Select a jar with a tight fitting lid. Killing jars can be made simply by adding a few strips of paper towels to a jar and then adding a few drops of *ethyl acetate*. Most nail polish remover contains ethyl acetate as an ingredient and can be used rather than special ordering ethyl acetate. The paper allows insects in the jar to keep separated and also picks up excess moisture. More permanent killing jars are made with a layer of vermiculite topped with a layer of plaster of paris (mixed with water) then allowed to dry before "charging" it with ethyl acetate. Label the jar clearly with a "poison" notice.

Avoid putting moths in the same killing jar with other insects. It is best to keep a separate jar for this group because scales from the wings rub off easily and will coat the other insects in the jar. Butterflies can be immobilized or killed while in the aerial net. Grab and squeeze the thorax of the specimen between the thumb and forefinger with the wings folded over the back. The butterfly will be stunned or killed, depending on force of squeezing and time. Thereafter, specimens can be slipped into a *glassine envelope* or paper triangle (see description below). Specimens can be stored in this manner or mounted, either directly or after "relaxing" the specimen.

Soft-bodied insects may be collected (and preserved) in alcohol. *Ethyl alcohol* or rubbing alcohol (70%) are fine for this purpose. Many insects, especially caterpillars, lose their color when preserved directly in alcohol. To improve the appearance of these insects they may be killed in *boiling water* for a few seconds or first killed in a solution called *KAAD* (available from a source of entomological supplies). KAAD consists of a solution of 1 part kerosene, 7–10 parts 95% ethyl alcohol, 2 parts glacial acetic acid, and 1 part dioxane.

Preserving Insects

Most insects have a sufficiently hardened exoskeleton to allow them to maintain their shape after they die. Basically, the hardened exoskeleton remains and the soft internal structures dry up. Insects are stored on insect pins, glued to cardboard points, in alcohol, in envelopes, or on microscope slides. Most insects are pinned through the thorax on the right side. Butterflies, moths, dragonflies and damselflies (Lepidoptera and Odonata) are often pinned through the center of the first thoracic segment (pronotum). Select good quality insect pins, which are longer than sewing pins and are made of materials that resist rust. Insect pins are available from biological supply houses. Number 2 or 3 pins are the most commonly used for insect collections. Thinner or thicker pins have special purposes.

When preserving insects, consider that the characteristic body parts should be observable. It is often wise to position legs and wings to help preserve them by folding them out of the way to make good use of space in the collection. Insects should also be positioned on the insect pins at consistent heights. Use a pinning block to standardize the height.

Small specimens, too small to pin directly, can be mounted on small *cardboard points*. Points are small cardboard triangles. A point punch can be purchased to make them consistently and in quantity. Two-ply bristle board can be used for points and labels, although index cards make a reasonable substitute. White glue (like Elmer's®) is used to glue small insects to points and also to repair damaged specimens. This glue is water soluble and can be soaked in water to reposition the specimen later.

Butterflies, moths, dragonflies, damselflies, crane flies, and a few other groups of insects are sometimes preserved in *glassine envelopes* or *paper triangles*. These insects can be laid flat and the envelopes help hold the delicate body parts that may break off. This method allows many specimens to be maintained in a little space. However, examination of the specimens is not as convenient as with pinned specimens. These same insects are often prepared with the wings spread out for easy viewing. To "relax" a dried specimen, place it in a container with moistened paper towels (add a disinfectant agent like Lysol® to keep fungus growth to a minimum) for several days (longer for large specimens). Appendages of relaxed specimens can be moved and repositioned. A spreading board is needed to spread the wings and hold them in position while specimens dry. Drying may take a week or more depending on the environmental conditions. Once dry, the wings will remain outstretched unless there is too much moisture.

Regardless of the preservation method, all insect specimens should be carefully *labeled* with information about when and where they were collected. Information on the labels is valuable from a scientific standpoint. Small, neatly printed labels of a consistent size really add to the scientific value and attraction of an insect collection. Labels should have information about the country, state, county, nearest town, collecting date, and collector's name. Additional information about the collecting method or host plant are also useful. A second label with the scientific name is usually added below the collection label. Keep the height of the labels consistent by using a pinning block. Labels should be placed on the pin with the insect, inserted in the alcohol vial, or written directly on the envelope.

Storing an Insect Collection

Insect collections can be maintained in almost any box large enough and deep enough to hold the pinned insects. Cigar boxes with styrofoam or cork layer on the inside bottom are useful. More permanent boxes are Schmitt boxes or Cornell drawers, which can be purchased commercially. Schmitt boxes typically have a pinning bottom and a closed hinged lid. Cornell drawers have a glass top, and often contain smaller boxes called unit trays that are used to fill the box and hold the specimens. Stored, dried insects are susceptible to attack by small dermestid beetles (Coleoptera), booklice (Psocoptera), and sometimes ants or other pests. Tight-fitting lids on collection boxes help prevent entry of these pests of insect collections. These pests do not attack specimens stored in well-lighted collections, because they avoid light. However, it may be necessary to use naphthalene (a repellent), paradichlorobenzene (a fumigant), or a regimen of periodic cold treatment (freezing) to maintain a collection free of dermestid beetles. These chemicals may react with styrofoam. Pesticide strips containing DDVP or dichlorvos are also available from suppliers of entomological equipment to protect insect collections from these pests. As with any insecticide, always follow the instructions on the product label.

Literature: Borror et al. 1989; Godwin 1996; Jackman 1996; Petersen 1962.

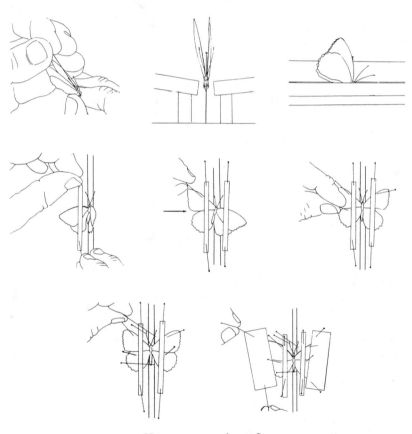

How to mount a butterfly

Appendix B

Threatened and Endangered Species of Insects in Texas[1]

Scientific Name	Common Name	Global, State, Federal[2] Status
Adhemarius blanchardorum	Blandchards' Sphinx Moth	G1, S1, C2
Aeshna dugesi	Arroyo Darner	G3, S?
Agathymus clisosensis		G2?, S2?
Agathymus gilberi		G2?, S?
Agathymus valverdiensis		G2?, S?
Amblychila picolominii	A tiger beetle	G3, S?
Anomala tibialis	Tibial Scarab	GH, SH, C2*
Apodemia chisosensis	Chisos Metalmark	G1, G3, S?
Argia leonorae	Balmorhea Damselfly	G2, G3, S2, C2
Asaphomyia texanus	Texas Asaphomyian Tabanid Fly	GH, SH, C2*
Atrytonopsis cestus		G1, G3, S?
Austrotinodes sp. 1	Texas Austrontinodes Caddisfly	G2, S2, C2
Batrisodes texanus	Coffin Cave Mold Beetle	G1, S1, LE
Batrisodes venyivi	Helotes Mold Beetle	G1, S1, C2
Calephelis freemani	Freeman's Metalmark	GH, SH
Calephelis rawsoni	Rawson's Metalmark	G3?, S?
Cheumatopsyche flinti	Flint's Net-spinning Caddisfly	G3, S3, 3C
Cheumatopsyche morsei	Morse's Net-spinning Caddisfly	G1, S1, C2
Chimarra holzenthali	Holzenthal's Philopotamid Caddisfly	G1, S1, C2
Cicindela cazieri	Cazier's Tiger Beetle	G1, S1, C2*
Cicindela chlorocephala smythi	Smyth's Tiger Beetle	GHTH, SH, C2*
Cicindela hornii	A tiger beetle	G3, S?
Cicindela nevadica olmosa	Los Olmos Tiger Beetle	G5T3, S1S2, C2

[1]Texas Parks and Wildlife, Texas Biological and Conservation Data System, Special Animal List, Jan. 29, 1996.
[2]See footnote at end of Appendix C.

Cicindela nigrocoerulea subtropica	Subtropical Blue-black Tiger Beetle	G5T2, SH, C2
Cicindela obsoleta neojuvenilis	Neojuvenile Tiger Beetle	G5T1, SH, C2*
Cicindela politula barbarannae	Barbara Ann's Tiger Beetle	G5T1, S1, C2
Cicindela politula petrophila	Guadalupe Mountains Tiger Beetle	G5T2, S1, C2
Cylindropsis sp. 1	Tooth Cave Blind Rove Beetle	G1, S1, 3A
Deronectes neomexicana	Bonita Diving Beetle	G1, S1, C2
Euproserpinus wiesti	Wiest's Sphinx Moth	G3, G4, S1, 3C
Eximacris superbum	Superb Grasshopper	GH, SH, C2*
Fixsenia polingi	Poling's Hairstreak	G1, S?
Gomphus modestus	Gulf Coast Clubtail	G3, S?
Haideophorus texanus	Edwards Aquifer Diving Beetle	G1, S1, C2
Haliplus nitens	Disjunct Crawling Water Betle	GH, SH, C2*
Heterelmis comalensis	Comal Springs Riffle Beetle	G1, S1, PE
Hydroptila ouachita	Purse Casemaker Caddisfly	G1, S1, C2
Libellula composita	Bleached Skimmer	G3, S?
Limnebius texanus	Texas Minute Moss Beetle	GH, SH, C2
Lordithon niger	Black Lordithon Rove Beetle	G1, SH, C2*
Megacephala affinis angustata	A tiger beetle	G5T3, S?
Ministrymon clytie	Clytie Hairstreak	G3?, S?
Neurocordulia molesta	Smoky Shadowfly	G3, S?
Nicrophorus americanus	American Burying Beetle	G1, SR, LE
Oxyethira florida	Florida Oxyethiran Micro Caddisfly	G1?, S?, C2
Phylocentropus harrisi		G1, S1
Piruna haferniki		G1?, S1?
Protoptila arca	San Marcos Saddle-case Caddisfly	G1, S1, C2
Protoptila balmorhea	Balmorhea Saddle-case Caddisfly	G2, S1, C2
Rhadine exilis	Ground Beetle	G1, S1
Rhadine infernalis	Ground Beetle	G1, S1, C2
Rhadine persephone	Tooth Cave Ground Beetle	G1, S1, LE
Schinia indiana	Phlox Moth	GU, SH, LE
Somatochlora margarita	Big Thicket Emerald Dragonfly	G2, S2, C2
Stallingsia maculosus	Maculated Manfreda Skipper	G2, S2, C2
Stygoparnus comalensis	Comal Springs Dryopid Beetle	G1, S1, PE
Taeniopteryx starki	Leon River Winter Stonefly	G1, S1, C2
Texamaurops reddelli	Kretschmarr Cave Mold Beetle	G1, S1, LE
Zizula cyna	Cyna Blue	G3, S?

Appendix C
Threatened and Endangered Species of Arachnids in Texas[1]

Scientific Name	Common Name	Global, State, Federal[2] Status
Archeolarca guadalupensis	Guadalupe Cave Pseudoscorpion	G1, S1, C2
Cicurina bandida	Bandit Cave Spider	G1, S1, C2
Cicurina baroni	Robber Baron Cave Spider	G1, S1, C2
Cicurina cueva	A Cave Spider	G1, S1, C2
Cicurina madla	Madla's Cave Spider	G1, S1, C2
Cicurina venii	Veni's Cave Spider	G1, S1, C2
Cicurina vespera	Vesper Cave Spider	G1, S1, C2
Cicurina wartoni	Warton's Cave Spider	G1, S1, C1
Neoleptoneta microps	Government Canyon Cave Spider	G1, S1, C2
Neoleptoneta myopica	Tooth Cave Spider	G1, S1, LE
Tartarocreagris texana	Tooth Cave Pseudoscorpion	G1, S1, LE
Texella cokendolpheri	Robber Baron Cave Harvestman	G1, S1, C2
Texella reddelli	Bee Creek Cave Harvestman	G1, S1, LE
Texella reyesi	Bone Cave Harvestman	G1Q, S1, LE

[1]Texas Parks and Wildlife, Texas Biological and Conservation Data System, Special Animal List, Jan. 29, 1996.

[2]**Global Rank**

G1—Critically imperiled globally, extremely rare, 5 or fewer occurrences. (Critically endangered throughout range.)
G2—Imperiled globally, very rare, 6 to 20 occurences. (Endanged throughout range.)
G3—Very rare and local throughout range or found locally in restricted range, 21 to 100 occurrences. (Threatened throughout range.)
G4—Apparently secure globally.
G5—Demonstrably secure globally.
GH—Of historical occurrence through its range.
G#T#—"G"= species rank; "T" = rank of variety or subspecies taxa.
GU—Possible in peril range-wide, but stats uncertain.
GX—Believed to be extinct throughout range.
Q—Qualifier denoting questionable taxonomic assignment.
?—Not ranked to date; or qualifier denoting uncertain rank.
C—Captive population exists.

Federal Rank
LE—Listed endangered.
LT—Listed threatened.
LELT—Listed endangered in part of range; threatened in a different part.
PE—Proposed to be listed endangered.
PT—Proposed to be listed threatened.

E(S/A) or T(S/A)—Listed endangered or threatened on basis of similiarity of appearance.

DL—Delisted endangered/threatened.

C1—Candidate, Category 1. USFWS has substantial information on biological vulnerability and threats to support proposing to list as endangered or threatened. Data are being gathered on habitat needs and/or critical habitat designations.

C1*—C1, but lacking known occurrences.

C1**—C1, but lacking known occurrences, except in captivity/cultivation.

C2—Candidate, Category 2. Information indicates that proposing to list as endangered or threatened is possibly appropriate, but substantial data on biological vulnerability and threats are not currently known to support the immediate preparation of rules. Further biological research and field study will be necessary to ascertain the status and/or taxonomic validity of the taxa in Category 2.

C2*—C2, but lacking known occurrences.

C2**—C2, but lacking known occurrences, except in captivity/cultivation.

3—Taxa no longer being considered for listed as threatened or endangered. Three subcategories indicate the reasons for removal from consideration.

3A—Former candidate, rejected because presumed extinct and/or habitats destroyed.

3B—Former candidate, rejected because not a recognized taxon; i.e., synonym or hybrid.

3C—Former candidate, rejected because more common, widespread, or adequately protected.

XE—Essential experimental population.

XN—Non-essential experimental population.

State Rank or Status

E—Listed as Endangered in Texas.

T—Listed as Threatened in Texas.

Blank—Not currently listed.

S1—Critically imperiled in state, extremely rare, very vulnerable to extirpation, 5 or fewer occurrences.

S2—Imperiled in state, very rare, vulnerable to extirpation, 6 to 20 occurrences.

S3—Rare or uncommon in state, 21 to 100 occurrences.

S4—Apparently secure in state.

S5—Demonstrably secure in state.

SA—Accidental in state.

SE—An exotic species established in state.

SH—Of historical ocurrence in state; may be rediscovered.

SP—Potential occurence in state.

SR—Reported, but without persuasive documentation.

SRF—Reported in error, but error persists in literature.

SU—Possible in peril in state, but status uncertain.

SX—Apparently extirpated from state.

SZ—Migratory/transient in state to irregular/dispersed locations.

B—Basic rank refers to the breeding population in the state.

N—Basic rank refers to the non-breeding population in the state.

?—Not ranked to date; or, qualifier denoting uncertain rank.

C—Captive population exists.

LITERATURE

Aaron, S. 1884. "Collecting on the Gulf Coast of Southern Texas." *Papilio* 4: 159–161.

Aaron, E. M. and S. F. Aaron. 1885. "List of a Collection of Diurnal Lepidoptera from Southern Texas." *Papilio* 4(19-10): 172–182.

Abbott, J. C., K. W. Stewart, and S. R. Moulton, 1997. "Aquatic Insects of the Big Thicket Region of East Texas." *Texas J. Sci.* 49: 35–50.

Acciavatii, R. E. 1980. "A Review of *Cicindela praetextata* from the Southwest United States." *Southw. Entomol.* 5(4): 231–244.

Adams, C. L. and R. B. Selander. 1979. "The Biology of Blister Beetles of the *Vittata* Group of the Genus *Epicauta* (Coleoptera: Meloidae)." *Bull. Amer. Museum of Natural History* 162(4).

Agnew, C. W., W. L. Sterling, and D. A. Dean. 1981. "Notes on the Chrysopidae and Hemerobiidae of Eastern Texas with Keys for Their Identification." Suppl. No. 4, *Southw. Entomol.*, 20 pp.

Akre, R. D., A. Greene, J. F. McDonald, P. J. Landolt, and H. G. Davis. 1981. "The Yellowjackets of America North of Mexico." United States Department of Agriculture Agric. Handbook No. 552. 102 pp.

Alex, A. H. 1947. "Notes on Robber Flies Preying on Honeybees in the San Antonio Area During 1946." *Bull. Brooklyn Entomol. Soc.* 42(5): 170–172.

Anon. 1982. "Southern Pine Beetle," Circular 259. Texas Forest Service, The Texas A&M University System, College Station, Texas.

Anon. 1986. "The Sevenspotted Lady Beetle—A Promising Biological Control Agent." APHIS Facts. USDA APHIS. 2 pp.

Arnett, R. H., Jr. 1965. "Species of Oedemeridae of the Big Bend Region of Texas." *Proc. U. S. Nat. Mus.*, No, 3523, Vol. 118, p. 47–55.

Arnett, R. H. 1985. *American Insects, A Handbook of the Insects of America North of Mexico.* Van Nostrand Reinhold Company, New York. 850 pp.

Baker, J. R. (ed.) 1982. "Insects and Related Pests of Flowers and Foliage Plants." AG-136. The North Carolina Agricultural Extension Service. Raleigh, North Carolina. 75 pp.

Baker, J. R. (unpublished) "Mealybug Pests of Foliage Plants and Other Ornamentals in the Greenhouse and Interiorscape," (mimeograph) November 17, 1988.

Baker, W. L. 1972. "Eastern Forest Insects." U.S.D.A., Forest Serv., Misc. Pub. No. 1175. 642 pp.

Barber, H. G. 1906. "Hemiptera from Southwestern Texas." Bull Mus. Brooklyn Inst. Arts Sci. 1(9): 255–289.

Barber, H. G. 1948. "Lygaeidae Collected in Western Texas, with a New *Lygaeopilus* from California." *Ohio J. Sci.* 48(2): 66–68.

Barr, T. C., Jr. 1974. "Revisions of *Rhadine* LeConte (Coleoptera, Carabidae. I. The *Subterranea* Group.)" *Amer. Mus. Novit.* No. 2539, pp. 1–30.

Barr, T. C. and J. R. Reddell. 1967. "The Arthropod Cave Fauna of the Carlsbad Caverns Region, New Mexico." *Southw. Nat.* 12(3): 253–274.

Barr, T. C., Jr., and H. R. Steeves, Jr. 1963. "*Texamaurops*, A New Genus of Pselaphids from Caves in Central Texas (Coleoptera: Pselaphidae)." *Colept. Bull.* 17: 117–120.

Batra, S. W. T. 1972. "Notes on the Behavior and Ecology of the Mantispid, *Climaciella brunnea occidentalis.*" *J. Kansas Entomol. Soc.* 45(3): 334–340.

Baumhover, A. H. 1966. "Eradication of the Screw-worm Fly." *J.A.M.A.* 196: 240–248.

Bay, D. E. and R. L. Harris. *Introduction to Veterinary Entomology* (A Guide to Livestock Insects). Stonefly Publishing, Bryan, Texas. 111 pp.

Bibby, F. F. 1931. "Coccoids Collected on Wild Plants in Semi-Arid Regions of Texas and Mexico (Homoptera)." *J. New York Entomol. Soc.* 39(4): 587–591.

Birkman, G. 1899. "List of Aculeate Hymenoptera, Taken at Fedor, Lee County, Texas." *Entomol. News* 10(8): 244–245.

Blanchard, A. 1968. "More New Moths from Texas (Noctuidae)." *J. Lepidop. Soc.* 26(1): 56–63.

Blanchard, A. 1968. "New Moths from Texas (Noctuidae, Tortricidae)." *J. Lepidop. Soc.* 22(3): 133–145.

Blanchard, A. 1970. "Observations on Some Phycitinae (Pyralidae) of Texas with Descriptions of Two New Species." *J. Lepidop. Soc.* 24(4): 249–255.

Blanchard, A. 1972. "More New Moths from Texas (Noctuidae)." *J. Lepidop. Soc.* 26(1):56–63.

Blanchard, A. 1973. "Record and Illustration of Some Interesting Moths Flying in Texas (Sphingidae, Ctenuchidae, Noctuidae, Notodontidae, Geometriade, Pyralidae, Cossidae)." *J. Lepidop. Soc.* 27(2): 103–109.

Blanchard, A., J. E. Gillaspy, D. F. Hardwick, J. W. Johnson, R. O. Kendall, E. C. Knudson. 1985. "Checklist of Lepidoptera of the Rob and Bessie Welder Wildlife Refuge near Sinton, Texas." *Southw. Ento.* 10(3): 195–214.

Blanchard, A. and E. C. Knudson. 1985. "The *Eupithecia* (Lepidoptera: Geometridae) of Texas with the Description of a New Species." *Proc. Entomol. Soc. Wash.* 87 (3): 662–674.

Blume, R. R. 1985. "A Checklist, Distributional Record, and Annotated Bibliography of the Insects Associated with Bovine Droppings on Pastures in America North of Mexico." *Southw. Entomol.*, Suppl. No. 9, 55 pp.

Boethel, D. J. and J. L. Bagnet. 1985. Bug Biz Coop. Ext. Pub. Louisiana Coop. Ext. Serv.

Bohmfalk, G. T., R. E. Frisbie, W. L. Sterling, R. B. Metzer, and A. E. Knutson. 1982. "Identification, Biology, and Sampling of Cotton Insects." B-933. Texas Agricultural Extension Service, Texas A&M University System, College Station, Texas. 43 pp.

Boldt, P. E., and T. O. Robbins. 1987. "Phytophagous and Pollinating Insect Fauna of *Baccharis neglecta* (Compositae) in Texas." Environ. Entomol. 16: 887–895.

Boring, E. P., III. 1981. "Lace Bugs on Trees and Shrubs." L-1739. Texas Agricultural Extension Service, Texas A&M University System, College Station, Texas. 2 pp.

Borror, D. J., C. A. Triplehorn, and N. F. Johnson. 1989. *An Introduction to the Study of Insects.* Sixth Ed., Saunders College Publishing, New York. 875 pp.

Bottimer, L. J. 1926. "Notes on Some Lepidoptera from Eastern Texas." *J. Agri. Res.* 33(9): 797–819.

Bottimer, L. J. 1969. "Bruchidae Associated with *Mimosa* with the Description of a New Species." *Can. Entomol.* 101(11): 1186–1198.

Bradley, J. C. 1919. "An Entomological Cross-section of the United States." *Sci. Monthly* (Apr., May, June): 356–420.

Brandenburg, R. L. and M. G. Villani. 1995. *Handbook of Turf Grass Insect Pests.* Entomol. Soc. Amer., Landham, Maryland. 140 pp.

Breland, O. P. 1952. "Keys to the Larvae of Texas Mosquitoes with Notes on Recent Synonymy. I. Key to General and to the Species of the Genus *Aedes.*" *Tex. J. Sci.* 4(1): 65–72.

Breland, O. P. 1953. "Keys to the Larvae of Texas Mosquitoes with Notes on Recent Synonymy. II. The Genus *Culex* Linnaeus." *Tex. J. Sci.* 5(1): 114–119.

Bromley, S. W. 1933. "Cicadas in Texas." *Psyche* 40(4): 138.

Bromley, S. W. 1934. The Robber Flies of Texas (Diptera: Asilidae). *Ann. Entomol. Soc. Amer.* 27(1): 74–113.

Bromley, S. W. 1935. "Notes on Texas Robber Flies with the Description of a New Species of *Proctacanthella* (Asilidae: Diptera)." *Occ. Pap. Mus. Zool. Univ. Mich.,* No. 304, 7 pp.

Brook, T. S., C. C. Carter, P. P. Cobb, C. S. Gorsuch, K. R. Horn, L. T. Lucas, K. Pinkston, D. K. Pollet, R. Price, R. L. Robertson, R. A. Scheibner and H. E. Williams (J. R. Baker, ed.) 1982. *Insects and Other Pests Associated with Turf.* Ag-268. Department of Agricultural Communications. North Carolina State University. Raleigh, North Carolina. 108 pp.

Browning, H. W., M. O. Way, and B. M. Drees. 1989. "Managing the Mexican Rice Borer in Texas." B-1620. Texas Agricultural Extension Service and Texas Agricultural Experiment Station, The Texas A&M University System, College Station, Texas. 8 pp.

Brues, C. T. 1903. "Studies on Texas Bees Part 1." *Entomol. News* 14: 79–84.

Bueno, de la Torre, J. R. 1912. "Records of Heteroptera from Brownsville, Texas (Hemip)." *Entomol. News* 23(3): 120–122.

Bueno, de la Torre, J. R. 1931. "Heteroptera Collected by G. P. Englehardt in the South and West II." *Bull. Brooklyn Entomol. Soc.* 26(3): 135–138.

Burke, H. R. 1959. "Notes on Some Texas Curculionidae with a Description of a New Species." *Coleopt. Bull.* 12: 36–41.

Burke, H. R. 1961. "Biological and Distributional Notes on Some Texas Weevils (Coleoptera, Curculionidae)." *Southw. Nat.* 6(3–4): 195–197.

Burke, H. R. 1963. "Coleoptera Associated with Three Species of *Solanum* in Texas." *Southwest. Nat.* 8(1): 53–60.

Burke, H. R. 1963. "Notes on Texas Riffle Beetles." *Southw. Nat.* 8(2): 111–114.

Burke, H. R. 1976. "The Beetle, *Zopherus nodulosus haldemani*: Symbol of the Southwestern Entomological Society." *The Southwestern Entomologist* 1: 105–106.

Burns, J. M. and R. O. Kendall. 1969. "Ecologic and Spatial Distribution of *Pyrgus oileus* and *Pyrgus philetas* (Lepidoptera: Hesperiidae) at Their Northern Distributional Limits." *Psyche* 76(1): 41–53.

Byers, G. W. 1984. "Tipulidae" (Chapter 24, pp. 491–514) in *An Introduction to the Aquatic Insects,* Second Ed. (R. W. Merrit and K. W. Cummins, ed.) Kendall/Hunt Pub. Co., Dubuque, IA 722 pp.

Capinera, J. L. and T. S. Sechrist. 1982. "Grasshoppers (Acrididae) of Colorado: Identification, Biology, and Management." Colorado State Univ., Exp. Sta., Ft. Collins, Bull. No. 5845. 161 pp.

Carter, C. C., K. F. Horn, D. Kline, J. R. Baker, J. Scott, and H. Singletary (J. R. Baker, ed.). 1980. *Insects and Related Pests of Shrubs.* AG-189. The North Carolina Agricultural Extension Service, North Carolina State University, Raleigh, North Carolina. 199 pp.

Carter, C. C., K. F. Horn, and J. R. Baker. 1982a. *Insects and Related Pests of Flowers and Foliage Plants, Some Important, Common and Potential Pests in North Carolina.* The North Carolina Agricultural Extension Service, North Carolina State University, Raleigh, North Carolina. 75 pp.

Carter, C. C., T. N. Hunt, D. L. Kline, T. E. Reagan, and W. P. Barney. 1982b. *Insects and Related Pests of Field Crops.* AG-271 (T. N. Hunt and J. R. Baker, eds.). North Carolina Agricultural Extension Service, North Carolina State University, Raleigh, North Carolina. 106 pp.

Caudell, A. N. 1902. "Notes on Orthoptera from Colorado, New Mexico, Arizona, and Texas, with Descriptions of New Species." *Proc. U. S. Nat. Mus.* 26(1333) pp. 775–810.

Caudell, A. N. 1904. "Orthoptera from Southwestern Texas Collected by the Museum Expeditions of 1903, 1904." *Bull. Mus. Brooklyn Inst. Arts and Sci.,* 1(4): 105–116.

Cave, G. L. and C. M. Smith. 1982. "Number of Instars of the Rice Water Weevil (Coleoptera: Curculionidae)." Annals Entomol. Soc. Amer. 76(2): 293–294.

Chambers, V. T. 1874–1875. "Tineina from Texas." *Can. Entomol.* 6: 229–249;7: 7–12, 30–35, 51–56, 73–75, 92–95, 105–108.

Chambers, V. T. 1877. "Tineina from Texas." *Can. Entomol.* 9: 22–26, 71–74.

Chandler, L. D. and M. D. Heilman. 1982. "Hymenoptera Associated with Sunflower in the Lower Rio Grande Valley of Texas with Notes on Relative Abundance, Visitation Times, and Foraging." *Southw. Entomol.* 7(3): 170–172.

Cocke, J., Jr. 1979. "Clothes Moths and Carpet Beetles." L-1736. Texas Agricultural Extension Service, Texas A&M University, College Station, Texas. 2 pp.

Cockerell, T. D. A. 1907. "Some Bees Collected by Mr. Pratt in Texas." Proc. Entomol. Soc. Washington, 9: 71–72.

Cockerell, W. P. 1917. Collecting Bees in Southern Texas. *J. New York Entomol. Soc.* 25(3): 187–193.

Cole, C. L. 1985. "Fungus Gnats." L-2041, Texas Agricultural Extension Service, Texas A&M University System, College Station, Texas.

Cole, C. L. 1982. unpublished. "Ants." Texas Agricultural Extension Service, Texas A&M University System, College Station, Texas.

Cole, C. L. and P. J. Hamman. 1984. "Springtails." L-2109, Texas Agricultural Extension Service, Texas A&M University System, College Station, Texas.

Coquillett, D. W. 1904. "Diptera from Southern Texas with Descriptions of New Species (Diptera)." *J. New York Entomol. Soc.* 12(1): 31–35.

Cresson, E. T. 1872. "Hymenoptera Texana." Trans. Amer. Entomol. Soc. 4: 153–292.

Crocker, R. L., D. L. Morgan, and M. T. Longnecker. 1987. "Effects of Microwave Treatment of Live Oak Acorns on Germination and on *Curculio* sp. (Coleoptera: Curculionidae) Larvae." *J. Econ. Entomol.* 80(4): 916–920.

Crocker, R. L. and J. B. Beard. 1982. "Southern Mole Cricket Moves Farther into Texas." PR4050Texas Turf Grass Research–1982. Texas Agricultural Experiment Station, The Texas A&M University System, College Station, Texas, pp. 58–61.

Cushing, E. C. 1934–1935. "Mosquitoes of Brazos County (Texas)." Trans. Texas Acad. Sci. 19: 7–10.

Cushman, R. A. 1911. "Notes on the Host Plants and Parasites of Some North American Bruchidae." *J. Econ. Entomol.* 4: 489–510.

Dadant and Sons, Inc. 1979. *The Hive and the Honey Bee.* A Dadant Publication, Carthage, Illinois.

Daniels, N. E. 1981. "Some Dryland Agricultural Arthropod Pests of the Great Plains." Texas Agricultural Experiment Station, Amarillo, Texas (mimeograph) 56 pp.

Daniels, N. E. and L. D. Chedester. 1973. "Grasshopper Collections on Three Land Types." Misc. Publ. 1100, Tex. Agri. Exp. Sta., 4 pp.

Davis, J. T. "Raising Crickets for Fish Bait." L-1311. Texas Agricultural Extension Service, Texas A&M University System, College Station, Texas.

Denmark, H. A. 1967. "Cuban-laurel Thrips, *Gynaikothrips ficorum*, in Florida." Entomol. Circular No. 59, Fla. Dept. Agric. Div. Plant Industry. 2 pp.

Dillon, L. S. 1952. "The Meloidae (Coleoptera) of Texas." *Amer. Midland Nat.* 48(2): 330–420.

Drake, C. J. 1920. "The Southern Green Stink Bug in Florida." Fla. State Plant. Bd. Quart. Bull. 4: 41–94.

Drees, B. M. 1990a. "Yellowmargined Leaf Beetle on Leafy Greens in Texas." UC-006. Texas Agricultural Extension Service, Texas A&M University, College Station, Texas.

Drees, B. M. 1990b. "Lovebugs." *House and Landscape Pests.* UC-009. Texas Agricultural Extension Service, Texas A&M University. College Station, Texas.

Drees, B. M. 1990c. "Soldier Flies." *House and Landscape Pests.* UC-011. Texas A&M University, College Station, Texas.

Drees, B. M. 1993. "Aphid Management." *House and Landscape Pests.* UC-031. Texas Agricultural Extension Service, The Texas A&M University, College Station, Texas. 9 pp.

Drees, B. M. 1994a. "Gall-Making Insects and Wasps." *House and Landscape Pests.* L-1299. Texas Agricultural Extension Service, The Texas A&M University System, College Station, Texas. 4 pp.

Drees, B. M. 1994b. "Sweetpotato/Silverleaf Whitefly Management on Texas Greenhouse-Grown Poinsettia." UC-029. Texas Agr. Ext. Serv., Texas A&M Univ., College Station, Texas. 7 pp.

Drees, B. M. 1994c. Greenhouse Mites and Their Control. *House and Landscape Pests.* UC-030. Texas Agricultural Extension Service, Texas A&M University System, College Station, Texas.

Drees, B. M. in press. "Southern Corn Rootworm or Spotted Cucumber Beetle," in *Corn Insect Pest Handbook,* Entomological Society of America.

Drees, B. M., C. L. Barr, S. B. Vinson, R. Gold, M. E. Merchant, and D. Kostroun. 1996. "Managing Red Imported Fire Ants in Urban Areas." B-6043. Texas Agricultural Extension Service, Texas A&M University, College Station, Texas. 18 pp.

Drees, B. M., G. McIlveen, R. L. Crocker, C. Allen, M. Merchant, and J. Reinert. 1994. "Integrated Pest Management of Texas Turf Grass." B-5083. Texas Agricultural Extension Service, Texas A&M University System.

Drees, B. M. and J. M. Owens. 1982. "Drain Flies." L-2037. Texas Agricultural Extension Service, Texas A&M University, College Station, Texas.

Drees, B. M. and M. O. Way. 1988. "Managing Soybean Insects." B-1501. Texas Agricultural Extension Service, Texas A&M University, College Station, Texas. 16 pp.

Drees, B. M. and M. Wicksten. 1990. "'Scud,' Beach Fleas and Sea Roaches." *House and Landscape Pests.* UC-012. Texas Agricultural Extension Service, Texas A&M University, College Station, Texas.

Eads, R. B. 1950. "The Fleas of Texas." *Bull. Tex. State Health Dept.*, 85 pp.

Eads, R. B., G. C. Menzies, and L. J. Ogden. 1951. "Distribution Records of West Texas Mosquitoes." *Mosquito News* 11(1): 41–47.

Eads, R. B., J. S. Wiseman, and G. C. Menzies. 1957. "Observations Concerning the Mexican Free-Tailed Bat, *Tadarida mexicana,* in Texas." *Tex. J. Sci.* 9(2): 227–242.

Ebeling, W. 1978. *Urban Entomology.* Division of Agricultual Sciences, Univ. Calif., Berkley, California. 695 pp.

Edwards, S. W. and C. R. Arnold. "The Caddisflies of the San Marcos River." *Tex. J. Sci.* 12(4): 398–415.

Elkins, J. C. 1951. "The Reduviidae of Texas." *Tex. J. Sci.* 3(3): 407–412.

Ferguson, A. 1940. "A Preliminary list of the Odonata of Dallas County, Texas." Field and Laboratory 8(1): 1–10.

Ferguson, A. 1942. "Scattered Records of Texas and Louisiana Odonata with Additional Notes on the Odonata of Dallas County, Texas." *Field and Laboratory* 11: 145–149.

Fincher, G. T., R. R. Blume, J. S. Hunter, III, and K. R. Beerwinkle. 1976. "Seasonal Distribution and Diel Flight Activity of Dung-Feeding Scarabs in Open and Wooded Pasture in East-Central Texas." *Southw. Ento. Suppl.* 10, 35 pp.

Fisk, F. W. and J. H. LeVan. 1940. "Mosquito Collections at Brownsville, Texas." *J. Econ. Entomol.* 33: 944–945.

Fletcher, K. 1930. "A Study of the Insect Fauna of Brazos County, Texas, with Special Reference to the Cicadellidae." *Ann. Entomol. Soc. Amer.* 23(1): 33–56.

Foster, D. E., D. N. Uecker, and C. J. De Loach. 1981. "Insects Associated with Broom Snakeweed (*Xanthocephalum sarothrae*) and Threadleaf Snakeweed (*Xanthocephalum microcephala*) in West Texas and Eastern New Mexico." *J. Range Management* 34(6): 446–454.

Frank, W. A. and J. E. Slosser. 1991. "An Illustrated Guide to the Predaceous Insects of the Northern Texas Rolling Plains." Misc. Publ. 1718, Tex. Agric. Exp. Sta. 23 pp.

Frankie, G. W., D. L. Morgan, M. J. Gaynor, J. G. Benskin, W. E. Clark, H. C. Reed and P. J. Hamman. 1978. "The Mealy Oak Gall on Ornamental Live Oak in Texas." MP-1315. The Texas Agricultural Experiment Station, The Texas A&M Univ. System. 12 pp.

Freeman, A. 1939. The Hesperiidae of Dallas County, Texas. Field and Laboratory 7(1): 21–28.

Freeman, H. A. 1945. "Notes on Some North American Hesperiidae, with Two New Records for the United States (Lepidoptera, Rhopalocera)." *Entomol. News* 56(1): 4–5.

Freeman, H. A. 1945. "Notes on Some Hesperiidae, with New Records for the United States (Lepidoptera, Rhopalocera)." *Entomol. News* 56(4): 102–104.

Freeman, H. A. 1947. "New Skipper Records for the United States." *Entomol. News* 58: 184–186.

Freeman, H. A. 1951. "Ecological and Systematic Study of the Hesperoidea of Texas." *Entomol. News* 58: 184–186.

French, J. V., D. S. Moreno, K. R. Summy, A. N. Sparks, Jr., and P. F. Lummus. 1989. "Citrus Blackfly." 89-1. Texas A&I University Citrus Center, Weslaco, Texas. 2 pp. mimeograph.

Fuchs, T. W., D. N. Ueckert, and B. M. Drees. 1990. "Desert Termites." *House and Landscape Pests*. UC-016. Texas Agricultural Extension Service, The Texas A&M University System, College Station, Texas. 2 pp.

Gaines, J. C. 1933. "Notes on Texas Coccinellidae." Bull. Brooklyn Entomol. Soc. 28(5): 211–215.

Gaines, J. C. 1933. "Trap Collections of Insects in Cotton in 1932." Bull. Brooklyn Entomol. Soc. 28(2): 47–54.

Gaumer, G. C. 1969. "Coastal Tiger Beetles of Texas in the Genus *Cicindela*." (Coleoptera: Cicindelidae). *Cicindela* 1(1): 2–16.

Gaumer, G. C. 1973. "Aestival Tiger Beetle Fauna of the Big Bend National Park." *Cicindela* 5(1): 12–19.

Gaumer, G. C. and R. R. Murray. 1971. "Checklist of the Cicindelidae of Texas with Regional Distributions." *Cicindela* 3(1): 9–12.

Gaumer, G. C. and R. R. Murray. 1972. "The Genus *Amblychila* in Texas." *Cicindela* 4(4): 85–88.

Gaumer, G. C., and R. R. Murray. 1972. "Distributional Records and Observations on *Cicindela nevadica* LeConte in Texas." *Cicindela* 4(4): 79-84).

Girault, A. A. 1913. "Fragments from an Entomological Diary, Texas 1904— Appearance of Insects in Spring." *Entomol. News* 24: 156–159.

Glick, P. A. 1957. "Collecting Insects by Airplane in Southern Texas," Tech. Bull. No. 1158, U. S. Dept. Agri. pp. 1–28.

Gloyd, L. K. 1958. "The Dragonfly Fauna of the Big Bend Region of Trans-Pecos Texas." Univ. Mich., Mus. Zool. Occ. Papers 593-27.

Goodwin, J. T. and B. M. Drees. 1996. "The Horse and Deer Flies (Diptera: Tabanidae) of Texas." Southwestern Entomologist Supplement No. 20 140 pp.

Habeck, D. H. 1991. "*Synclita obliteralis* (Walker), the Waterlily Leafcutter (Lepidoptera: Pyralidae: Nymphalinae)." Fla. Dept. Agric. and Consumer Services, Div. Plant Industry, Entomology Circular No. 345. 2 pp.

Halbert, S., L. E. Sandvoi, B. Stoltz, and R. Johnson. 1988. "Russian Wheat Aphid." Current Info. Series No. 817. Coop. Ext. Serv., Agric. Exp. Sta., Univ. Idaho. 2 pp.

Hall, C. C. 1950. "The Trichoptera or Caddisflies of Dallas County, Texas." *Field and Laboratory* 18: 165–177.

Hall, M. J. 1982. "Hickory Shuckworm." Bug Biz, Coop. Ext. Pub. 2166. Louisiana Coop. Ext. Serv.

Hamman, P. J. 1980. "Bees in Homes." L-1791. Texas Agricultural Extension Service, The Texas A&M University System, College Station, Texas. 2 pp.

Hammon, P. J. 1981a. "Bagworms." L-1802. Texas Agr. Ext. Serv., Texas A&M Univ. System, College Station, Texas. 2 pp.

Hamman, P. J. 1981b. "Chinch Bugs in Home Lawns." L-1766. Texas Agricultural Extension Service, Texas A&M University System, College Station, Texas. 2 pp.

Hamman, P. J. 1983a. "Stinging Caterpillars." L-1312. Texas Agricultural Extension Service, Texas A&M University System, College Station, Texas. 3 pp.

Hamman, P. J. 1983b. "Chiggers." L-1223. Texas Agricultural Extension Service, Texas A&M University System, College Station, Texas. 2 pp.

Hamman, P. J. 1983c. "Ticks Attacking Humans." L-1403. Texas Agricultural Extension Service, Texas A&M University System, College Station, Texas. 4 pp.

Hamman, P. J. 1985. "Boxelder Bugs." L-1830. Texas Agricultural Extension Service, Texas A&M University System, College Station, Texas. 2 pp.

Hamman, P. J. 1989. "Subterranean Termites." L-1781. Texas Agricultural Extension Service, Texas A&M University System, College Station, Texas. 6 pp.

Hamman, P. J., B. S. Brewer, J. D. Stone and R. L. Crocker. 1985. "White Grubs in Texas Turf Grass." L-1131. Texas Agricultural Extension Service, Texas A&M University System.

Hamman, P. J. and R. E. Gold. 1992. "Drywood Termites." L-1782. Texas Agricultural Extension Service, Texas A&M University System, College Station, Texas. 5 pp.

Hamman, P. J. and H. A. Turney. 1983. "Cockroaches: Recognition and Control." B-1458. Texas Agricultural Extension Service, Texas A&M University System, College Station, Texas. 7 pp.

Hamman, P. J. and J. K. Olson. 1985. "Human Lice." L-1315. Texas Agricultural Extension Service, Texas A&M University System, College Station, Texas. 3 pp.

Hamman, P. J. and J. Owens. 1981. "Controlling Cockroaches Without Synthetic Organic Insecticides." L-1373. Texas Agricultural Extension Service, Texas A&M University System, College Station, Texas. 4 pp.

Hamman, P. J., and J. M. Owens. 1981. "Carpenter Bees." L-1826. Texas Agricultural Extension Service, Texas A&M University System, College Station, Texas. 2 pp.

Hamman, P. J., and J. M. Owens. 1981. "Carpenter Ants." L-1783. Texas Agricultural Extension Service, Texas A&M University System, College Station, Texas. 3 pp.

Hamman, P. J. and G. McIlveen. 1983. "Destructive Mites in the Garden and Home Landscape." L-1244. Texas Agricultural Extension Service, Texas A&M University System, College Station, Texas. 6 pp.

Hamman, P. J. and C. W. Neeb, 1981. "Cicadas." Texas Agricultural Extension Service, Texas A&M University System, College Station, Texas. 2 pp.

Haney, R. L. 1993. "The Scientists Tell Me Termites Are a Costly Hidden Hazard to Both Rural and Urban Structures." Research report, Texas Agric. Exper. Sta., Texas A&M University System, College Station, Texas.

Hart, C. 1906. "Notes of Winter Trip in Texas, with an Annotated List of the Orthoptera." *Ento. News* 154–160.

Hartman, C. 1905. "Observations on the Habits of Some Solitary Wasps of Texas." Bull. Univ. Tex., 65, Sci. Ser. 7, pp. 1–73.

Hartwell, J. E. 1951. "Notes on the Odonata of Northeastern in Texas." *Tex. J. Sci.* 3: 204–207.

Hebard, M. 1943. "The Dermaptera and Orthopterous Families Blattidae, Mantidae, and Phasmidae of Texas." Trans. Amer. Entomol. Soc. 68: 239–310.

Henn, T. and R. Weinzeri. 1990. "Beneficial Insects and Mites." Circular 1298. Coop. Ext. Serv. U. Illinois at Urbana-Champaign. 24 pp.

Henry, B. C., Jr. 1986. "Mayflies (Ephemeroptera) of the Concho River." *Texas. Southw. Nat.* 31(1): 15–21.

Herrick, G. W. 1911. "Some Scale Insects of Mississippi with Notes on Certain Species" Texas. Tech. Bull. No. 2, Mississippi Agr. Exp. Sta., 78 pp.

Hess, C. G. 1958. "The Ants of Dallas County, Texas, and Their Nesting Sites; with Particular Reference to Soil Texture as an Ecological Factor." *Field and Laboratory* 26(1 & 2): 3–72.

Hine, J. S. 1918. "Notes on Robberflies from Southwest Texas, Collected by the Bryant Walker Expedition, with a Description of a New Species of *Erax*." Occ. Paper Mus. Zool. Univ. Mich., No. 61, 7 pp.

Hoelscher, C. E., J. G. Thomas and G. L. Teetes. 1987. "Aphids on Texas Small Grains and Sorghum." B-1572. Texas Agricultural Extension Service, Texas A&M University System, College Station, Texas. 6 pp.

Hoelscher, C. E., et al. 1997. "Management of External Parasites of Cattle and Poultry." B-1306. Texas Agricultural Extension Service, Texas A&M University System, College Station, Texas. 23 pp.

Hoff, C. C. 1949. "The Pseudoscorpions of Illinois." *Bull. of the Ill. Nat. Hist Survey.* 24(4): 413–498.

Holland, W. J. 1913. *The Butterfly Book.* Doubleday, Page and Co., Garden City, New York. 382 pp.

Holland, W. J. 1968. *The Moth Book: A Guide to the Moths of North America.* Dover Publications, Inc., New York. 479 pp.

Hollingsworth, W. P. 1948. "Mosquitoes in the Vicinity of Nacogodoches (Texas)." Trans. Proc. Tex. Acad. Sci. 39: 125–129.

Holloway, R. L. 1980. "Sampling for Adult Pecan Weevils in Texas." L-1808. Texas Agricultural Extension Service, The Texas A&M University System, College Station, Texas. 4 pp.

Holloway, R. L. 1985. "The Peachtree Borer." Texas Agricultural Extension Service, Texas A&M University System, College Station, Texas. 2 pp.

Holloway, R. L., M. K. Harris, H. W. Van Cleave and J. N. Cooper. 1984. "Pecan Insects of Texas." B-1238. Texas Agricultural Extension Service, The Texas A&M University System, College Station, Texas. 18 pp.

Hovore, F. T., R. L. Penrose, and R. W. Neck. 1987. "The Cerambycidae, or Longhorned Beetles, of Southern Texas: A Faunal Survey (Coleoptera)." *Proc. Calif. Acad. Sci.* 44 (13): 283–334.

Howden, H. F. 1960. "A New Species of *Phyllophaga* from the Big Bend Region of Texas and Coahuila, with Notes on Other Scarabaeidae of the Area." *Can. Entomol.* 92(6): 457–464.

Howe, W. H. 1975. *The Butterflies of North America.* Doubleday and Company, Inc. Garden City, New York. 633 pp.

Howell, Jr., H. N., P. J. Hamman, and T. A. Granovsky. 1987. "The Geological Distribution of the Termite Genera *Reticulitermes, Coptotermes,* and *Incisitermes* in Texas." *Southw. Entomol.* 12(2): 119–125.

Huffman, R. 1996. "Classical Biological Control of the Citrus Blackfly in Corpus Christi, Texas." Texas Agric. Ext. Serv., The Texas A&M University System, College Station, Texas. 4 pp. mimeograph.

Huffman, F. R. and J. A. Harding. 1980. "Pitfall Collected Insects from Various Lower Rio Grande Valley Habitats." *Southw. Entomol.* 5(1)33–44.

Hunter, W. D., F. C. Pratt and J. D. Mitchell. 1912. "The Principal Cactus Insects of the United States." *Bull. 113, USDA Bur. Entomol.,* 71 pp.

Hunter, J. S., D. E. Bay, and G. T. Fincher. 1986. "A Survey of Staphylinidae Associated with Cattle Droppings in Burleson County, Texas." *Southw. Entomol.* 11(2): 83–88.

Ihrke, T. R. and D. P. Bartell. 1979. "Insects Associated with Potatoes in West Texas." *Southw. Entomol.* 4(4): 289–293.

Irwin, M. E. and M. Shepard. 1980. Chapter 25: "Sampling Predaceous Hemiptera on Soybean." pp. 505–532, in *Sampling Methods in Soybean Entomology* (M. Kogan and D. C. Herzog, eds.). Springer-Verlag, New York. 587 pp.

Isley, F. B. 1934. "Field Notes on Texas Orthoptera." *Entomol. News* 45(1): 5–8.

Isley, F. B. 1935. "Acridian Researchers Within Northeastern Texas (Orthoptera)." *Entomol. News* 46: 37–43, 69–75.

Isley, F. B. 1941. "Researchers Concerning Texas Tettigoniidae." Ecological Monographs 11: 457-475. See also *Entomological News* 45: -8;46: 37–43; 69–75. *Ecological Monographs* 7: 319–44; 8: 551–604. *Ecology* 19: 370–389.

Jackman, J. A. 1981a. Armyworms in the Texas Landscape. L-1725. Texas Agricultural Extension Service, Texas A&M University System, College Station, Texas. 2 pp.

Jackman, J. A. 1981b. "Silverfish and Firebrats." L-1833 Texas Agricultural Extension Service, Texas A&M University System, College Station, Texas. 2 pp.

Jackman, J. A. 1981c. "Earwigs." L-1834. Texas Agricultural Extension Service, The Texas A&M University System, College Station, Texas. 2 pp.

Jackman, J. A. 1981d. "Cankerworms." L-1829 Texas Agricultural Extension Service, Texas A&M University, College Station, Texas. 2 pp.

Jackman, J. A. 1981e. "The Walnut Caterpillar." L-1835. Texas Agricultural Extension Service, Texas A&M University, College Station, Texas. 2 pp.

Jackman, J. A. 1988. "Tent Caterpillars." L-1637. Texas Agricultural Extension Service, Texas A&M University System, College Station, Texas. 6 pp.

Jackman, J. A. and C. R. Nelson. 1995. "Diversity and Phenology of Tumbling Flower Beetles (Coleoptera: Mordellidae) Captured in a Malaise Trap." *Ent. News* 106(3): 97–107.

James, M. T. and R. F. Harwood. 1969. *Herms' Medical Entomology* (6th Ed.). The Macmillan Co., Collier-Macmillan Ltd., London. 484 pp.

Joern, A. 1979. "Resource Utilization and Community Structure in Assemblages of Arid Grassland Grasshoppers (Orthoptera: Acrididae)." Trans. Amer. Entomol. Soc. 105: 253–300.

Johnson, C. 1972. "The Damselflies (Zygoptera) of Texas." Bull. Florida State Museum, Biol. Sci. 16(2): 55-128.

Johnson, W. T. and H. H. Lyon. 1988. *Insects that Feed on Trees and Shrubs.* (2nd Ed.). Cornell University Press, Ithaca, New York. 556 pp.

Johnston, H. G. 1929. "A Partial list of Miridae from Texas (Order Hemiptera)." Bull. Brooklyn Entomol. Soc. 24: 217–219.

Jones, F. M. and H. B. Parks. 1928. "The Bagworms of Texas." Tex. Agr. Exp. Sta. Bull. No. 382, 36 pp.

Kendall, R. O. 1959. "More Larval Food Plants from Texas. "*J. Lepidop. Soc.* 13(4): 221–228.

Kendall, R. O. 1964. "Larval Food Plants for Twenty-Six Species of Rhopalocera (Papilionoidea) from Texas." *J. Lepidop. Soc.* 18(3): 129–157.

Kendall, R. O. 1965. "Larval Food Plants and Distribution Notes for Twenty-Four Texas Hesperiidae." *J. Lepidop. Soc.* 19(1): 1–32.

Kendall, R. O. 1966. "Larval Food Plants and Distributional Notes for Three Texas Hesperiidae." *J. Lepidop. Soc.* 20(4): 229–232.

Kendall, R. O. 1970. "A Day-Flying Moth (Pericopidae) New to Texas and the United States." *J. Lepidop. Soc.* 24(4): 310–303.

Kendall, R. O. 1970. "*Lerma ancillaris* (Hesperiidae) New to Texas and the United States." *J. Lepidop. Soc.* 24(4): 266.

Kendall, R. O. 1972. "Three Butterfly Species (Lycaenidae, Nymphalidae, and Heliconiidae) New to Texas and the United States." *J. Lepidop. Soc.* 26(1): 49–56.

Kendall, R. O. 1974. "Two Moth Species (Pericopidae and Notodontidae) New to Texas and the United States." *J. Lepidop. Soc.* 28(3): 243–245.

Kendall, R. O. 1976. "Larval Food Plants and Life History Notes for Eight Months from Texas and Mexico." *J. Lepidop. Soc.* 30(4): 264–271.

Kendall, R. O. 1976. "Larval Food Plants and Life History Notes on Some Metalmarks (Lepidoptera: Riodinidae) from Mexico and Texas." *Bull. Allyn Mus.* No. 32, pp 1–12.

Kendall, R. O. and P. A. Glick. 1972. "Rhopalocera Collected at Light in Texas." *J. Res. Lepid.* 10(4): 273–283.

Kendall, R. O. and C. A. Kendall. 1971. "Lepidoptera in the Unpublished Field Notes of Howard George Lacey, Naturalist (1856–1929)." *J. Lepidop. Soc.* 25(1): 29–44.

Kendall, R. O. and M. A. Rickard. 1976. "Larval Food Plants, Spatial, and Temporal Distribution for Five Skippers (Hesperiidae) from Texas." *J. Lepidop. Soc.* 30(2): 105–110.

Kendall, R. O. and W. W. McGuire. 1984. "Some New and Rare Records of Lepidoptera Found in Texas." *Bull. Allyn Mus.* 86, 50 pp.

Kerr, S. H. 1955. "Life History of the Tropical Sod Webworm *Pachyzancla phaeopteralis* Guenée." *The Florida Entomologist* 38(1): 3–11.

Klots, A. B. 1960. *A Field Guide to the Butterflies.* (5th printing) Houghton Mifflin Co., Boston, Mass. 349 pp.

Knaus, W. 1905. "Central Texas Coleoptera." *Can. Entomol.* 37(10): 348–352.

Knutson, A., B. Ree, Jr., and D. Stephenson. 1994. "The Harmonia Lady Beetle." ENTD4015. Texas Agricultural Extension Service, Texas A&M University System, College Station, Texas. 4 pp.

Knutson, H. 1940. "A Key to the Acrididae (Orthoptera) of Northeastern Texas with Ecological Notes." *Field and Laboratory* 8(2): 33–58.

Knutson, A. 1990. "The Field Skipper—A Pest of Bermuda Grass." *House and Landscape Pests.* UC-015. Texas Agricultural Extension Service, Texas A&M University System, College Station, Texas. 3 pp.

Knutson, A. and B. Ree. 1995. "Controlling the Pecan Nut Casebearer." L-5134. Texas Agricultural Extension Service, Texas A&M University System, College Station, Texas. 4 pp.

Kogan, M. and D. E. Kuhlman. 1982. "Soybean Insects: Identification and Management in Illinois." Bull. 773. Agric. Ext. Sta., U. IL., Urbana-Champaign, IL. 58 pp.

Kohls, G. M. and W. L. Jellison. 1948. "Ectoparasites and Other Arthropods Occurring in Texas Bat Caves." *Bull. Nat. Speleol. Soc. 10:* 116–117.

Kovarik, P. W. and H. R. Burke. 1989. "Observations on the Biology and Ecology of Two Species of *Eudiagogus* (Coleoptera: Curculionidae)." *The Southwestern Naturalist* 34(2): 196–212.

Leonard, M. D. and N. Tissot. 1965. "A Preliminary List of Texas Aphids." *Florida Entomol.* 48(4): 255–264.

Leser, J. F. 1980. "Crickets." L-1809. Texas Agriculture Extension Service, The Texas A&M University System, College Station, Texas. 2 pp.

Liljeblad, E. 1945. "Family Mordellidae (Coleoptera) of North America, North of Mexico." Monograph Univeristy of Michigan Press. 229 pp.

Lindquist, R. K. 1994. "Integrated Management of Fungus Gnats and Shore Flies" in Proc. 10th Conf. Insect and Disease Management on Ornamentals (Ed. K. Robb), pp. 58–67, Society of American Florists, Alexandria, Virginia.

Linsley, E. G. and J. O. Martin. 1933. "Notes on Some Longicorns from Subtropical Texas (Coleop. Cerambycidae)." *Entomol. News* 44;178–183.

Lintner, J. A. 1884. "On Some Rio Grande Lepidoptera." 4(7–8): 135–147.

Lipes, J. E. 1962. "More Butterfly Records from Brownsville, Texas, Including a Food Plant of *Phocides polybius* (Hesp.)" *J. Lepidop. Soc.* 15(2): 114.

Little, V. A. 1926. "Notes on the Acrididae of Brazos County, Texas (Orthoptera)." *Entomol. News* 37(10): 316–319.

Little, V. A. 1963. *General and Applied Entomology.* Third edition. Harper and Row, Publishers, New York.

Mahr, S. 1994. "Know Your Friends: Green Lacewings." *Midwest Biological Control News.* Univ. Wisconsin 1(3): 3.

Mahr, S. 1995. "Know Your Friends: Hover Flies." *Midwest Biological Control News.* Univ. Wisconsin 2(11): 3.

Mahr, D. L. and N. M. Ridgway. 1993. "Biological Control of Insects and Mites: An Introduction to Beneficial Natural Enemies and Their Use in Pest Management." North Central Regional Publication 481, Univ. Wisconsin, Madison, Wisconsin. 92 pp.

Manley, G. V. and J. V. French. 1976. "Wood Boring Beetles Inhabiting Citrus in the Lower Rio Grande Valley of Texas. Part 1: Cerambycidae." J. Lower Rio Grande Valley Hort. Soc. 30: 45–53.

Mann, J. 1969. "Cactus-Feeding Insects and Mites." Bull. 256 Smithsonian Institution, 158 pp.

McAlister, W. H. and M. K. McAlister. 1987. Guidebook to the Aransas National Wildlife Refuge. Mince Country Press, Victoria, TX 298 pp.

McCafferty, W. P. 1981. *Aquatic Entomology, The Fisherman's and Ecologists' Illustrated Guide to Insects and Their Relatives.* Science Books International. Boston, Massachusetts. 448 pp.

McClendon, J. F. "Notes on the True Neuroptera 3: A Catalogue of Texas Neuroptera." *Entomol. News* 17: 169, 173.

McClesky, O. L. 1951. "The Bionomics of the Culicidae of the Dallas Area." *Field and Laboratory* 19(1): 5–14.

McCook, H. C. 1879. "The Natural History of the Agricultural Ants of Texas." J. B. Lippincott and Co., Philadelphia, PA. 311 pp.

McDaniel, B., Jr. 1961. "A Taxonomic Study of the Scale Insects of the Family Diaspididae in Texas (Homoptera-Coccoidea)." Master's Thesis, A&M College of Texas. 246 pp.

McDaniel, B., Jr. 1964. Key to Texas Species of the Genus *Eriococcus* and a Description of a New Species." *Tex. J. Sci.* 16(1): 1001–106.

McDaniel, B., Jr. 1968–1972. The Armored Scale Insects of Texas (Homoptera: Coccoidea: Diaspididae). Part I *Southw. Natur.* 13(2): 201–242; Part II. 1969. 14(1): 89–113, Part III. 1970 14(4): 411–440; Part IV. 1971. 15(3): 275–308; Part V. 1972. 16(3 and 4): 321–340.

McGregor, W. S. and O. C. Schomberg. 1952. "A Partial Annotated List of Species of the Tabanidae." *J. Econ. Entomol.* 45(4): 746.

McGuire, W. W. 1976. "New Hesperiidae Records of Texas and the United States." *J. Lepidop. Soc.* 30(1): 5–11.

McIlveen, Jr., G. 1986. "The Urban Insecta." The Texas Agricultural Extension Service, Texas A&M University System, College Station, Texas (mimeograph).

McIlveen, G. 1991. "Wasps and Yellowjackets." L-1828. Texas Agricultural Extension Service, Texas A&M University System, College Station, Texas. 4 pp.

Mead, F. W. 1983. "Yaupon Psyllid, *Gyropsylla ilicis* (Ashmead) (Homoptera: Psyllidae)." Fla. Dept. of Agric., and Consumer Serv. Entomol. Circ. 247. 2 pp.

Menzies, G. C., T. B. Eads, and B. G. Hightower. 1951. "List of Anoplura from Texas." Proc. Entomol. Soc. Washington 53(3): 150–152.

Merchant, M. 1995. "Bee Mites." Texas Agricultural Extension Service. ENTD4024. College Station, TX.

Metcalf, C. L., W. P. Flint and R. L. Metcalf. 1962. *Destructive and Useful Insects: Their Habits and Control.* McGraw-Hill Book Company. New York. 1087 pp.

Michener, C. D. 1951. "Records and Descriptions of Magachilid Bees from Texas (Hymenoptera)." *Pan-Pacific Ento.* 27(2): 61–71.

Millspaugh, D. D. 1939. "Bionomics of the Aquatic and Semi-aquatic Hemiptera of Dallas County, Texas." *Field and Laboratory* 7(2): 67–86.

Mitchell, J. D. and W. D. Pierce. 1911. "The Weevils of Victoria County, Texas." *Proc. Entomol. Soc.* Washington 13(1): 45–62.

Mitchell, P. L., R. Olszak, M. B. Stoetzel, and M. K. Harris. 1984. "Fauna Associated with Galls of *Phylloxera* spp." *Southw. Entomol.* 9(2): 117–124.

Mitchell, J. D. and W. D. Pierce. 1972. "The Ants of Victoria County, Texas." Proc. Entomol. Soc. Washington 14(2): 67–76.

Mock, D. E., H. L. Brooks, J. J. Durkin, J. M. Good, W. M. Hantsbarger, D. L. Kieth, W. B. Massey, and W. P. Morrison. 1981. "Insect Pest Management for Corn on the Western Great Plains." Texas Agricultural Extension Service, Texas A&M University System, College Station, Texas. 36 pp.

Mockford, E. L. and A. B. Gurney. 1956. "A Review of the Psocids, or Book Lice and Bark Lice of Texas (Psocoptera)." *J. Washington Acad. Sci.* 46(11): 353–368.

Moody, J. V. and O. F. Franke. 1982. "The Ants (Hymenoptera, Formicidae) of Western Texas Part 1: Subfamily Myrmicinae." Graduate studies No. 27, Texas Tech University, Texas Tech press, Texas, 80 pp.

Moore, L. E., Jr. 1950. "Distribution of Mayfly Nymphs (Ephemeroptera) in Streams of Dallas County, Texas." *Field and Laboratory* 18(3): 103–112.

Moser, J. C., R. C. Thatcher, and L. S. Pickard. 1971. "Relative Abundance of Southern Pine Beetle Associates in East Texas." Ann. Entomol. Soc. Amer. 64(1): 72–77.

Mueller, A. J. 1980. "Sampling Threecornered Alfalfa Hopper in Soybean." Pp. 382–393 in *Sampling Methods in Soybean Entomology* (M. Kogan and D. C. Herzog, eds.). Springer-Verlag, New York.

Muma, M. H. 1951. "The Arachnid Order Solpugida in the United States." Bull. Amer. Mus. Nat. Hist., 97(2): 35–141.

Muma, M. H. 1962. "The Arachnid Order Solpugida in the United States," Supplement I. *Amer. Mus. Novitates* 2092. 44 pp.

Naresh, J. S. and C. M. Smith. 1982. "Development and Survival of Rice Stink Bugs (Hemiptera: Pentatomidae) Reared on Different Host Plants at Four Temperatures." *Environ. Entomol.* 12(5): 1496–1499.

Naresh, J. S. and C. M. Smith. 1984. "Feeding Preferences of the Rice Stink Bug on Annual Grasses and Sedges." *Entomol. Exp. Appl.* 35: 89–92.

Neck, R. A. 1996. *A Field Guide to Butterflies of Texas.* Texas Monthly Field Guide Series. Gulf Publishing Company, Houston, Texas. 323 pp.

Neeb, C. 1980. "Ground Pearls in Home Lawns." L-1740. Texas Agricultural Extension Service, Texas A&M University System, College Station, Texas. College Station, TX. 2 pp.

Neece, K. C. and D. P. Bartell. 1981. "Insects Associated with *Solenopsis* in Southeastern Texas." *Southw. Entomol.* 6(4): 307–311.

Neunzig, H. H. 1964. "The Eggs and Early-Instar Larvae of *Heliothis zea* and *Heliothis virescens* (Lepidoptera: Noctuidae)." Ann. Entomol. Soc. Amer. 57: 98–102.

Niemczyk, H. 1981. *Destructive Turf Insects.* The Gray Printing Co., Fostoria, OH. 48 pp.

Nilakhe, S. S. 1976. "Overwintering Survival, Fecundity, and Mating Behavior of the Rice Stink Bug." Ann. Entomol. Soc. Amer. 69(4): 717–720.

Noble, L. W. 1955. "Investigations on the pink bollworm and hemipterous cotton insects." U. S. Dept. Agri. Circ. 957, 16 pp.

O'Neill, K., L. J. Odgen, and D. E. Eyles. 1944. "Additional Species of Mosquitoes Found in Texas." *J. Econ. Entomol.* 37(4): 555–556.

Oldroyd, H. 1964. *The Natural History of Flies.* W. W. Norton and Co., Inc. New York. 324 pp.

Olkowski, W., S. Daar, and H. Olkowski. 1991. *Common-Sense Pest Control.* The Taunton Press, Newtown, CT. 716 pp.

Olson, J. K. 1996. Presentation: "Establishing Mosquito Control in Subdividions and Other Sensitive Areas." Winter Pest Control Workshop, College Station, Texas.

Opler, P. A. and G. O. Rizek. 1984. *Butterflies East of the Great Plains.* The John Hopkins University Press, Baltimore, Maryland. 294 pp.

Owens, J. M. 1983. House Infesting Ants. L-2061. Texas Agricultural Extension Service, Texas A&M University System, College Station, Texas. 4 pp.

Parks, H. G., C. Smith, and J. Garrett. 1939. "The East Texas Crayfish and Lepidopterous Insects." Tech. Bull., Stephen F. Austin State College, Nacogdoches, Texas.

Patrick, C. D. 1995. "Windscorpions." Texas Agricultural Extension Service. Unnumbered publication. 2 pp.

Patrick, C. D., and P. J. Hamman. 1980. "Fleas." L-1738. Texas Agricultural Extension Service, Texas A&M University System, College Station, Texas. 3 pp.

Pawson, B. 1995. "Research Vignettes, Termites." Presentation at the 49th Midwinter PCO Workshop for Advanced Learning, College Station Hilton and Conference Center, College Station, Texas, Jan. 3–6.

Peairs, L. A. and R. H. Davidson. 1956. *Insect Pests of Farm, Garden, and Orchard,* 5th Ed. John Wiley and Sons, Inc. New York.

Pearsall, R. F. 1906. "List of Geometridae Collected in Utah, Arizona, and Texas." *Mus. Brooklyn Inst. Arts and Sci., Sci. Bull.* June.

Peterson, A. 1973. *Larvae of Insects, An Introduction to Nearctic Species, Part II.* Sixth Ed. Edwards Brothers, Inc., Ann Arbor, Michigan. 416 pp.

Pettis, J. S. and W. T. Wilson. 1990. "Life Cycle Comparisons Between *Varroa jacobsoni* and *Acarapis woodi.*" *American Bee Journal.* 130(9): 597–599.

Pierce, W. D. 1907. "Contributions to the Knowledge of Rhyncophora." *Entomol. News* 18(8): 356–363; (9): 379–385.

Polhemus, J. T. 1973. "Notes on Aquatic and Semi-Aquatic Hemiptera from the Southwestern United States (Insecta-Hemiptera)." *Great Basin Nat.* 33(2): 113–119.

Porter, C. 1981. "Ecological Notes on Lower Rio Grande Valley *Xylocopa* (Hymenoptera: Anthoporidae)." *Florida Entomol.* 64(1): 175–182.

Porter, C. 1975. "New Records for *Zethus* from Texas." *Florida Entomol.* 58: 303–306.

Porter, C. 1976. "New Records for *Thyreodon* from South Texas." *Psyche* 83: 304–309.

Porter, C. 1977. "Ecology, Zoogeography and Taxonomy of the Lower Rio Grande Mesotenines." *Psyche* 84: 28–91.

Porter, C. 1978. "Ecological Notes on Lower Rio Grande Valley Sphecini." *Florida Entomol.* 61: 169–178.

Porter, C. 1978. "Ecology and Taxonomy of Lower Rio Grande Valley *Zethus.*" *Florida Entomol.* 61: 159–167.

Randolph, N. M. and K. O'Neill. 1944. "The Mosquitoes of Texas." Texas State Health Dept. Bull., 100 pp.

Randolph, N. M., C. F. Garner. 1961. "Insects Attacking Forage Crops." B-975. Texas Agricultural Extension Service, Texas A&M University System, College Station, Texas. 26 pp.

Redborg, K. E. and E. G. Macleod. 1983. "*Climaciella brunnea* (Neuroptera: Mantispidae): A Mantid that Obligately Boards Spiders." *J. Natural History* 17: 63–73.

Reddell, J. R. 1966. "A Checklist of the Cave Fauna of Texas. II. Insects." *Tex. J. Sci.* 8(1): 25–56.

Reddell, J. R. 1970. "A Checklist of the Cave Fauna of Texas. V. Additional Records of Insects." *Tex. J. Sci.* 22(1): 47–65.

Ree, W. 1994. "Asian Ambrosia Beetle Active on Pecans in East Texas." UC-026. Texas Agr. Ext. Serv., Texas A&M Univ., College Station, Texas. 2 pp.

Rehn, J. A. G. 1903. "Notes and Remarks on North American Blattidae, Mantidae, and Phasmidae, with a Catalogue of the Forficulidae, Blattidae, Mentidae, and Phasmidae Recorded from Texas." *Entomol. News* 14(10): 325–331.

Rehn, J. A. G. 1907. "Records of Orthoptera from the Vicinity of Brownsville, Texas." *Entomol. News.* 18(5): 209–212.

Rehn, J. A. G. and M. Hebard. 1909. "An Orthopterological Reconnaissance of the Southwestern United States. Part II. New Mexico and Western Texas." *Proc. Acad. Nat. Sci. Philadelphia* 61: 111–175.

Reinert, J. A. 1983. "Controlling Cuban Laurel Thrips in Nurseries and Landscapes." *American Nurseryman* 157 (8): 63–66.

Reinert, J. A., P. R. Heller, and R. L. Crocker. 1995. *Handbook of Turf Grass Insect Pests* (R. L. Brandenburg, and M. G. Villani, eds.) pp. 38–42. The Entomological Society of America. Landham, MD, 140 pp.

Reinhard, H. J. 1919. "Preliminary Notes on Texas Tachinidae (Diptera)." *Entomol. News* 30(10): 279–285.

Reinhard, H. J. 1922. "Host Records of Some Texas Tachinidae (Diptera)." *Entomol. News* 33(3): 72–73.

Reinhard, H. J. 1924. "Notes on Texas Sarcophagidae (Diptera)." *Entomol. News* 35940;127–129.

Reinhard, H. J. 1950. "The Phyllophaga of Texas (Scarabaeidae, Coleoptera)." *J. Kansas Entomol. Soc.* 23(1): 27–41; (2): 41–51.

Reuger, M. E. and S. Druce. 1950. "New Mosquito Distribution Records of Texas." *Mosquito News* 10920;60–63.

Rice, M. E. 1985. "New Host Associations for Cerambycidae (Coleoptera) from Selected Species of Leguminosae and Rutaceae." *J. New York Entomol. Soc.* 93(4): 1223–1225.

Rice, M. E. 1986. "Communal Ovipostion by *Mantispa fuscicornis* (Say) (Neuroptera: Mantispidae) and Subsequent Larval Parasitism on Spiders (Arachnida: Araneida) in South Texas." *J. Kansas Entomol. Soc.* 59(1): 121–126.

Rice, M. E. 1989. "Branch Girdling and Oviposition Biology of *Oncideres pustulatus* (Coleopera: Cerambycidae) on *Acacia farnesiana.*" Ann. Entomol. Soc. Am. 82(2): 181–186.

Rice, M. E. 1995. "Branch Girdling by *Oncideres pustulatus* (Coleopera: Cerambycidae) and Relative Host Quality of Persimmon, Hickory, and Elm." Ann. Entomol. Soc. Am. 88(4): 451–455.

Rice, M. E. and B. M. Drees. 1990. "Twig Girdlers." UC-018. Texas Agricultural Extension Service, The Texas A&M University System, College Station, Texas. 3 pp.

Rice, M. E. and W. B. Peck. 1991. "*Mantispa sayi* (Neuroptera: Mantispidae) Parasitism on Spiders (Araneae) in Texas, with Observations on Oviposition and Larval Survivorship." Ann. Entomol. Soc. Am. 84(1): 52–57.

Riherd, P. T. and G. P. Wene. 1955. "A Study of Moths Captured at a Light Trap at Weslaco, Texas." *J. Kans. Ento. Soc.* 28(3): 102–107 (collection records and temporal distributions).

Riley, D. G. 1992. "A New Occurrence of Broad Mites in Peppers in the Lower Rio Grande Valley of Texas." *Subtropical J. Sci.* 45: 46–48.

Rings, R. W. and G. J. Musik. 1976. "A Pictorial Key to the Armyworms and Cutworms Attacking Corn in the North Central States." Research Circular 221. Ohio Agricultural Research and Development Center, Wooster, Ohio.

Robinson, J. V. and P. J. Hamman. 1980. "Fall Webworms." L-1811. Texas Agricultural Extension Service, Texas A&M University System, College Station, Texas. 2 pp.

Robinson, J. V. 1984. "The Nantucket Pine Tip Moth." L-946. Texas Agricultural Extension Service, The Texas A&M University, College Station, Texas. 4 pp.

Schaffer, C. 1908. "List of the Longicorn Coleoptera Collected on the Museum Expeditions to Brownsville, Texas, and the Huachuca Mts., Arizona, with Descriptions of New Genera and Species and Notes on Known Species." *Mus Brooklyn Inst. Arts and Sci., Sci. Bull.* 1(12): 325–352.

Schuster, F. M. and J. C. Boling. 1971. "Biological Control of Rhodes Grass Scale in Texas by *Neodusmetia sangwawi* (Rao)—Effectiveness and Colonization Studies." B-1104. Texas Agric. Exper. Sta., College Station, Texas. 7 pp.

Schwarz, E. A. 1896. "Termitidae Observed in Southwestern Texas in 1895." *Proc. Entomol. Soc.* Washington 4 (1): 38–41.

Selman, C. L. 1975. "A Pictorial Key to the Hawkmoths (Lepidoptera: Sphingidae) of Eastern United States (except Florida)." Biological Notes No. 9, Ohio Biological Survey, Ohio State University, Columbus, Ohio.

Slater, J. A. and R. M. Baranowski. 1978. *How to Know the True Bugs.* Wm. C. Brown Company Publishers, Dubuque, Iowa. 256 pp.

Smith, C. M. 1983. "The Rice Water Weevil, *Lissorhoptrus oryzophilus* Kuschel." Exotic Quarantine Pests and Procedures for Introduction of Plant Materials. 3–9.

Smith, C. M., J. L. Bagnet, S. D. Linscombe and J. F. Robinson. 1986. "Insect Pests of Rice in Louisiana." Louisiana Agric. Exp. Sta. Bull. No. 774. Louisiana State Univ.

Smith, M. R. 1936. "A List of the Ants of Texas." *J. New York Entomol. Soc.* 44(2): 155–170.

Snow, F. H. 1905. "Some Results of the University of Kansas Entomological Expeditions on Galveston and Brownsville, Texas, in 1904 and 1905." Trans. Kansas Acad. Sci. 20(1): 136–154.

Solomon, J. D. 1995. "Guide to Insect Borers in North American Broadleaf Trees and Shrubs." USDA, Forest Service, Agricultural Handbook AH-706. 735 pp.

Stallings, D. B. and J. R. Turner. 1946. "Texas Lepidoptera (Rhopalocera: Papilionoidea)." *Entomol. News* 57(2): 44–49.

Stallings, D. B. and J. R. Turner. 1947. "Texas Lepidoptera (with Description of a New Subspecies)." *Entomol. News* 58(1): 36–41.

Sterling, W. L., G. C. Gaumer, J. Hafernik, and D. A. Dean. 1978. "A Checklist of Insects Found on Cotton in East Texas." Texas Agric. Expt. Sta. MP-1366.

Stewart, J. W. 1979. "Centipedes and Millipedes." L-1747. Texas Agricultural Extension Service, Texas A&M University System, College Station, Texas. 2 pp.

Stewart, J. W. 1982. "Texas Leaf Cutting Ant." L-1222. Texas Agricultural Extension Service, Texas A&M University System, College Station, TX. 4 pp.

Stewart, W. 1985. "Cutworms in the Home Garden and Landscape." L-1504. Texas Agricultural Extension Service, Texas A&M University System, College Station, TX. 2 pp.

Stewart, J. W. 1993. "Wintergarden Insect Report." Mimeograph. Texas Agricultural Extension Service, Texas A&M University System, Uvalde, TX. 2 pp.

Stewart, K. W., R. W. Baumann, and B. P. Stark. 1974. "The Distribution and Past Dispersal of Southwestern United States Plecoptera." Trans. Amer. Ento. Soc. 99: 507–546.

Stinner, R. E., J. R. Bradley, Jr. and J. W. Van Duyn. 1980. "Sampling *Heliothis* spp. on Soybean," in *Sampling Methods in Soybean Entomology* (M. Kogan and D. C. Herzog, eds.), Springer-Verlag, New York, pp. 407–421.

Stoetzel, M. B. 1989. *Common Names of Insects and Related Organisms 1989*. Entomological Society of America, Landham, Maryland. 199 pp.

Stojanovich, C. J. 1964. "Pictorial Key to Adult Female Mosquitoes of Texas." U. S. Dept. Health, Education and Welfare, Communicable Disease Center, Atlanta, Georgia.

Strecker, J. K. 1925. "Additions to a List of Diurnal Lepidoptera of the Vicinity of Waco, Texas." Contrib. Baylor Univ. Mus., No. 1, in *Natural History of Texas*, Vol. 2.

Strecker, J. K. 1935. "Moths from the Vicinity of Waco, Texas." *Baylor Bull.* 38(3): 46–47.

Sublette, J. E. and M. S. Sublette. 1967. "The Limnology of Playa Lakes on the Llano Estacado, New Mexico, and Texas." *Southw. Natur.* 12(4): 396-406.

Sundman, J. A. 1965. "Checklist and Descriptions of a New Species of the Genus *Cryptocephalus* in Texas (Coleoptera: Chrysomelidae)." *Southw. Natur.* 19(11): 1–8.

Swan, L. A. and C. S. Papp. *The Common Insects of North America*. Harper and Row, Publishers, New York. 750 pp.

Swanson, M. C. and L. D. Newsom. 1962. Effect of Infestation by the Rice Stink Bug, *Oebalus pugnax*, on Yield and Quality of Rice. *J. Econ. Entomol.* 55(6)877–879.

Tedders, W. L. 1978. "Important Biological and Morphological Characteristics of the Foliar-Feeding Aphids of Pecan." USDA Tech. Bull. 1579. Washington, D. C. 29 pp.

Teetes, G. L., K. V. Seshu Reddy, K. Leuschner, and L. R. House. 1983. "Sorghum Insect Identification Handbook." International Crops Research Institute for the Semi-Arid Tropics. Info. Bull. 12. 121 pp.

Thatcher, R. C., J. L. Searcy, J. E. Coster, and G. D. Hertel. 1980. "The Southern Pine Beetle." U.S.D.A. Forest Service, Tech. Bull. 1631.

Thomas, J. G. 1968. "Catalpa Sphinx and Catalpa Trees." Texas Agricultural Extension Service, Texas A&M University System, College Station, Texas (mimeograph).

Thomas, J. G., W. H. Newton, and P. J. Hamman. 1972. "Peach and Plum Insects." MP-685. Texas Agricultural Extension Service, Texas A&M University System, College Station, Texas. 16 pp.

Tilden, J. W. 1974. "Unusual and Interesting Butterfly Records from Texas." *J. Lepidop. Soc.* 28(1): 22–25.

Tinkham, E. R. 1934. "The Dragonfly Fauna of Presidio and Jeff Davis Counties of the Big Bend Region of Trans-Pecos Texas." *Can. Entomol.* 66(10): 211–218.

Tinkham, E. R. 1935. "The Mutillidae of Presidio and Jeff Davis Counties of the Big Bend Region of Trans-Pecos Texas." *Can Entomol.* 67(10): 207–211.

Tinkham, E. R. 1938. "Western Orthoptera Attracted to Lights." *J. New York Entomol. Soc.* 46(3): 339–353.

Tinkham, E. R. 1941. "Biological and Faunistic Notes on the Cicadidae of the Big Bend Region of Pecos Texas." *J. New York Entomol. Soc.* 49: 165–183.

Tinkham, E. R. 1944. "Faunistic Notes on the Diurnal Lepidoptera of the Big Bend Region of Trans-Pecos, Texas, with the Description of a new *Melitaea*." *Can. Entomol.* 76(1): 11–18.

Tinkham, E. R. 1948. "Faunistic and Ecological Studies on the Orthoptera of the Big Bend Region of Trans-Pecos Texas." *Amer. Midl. Natur.* 40: 521–663.

Townsend, C. H. T. 1897. "Diptera from the Rio Grande or Tamaulipan region of Texas I." *J. New York Entomol. Soc.* 5(4): 171–178.

Townsend, C. H. T. 1898. "Diptera from the lower Rio Grande or Tamaulipan region of Texas. II." *J. New York Entomol. Soc.* 6(6): 50–52.

Townsend, C. H. T. 1903. "A Contribution to the Knowledge of the Coleopterous Fauna of the Lower Rio Grande Valley of Texas and Tamaulipas, with Biological Notes and Special Reference to Geographical Distribution." *Trans. Texas Acad. Sci.* 5: 51–101.

Tucker, E. S. 1906. "Determinations of Some Texas Coleoptera with Records." *Entomol. News* 17(1): 10–14.

Tucker, E. S. 1908. "Incidental Captures of Neuropterous Insects at Plano, Texas." *Psyche* 15: 97–100.

Tucker, E. S. 1909. "Incidental Captures of Apterous and Orthopterous Insects at Plana (Plano), Texas." *Entomol. News* 20(7): 294–297.

Tucker, E. S. 1910. "Incidental Captures of Coleoptera at Plano, Texas." *Can. Entomol.* 42(7): 229–237.

Turnbow, R. H. and J. E. Wappes. 1978. "Notes on Texas Cerambycidae (Coleptera)." *Coleopt. Bull.* 32: 367–372.

Turnbow, R. H. and J. H. Wappes. 1981. "New Host and Distributional Records for Texas Cerambycidae." *Southw. Entomol.* 6(2): 75–80.

Turney, H. A. and R. Crocker. 1980. Elm leaf beetles. L-1812. Texas Agricultural Extension Service, Texas A&M University System, College Station, Texas.

Valentine, B. D. 1947. "Cicindelid Collecting in Texas." *Coleopt. Bull.* 1(7): 61–62.

Van Pelt, A. 1983. "Ants of the Chisos Mountains, Texas (Hymenoptera: Formicidae)." *Southw. Nat.* 28(2): 137–142.

Vickery, R. A. 1925. "List of Parasitic insects Reared from Host insects Collected in the Vicinity of Brownsville, Texas." *Proc. Entomol. Soc.* Washington 27(7): 137–141.

Vogt, G. B. 1949. "Three New Cicindelidae from South Texas with Collecting Notes on Other Cicindelidae (Coleoptera)." *Bull. Brooklyn Entomol. Soc.* 44(1): 1–9.

Vogt, G. B. 1949. "Notes on Cerambycidae from the Lower Rio Grande Valley, Texas (Coleoptera)." *Pan-Pacific Entomol.* 25(3): 137–144, 175–184.

Webster, F. M. 1893. "Notes on Some Injurious Insects in Texas." *Can. Entomol.* 25(1): 35–36.

Werner, F. and C. Olson. 1994. *Insects of the Southwest.* Fisher Books, Tuscon, Arizona. 162 pp.

Westcott, C. 1973. *The Gardener's Bug Book.* 4th Ed. Doubleday and Company, Inc., Garden Coty, New York. 689 pp.

Wheeler, W. M. 1900. "A Study of Some Texas Ponerine." *Biol. Bull.* 2: 1–31.

Wheeler, G. C. and J. Wheeler. 1985. "A Checklist of Texas Ants." *Prairie Naturalist.* 17(2): 49–64.

Wheeler, W. M. 1903." A Decade of Texas Formicidae." *Psyche* 10(323): 93–111. *Mus. Nat. Hist. Bull.* 24: 339–485.

Whitcomb, C. E. 1983. *Know It and Grow It.* Lacebark Publications, Stillwater, Oklahoma, 739 pp.

Wickham, H. F. 1893. "Field Notes from Texas and Louisiana." *Can. Entomol.* 25(6): 139–143.

Wickham, H. F. 1897. "The Coleoptera of the Lower Rio Grande Valley." *Bull. Lab. Nat. Hist., State Univ. Iowa* 4: 96–114.

Wickham, H. F. 1898. "Recollections of Old Collecting Grounds. II: The Lower Rio Grande Valley." *Entomol. News* 9: 22–24, III. 9: 39–41, IV 9: 81–84.

Williamson, E. B. 1914. "Dragonflies (Odonata) Collected in Texas and Oklahoma." *Entomol. News* 25(9): 411–415.

Wirth, W. W. and L. J. Bottimer. 1956. "A Population Study of the *Culicoides* Midges of the Edwards Plateau Region of Texas." *Mosquito News* 16940: 256–266.

Wiseman, J. S. 1965. "A List of Mosquito Species Reported from Texas." *Mosquito News* 25(1): 58–59.

Wiseman, J. S. and R. B. Eads. "1960 Texas Blackfly Records (Diptera: Simuliidae)." *Mosquito News*: 20(1): 45–49.

Wright, A. B. 1993. *Peterson First Guides® to Caterpillars.* Houghton Mifflin Co., New York. 128.

Yanega, D. 1996. "Field Guide to Northeastern Longhorned Beetles (Coleoptera: Cerambycidae)." Illinois Natural History Survey, Manual 6. 184 pp. Champaign, IL.

Young, D. G. 1972. "Phleotomine Sandflies from Texas and Florida (Diptera: Psychodidae)." *Florida Entomol.* 55(1): 61–64.

Zim, H. S. and C. Cottam. 1956. *Insects, A Guide to Familiar American Insects.* A Golden Nature Guide. Golden Press. New York. 160 pp.

INDEX

Acanthocephala declivis, 58
Acanthoscelides obtectus, 185
Acarapsis woodi, 306
Acari, 301–306
Acheta domesticus, 22
Acmaeodera, 103, 105
Acorn weevils, 192
Acraspis erinacei, 276
Acrididae, 19–21
Acrobasis nuxvorella, 237
Acrobat ants, 287
Actias luna, 257
Aculops lycopersici, 303
Aedes, 207
Aedes aegypti, 207
Aedes albopictus, 207
Aerial nets, 312
Aeschnidae, 14
African violet, 84
Africanized honey bee, 281
Ageneotettix deorum, 19
Agraulis vanillae
    incarnata, 252
Agraulis vanillae nigrior, 252
Agrilus, 103
Agromyzidae, 214
Agrotis ipsilon, 265
Agrotis orthogonia, 265
Agrotis subterranea, 265
Alates, 32
Alaus oculatus, 105
Alderflies, 90
Aleurocanthus woglumi, 69
Aleyrodidae, 69–70
Alfalfa, 49, 66, 101, 105,
    115, 190, 192, 217, 268
Alfalfa caterpillar, 246
Alfalfa leafcutting bee, 279
Alfalfa weevil, 190
Allergic reactions, 28, 311
Alsophila pometaria, 254
Altica litigata, 186
Alydidae, 58
Alypia octomaculata, 265
Amblyomma
    americanum, 301
Ambrosia fungus, 197
American dog tick, 301
American elm, 188
American grasshopper, 20
American house dust
    mite, 306

American painted lady, 249
American plum borer,
    231–232
Ammotrechidae, 309
Amphibolips, 276
Amphipoda, 310
Amphipods, 310
Anacua, 190
Anaea aidea, 252
Anaea andria, 251
Anaphylactic shock, 209
Anaplasmosis, 211
Anarsia lineatella, 234
Anasa tristis, 57
Anax junius, 14
Andricus laniger, 276
Anemia, 302
Angoumois grain moth, 227,
    229, 242
Animal matter, 216
Animal products, 108
Animal skins, 108
Animals, 208–209, 211, 304
Anisoptera, 14
Annual cicada, 64
Anobiid beetles, 109
Anobiidae, 109–110
Anopheles, 207
Ant farms, 289
Anthanassa texana, 250
Antheraea polyphemus, 257
Anthocoridae, 51
Anthomyiidae, 216–217
Anthonomus grandis, 191
Anthophoridae, 279
Anthrenus, 107
Anthrenus flavipes, 107
Anthrenus verbasci, 107
Antlions, 14, 90, 93
Antonina graminis, 84
Ants, 272
Aphelinidae, 275
Aphid lions, 90
Aphid mummies, 275
Aphididae, 71–77
Aphidiinae, 275
Aphidius, 275
Aphids, 63, 276, 287
Aphis gossypii, 71, 77
Aphis nerii, 72
Aphodius, 102
Aphonopelma, 295

Apidae, 280–281
Apis, 281
Apis mellifera, 3, 281
Apoidea, 281
Apple, 18, 59, 73, 82–84, 233,
    248, 256, 259, 261–262
Apples, 192, 234
Apricot, 232, 234
Aquatic, 13, 37, 46, 90,
    97–98, 207–208, 211,
    213, 224
Aquatic grasses, 194
Aquatic habitats, 10
Aquatic moth, 225
Aquatic nets, 313
Aquatic predators, 45
Arachnida, 4
Araneae, 295-297
Arborvitae, 229
Archilestes grandis, 15
Archipsocidae, 40
Archipsocus nomas, 40
Arctiidae, 256, 262–264
Argasidae, 302
Arilus cristatus, 54
Armored scales, 80
Army cutworm, 265
Armyworms, 226,
    265–269
Arphia pseudonietana, 20
Arthropoda, 3, 291
Ascalaphidae, 93
Ash, 48, 59, 70, 117, 233,
    273, 279
Ash paneling, 110
Ash sawfly, 273
Ash-gray lady beetle, 112
Asian ambrosia beetle, 196
Asian tiger mosquito, 207
Asilidae, 212
Asp, 236–237, 258
Asparagus, 71
Assassin bugs, 52, 58
Aster, 215
Aster leafhopper, 66
Asterocampa celtis, 251
Asterocampa celtis
    antonia, 251
Asterocampa celtis
    clyton, 251
Asterocampa celtis
    louisa, 251

*Asterocampa celtis
 texana,* 251
Asterocampa clyton, 251
Asterocampa leilia, 251
Asters, 250
Ataenius, 102
Atalopedes campestris, 244
Atlides halesus, 247
Atta texana, 286
Attagenus, 107
Attagenus unicolor, 107
Atteva punctella, 265
Aulocara elliotti, 19
Automeris io, 236, 258
Avocado, 70, 84
Axonopus compressus, 253
Azalea, 47, 259, 279
Azalea lace bug, 47

Backswimmers, 46
Bacon, 288
Baetidae, 11
Bagworms, 228–229,
 257, 263
Bahia grass, 24, 55, 241
Baits, 313
Baldfaced hornet, 283–284
Banana fly, 215
Banded cucumber beetle, 186
Banded woollybear, 264
Banded-winged
 grasshopper, 20
Bark beetles, 196
Bark scorpions, 293
Barklice, 39–41
Barklouse, 40
Barley, 75–76, 193, 206
Barley yellow dwarf virus, 76
Barnacle scale, 79
Barnyard grass, 62
*Basilarchia (Limenitis)
 archippus,* 249
*Basilarchia (Limenitis)
 arthemis,* 249
Basilarchia archippus, 253
Basswood, 18, 262
Bathrooms, 212
Battus philenor, 245
Bean weevil, 185
Beans, 49–50, 58, 71, 105,
 187, 215, 217, 267,
 305–306
Beating sheet, 313
Bed bugs, 53
Bedding plants, 75, 105,
 270, 310
Bee bread, 279
Bee flies, 212
Bee hives, 240–241
Beebalm, 49

Beech, 233, 274
Bees, 272
Beeswax, 281
Beet armyworm, 268–269
Beetles, 94, 225, 275, 285
Beets, 49–50, 102, 105, 271
Begonia, 71
Belastomatidae, 45
Bembix, 277
Bemisia agrentifolii, 70
Berlese funnel, 314
Bermuda grass, 24, 55, 85,
 100, 241, 244, 269
Bermuda grass mites, 303
Bess beetles, 99
Bibionidae, 204
Big Bend recluse, 296
Bigheaded grasshopper, 19
Birch, 18
Bird cherry-oat aphid, 76
Birds, 200, 209
Biscuits, 242
Bison, 222
Bites of arthropods 51–54,
 86–88, 91, 99,
 200–201, 207–211
Blaberidae, 28
Black blow fly, 219
Black carpenter ant, 287
Black carpet beetle, 107
Black citrus aphids, 77
Black cutworm, 265
Black flies, 70, 208–209
Black gum, 257
Black larder beetle, 107–108
Black lights, 313
Black and yellow mud
 dauber, 278
Black pecan aphid, 74
Black soldier fly, 211–212
Black swallowtail, 245
Black turpentine beetle, 196
Black-eyed peas, 58
Blackberries, 303
Blackberry, 248, 286
Blackmargined aphid, 73
Blackwinged damselflies, 15
Bladder, 87
Blanket flower, 21
Blatella vaga, 28
Blatellidae, 28
Blatta orientalis, 27
Blattaria, 27–28
Blattella germanica, 28
Blattellidae, 28
Blattidae, 27
Blissus insularis, 54
*Blissus leucopterus
 leucopterus,* 55
Blister beetles, 114–115

Bloodsucking conenose, 53
Bloodworms, 210
Blow flies, 219
Blue mud dauber, 278
Blue-green sharpshooter,
 66–67
Blues, 247
Body louse, 43
Boisea trivittata, 58
Bok choy, 189
Boll weevil, 191, 299
Bollworm, 226, 248, 265–266
Bombus, 280
Bombyliidae, 212
Booklice, 39–40, 314
Booklouse, 40
Bordered patch, 250
Boston ivy, 83
Bostrichid beetles, 109
Bostrichidae, 109
Bot flies, 221
Bothynus gibbosus, 101
Bots, 222
Bougainvillea, 279
Bourletiella hortensis, 6
Boxelder, 59, 229
Boxelder bug, 58
Boxwood, 83
Brachypsectra fulva, 105
Brachypsectridae, 105
Brachystola magna, 21
Braconidae, 72, 275
Bradysia, 205
Brazilian skipper, 243
Breads, 288
Brephidium exilis, 247
Bristletails, 8
Broad mites, 305
Broad-headed bugs, 58
Broad-shouldered water
 striders, 47
Broadbean weevil, 185
Broccoli, 217
Brown dog tick, 301
Brown recluse, 296
Brown soft scale, 80
Brown spiders, 296
Brown stink bug, 60
Brown widow, 298
Brown-winged earwig, 36
Brownbanded cockroach, 28
Brownheaded ash sawfly, 273
Bruchidae, 185
Bruchus pisorum, 185
Bruchus rufimanus, 185
Brushfooted butterflies,
 249–252
Brussel sprouts, 217
Buck moth, 236, 257–259
Buckeye, 249

Buffalo gnats, 208
Buffalo treehopper, 64
Buildings, 30
Bumble bees, 272, 280, 283
Buprestidae, 103, 116, 232
Buprestis lineata, 103
Bur clover, 190
Burrower bug, 59
Burying beetles, 97
Buthidae, 292
Butter, 288
Butterflies, 226, 275
Butterfly net, 312
Butterfly weed, 72

Cabbage, 49, 50, 217,
   266, 271
Cabbage looper, 270, 271
Cabbage maggot, 217
Cabbageworm, 226, 270
Caddisflies, 224–225
Caenidae, 11
Cakes, 288
Caliroa, 273
Calliphora, 219
Calliphora vomitoria, 219
Calliphoridae, 219–220
Callirhytis, 276
Callirhytis seminator, 276
*Callosobruchus
   maculatus,* 185
Calopteryx, 15
Calosoma scrutator, 95
Calpodes ethlius, 243
Calyopterygidae, 15
Camel crickets, 22
Camellia, 82
Camponotus, 287
*Camponotus
   pennsylvanicus,* 287
Camponotus rasilis, 287–288
Camponotus sayi, 287
Candy, 242
Cankerworms, 254–255
Canna lilies, 243
Cantaloupe, 215
Cantharidae, 106
Cantharidin, 115
Canthon, 102
Capnodium, 70, 77
Carabidae, 95
Cardboard points, 315
Carnation, 271
Carolina grasshopper, 20
Carolina mantid, 25
Carpenter ants, 287–288
Carpenter bees, 279–280
Carpenterworm, 232–233
Carpet beetles, 107, 108, 227
Carpophilus, 109

Carrion, 219
Carrion beetles, 97
Carrot beetle, 101
Carrots, 102, 215, 245
Carton, 33–34
Casemaking clothes moth,
   227–228
Cassia, 195, 247
Castes, 30
Cat flea, 200
Cat-facing, 49, 60
Catalpa, 71, 81, 260
Catalpa sphinx, 259
Catawba worms, 260
Caterpillar hunter, 95
Caterpillars, 226, 285, 290
Cattle, 220–222
Cattle fever, 301
Cattle grub, 222
Cauliflower, 49, 217
Cave crickets, 22
Cecidomyiidae, 68, 205–206
Cecropia moth, 257
Cedar, 229
Cedar elm, 188
Celastrus, 82
Celery, 49, 50, 102, 215
Celery looper, 270
Celticecis spiniformis, 68
Celtis, 248, 251
Centipede grass, 55, 241
Centipedes, 4, 291, 311
Centruroides, 293
Centruroides vittatus, 292
Cerambycidae, 116,
   118–120, 232
Ceratipsocus venosus, 40
Ceratomia catalpae, 259
Ceratopogonidae, 209
Cerci, 11
Cercopidae, 65
Cereal psocid, 39
Cereals, 102, 108, 114
*Ceroplastes
   cirripediformis,* 79
Ceroplastes floridensis, 79
Cerrina unicolor, 274
Ceryonis pegala, 253
Chagas' disease, 54
Chalcophora virginiensis, 103
Chalybion californicum, 278
Chamaecrista cinerea, 247
Chaoborinae, 207
Chard, 49
Charidotella bicolor, 189
Charidryas nycteis, 168, 250
*Chaulognathus
   pennsylvanicus,* 106
Cheeses, 108
Chelicerae, 296

Chenopodium, 247
Cherry, 18, 59, 197, 232,
   256, 259, 261
Chestnut, 66
Chewing lice, 42
Chicken head louse, 42
Chickweed, 259, 303
Chiggers, 290, 304–305
Chilo plejadellus, 239
Chilocorus cacti, 112
Chilocorus stigma, 111
Chilopoda, 4, 311
Chin fly, 221
Chinaberry, 59, 81
Chinch bug, 54
Chinese cabbage, 189
Chinese elm, 197
Chinese lantern, 68
Chinese praying mantid, 25
Chironomidae, 210
Chironomus, 210
Chlorochroa ligata, 60
Chloropid flies, 216
Chloropidae, 216
Chlosyne janais, 250
Chlosyne lacinia, 250
Chocolate, 114, 242
Christmas trees, 236
Chrysalis, 226
Chrysobothris, 103
Chrysomela scripta, 187
Chrysomela texana, 187
Chrysomelidae, 50,
   185–189, 214
Chrysoperla carnea, 92
Chrysoperla oculata, 92
Chrysoperla rufilabris, 92
Chrysopidae, 92
Chrysops, 210
Cicada killer, 277
Cicadas, 63
Cicadellidae, 65–66
Cicadidae, 63
Cicindela, 95
Cicindelidae, 95
Cigar case makers, 228
Cigarette beetle, 110
Cimbex americana, 273
Cimbicidae, 273
Cimex lectularius, 53
Cimicidae, 53
Cisseps fulvicollis, 264
Citheronia regalis, 258
Citrus, 70, 71, 84, 87, 89,
   119, 246, 268, 306
Citrus blackfly, 69–70
Citrus mealybug, 83
Citrus rust mite, 303

Citrus thrips, 87
Classification, 3
Clearwing moths, 232
Click beetles, 105–106
Climaciella brunnea, 91
Climbing cutworms, 265
Clostridium, 288
Clothes moth, 226–228, 242
Clothing, 108, 228
Cloudless sulphur, 246
Clover, 71, 105, 190
Clubtails, 14
Cluster fly, 219
Coccidae, 79–80
Coccids, 80
Coccinella septempunctata, 112
Coccinellidae, 111–112
Coccotorus scutellaris, 192
Coccus hesperidum, 80
Cochineal insect, 83
Cochliomyia hominivorax, 220
Cochliomyia macellaria, 220
Cocklebur, 120
Cockroaches, 27
Cocoon, 226
Codling moth, 226, 233–234
Coenagrionidae, 15
Coffee, 70
Coleomegilla maculata, 111
Coleoptera, 1, 50, 94–120, 185–196, 214, 225, 227, 232, 234, 242, 274, 275, 283, 314
Colias eurytheme, 246
Collard greens, 189
Collecting insects, 312
Collembola, 6
Collops balteatus, 108
Collops quinquemaculatus, 108
Colorado potato beetle, 188
Common blue bottle fly, 219
Common cattle grub, 222
Common chinch bug, 55
Common green darner, 14
Common green lacewing, 92
Common names, 3
Common skimmers, 14
Common wood nymph, 253
Compositae, 250
Compsus auricephalus, 192
Conchuela, 60
Confused flour beetle, 114
Conifer sawflies, 273
Conifers, 229
Conjunctivitis, 216
Conocephalus, 21

Conotrachelus nenuphar, 191, 234
Contarinia sorghicola, 206
Convergent lady beetle, 111
Copidosoma, 275
Coppers, 247
Copris, 102
Coptotermes formosanus, 33
Coquilettidia, 207
Coreidae, 52, 57–58
Coreids, 57
Corimelaena pulicaria, 59
Corixa, 46
Corixidae, 46
Corn, 20, 50, 55, 76, 100–102, 105, 193, 217, 229, 239–240, 248, 266–269, 290
Corn earworm, 266–267
Corn leaf aphid, 76
Cornmeal, 242
Corydalidae, 90, 225
Corydalus, 90
Corythuca arcuata, 48
Corythuca ciliata, 48
Corythuca cydoniae, 48
Corythuca gossypii, 48
Cossidae, 232
Cotinis nitida, 100
Cotinis mutabilis, 100
Cotton, 20, 21, 49, 58–60, 67, 70–71, 102, 109, 191, 230, 248, 267, 270–271, 303, 305–306
Cotton aphid, 71, 77
Cotton bollworm, 266
Cotton fleahopper, 49
Cotton lace bug, 48
Cotton square borer, 247
Cottonwood, 78, 120, 187
Cottonwood borer, 117, 119–120
Cottonwood leaf beetles, 187
Cottony camellia scale, 83
Cottony cushion scale, 83
Cottony-white waxy filaments, 67
Cow killer, 282–283
Cow manure, 220
Cowpea weevil, 185
Cowpeas, 50, 185
Crab louse, 43
Crabapple, 261
Crabs, 310
Crackers, 242
Crambus, 241
Crane flies, 203
Crapemyrtle aphid, 77
Crapemyrtles, 77
Crawdads, 310

Crawlers, 69, 79–83
Crayfish, 310
Crazy ant, 288
Crematogaster, 287
Crickets, 19
Crochets, 226, 231–232, 272–273
Crops, 22, 65, 105
Croton, 252
Ctenocephalides canis, 200
Ctenocephalides felis, 200
Cuban cockroach, 28
Cuban laurel thrip, 88–89
Cuclotogaster heterographus, 42
Cucujidae, 110
Cucumbers, 50, 186, 215, 231, 310
Cucurbits, 57, 71, 187, 217
Culex, 207
Culicidae, 207
Culiseta, 207
Curculio caryae, 192
Curculio fulvus, 192
Curculionidae, 185, 190–195, 234, 242
Cut ant, 286
Cutleaf evening primrose, 49
Cutworms, 226, 265
Cyclamen mites, 305
Cyclas formicarius elegantulus, 195
Cyclocephala, 99
Cyclocephala lurida, 100
Cycloneda munda, 112
Cydia caryana, 234, 238
Cydia pomonella, 233–234
Cydnidae, 59
Cyllopsis gemma, 253
Cynipid wasp, 276–277
Cynipidae, 272, 276
Cynodon dactylon, 253
Cyperus, 62
Cypress, 83, 229
Cyrtopeltis notata, 50
Cysteodemus armatus, 115

Dactylophidae, 83
Dactylopius coccus, 83
Dactylotum, 21
Dactyls, 23
Daddylonglegs, 300
Dahlias, 102, 215, 306
Daisy, 215
Daktulosphaira vitofoliae, 77
Dallis grass, 75
Damsel bugs, 51
Damselfly, 13, 15
Danaidae, 249, 253

Danaus gilippus, 254
Danaus plexippus, 249, 253
Dark mealworm, 114
Darkwinged fungus gnats, 205, 216
Dasymutilla gloriosa, 283
Dasymutilla occidentalis, 282
Dasymutilla vestita, 283
Datana integerrima, 261
Datana ministra, 261
Datura, 303
DDVP, 314
Dead animals, 97
Dead trees, 105
Deadheart, 240
Dealates, 32
Decaying logs, 99, 113
Decaying organic matter, 98, 100, 109, 204–205, 207, 210–211, 216–219, 310–311
Decopoda, 310
Dectes texanus, 120
Deer fly, 210–211
Deilelater, 105
Delia antiqua, 217
Delia platura, 216
Delia radicum, 217
Deltochilum, 102
Dendroctonus frontalis, 195
Dendroctonus terebrans, 196
Dengue, 208
Dermacentor variabilis, 301
Dermaptera, 35–36
Dermatophagoides farinae, 306
Dermatophagoides pteronyssinus, 306
Dermestes ater, 107
Dermestes lardarius, 107
Dermestes maculatus, 107
Dermestid beetles, 107, 314
Dermestidae, 107
Desert fire ant, 289
Desert termites, 34
Detritivores, 1, 6, 99, 101–102, 203–205, 210, 212, 215–216, 218–219, 310–311
Diabrotica balteata, 186
Diabrotica barberi, 187
Diabrotica undecimpunctata howardi, 186
Diabrotica virgifera virgifera, 186
Diabrotica virgifera zeae, 186
Diapause, 191, 194
Diapheromera femorata, 17
Diaspididae, 80–82
Diatraea crambidoides, 239

Diatraea grandiosella, 239
Diatraea saccharalis, 239
Dichlorvos, 314
Dichotomius, 102
Dictamnus, 246
Differential grasshopper, 19
Digger wasps, 277
Dill, 245
Dineutus, 97
Dione moneta poeyi, 252
Dioryctria amatella, 235
Diplopoda, 4, 311
Diprionidae, 273
Diptera, 70, 106, 202–223, 273, 275
Disease, 44, 65–66, 208, 211
Disholcaspis cinerosa, 276
Dissosteira carolina, 20
Dissosteira longipennis, 19
Diuraphis noxia, 75
Dixid midges, 207
Dixinae, 207
Dobsonfly, 90–91, 225
Dog flea, 200
Dog food, 242
Dog-day cicadas, 63
Dogs, 221
Dogwood, 18
Dolichopodidae, 213
Dolichopus, 213
Dolichovespula maculata, 283–284
Donkeys, 221
Doodlebugs, 93
Doru lineare, 36
Dorymyrmex insana, 288
Dragonfly, 13–14, 203
Drain flies, 207
Dried beans, 114
Dried fruit, 109, 242
Dried insects, 108
Dried plant material, 110
Drone flies, 214
Drosophila melanogaster, 215
Drosophilidae, 215
Drugs, 110, 114
Drugstore beetle, 110
Dryas julia moderata, 252
Drywood termite, 31–34
Dung beetle, 102
Dust, 228
Dynastes tityus, 101
Dytiscidae, 96, 98

Eacles imperialis, 258
Earthworm beds, 212
Earthworms, 211
Earwigs, 35–36

Earworm, 266
Eastern hercules beetle, 101
Eastern lubber grasshopper, 19
Eastern tent caterpillar, 256–257, 263
Eastern yellowjacket, 285
Echinophaga gallinacea, 200
Ecpantheria scribonia, 264
Edwardsiana rosae, 66
Eggplant, 50, 68, 186, 189, 215, 230, 260, 303
Eggplant flea beetle, 185
Eightspotted forester, 265
Elasmopalpus lignosellus, 120
Elateridae, 105–106
Electric light bugs, 46
Elephant beetle, 101
Elm, 73, 102, 117, 119, 229, 233, 255, 259, 261–262, 273–274
Elm leaf beetle, 187
Elm sawfly, 273
Elytra, 94
Empoasca fabae, 66
Empress leilia, 251
Encarsia formosa, 275
Encephalitis, 208
Enchenopa binotata, 64
Encyrtidae, 275
Endangered arachnids, 319
Endangered insects, 317
English grain aphid, 76
English ivy, 84
English walnut, 233
Engraver beetles, 196
Entomology, 4
Eoreuma loftini, 239
Ephemeridae, 11
Ephemeroptera, 10–11
Ephestia, 229
Ephydridae, 205
Epicauta occidentalis, 115
Epicauta pennsylvanica, 115
Epicauta temexa, 115
Epidemic typhus, 43
Epidermoptidae, 306
Epitrix cucumeris, 185
Epitrix fuscula, 185
Eradication program, 220
Eremobates, 309
Eremobatidae, 309
Eriophyes cynodoniensis, 303
Eriophyidae, 303
Eriosoma, 73
Erisoma lanigerum, 73
Eristalis, 214
Ermine moth, 265
Erythroneura, 66
Estigmene acrea, 264

Ethyl acetate, 314
Ethyl alcohol, 315
Euborellia annulipes, 36
Euborellia riparia, 36
Euchistus, 62
Eucnemidae, 105
Eudiagogus pulcer, 194
Eudiagogus rosenschoeldi, 194
Eugenia, 82
Eumenes fraternus, 278
Eumeninae, 278
Euonymus japonica, 82
Euonymus kiautschovica, 82
Euonymus scale, 82
Euphorbiaceae, 252
Euptoieta claudia, 249
European corn borer, 239, 266
European earwig, 36
European elm, 188
European honey bee, 282
European house dust mite, 306
Euschistus servus, 60
Euxoa auxiliaris, 265
Euzophera semifuneralis, 231–232
Evening primrose, 259
Evergreen trees, 229
Excrement, 102
External parasite, 91
Eye gnats, 216
Eyed click beetle, 105

Fall armyworm, 266, 268–269
Fall cankerworm, 254–255
Fall webworm, 256–257, 263
False chinch bugs, 55
False click beetles, 105
False loosestrife, 250
False workers, 33
Feathers, 108, 228
Fecal material, 102
Fennel, 245
Fermenting fruit, 101, 109
Fescue, 269
Feverfew, 21
Ficus, 79, 84, 89
Field cockroach, 28
Field crickets, 22
Field crops, 88, 217
Field skipper, 244
Filariasis, 208
Filter feeders, 209
Fiorionia theae, 81
Fire ant, 289, 290, 305
Firebrat, 8
Fireflies, 106

Fish, as food/prey for insects, 11–13, 20, 37–38, 46, 91, 96, 210, 224–225, 260
Fish meal, 228
Fishflies, 90
Flagging, 234
Flat-headed borers, 103–104, 232
Flatidae, 67
Flaxseed, 205
Flea, 200–201
Flea beetles, 50, 185
Flesh fly, 219, 223
Flies, 106, 202, 275, 276, 285
Florida wax scale, 79
Flour, 108, 111, 114
Flour moths, 229
Flower flies, 213
Flowering plants, 75, 80
Flowers, 6, 22, 101, 116
Fly spots, 218
Forage, 85, 100, 244, 270, 286
Forage grasses, 20, 34
Forest tent caterpillar, 257
Forficula auricularia, 36
Forficulidae, 36
Formicidae, 286–289, 305
Formosan termites, 33
Frankliniella fusca, 87
Frankliniella occidentalis, 87
Freezer, 314
French mulberry, 81
Fruit, 114, 196, 229
Fruit flies, 215
Fruit tree, 22, 119, 286
Fruitworm, 266
Fulgoroidea, 67
Fungus ant, 286
Fungus gnats, 205
Fur, 228
Furcula, 6
Furniture, 108
Furniture carpet beetle, 107

Gall-forming aphids, 78
Gall-forming chalcids, 272
Gall-forming midge, 68
Gall-forming psyllids, 68
Gall-makers, 276
Gall-making psyllid, 69
Galleria mellonella, 240
Gallery patterns, 196
Galls, 78
Garden fleahopper, 50
Garden millipede, 311
Garden springtail, 6

Garden vegetables, 116
Gardenia, 71, 79, 84
Gas plant, 246
Gas station spiders, 298
Gasterophilus haemorrhoidalis, 221
Gasterophilus intestinalis, 221
Gasterophilus nasalis, 221
Gelechiidae, 191, 227, 229, 230, 242
Gemmed satyr, 253
Genista caterpillar, 241, 263
Geometridae, 254, 270
Gerardia, 250
Gerber daisy, 306
German cockroach, 28
Gerridae, 46
Gerris, 46
Geshna cannalis, 241, 243
Giant leopard moth, 264
Giant stag beetle, 98
Giant swallowtail, 245
Giant water bugs, 45–46
Girdle, 64
Girdling, 118, 232
Gladiolus thrips, 87
Glassine envelopes, 315
Glowworms, 106
Gloxinia, 87
Gnathamiteres tubiformans, 34
Gnats, 202, 205, 216
Goats, 221
Goatweed, 252
Goatweed butterfly, 251
Golden rain tree, 197
Golden tortoise beetle, 189
Goldenheaded weevil, 192
Goldenrod, 265, 285
Gomphidae, 14
Gouty oak gall, 276
Grain, 107, 193, 242
Grammia parthenice intermedia, 264
Granary weevil, 193, 242
Granulate cutworm, 265–266
Grape, 59, 78, 117
Grape phylloxera, 77
Graphocephala, 66
Graphocephala atropunctata, 67
Grapholita molesta, 234
Grasses, 49, 55, 65, 85, 87, 100, 102, 105, 240, 265, 268
Grasshoppers, 19, 299
Grasslands, 21

Gray hairstreak, 247
Gray velvet-ant, 283
Greasy, 288
Great blue hairstreak, 247
Greater wax moth, 240
Green bottle fly, 219
Green cloverworm, 271
Green June beetle, 100
Green lacewings, 92
Green peach aphid, 71, 74
Greenbug, 75–76
Greenhouse, 7, 35, 50, 68,
    70, 83, 205, 215, 230
Greenhouse thrips, 87
Ground beetles, 95–96
Ground cherry, 68
Ground ivy, 71
Ground mealybugs, 84
Ground pearls, 84
Groundcherry, 303
Gryllacrididae, 22
Gryllidae, 22
Gryllinae, 22
Gryllotalpidae, 23
Gryllus, 22
Guava, 70
Gulf fritillary, 252
Gynailothrips ficorum, 88
Gypsy moth, 262
Gyrinidae, 97
Gyrinus, 97
Gyropsylla ilicis, 69

Hackberry, 18, 69, 83, 119,
    248, 251
Hackberry blister gall
    maker, 69
Hackberry bud gall maker,
    68–69
Hackberry butterfly, 251
Hackberry gall psyllids, 68
Hackberry nipplegall
    maker, 69
Haematobia irritans, 219
Haematopinidae, 42
Haematopinus suis, 42
Hag moth, 236
Hair, 228
Hairstreaks, 247
Halteres, 202
Halticus bractatus, 50
Halysidota harrisii, 262
Halysidota tessellaris, 262
Hard ticks, 302
Harlequin bug, 60
Harmonia axyridis, 112
Harmonia lady beetle, 112
Harvester ants, 289
Harvesters, 247
Harvestmen, 300

Hawk moth, 259
Hawthorn, 73, 79, 256
Hawthorn lace bug, 48
Hay, 108
Head louse, 43
Headworm, 266
Hedgehog gall, 276
Heel fly, 222
Heliconiidae, 252
Heliconius charitonius
    vazquezae, 252
Helicoverpa zea, 266
Heliothis virescens, 266
Heliothrips
    haemorrhoidalis, 87
Hellgrammites, 90–91
Hemelytra, 51, 59
Hemileuca maia, 236,
    257–258
Hemileuca oliviae, 258
Hemiptera, 17, 45–62, 106
Hemp, 228
Heraclides, 245
Heraclides (Papilio)
    cresphontes, 245
Herbaceous plants, 113
Herbs, 50
Hermes satyr, 253
Hermetia illucens, 211
Hermeuptychia hermes, 253
Herpetogramma
    phaeopteralis, 241
Hesperiidae, 243–244, 265
Hessian fly, 205–206
Hetaerina, 15
Hexagenia limbata, 11
Hexapoda, 4
Hibernacula, 238
Hibiscus, 70, 248
Hickory, 18, 48, 79, 119,
    258, 261, 263
Hickory horned devil, 258
Hickory nuts, 235
Hickory shuckworm,
    234, 238
Hide beetle, 107
High Plains grasshopper, 19
Hippelates, 216
Hippodamia convergens, 111
Hog louse, 42
Hogs, 221
Holly, 79, 82, 84
Homalodisca, 66
Homalodisca triquetra, 67
Home gardens, 50
Homes, 9, 27, 35
Homoptera, 63–84, 287
Honey, 281, 288
Honey bee, 3, 272, 281, 307
Honey bee mite, 306

Honey bee tracheal
    mites, 306
Honey locust, 261
Honey sac, 282
Honeycombs, 240, 241, 282
Honeydew, 69–74, 75, 77,
    79, 80, 83–84, 93,
    284, 287
Hopperburn, 66
Hops, 71
Horn fly, 219, 220
Horned lizard, 361
Horned oak gall, 276
Hornet, 283
Horns, 108
Horntail, 272, 274
Hornworm, 226, 259
Horse bot fly, 221
Horse flies, 210–211
Horsemint, 49
Horses, 221
Host feeding, 276
House centipede, 311
House crickets, 22
House dust mite, 306
House fly, 217–219
Household, 28, 108
Houseplants, 80, 205
Houses, 59
Hover flies, 213
Huisache, 119
Huisache girdler, 118
Human louse, 43–44
Humans, 42, 53, 201, 221,
    304, 305
Hummingbirds, 259
Hyalella, 310
Hyalophora cecropia, 257
Hydrangea, 71
Hydrophilidae, 96, 98
Hyles lineata, 259
Hylotrupes bajulus, 118
Hymenoptera, 72, 214,
    272–289, 305
Hypera postica, 190
Hypercompe scribonia, 232
Hypermetamorphosis, 115
Hyperparasites, 275–276
Hyphantria cunea, 256, 263
Hypoderma lineatum, 222
Hypostome, 302
Hypselonotus, 57

Icerya purchasi, 83
Ichneumonidae, 274–275
Ichneumonids, 272
Ichneumons, 274
Identify insects, 2
Imagoes, 11
Impatiens, 87

Imperial moth, 258
Inchworms, 254, 270
Incisitermes, 31
Indianmeal moth, 227, 234, 242
Insect orders, 5
Insect traps, 313
Insecta, 4
Insidious flower bug, 51
Interiorscapes, 88
Io moth, 236–237, 258
Irish potato, 189
Ironclad beetle, 116
Isabella tiger moth, 264
Isopoda, 310
Isoptera, 30–34, 287
Ixodidae, 301–302

Jadera haematoloma, 58
Janais patch, 250
Japanese beetle, 100
Jasmine, 84
Jelly, 288
Jiggers, 304
Johnson grass, 75–76, 85, 206, 269
Julia longwing, 252
Jumping plant lice, 67
June beetles, 99, 299
June bugs, 99
Juniper, 229
Junonia (Precis) coenia, 249
Junonia (Precis) coenia nigrosuffusa, 249
Junonia (Precis) evarete, 249

KAAD, 315
Kale, 271
Kalotermitidae, 31
Katydids, 19, 21
Keiferia lycopersicella, 230
Keratin, 108
Khapra beetle, 107
Killer bees, 281
Kissing bugs, 53
Kitchens, 212

Labels, 316
Labiduridae, 36
Labium, 13
Lacewings, 90
Lady beetles, 111
Ladybird beetles, 111
Ladybugs, 111
Lampyridae, 105, 106
Landscape trees, 79
Lantana, 248
Lantana lace bug, 48
Laothe juglandis, 259
Larder beetle, 107

Large elm leaf beetle, 187
Large milkweed bug, 55
Larger canna leafroller, 243
Larger pale trogiid, 39
Largidae, 56
Largus bug, 56
Largus cuccinctus, 56
Lasciocampidae, 256, 263
Lasioderma serricorne, 110
Latrines, 212
Latrodectus geometricus, 298
Latrodectus hesperus, 298
Latrodectus mactans, 297
Latrodectus variolus, 298
Lawn, 241
Leaf galls, 78
Leaf insects, 17
Leafcutting bees, 278, 286
Leaffooted bug, 52, 58
Leafhopper assassin bug, 52
Leafhoppers, 63, 65–66
Leafminer flies, 214
Leafminers, 103, 214, 230, 273
Leather, 228
Lecanium, 80
Legumes, 34, 192, 195, 248, 268
Leopard moth, 232–233, 264
Lepidoptera, 1, 120, 191, 214, 225–272, 275, 315
Lepinotus inquilinus, 39
Leptinotarsa decemlineata, 188
Leptinotarsa texana, 188
Leptoglossus clypealis, 58
Leptoglossus phyllopus, 58
Lespisma saccharina, 8
Lespismatidae, 8
Lesser canna leafroller, 241, 243
Lesser cornstalk borer, 120
Lesser peachtree borer, 231
Lestidae, 15
Lethocerus, 45
Lettuce, 21, 50, 75, 215, 271
Libellulidae, 14
Libytheana bachmanii bachmanii, 248
Libytheana bachmanii larvata, 248
Libytheana carinenta mexicana, 248
Libytheidae, 248
Lice, 42
Lichens, 116
Light production, 105–106
Lightning beetles, 106
Lightningbugs, 105–106
Ligia, 310

Ligyrus gibbosus, 101
Lilac, 81, 233
Lily pads, 243
Limacodidae, 236
Linear earwig, 36
Lint, 228
Lip bot fly, 221
Liposcelidae, 39
Liposcelis corrodens, 39
Liposcelis divinatorius, 39
Liriomyza brassicae, 214
Liriomyza sativae, 214
Liriomyza trifolii, 214–215
Lissorhoptrus oryzophilus, 194
Live oak, 192, 229
Liver, 288
Livestock, 220, 290
Loblolly pine sawfly, 273
Lobsters, 310
Locust, 18, 64, 83, 229
Locust borer, 116–117
Logs, 105
Lone star tick, 301
Long-horned beetle, 116–117
Long-horned borer, 232
Long-horned grasshoppers, 21
Long-horned wood borers, 104
Longlegged flies, 213
Longtailed mealybug, 83
Longwing butterflies, 252
Loopers, 270
Lovebugs, 204
Loxagrotis albicosta, 266
Loxosceles, 296
Loxosceles apachea, 297
Loxosceles blanda, 296
Loxosceles devia, 297
Loxosceles reclusa, 296–297
Loxosceles rufescens, 297
Lubber grasshopper, 21
Lucanidae, 98
Lucanus elephas, 98
Lucanus placidus, 98
Luciferase, 106
Luciferin, 106
Lumber, 110
Luna moth, 257–258
Lycaenidae, 247
Lycium, 68
Lyctidae, 109
Lyctus planicollis, 109
Lygaeidae, 51, 54–55
Lygaeus, 55
Lygus bugs, 48
Lygus hesperus, 48
Lygus lineolaris, 48

Lymantria dispar, 262
Lymantriidae, 262
Lyme disease, 302
Lysiphlebus testaceipes, 72

Macaroni, 193
Macrosteles
    quadrilineatus, 66
Maggots, 202, 217, 219
Magicicada septendecim, 63
Magnolia, 197
Maize dwarf mosaic virus, 76
Maize weevil, 193
Malacosoma americanum,
    256–257, 263
Malacosoma
    californicum, 256
Malacosoma disstria, 256
Malacosoma tigris, 256–257
Malaria, 202, 208
Malvaceous plants, 191
Man, 208–209, 211, 293
Manduca
    quinquemaculata, 260
Manduca sexta, 260
Mango, 70
Mantidae, 25, 91
Mantidflies, 91
Mantispidae, 91
Mantispids, 91
Mantodea, 25, 45, 91
Maple, 59, 66, 83, 229, 233,
    258, 261, 274
March flies, 204
Margarodes, 84
Margarodidae, 83–84
Marigold, 215
Masked hunter, 53
Mastigoproctus
    giganteus, 294
Matrimony vine, 68
May beetles, 99
Mayetiola destructor, 205
Mayflies, 10–11
Mayhaws, 192
Meadow grasshoppers, 21
Mealy oak gall wasp, 276
Mealybugs, 63
Meats, 108
Mecoptera, 198
Medical, 237, 290
Megachile, 278
Megachile rotundata, 279
Megachilidae, 278–279
Megacyllene caryae, 118
Megacyllene robiniae, 116
Megalopyge opercularis, 236
Megalopygidae, 236
Megaphasma dentricus, 17
Megarhyssa macrurus,
    274–275

Megisto cymela cymela, 253
Megisto rubricata, 253
Melandryidae, 108
Melanocallis caryaefoliae, 74
Melanoplus bivittatus, 19
Melanoplus differentialis, 19
Melanoplus
    femurrubrum, 19
Melanoplus sanguinipes, 19
Melipotis, 269
Melittia calabaza, 230
Melittia cucurbitae, 230
Meloidae, 115
Melon aphid, 71, 77
Melons, 231
Membracidae, 64
Merchant grain beetle, 110
Mercury vapor lights, 313
Mesoveliidae, 47
Mesquite, 269
Mesquite twig girdlers, 118
Metallic wood borers,
    103–104, 232
Metalmarks, 247
Metcalfa pruinosa, 67
Mexican bed bug, 53
Mexican corn rootworm, 186
Mexican rice borer, 239
Mexican silverspot, 252
Microcentrum, 21
Microorganisms, 30
Microtheca ochroloma, 189
Midges, 202, 206, 210
Migratory grasshopper, 19
Milk powders, 228
Milkweed, 72, 254
Millers, 265
Millipedes, 4, 311
Mimosa, 119, 262
Mint apple jelly, 288
Minute pirate bug, 51
Miridae, 48–50
Mistletoe, 247
Mites, 4, 276, 301, 304
Monarch butterfly, 249,
    253–254
Monellia caryella, 73
Monelliopsis pecanis, 73
Monkey flower, 250
Monocesta coryli, 187
Monomorium
    pharaonis, 288
Moon moths, 258
Mordella atrata, 113
Mordella marginata, 113
Mordellidae, 113
Mordellistena, 113
Mosquito hawk, 14, 203
Mosquitoes, 202, 207–208
Moth flies, 206–207
Moths, 226, 275

Mountain ash, 73
Mountain laurel, 47
Mud daubers, 277–278
Mulberry, 263
Mules, 221
Multicolored Asia lady
    beetle, 111–112
Murgantia histrionica, 60
Musca domestica, 217
Muscidae, 217, 219
Museum specimens, 114
Mustard greens, 189
Mutillidae, 282
Myiasis, 212
Myrmeleon, 93
Myrmeleonidae, 93
Myrmeleontoidea, 93
Myzinum, 283
Myzus persicae, 71, 74

Nabidae, 51
Nabis capsiformis, 51
Nantucket pine tip
    moth, 235
Naphthalene, 314
Narceus americanus, 311
Narnia, 58
Nasturtium, 271
Nicrophorus, 97
Nectar, 284
Nectarines, 192
Neoclytus acuminatus, 117
Neocurtilla hexadactyla, 23
Neodiprion taedae
    linearis, 273
Neodusmetia sangwawi, 85
Nepidae, 45
Neuroptera, 14, 90–93, 225
Nezra viridula, 60
Niesthrea, 58
Night ant, 286
Nightshade, 189
Nitidulidae, 36, 109
Nits, 42–43
No-see-ums, 209
Noctuid moth, 174
Noctuidae, 265–270
Nola sorghiella, 266
Nomenclature, 2
Northern black widow, 298
Northern corn
    rootworm, 187
Northern mole cricket, 23
Northern true katydid, 22
Norway maple, 262
Nose bot fly, 221
Notodontidae, 261
Notonectidae, 46
Nursery crops, 83, 215
Nut trees, 49, 229, 286
Nuts, 111, 242

Nymphalidae, 249–253
Nysius ericae, 55
Nysius raphanus, 55

Oak, 18, 83, 102, 105, 117,
   233, 256, 258–259,
   261–263, 274
Oak apple, 276
Oak trees, 192, 255
Oak wilt disease, 109
Oats, 75–76, 101, 193
Odonata, 13–15, 203, 315
Odontotaenius, 99
Oebalus pugnax, 60–61
Oecanthus fultoni, 22
Oestridae, 221–222
Okra, 67, 71, 186, 290
Old house borer, 117–118
Oleander, 72, 84
Oleander aphid, 72
Oligonychus ilicus, 302
Olla, 112
Olla v-nigrum, 111–112
*Olla v-nigrum
   abdominalis,* 112
Onagraceae, 186
Oncideres cingulata, 118
Oncideres pustulatus, 118
Oncideres rhodosticta, 118
Oncopeltus fasciatus, 55
Onion, 217, 268
Onion maggot, 217
Onion thrips, 87
Onthophagus gazella, 102
Ophion nigrovarius, 274
Opiliones, 300
Orange dog, 245
Orchard trees, 261
Orders, 5
Organic matter, 210
Orgyia leucostigma, 262
Oriental cockroach, 27
Oriental fruit moth,
   233–234
Oriental rat flea, 200
Orius, 52
Orius insidiosus, 51
Orius tisticolor, 51
Ormenoides, 67
Ornamental pear, 79
Ornamental plants, 50, 60,
   65, 67, 70, 75, 83,
   100–101, 115, 187, 196,
   215, 234, 261–262,
   266–267, 286, 303
Orthoptera, 19–23
Oryzaephilus mercator, 110
*Oryzaephilus
   surinamensis,* 110
Osage orange, 82

Osmeteria, 245
Ostrinia nubilalis, 239, 266
Overripe fruit, 101, 109
Ovisac, 84
Owlflies, 14, 90, 93
Ox beetle, 101
Ox bot, 222
Ox warble, 222
Oxidus gracilis, 311
*Pachypsylla
   celtidisgemma,* 68
*Pachypsylla
   celtidismamma,* 69
*Pachypsylla
   celtidisvesicula,* 69
Pachysandra, 82
Painted hickory borer, 118
Palamedes swallowtail, 246
Pale damsel bug, 51
Pale tussock moth, 262
Pale western cutworm, 265
Pale-bordered field
   cockroach, 28
Paleacrita vernata, 254
Pallid-winged grasshopper, 20
Pampas grass, 240
Panchlora nivea, 28
Pangaeus bilineatus, 59
Panorpa, 198
Panorpidae, 198
Paper, 228
Paper triangle, 315
Paper wasps, 283–285
Papilio, 245–246
*Papilio polyxenes
   asterius,* 245
Papilionidae, 245
Paradichlorobenzene, 314
Paradoxosomatidae, 311
Paraprociphilus, 73
Parasites, 1, 42–44, 115,
   200–201, 220–223,
   274–276, 283,
   301–302, 304–309
Parasitic flies, 223
Parasitic insects, 42
Parasitic wasp, 72, 85, 275
Parasitiformes, 307
Parasol ant, 286
Paratrechina longicornis, 288
Paratrioza cockerelli, 67
Parcoblatta, 28
Parsley, 245, 271
Parsleyworm, 245
Parsnips, 102
Parthenogenesis, 39, 63, 73,
   74, 77, 78
Partridge pea, 247
Passalid beetles, 99
Passalidae, 99

Passiflora, 252
Passion flower, 252
Pea, 268
Pea weevil, 185
Peach(es), 58–60, 75, 81–83,
   101, 192, 197,
   232–234, 256, 261, 286
Peach bark beetle, 196
Peach twig borer, 234
Peachtree borer, 231–232
Peanuts, 59, 230, 267
Pear, 70, 73, 82,
   233–234, 262
Pearls, 84
Pears, 83, 192
Peas, 50, 114, 215, 217, 271
Pecan, 18, 60, 79, 83, 116,
   119, 193, 197, 235,
   238–239, 261, 263, 273
Pecan leaf phylloxera, 79
Pecan nut casebearer, 234,
   237–238
Pecan phylloxera, 78, 235
Pecan weevil, 192, 234
Pecky rice, 62
Pectinophora gossypiella,
   191, 230
*Pediculus humanus
   capitus,* 43
*Pediculus humanus
   humanus,* 43
Pemphigus, 78
Pentatomidae, 60–62
Pepper, 50, 59, 68, 114, 186,
   217, 260, 268, 303, 306
Pepsis, 277
Peridroma saucia, 265
Periplaneta americana, 27
Periplaneta fuliginosa, 27
Periodical cicada, 63
Persimmon, 81, 84, 119,
   197, 229, 258
Pets, 201, 290
Petunia, 215, 303
Phaenicia, 219
Phaenicia sericata, 219
Phalangiidae, 300
Phanaeus vindex, 102
Phaneropterinae, 21
Phantom midges, 207
Pharaoh ants, 288
Phasmida, 17
Pheromones, 313
Philopteridae, 42
Phlaeothripidae, 88
Phloeotribus liminaris, 196
Phobetron pithecium, 236
Phoebis sennae eubule, 246
*Phoebis sennae
   marcellina,* 246

Phoradendron, 247
Phoretic, 91
Phormia regina, 219
Photinia, 234
Photuris pennsylvanicus, 106
Phthia picta, 57
Phthiraptera, 42–43
Phyllocoptruta oleivora, 303
Phyllophaga crinita, 99–100
Phyllotreta, 185
Phyllotreta striolata, 185
Phylloxera, 276
Phylloxera devastatrix, 78–79
Phylloxera galls, 235
Phylloxera notabilis, 79
Phylloxeridae, 77, 78
Phytonemus pallidus, 305
Piano strikers, 228
Pictured grasshopper, 21
Pierce's disease, 67
Pieridae, 246, 270
Pieris rapae, 270
Pies, 288
Pigeon tremex, 274
Pigweed, 102, 268
Pillbugs, 291, 310
Pinchers, 36
Pines, 83, 104, 229
Pink bollworm, 191, 230
Pinkeye, 216
Pipe organ mud dauber, 278
Pipevine swallowtail, 245
Piss ant, 288
Pit fall traps, 313
Pittosporum, 83–84
Placosternus difficilis, 118
Planococcus citri, 83
Plant bugs, 48
Plant diseases, 67, 76, 186, 205
Plant feeders, 1, 6, 17–24, 33, 34, 40, 47–50, 54–62, 63–93, 99–105, 113–120, 185–197, 205–206, 214–271, 228–271, 273–274, 276–278, 286–289, 302–303, 305–306, 310
Plantain, 250, 268
Planthoppers, 63, 67
Plecia nearctica, 204
Plecoptera, 37
Plectrodera scalator, 119
Plodia interpunctella, 227, 229, 242
Plum, 59, 70, 81–83, 192, 197, 232–234, 256, 262, 286
Plum curculio, 191, 234
Plum gouger, 192

Podisus maculiventris, 60, 62
Podura aquatica, 7
Poduridae, 7
Podworm, 266
Pogonomyrmex barbatus, 286, 289
Poinsettia, 70
Poison sac, 282
Pokeweed, 303
Polistes, 284
Polistes carolina, 284
Polistes exclamans, 284
Pollen, 114
Pollen basket, 282
Pollenia rudis, 219
Pollinators, 272, 279–282
Polydesmida, 311
Polyembryony, 275
Polyphagotarsonemus latus, 305
Polyphemus moth, 257–258
Pomegranate, 70, 83
Pompilidae, 277
Popilius, 99
Popillia japonica, 100
Poplars, 120, 233, 262–263
Portulaca, 259
Post oak, 276
Postabdomen, 292
Potato, 50, 58, 68, 75, 102, 105, 115, 189, 215, 230, 260, 268, 271, 290, 303, 306
Potato flea beetle, 185
Potato leafhopper, 66
Potato psyllid, 67
Potatobugs, 189
Pothos, 84
Potter wasp, 278
Potting media, 101
Poultry houses, 218
Powdered milk, 242
Powderpost beetle, 109, 117
Praying mantids, 17, 25, 45, 91
Predaceous, 54–55, 62, 87, 90–91, 95–98, 112, 115, 211, 213–214, 225
Predaceous diving beetles, 96, 98
Predators, 1, 13–16, 21, 25–26, 38, 45–47, 51–55, 62, 91–92, 95–97, 106, 108, 111–113, 211–214, 277–278, 284, 290, 294–299, 308–309, 311
Preserving insects, 312
Prey, 51, 53, 86

Prickly ash, 246
Prickly pear, 100
Primary reproductives, 32–33
Primrose, 186
Prionoxystus robiniae, 232
Prionus imbricornis, 119
Privet, 81
Prolegs, 226, 232, 254, 270, 272–273
Prosapia bicincta, 65
Protoneuridae, 15
Protozoan, 30
Prunus, 67, 83, 232
Psalidonota texana, 189
Pseudaletia unipuncta, 268
Pseudatomoscelis seriatus, 49
Pseudaulacaspis pentagona, 80
Pseudergates, 33
Pseudococcidae, 83–84
Pseudococcus longispinus, 83
Pseudomonas, 288
Pseudomops septentrionalis, 28
Pseudophylinae, 22
Pseudoplusia includens, 270
Pseudopupa, 115
Pseudoscorpiones, 308
Pseudoscorpions, 308
Psithyrus, 280
Psocidae, 40
Psocids, 39–41
Psocoptera, 39–40, 314
Psorophora, 207
Psychidae, 228, 263
Psychodidae, 206
Psyllid yellows, 68
Psyllidae, 67–69
Psyllids, 63, 276
Pterophylla camellifolia, 22
Pterourus (Papilio) glaucus, 245
Pterourus (Papilio) multicaudatus, 246
Pterourus (Papilio) palamedes, 246
Pterourus (Papilio) triolus, 246
Pthiridae, 43
Pthirus pubis, 43
Pulicidae, 200
Pulvinaria floccifera, 83
Pumpkin, 50, 57
Punkies, 209
Puparium, 205
Purple-top, 68
Purslane, 259
Puss caterpillar, 236–237, 258
Pyemotes tritici, 305
Pyemotidae, 305

Pygmy blue, 247
Pyracantha, 79, 262
Pyralid stalk borer, 239
Pyralidae, 120, 227, 229, 231–232, 235, 237, 239–243, 263, 266
Pyramid ant, 288
Pyrrharctia isabella, 264

Quadraspidiotus perniciosus, 81
Queen, 254
Queen Anne's lace, 245
Quince, 73, 83

Radish, 189, 217
Ragweed, 21, 120
Rainbow grasshopper, 21
Rainbow scarab, 102
Range caterpillar, 258
Range grasses, 258
Raphidiidae, 91
Rasping, 86, 88
Rattailed maggots, 214
Recluse spiders, 295
Red admiral, 249
Red bugs, 56.
    See also Redbugs.
Red cross beetle, 108
Red flour beetle, 114
Red harvester ant, 286, 289
Red imported fire ant, 286, 289, 299, 305
Red oak, 119, 276
Red peppers, 242
Red satyr, 253
Red-spotted purple, 249
Red velvet-ant, 282
Redbud, 262–263, 279
Redbugs, 304
Redheaded ash borer, 117
Redlegged grasshopper, 19
Rednecked peanutworm, 230
Redshouldered bug, 58
Reduviidae, 17, 52–54, 58
Reduvius personatus, 53
Repugnatorial fluids, 311
Retama, 119
Reticulitermes flavipes, 32
Reticulitermes hageni, 32
Reticulitermes tibialis, 32
Reticulitermes virginicus, 32
Rhinoceros beetle, 101
Rhinotermitidae, 31–32
Rhipicephalus sanguineus, 302
Rhizoecus, 84
Rhodesgrass mealybug, 84–85
Rhododendron, 84

Rhopalidae, 58
Rhopalosiphum maidis, 76
Rhopalosiphum padi, 76
Rhyacionia frustrana, 235
Rhyssella, 274
Rice, 20, 61, 194, 208, 239–240, 269
Rice stalk borer, 239
Rice stink bug, 60–61
Rice water weevil, 194
Rice weevil, 193, 242
Riffle bugs, 47
Ringlegged earwig, 36
Riodinidae, 247
Robber flies, 212
Rocky Mountain spotted fever, 301–302
Roly-polies, 310
Romalea guttata, 20
Root galls, 78
Rootworm, 186
Rose leafhopper, 66
Roses, 83, 189, 261–262, 279
Rosetting, 68
Rotten logs, 101
Rotting fruit, 215
Rotting stumps, 105
Rough stink bug, 60
Round-headed borer, 103, 116, 117, 232
Rove beetles, 36
Royal jelly, 281
Rubyspots, 15
Rue, 246
Russian wheat aphid, 75–76
Ruta graveolens, 245–246
Rutaceae, 245
Rye, 75–76, 206
Rye grass, 269

Sacred scarab, 102
Saddleback caterpillar, 236–237
Salmonella, 288
Salt cedar, 229
Saltmarsh caterpillar, 264
Saltwater isopods, 310
San Jose scale, 81
Sand wasps, 277
Sandwich man, 242
Sap, 109
Sap beetles, 36, 109
Sarcophaga haemorrhoidalis, 219
Sarcophagidae, 219, 223
Saturnidae, 236, 257–258
Satyridae, 253
Satyrs, 253
Sawflies, 214, 272–273, 275
Sawtoothed grain beetle, 110

Scale insects, 63
Scapteriscus borellia, 23
Scapteriscus vicinus, 23
Scarab beetles, 101
Scarabaeidae, 99–102, 274, 283
Scarabeus sacer, 102
Scarites subterraneous, 95
Scavengers, 1, 27–29, 35–38, 40–41, 98, 107, 156, 198–199, 224–225, 285, 288–290, 292–293, 300, 306
Sceliphron caementarium, 278
Schistocerca americana, 20
Schizaphis graminum, 75
Schizura unicornis, 261
Scientific names, 3
Scindapsus, 84
Scirtothrips citri, 87
Scolopendra, 311
Scolopendridae, 311
Scolytidae, 195–196
Scolytus rugulosus, 196
Scorpionflies, 198–199
Scorpionida, 292
Scorpions, 4, 291–293, 299
Screwworm, 220–221
Scud, 310
Scudderia, 21
Scutellaridae, 59
Scutigera coleoptrata, 311
Scymnus loewii, 112
Sea roaches, 310
Secondary reproductives, 32
Secondary screwworm, 220
Sedges, 62, 194
Seed ticks, 302
Seedcorn beetle, 96
Seedcorn maggot, 216–217
Seedlings, 290
Seeds, 57, 60, 107, 110, 242, 290
Serpentine leafminer, 214
Sesbania, 195
Sesbania weevils, 194
Sessidae, 230–232
Seven-spotted lady beetle, 112
Shade trees, 82
Sharpshooters, 66–67
Sheep, 221
Shelled corn, 242
Shelled nuts, 114
Shield bugs, 59
Shore flies, 205
Shothole borer, 196
Shrimp, 310
Shrubs, 79, 82, 262
Shumard oak, 197

Sialidae, 90
Siberian elms, 188
Sibine stimulea, 236
Sicariidae, 296
Siciariidae, 205
Silk moths, 257
Silken mat, 242
Silken tents, 256
Silken webs, 230, 263
Silkworm, 257
Silpha, 97
Silphidae, 97
Silver maple, 262
Silverfish, 8
Silverleaf nightshade, 49, 188
Silverleaf whitefly, 70
Silvery cherckerspot, 168, 250
Simuliidae, 70, 208
Simulium, 208
Sinea diadema, 52
Sipha flava, 75
Siphonaptera, 200
Siricidae, 274
Sitobion avenae, 76
Sitophilus granarius, 193, 242
Sitophilus oryzae, 193, 242
Sitophilus zeamais, 193
Sitotroga cerealella, 227, 229, 242
Six-spotted leafhopper, 66
Skin rash, 237
Skipper butterfly, 265
Skippers, 226
Small berries, 192
Small fruit, 49
Small fruit flies, 215
Small grains, 75–76, 105, 206, 269, 286, 303, 305
Sminthuridae, 6
Smokybrown cockroach, 27
Snake doctors, 14
Snakeflies, 90–91
Snapdragon, 250
Snout butterflies, 248
Snowy sundrops, 49
Snowy tree cricket, 22
Snuff, 114
Social insects, 272, 281, 285–286
Soft scales, 79–80
Soft ticks, 302
Soft-bodied insects, 315
Solanum, 189
Soldier beetles, 106
Soldier fly, 211
Soldiers, 32
Solenaceous, 303
Solenopsis aurea, 289
Solenopsis geminata, 289
Solenopsis invicta, 286, 289, 305

Solenopsis xyloni, 289
Solifugae, 309
Sonoran tent caterpillar, 256–257
Sooty mold, 70, 75, 77, 83–84
Sorghum, 55, 58, 60, 76, 100, 101, 193, 206, 240, 266–267, 269, 290
Sorghum midge, 206
Sorghum webworm, 266
Southern black widow, 297
Southern chinch bug, 54
Southern corn rootworm, 186
Southern cornstalk borer, 239
Southern fire ant, 289
Southern green stink bug, 60
Southern lyctus beetle, 109
Southern masked chafer, 100
Southern mole cricket, 23
Southern pine beetle, 195–196
Southern pine coneworm, 235
Southern pines, 235
Southern red mite, 302
Southern yellowjackets, 283–285
Southwestern corn borer, 239
Southwestern squash vine borer, 230
Sowbugs, 291, 310
Soybean, 20, 60, 116, 120, 186, 217, 264, 268, 271, 303
Soybean looper, 270–271
Soybean stem borer, 120
Sphecidae, 277–278, 283
Sphecius speciosus, 277
Sphingidae, 259–260
Spicebush swallowtail, 246
Spices, 110, 114, 228
Spider wasps, 277
Spiders, 4, 291, 295–299
Spinach, 59, 71, 75, 271
Spinach aphid, 75
Spined assassin bug, 52
Spined soldier bug, 60, 62
Spirobolida, 311
Spissistilus festinus, 64
Spodoptera exigua, 268
Spodoptera frugiperda, 266, 268
Spodoptera ornithogalli, 269
Spotted cucumber beetle, 186
Spotted lady beetle, 111
Spring cankerworm, 254–255
Springtails, 6
Squash, 50, 57, 231
Squash bug, 57
Squash vine borer, 230

St. Augustine grass, 24, 85, 100, 241, 244
Stable fly, 217, 220
Stag beetles, 98
Stagmomantis, 25
Stagmomantis carolina, 25
Staphylinidae, 36
Staphylococcus, 288
Stegasta bosqueella, 230
Stegobium paniceum, 110
Stegophylla, 73
Stem galls, 78
Stenolophus lecontei, 96
Stephanitis pyriodes, 47
Sticktight flea, 200
Stictocephala bisonia, 64
Stinging, 272, 275, 277–280, 283–285, 289, 290, 292
Stomoxys calcitrans, 217, 220
Stonecrop, 250
Stoneflies, 37
Stored food, 114, 242
Stored grain, 111, 185, 193, 229, 305
Stored product pests, 9, 39–40, 107, 110–111, 114, 185, 193, 195, 227, 229
Storing, 314
Strategus, 101
Stratiomyidae, 211
Straw, 108, 305
Straw itch mite, 305
Strawberry, 71, 248
Striped bark scorpion, 292
Striped earwig, 36
Striped flea beetle, 185
Structural pests, 30–33, 109, 118, 279–280, 287
Strymon melinus, 247
Subfamily, 3
Subimago, 10, 11
Subterranean cutworms, 265
Subterranean termite, 31–32
Suckfly, 50
Sucking lice, 42
Sucking mouthparts, 63
Sudan grass, 269
Sugar, 111, 288
Sugar ant, 288
Sugar beets, 268
Sugarcane, 100, 240
Sugarcane borer, 239–240
Sulphur butterflies, 246
Sumac, 229
Sunflower, 21, 113, 215, 268, 290
Sunscorpions, 309
Sunspiders, 309
Supella longipalpa, 28
Superfamily, 3

Surface feeders, 265
Swallowtail butterflies, 245
Swarmers, 31
Swarming, 281
Sweep net, 313
Sweet gum, 197, 257
Sweet potato, 50, 105, 190, 195, 197
Sweet yellow clover, 190
Sweetgum, 258, 263
Sweetpotato weevil, 195
Sycamore, 48, 229, 262
Sycamore lace bug, 48
Sycamore tussock moth, 262
Synanthedon exitiosa, 231
Synanthedon pictipes, 231
Synclita obliteralis, 242
Syrphid flies, 213
Syrphidae, 213
Syrphinae, 214

Tabanidae, 210
Tabanus, 210, 211
Tachinidae, 223
Tall fescue, 100
Tapeworms, 201
Tar, 102
Tarantula hawk, 277
Tarantulas, 295–296
Tarnished plant bug, 48
Tarsonemidae, 305–306
Tawny emperor, 251
Tawny mole cricket, 23
Taxonomists, 3
Tea scale, 81
Teleonemia scrupulosa, 48
Tenaculum, 6
Tenebrio molitor, 114
Tenebrio obscurus, 114
Tenebrionidae, 114, 116
Tenodera aridifolia sinensis, 25
Tenthredinidae, 214, 273
Tepehuaje, 119
Terminology, 3
Termites, 30, 280, 287
Tethida barda, 273
Tetranychidae, 302
Tetranychus urticae, 302
Tettigoniidae, 21
Texas beetle, 105
Texas crescent, 250
Texas ebony, 119
Texas leafcutting ant, 286
Texas mountain laurel, 241
Texas recluse, 297
Thamnosma texana, 245
Thelyphonidae, 294
Theraphosidae, 295
Thermobia domestica, 8

Thistle down mutillid, 283
Thorn gall, 68
Thread bugs, 17
Threatened arachnids, 319
Threatened insects, 317
Threecornered alfalfa hoppers, 64–65
Thripidae, 87
Thrips, 86, 276
Thrips simplex, 87
Thrips tabaci, 87
Throat bot fly, 221
Thyreocoridae, 59
Thyridopteryx ephemeraeformis, 228
Thysanoptera, 86–88
Thysanura, 8
Tibicen, 63
Tick paralysis, 302
Ticks, 4, 290, 301
Tiger beetles, 95
Tiger moth, 173, 264
Tiger swallowtail, 245
Tilehorned prionus, 119
Timothy, 269
Tinea bisselliella, 227
Tinea pellionella, 227
Tineidae, 227, 242
Tingidae, 47–48
Tinocallis kahawaluokalani, 77
Tip moth, 235
Tip-burn, 66
Tiphiid wasp, 283
Tiphiidae, 283
Tipulidae, 203
Toadflax, 250
Tobacco, 75, 110, 228
Tobacco aphid, 75
Tobacco budworm, 248, 266–267
Tobacco hornworm, 260
Tobacco thrips, 87
Tomatillo, 68
Tomato, 50, 58, 60, 68, 71, 75, 87, 186, 230, 260, 266–271, 303, 306
Tomato fruitworm, 266
Tomato hornworm, 260
Tomato pinworm, 214, 230
Tomato psyllid, 67
Tomato russet mite, 303
Tomostethus multicinctus, 273
Torticidae, 235, 238
Tortoise beetle, 189–190
Tortricidae, 233–234
Town ant, 286
Toxic, 55, 75
Toxoptera aurantii, 77

Tracheal bee mites, 306–307
Tree crickets, 22
Tree roots, 64
Tree stink bug, 60
Treehoppers, 63
Trees, 67, 257–258, 262
Tremex columba, 274
Triatoma sanguisuga, 53
Tribolium castaneum, 114
Tribolium confusum, 114
Tricentrus albomaculatus, 64
Trichogramma, 276
Trichogrammatidae, 276
Trichoplusia ni, 270
Trichoptera, 224
Tricorythidae, 11
Trimerotropis pallidipennis, 20
Triticale, 75
Triungulin, 115
Trogium pulsatorium, 39
Trogoderma granarium, 107
Trombicula alfreddugesi, 304
Trombicula splendens, 304
Trombiculidae, 304
Tropical fire ant, 289
Tropical leaf wing, 251
Tropical sod webworm, 241
True armyworm, 268
True bugs, 45, 106
Trypanosoma cruzi, 54
Trypoxylon politum, 278
Tularemia, 302
Tumbling flower beetles, 113
Tunnel dwellers, 265
Tupelo gum, 257
Turf, 84, 266, 269, 286
Turf grass, 24, 100–101, 241, 270
Turkey gnats, 208
Turnip, 217
Turnip greens, 189
Twicestabbed lady beetles, 111
Twig galls, 78
Twig girdlers, 118
Twinberry, 82
Twolined spittlebug, 65
Twomarked treehopper, 64
Twospotted spider mite, 302
Twostriped grasshopper, 19
Two-tailed swallowtail, 246
Typhus, 43

Ulmaceae, 251
Umbelliferae, 245
Unaspis euonymi, 82
Unicorn caterpillar, 261
Upholstered furniture, 228
Upholstery, 110

Uresiphita reversalis, 241, 263
Uropygi, 294
Vanessa atalanta, 249
Vanessa virginiensis, 249
Varied carpet beetle, 107
Variegated cutworm, 265
Variegated fritillary, 249
Varroa jacobsoni, 307
Varroa mite, 307
Varroidae, 307
Vegetable(s), 6, 59, 70, 87, 88, 100, 101, 105 187, 215, 217, 266, 303, 310
Vegetable leafminer, 214
Vegetable transplants, 100
Veliidae, 47
Velvetbean caterpillar, 271
Verbena, 83
Verbenaceae, 250
Vespidae, 278, 283– 285
Vespula maculifrons, 285
Vespula squamosa, 284– 285
Vetch, 190
Viburnum, 89
Viceroy, 249, 253
Vinegar flies, 215
Vinegaroons, 294
Violets, 71
Violin spiders, 296
Virginia creeper, 259
Virginia pines, 236
Viviparous, 293
Vostox brunneipennis, 36

Walkingsticks, 17
Wallengrenia otho, 165
Walnut, 81, 83, 119, 258, 261
Walnut caterpillar, 261
Walnut sphinx, 259
Warbles, 222
Wasp moths, 264
Wasps, 272, 275
Water boatmen, 46
Water garden plants, 243
Water lily, 243
Water lily leafcutter, 242
Water scavenger beetles, 96, 98
Water scorpions, 45
Water springtail, 7
Water striders, 46
Water tigers, 96
Water treaders, 47

Watercress, 189
Wax, 79, 83– 84, 282
Wax masses, 73
Wax scales, 79
Webbing clothes moth, 227
Webworms, 241, 263
Weeds, 22, 49, 55, 65, 67, 71, 88, 100, 120, 249, 260, 303
Western bean cutworm, 266
Western black widow, 298
Western corn rootworm, 186
Western flower thrips, 87
Western soapberry, 59
Western tent caterpillar, 256
Wheat, 75– 76, 193, 206, 229, 242
Wheel bug, 54
Whipscorpion, 294
Whirligig beetles, 97
White butterflies, 246, 270
White grubs, 99, 101, 274, 283
White heads, 240
White peach scale, 80
White pigweed, 247
White-whiskered grasshopper, 19
Whiteflies, 63
Whitelined sphinx, 259
Whitemarked treehopper, 64
Whitemarked tussock moth, 262
Widow spiders, 295, 299
Wild cherry, 18, 229
Wild grasses, 76, 206
Wild mustard, 303
Wild plants, 60, 88
Wild plums, 256
Wild senna, 247
Wildlife, 290
Willow, 83, 120, 229, 233, 258– 263, 273
Window pane traps, 313
Windscorpions, 291, 309
Windspiders, 309
Winged elm, 188
Wireworms, 105
Wisteria, 262
Wolfberry, 68
Wood borers, 103–105, 116–120, 232, 274, 287
Wood nymphs, 253

Wood roaches, 28
Wood ticks, 301
Wood wasp, 274
Woodlice, 34
Woods firefly, 106
Woody ornamentals, 83
Woody twig gall, 276
Wool, 228
Wool sower gall, 276
Woolens, 228
Woolly apple aphid, 73
Woolly leaf gall, 276
Woolly tidestromia, 49
Woollybear, 264

Xanthogaleruca luteola, 187
Xanthoxylum, 195, 246
Xenopsylla cheopis, 200
Xiphydriidae, 274
Xylocopa, 279
Xyloryctes jamaicensis, 101
Xylosandrus crassiusculus, 196

Yarn, 228
Yaupon hollies, 69
Yaupon psyllid gall, 69
Yellow fever, 202, 208
Yellow mealworm, 114
Yellow pecan aphid, 73
Yellow sugarcane aphid, 75
Yellowcollared scape moth, 264
Yellowfever mosquito, 207
Yellowjacket, 283, 285
Yellowmargined leaf beetle, 189
Yellownecked caterpillar, 261
Yellowstriped armyworm, 269
Yponomeutidae, 265

Zebra longwing, 252
Zelus renardii, 52
Zeuzera pyrina, 232
Zinnias, 215, 306
Zopheridae, 116
Zopherus nodulosus haldemani, 116
Zoysia grass, 55, 241
Zygoptera, 15